Nov 81
To Irena
Love LJ.

Penguin Handbooks
Women's Rights: A Practi

Anna Coote is Deputy Editor of the *New Statesman*. She
read Modern History and Politics at Edinburgh University.
She has worked as a journalist since 1968, first on the staff of
the *Observer* and then as a freelance writer until joining the
*New Statesman* in 1978. Her other publications include
*Equal at Work?* on women in jobs traditionally done by men
(1979); *Hear This, Brother: Women workers and union power*
(with Peter Kellner, 1981); *Family in the Firing Line* (with
Jean Coussins, 1981); and *Positive Action for Women* (with
Sadie Robarts and Elizabeth Ball, 1981).

Tess Gill is Legal Officer of the General and Municipal
Workers' Union. She read History and Politics at Manchester
University and before joining the GMWU worked as a
solicitor in private practice, specializing in law relating to
women's rights and employment. She has three children. As
this edition went to press, she was writing a collective
bargaining guide for women at work, to be published by
Penguin in 1982.

Both authors are active in the women's movement; they are
members of the executive of the National Council for Civil
Liberties and its Rights for Women Group. They are also
co-authors of *Battered Women and the Law*.

ANNA COOTE and TESS GILL

# Women's Rights:
# A Practical Guide

*Drawings by Posy Simmonds*

THIRD EDITION

PENGUIN BOOKS

Penguin Books Ltd, Harmondsworth, Middlesex, England
Penguin Books, 625 Madison Avenue, New York, New York 10022, U.S.A.
Penguin Books Australia Ltd, Ringwood, Victoria, Australia
Penguin Books Canada Ltd, 2801 John Street, Markham, Ontario, Canada L3R 1B4
Penguin Books (N.Z.) Ltd, 182–190 Wairau Road, Auckland 10, New Zealand

First published as a Penguin Special 1974
Reprinted with revisions 1974
Second edition published in Penguin Handbooks 1977
Third edition published 1981

Filmset, printed and bound in Great Britain by
Hazell Watson & Viney Ltd, Aylesbury, Bucks
Set in VIP Times

# Contents

**The following pages may be of particular interest to you . . .**

## 1. If you are single

## 2. If you are married

## 3. If you are divorced

### 4. If you are separated or getting a divorce

### 5. If you are living with a man who is not your husband

### 6. If you have children

## 7. If you are under 18

Sex, p. 210
Contraception under 16, p. 214
Getting married, p. 252
Leaving home, p. 368

## 8. If you live in Scotland

*These sections apply almost entirely to Scotland,
with only very minor differences*

Introduction to the Sex Discrimination Act,
pp. 23–31
Work, pp. 32–114
Money, pp. 115–209, with the important exception
of Widows' inheritance, pp. 182
Women and immigration, pp. 421–31
Equal Opportunities Commission, pp. 481–7
Tribunals, pp. 488–96

*These sections apply to Scotland, with minor
differences noted in Appendix 2*

Goods, Facilities and Services, pp. 402–20
Women and Prison, pp. 432–48
Approaching the Law, pp. 449–80

*Only parts of these sections apply to Scotland;
there are major differences, described in
Appendix 2*

Widows' inheritance, pp. 182–5
Sex, pp. 210–46
Marriage, pp. 247–61
Domestic violence, pp. 261–77
Divorce and separation, pp. 278–313
Children, pp. 314–70
Housing, pp. 371–401

## 9. If you live in Northern Ireland

# Acknowledgements

This book could not have been assembled without the expertise and assistance of a great many individuals and organizations. We are deeply indebted to Fran Bennett for her patient, meticulous and extensive work on national insurance and social security: those chapters are now hers. For the Appendix on Scotland, thanks to Eveline Hunter, author of the Scottish equivalent to this Guide, *A Scottish Woman's Place*; and for the Northern Ireland Appendix, thanks again to Eileen Evason, for updating the excellent work she produced for the second edition.

Julia Vellacott, our original editor, has now left Penguin Books, but she has given us invaluable help again, assembling our material, checking it and making it presentable. In many ways she is the third author of this book. Cathy Pulley did much of the hard work on checking and updating addresses and other details.

Thanks, too, to Audrey Sander for her advice on family law; to Jo Dodson, for updating the housing chapter; to Sue Shutter for her expertise on immigration law; to Frances Glover for her help with the education chapter; to Linda Millington and David Tench for checking the chapter on goods, facilities and services; to Pauline Hoare and Paul Cavadino for checking the chapter on women and prison; to Linda Smith, Phil King, Sue Edwards and Caroline Langridge for their advice (respectively) on child care, county court procedure, student grants and birth control; and to the long-suffering officials at the Inland Revenue and the Manpower Services Commission for helping us to update the chapters on taxation and training.

For their help on earlier editions, still very relevant to this one, thanks to Patricia Hewitt, Jean Coussins, Gail Coles, Margaret

Tuttle, Lindsay Mackie, Polly Patullo, Ruth Lister, Mary Chamberlain, Barbara Calvert, Mary Dines, Beryl McAlhone, David Pearlman and Alison Truefitt. Finally, we are indebted to Christine Jackson for introducing us to each other and thereby making the book happen in the first place.

# Introduction

We began work on the first edition of this guide almost exactly ten years ago. At that time, in the early 1970s, we were optimistic that the position of women would improve – and it seemed that we had reason to feel that way. The economy was relatively healthy; nurseries and other provisions of the welfare state were expanding; the women's liberation movement was just beginning to make its presence felt; and campaigns for a Sex Discrimination Act and other legal reforms were gathering strength.

We did not foresee that by the end of the decade a massive attack would have been launched on the rights of women and on the material conditions of their lives. Yet that is what happened. Britain was hit by a severe economic recession. Inflation soared. Industry went into decline and factories closed down all over the country. Dole queues lengthened until, by 1981, there were nearly three million unemployed. Workers were unable to negotiate wages that kept abreast of the cost of living. A monetarist Conservative government came to power, savagely cutting public expenditure. Nurseries were closed down; health and social services were drastically curtailed. Women, who were often the first victims of redundancy and who had always been the main beneficiaries of the welfare state, were hardest hit by these developments. Margaret Thatcher, Britain's first woman Prime Minister, claimed that the Conservatives were 'the party of the family'; however, her idea of improving the quality of family life was to force women out of the labour market and back into their homes, where they would carry on working – unpaid – to fill the gaps left by the crumbling welfare state.

This is the 'Brave New World' in which women are now fighting to defend their hard-won rights. And in spite of the presence of a woman in Downing Street, it is a world built and maintained almost entirely by men. As we know, men devised the framework of government which controls our daily lives. Our rulers, representatives and arbitrators have almost all been men. Male judges and Justices of the Peace compiled our system of common law. Men drafted and interpreted our statute laws. Men constructed a bureaucracy to administer the law. Men cultivated the jungle of red tape which often threatens to engulf us.

A decade has passed, yet men still vastly outnumber women in Parliament, on local councils, on magistrates' benches, in the legal profession, the police force, on tribunal panels, in the upper ranks of the civil service, and among trade-union officials. The authority which men exercise over women remains a major source of oppression in our society. The fact that most of the nation's wealth is concentrated in the hands of a few means that the vast majority of women *and* men are deprived of their rights; but women are doubly deprived. At no level of society do they have equal rights with men.

At the beginning of the nineteenth century, women had virtually no rights at all. They were the chattels of their fathers and husbands. They were bought and sold in marriage. They could not vote. They could not sign contracts. When married, they could not own property. They had no rights over their children and no control over their own bodies. Their husbands could rape and beat them without fear of legal reprisals. When they were not confined to the home, they were forced by growing industrialization to join the lowest levels of the labour force.

Since then, progress towards equal rights for women has been very slow indeed. There have even been times when the tide seemed to turn against them. The first law against abortion was passed in 1803. It imposed a sentence of life imprisonment for termination within the first fourteen weeks of pregnancy. In 1832 the first law was passed which forbade women to vote in elections. In 1877 the first Trades Union Congress upheld the tradition that woman's place was in the home whilst man's duty was to protect and provide for her.

Nevertheless, the latter half of the nineteenth century saw the gradual acceptance of women into the unions and the informal adoption of resolutions on the need for equal pay. Between 1831 and 1872 the major Factory Acts were passed, which checked the exploitation of women workers by placing restrictions on hours and conditions of labour and by limiting their employment at night. In 1882 married women won the right to own property.

Wartime inevitably advanced the cause of women's rights – women became indispensable as workers outside the home, as they had to keep the factories and government machinery running while the men went out to fight. They were allowed into new areas of employment and were conceded new degrees of responsibility. In 1918 they got the vote. Again, during the Second World War, state nurseries were built on a considerable scale to enable women to go out to work. When peace came, however, women were unable to hold on to their gains. Men reclaimed their jobs, and women were forced back into the home and confined to their traditionally low-paid, menial and supportive forms of work. The government closed down most of the nurseries. Theories about maternal deprivation emerged – women who had been told it was patriotic to go out to work during the war were now told that their children would suffer if they did not stay at home. Little progress was made for the next two decades.

In the wake of the postwar population explosion, men invented the Pill the first really effective method of birth control. It was not altogether satisfactory. In its early forms it carried a considerable risk of thrombosis, and its long-term effects are still unknown. For many years it was not available under the National Health Service. But gradually it began to affect the lives of more and more women. For the first time in history, they were able to decide just when and how often they would give birth – which meant they had greater freedom to decide when to work and when to marry. Meanwhile rising standards of living and the development of household appliances and processed foods made domestic work less taxing.

Increasing numbers of married women went out to work. Woman's role was changing. The women's liberation movement was born in Britain in 1968. Its first national conference was held at Oxford in 1970.

It was no coincidence that the late sixties and early seventies saw a series of legislative reforms to improve the position of women. In 1967 the Abortion Act was passed, enabling women to have abortions for 'social' reasons. In 1970, the Equal Pay Act asserted women's rights to equal pay for doing the same work as men. In the same year the Matrimonial Proceedings and Property Act recognized that a woman's contribution to the family home by her work as wife and mother should earn her a share of the property after divorce. Contraceptive advice was made available free through family planning clinics, and some local councils offered free supplies too. In 1973, two new statutes gave mothers and fathers equal guardianship rights over their children, and enabled married women to choose their own domicile; the Law Commission recommended co-ownership of the family home by husband and wife.

There have been considerable improvements in women's legal rights since the first edition of this book was published in January 1974. In March of that year, the qualification for jury service was changed to enable women and men to be represented on juries in equal numbers. That summer, British women married to foreigners were allowed for the first time to extend their right of residence to their husbands. The 1975 Social Security Act introduced a new pensions system, to start in 1978, enabling women to earn a good pension in their own right even after spending several years at home looking after their families. In December 1975 the Sex Discrimination and Equal Pay Acts came into force, giving women the right (in theory at least) to equal opportunities in employment, education and the provision of goods, facilities and services. In 1976, the Domestic Violence Act gave battered women more effective legal protection and the Sexual Offences (Amendment) Act changed the law on rape in an attempt to end the practice at rape trials of submitting the victim to a gruelling and well-publicized examination of her personal life.

But these legal rights have made little impact on the lives of ordinary women. They are still treated as men's inferiors and dependants. Their take-home pay is still less than two-thirds that of men. Most employers have been able to avoid any obligations under the Equal Pay Act by keeping women in low-paid grades of work, and in women-only jobs where they have no chance of comparing their pay and conditions with male workers. A study published by the Department of Employment in 1980 showed that 45 per cent of women and 75 per cent of men were in jobs that were totally segregated.

Even when the Equal Pay Act can be applied, it turns out to be full of loopholes, so that women only benefit in the most clear-cut situations. Tribunals and the Court of Appeal have often interpreted the Act so narrowly as to defy its original purpose. The Sex Discrimination Act, also full of loopholes, has the added disadvantage of being so complex that few can understand it and most are unwilling to attempt to enforce it. The Equal Opportunities Commission – which is under-financed, over-cautious, and fearful of being cut back still further by the Tory government – is far from being a vigorous champion of the cause of equality.

Women who believed that the new legislation would bring them equal rights have been bitterly disappointed. It is now clear that equality cannot be achieved, even in a favourable economic climate, just by passing laws *against* discrimination and unequal pay: it is necessary to introduce positive measures which will compensate for past discrimination and help women to come forward and compete for jobs on equal terms with men. In employment, for example, special steps need to be taken to recruit and train women for jobs traditionally done by men.

Sadly, however, the prospects for positive action do not look bright in the early 1980s. It is hard enough for women and men to find any jobs at all – and in this climate it is unlikely that employers will make real efforts to open up more jobs to women, or that unions will make this a priority in collective bargaining. At the same time, public spending cuts have put an end to hopes that more child-care facilities will be provided in the foreseeable future.

And women's right to paid maternity leave, inadequate when it was introduced in 1975, is being eroded still further.

Many overt and legal forms of discrimination persist. For instance, unless a married woman applies for separate tax assessment, her income is treated as part of her husband's by the Inland Revenue. A married woman cannot claim supplementary benefit in her own right: her husband must claim it for her. A single woman loses her right to supplementary benefit if she is thought to be living with a man, because she is expected to be supported by him.

The law does not recognize that a woman has the right to control her own body. The ultimate decision on abortion rests with the doctor, not with the pregnant woman; National Health abortions are increasingly difficult to obtain and many women still pay more than £100 for the operation. Vigorous attempts have been made to restrict the abortion law still further, and although they remained unsuccessful until 1981, a new attempt is expected at any time.

A man can still rape his wife without contravening the letter of the law. Despite the good intentions of the Matrimonial Proceedings and Property Act, judges have reverted to the old rule of awarding a divorced woman only one third of the income and capital owned by herself and her husband during the marriage. The right of British women married to foreigners to live in Britain with their husbands has been severely restricted and may soon be removed altogether. Women who are not British citizens, but who have been working here for years (particularly Filipino women), have been deported when they asked to bring their children here to live with them.

In addition to these practical inequalities, women still suffer discrimination in the way they experience the world from the moment of birth. Girls and boys are treated differently by their parents and teachers, and encouraged to behave differently. Toys and books reinforce the traditional male and female roles. The Sex Discrimination Act has done next to nothing to change the way schools treat girls and boys, and cuts in education spending have put an end to hopes of improvement. Girls are still brought up to believe that their main function in life is to marry, have babies and find satisfaction through their children and husbands – rather than to recognize their full potential and to determine their lives according to their real abilities and inclinations. There remains a clear distinction between male and female roles in employment and at home. Men are still regarded as the main breadwinners for their families, even though a woman's wage is indispensable to most households. And women are still expected to be responsible for housework and child care, regardless of whether or not they go out to work.

So some progress has been made since the beginning of the nineteenth century, but there is still a long way to go and the obstacles look formidable. The most important positive development has been the emergence of the women's movement. In the course of ten years it has made a significant impact on public attitudes – and it is still a force to be reckoned with. More women are now aware that they are excluded from power and that men have control over the framing and enforcement of laws, and over the machinery of government. Women have begun to play a fuller part in trade unions and in politics generally. We have built up a sense of solidarity and a determination to fight back. We are better prepared now than we were at the beginning of the 1970s to defend ourselves against attack and to carry on the fight for equality.

This guide is designed to assist in that fight. Its main purpose is as a practical handbook, to help women gain a useful knowledge of the laws, traditions, rules and regulations which affect their rights – so that they can know best how to defend them when they come under attack.

The material is arranged under broad subject headings. You will find some areas more relevant to you than others, depending on whether you are married or single, with or without children. The special contents table on pp. 9–12 is designed to direct you to parts of the book most useful for your particular situation. For women in Scotland and Northern Ireland, where some areas of the law are very different, the same contents table, pp. 11–12, shows you where the main differences lie. You will find special notes, designed to adapt this book to your needs, in Appendix 2, pp. 503–30.

We cannot provide the ideal solution to every problem. In a straightforward situation, we hope we have provided enough information to enable you to take action on your own. If your problem is more complex, the information will give you a basic idea of what your rights are, so that you may be encouraged to seek expert advice – either from a solicitor, or from one of the specialist organizations listed at the end of most chapters or on pp. 497–502. The law is rapidly changing in this field and it is almost impossible to be completely up to date. The last date on which we were able to make any alterations to the text was 1 July 1981.

The guide is also intended to be more than just a practical handbook. It explains aspects of the law which have particular significance for women. It shows where the law can be used to help women to assert and defend their rights. It also points out ways in which the law discriminates against women. For the same purpose it attempts to unravel some of the red tape produced by government machinery. It suggests changes of all kinds that might be made to improve the position of women. In other words it is a self-help guide, a catalogue of evils and something of a manifesto.

Anna Coote
Tess Gill

# 1. An Introduction to the Sex Discrimination Act

The Sex Discrimination Act came into force on 29 December 1975. It was only passed after an intensive campaign lasting eight years. It was never seen as perfect nor as the main way to deal with sex discrimination. If we are to achieve real equality, it is essential that women are determined not to accept second-class status and that men are prepared to back them. We also need an educational system geared to equal opportunities and trade unions prepared to work for change.

The terms of the Act are limited and the enforcement machinery inadequate. But it is better than nothing. For centuries discrimination against women has been perfectly legal. Now – in theory – it is against the law.

However, in practice the Act has been very disappointing. Few cases have been brought and even fewer have succeeded. Our tribunals and courts seem to be distinctly uneasy in the role of eradicators of prejudice and tradition. For every decision upholding the new standards of non-discrimination one can find ten that let the employer off the hook by using the kind of arguments that the law is supposed to extinguish. The economic climate has not helped. Unemployment and job insecurity do not provide an ideal base from which to launch bold initiatives. Nonetheless, the Act is still an advance and has not yet been fully utilized. Women still need to know what it says and how to use it.

The Sex Discrimination Act affects many different aspects of women's lives and so is relevant to a number of chapters in this book. Here we describe the broad outlines of the Act. It is dealt with in more detail elsewhere in relation to:

- employment and training, p. 41
- education, p. 335
- provision of goods, facilities and services, p. 402
- housing, p. 392; mortgages, p. 397
- enforcement through industrial tribunals, p. 488
- enforcement through county courts, p. 461
- powers of the Equal Opportunities Commission, p. 481

### What does the Act say?

It is illegal to discriminate on grounds of sex in the fields of employment and training; education; housing; and the provision of goods, facilities and services.

In employment and training, it is also illegal to discriminate against married people.

*It applies to women and men.* This chapter concentrates on the way the law affects women. But the Act applies to men in exactly the same way, except in relation to: (a) protective laws for women factory workers; and (b) maternity provisions.

### What does discrimination mean?

Discrimination means treating a woman less favourably than a man would be treated in the same circumstances, just because she is a woman. It can also mean (in employment and training) treating a married woman less favourably than a single woman would be treated in the same circumstances, just because she's married.

### Not all discrimination is unlawful

1. There are plenty of exceptions in each of the major areas covered by the Act. We have listed these under the separate headings.
2. The Act does not cover tax, Social Security, conditions relating to retirement (including pensions), immigration law and health and birth control provisions.
3. Discrimination against married people is lawful in areas other

than employment and training. Discrimination against single people (treating a single woman less favourably than a married woman, just because she is single) remains lawful in all fields.

## There are two kinds of unlawful discrimination: direct and indirect

*Direct discrimination* is a straightforward matter of treating a woman less favourably than a man, or a married woman less favourably than a single woman. Here are two examples:

1. You apply for a training course. You have the necessary qualifications, but you are turned down. Only men are accepted for the course. Their qualifications are no better than yours. Women have never been on the course before.
2. You go into a bar and order a drink. The barman tells you women are not allowed to buy drinks and asks you to sit down. He says you can only stay in the bar if you remain seated while a man buys you drinks.

*Indirect discrimination* means imposing certain conditions which can be met by more people of one sex than another (or by more single than married people). Unlike direct discrimination, it is only

against the law if it cannot be shown to be *justifiable*. Here are two examples of indirect discrimination:

1. You are 30. Now that your two children have reached school age, you want to go back to work. You apply for a job for which you have all the necessary qualifications. Then you learn that the company will not consider applicants over the age of 29. Since so many women have a break from employment in their twenties, it could be argued that this is a case of indirect discrimination. If the employer cannot show that it is justifiable, in terms of the requirements for this particular job, to exclude applicants over 29, it might be proved unlawful under the Act.
2. A company offers cheap mortgages to all employees in the 'executive' grade, which happens to be almost exclusively male. This would amount to unlawful discrimination unless the company could show that it was justified in restricting cheap mortgages to the executive grade.

In some circumstances, indirect discrimination has been so deeply rooted for so long that no woman is likely to get as far as raising a complaint. Here is an example:

A company offers a training course to school leavers. In theory girls are not excluded, but none has ever applied because the recruitment literature is aimed chiefly at boys and the training is for a traditionally male craft. There is no individual complaint because there is no girl who feels she has been treated less favourably. The company is breaking the law by aiming its recruitment at boys only (by showing only boys in the illustrations of its recruitment literature and making no mention of the fact that girls are eligible).

This is known as *discriminatory practice* and it is unlawful. It is up to the Equal Opportunities Commission to take action to stop it – for instance by making sure that the company changes its recruitment literature and distributes it to girls. If you know of a case of discriminatory practice, report it to the Commission (see p. 481).

### How to make the law work

Sex discrimination is not a criminal offence. The police have no power to enforce it. The Equal Opportunities Commission can investigate areas of discrimination and take some action to stop people breaking the law, as shown on p. 482. But its powers and resources are very limited. The fact that the law exists does not mean that discrimination will disappear like magic. If you think you are a victim of unlawful discrimination, it's up to *you* to take action. If you don't, it's unlikely that anyone else will.

Complaints of discrimination in employment and training should be made to an industrial tribunal. Complaints of discrimination in education should be made to the Secretary of State for Education and then to the county court if, after two months, your complaint has not been dealt with to your satisfaction. Complaints of discrimination in housing and the provision of goods, facilities and services should be made to the county court. We explain how to do all this when we deal in detail with each different type of discrimination. In some cases, complaints must be made to the Equal Opportunities Commission. You may be able to get free or partly free advice from a solicitor before you take this action (see p. 452). In employment cases, trade-union support can be invaluable. Don't be afraid to claim your rights. You should have nothing to lose and you may have a lot to gain.

## Victimization is illegal

It is against the law to victimize you for taking any action under the Sex Discrimination or Equal Pay Act. This means it is illegal to treat you less favourably than anyone else just because:

1. You have made a complaint under the Sex Discrimination or Equal Pay Act; *or*
2. You have helped someone else to make a complaint; *or*
3. You have given evidence at a court or tribunal hearing in connection with a complaint under one of the Acts; *or*
4. You have accused someone of breaking either law; *or*
5. You have taken any other action in connection with the Sex Discrimination or Equal Pay Act.

If you are victimized you should deal with it in the same way as you would deal with discrimination. Complaints of victimization in employment or training should be made to an industrial tribunal. Complaints of victimization outside the employment field should be made to the county court.

## Employment and training

It is illegal to treat women less favourably than men just because they are women in: training; recruitment; hiring; additional benefits; promotion or transfer to another job; reduction of working hours; redundancy and dismissal. In the same way it is illegal to treat a married woman less favourably than a single woman.

However, *there are plenty of exceptions*. For instance, the Act does not cover jobs in: private households; firms with less than six employees; the Church; the armed forces; mining; acting; modelling; changing rooms or lavatories.

### THESE ORGANIZATIONS MUST NOT DISCRIMINATE

Training bodies; trade unions; employers' associations; professional associations; employment agencies; organizations which license people to perform particular kinds of work; and the government, in appointing people to public bodies (such as the BBC and boards of nationalized industries).

### POSITIVE DISCRIMINATION IS ALLOWED IN SOME CIRCUMSTANCES

Employers, training bodies and trade unions can sometimes treat women more favourably than men in order to counteract past patterns of discrimination. For instance, an employer can take positive steps to train women for a particular type of work, or to encourage them to apply for particular jobs, if the work has been done only (or mainly) by men in the past.

*The protective laws* which apply to women factory workers are not affected by the Act.

*To obtain your rights*, complain to an industrial tribunal within three months of the date on which you suffered discrimination.

*For a full account of unlawful discrimination in employment and training, and how to obtain your rights, see p. 41.*

## Education

Local Education Authorities must offer equal educational facilities to girls and boys in schools and colleges. Single-sex schools and schools run by registered charities are exempt.

*To obtain your rights* you must write to the Secretary of State for Education (if you live in Scotland, write to the Secretary of State for Scotland), but if nothing is done within two months of that, you should make a complaint to the county court.

*For a full account of unlawful discrimination in education and how to obtain your rights, see p. 335.*

## Housing

It is illegal to treat a woman less favourably than a man in renting or selling accommodation. Owner-occupied properties, small boarding houses and shared flats are not covered by the Act.

*For a full account of unlawful discrimination in housing and how to obtain your rights, see p. 392.*

## Goods, facilities and services

It is illegal to treat a woman less favourably than a man in providing goods, facilities and services to the public. This includes pubs, cafés, restaurants, hotels, transport, banking, insurance, H.P., recreation and entertainment.

*There are a great many exceptions*, including private clubs, charities, political organizations, hospitals, old people's homes, and competitive sport.

*To get your rights*, make a complaint to the county court within six months of the date on which you suffered discrimination.

*For a full account of unlawful discrimination in the provision of goods, facilities and services, and how to get your rights, see p. 402.*

### Advertising

It is illegal to publish any advertisement which implies that the advertiser intends to discriminate unlawfully. This includes job advertisements, and advertisements for entertainment or accommodation. If you see an advertisement that you think may be unlawful under the Sex Discrimination Act, report it to the Equal Opportunities Commission. If it is a job advertisement, you may be able to complain directly to an industrial tribunal if you feel it discriminates against you personally. There is more about unlawful discrimination in advertising on pp. 52 and 484.

The Act does not affect the vast majority of advertisements

which are just selling products in ways that exploit women, by casting them in stereotyped roles (dumb blondes, housewives, sex symbols, etc.). But if you think *any* advertisement is illegal, indecent, dishonest or untruthful, complain to the Advertising Standards Authority, Brook House, 2/16 Torrington Place, London WC1.

## Encouraging or aiding unlawful discrimination

It is illegal to put pressure on another person to discriminate unlawfully, either by offering an incentive or by threatening some kind of deterrent. It is also illegal to help someone to discriminate unlawfully, unless the person who gives help has reason to believe a statement (falsely given by the person he helps) that they would not be breaking the law. If someone gives false information, knowing that it is false, or not caring whether it is false or not, to someone else who then helps him break the law, he can be fined up to £400.

If you suspect anyone of encouraging or aiding unlawful discrimination report it to the Equal Opportunities Commission. Only the Commission has power to take action in cases like this.

## The Equal Opportunities Commission

The EOC has been set up to monitor the workings of the Sex Discrimination and Equal Pay Acts and to fight discrimination generally. It has powers to conduct investigations into areas where discrimination is suspected and, where it finds it, to take action to end it.

Its powers are described in full on pp. 481–6.

# 2. Work

## Equal training and job opportunities

Most women work in low-paid, low-status, semi-skilled or unskilled jobs, with little expectation of moving on to better things. While girls are at school there are already strong influences at work to restrict their opportunities. Their interests are directed away from maths and sciences, so that fewer girls than boys take qualifying exams in these subjects. Careers advice is often inadequate and sex-biased: girls are given little encouragement to train outside the conventional female spheres of work. At a time of high unemployment all school leavers are hard pushed to find jobs. But girls head for shop work, catering, hairdressing, low-skilled factory jobs and dead-end office jobs, leaving boys to compete for skilled work in manufacturing and engineering, and for the potentially better-paid white collar work. As Tables 1 and 2 show, most girls go into clerical employment or other jobs with less than eight weeks' training.

Those who go on to universities and colleges find there is little overt discrimination. But a large majority of girls sign on for courses in arts and social sciences. By this stage, they don't have much option – they haven't taken the right exams at school to qualify for the traditionally male-dominated fields of study.

Under the Industrial Training Act 1964, employers have a duty

TABLE 1   16-YEAR-OLD GIRLS AND BOYS
ENTERING EMPLOYMENT, 1978

| Occupation group* | Male All % | Apprentices % | Others % | Female All % | Apprentices % | Others % |
|---|---|---|---|---|---|---|
| Professional and related in science, supporting management and administration | 8·4 | 18·7 | 2·3 | 0·7 | 2·4 | 0·6 |
| Clerical and related occupations | 4·7 | 1·0 | 6·9 | 31·9 | 9·2 | 33·8 |
| Selling occupations | 6·2 | 0·5 | 9·6 | 18·9 | 1·0 | 20·4 |
| Catering, cleaning, hairdressing and other personal service occupations | 3·7 | 2·5 | 4·5 | 12·8 | 70·6 | 8·0 |
| Making and repairing occupations (excluding metal and electrical) | 9·2 | 10·5 | 8·4 | 11·7 | 2·3 | 12·5 |
| Processing, making, repairing and related occupations (metal and electrical) | 24·2 | 44·5 | 12·3 | 1·8 | 2·3 | 1·8 |

* Figures show selected occupations only, as a percentage of all occupations entered in the survey (D.E. Gazette, December 1980).

to provide day-release training for young male and female employees. But the law has never been implemented.

About one in three male employees receive day-release training,
compared with one in ten female employees. The Industrial Training

Boards were set up under the 1964 Act. Their approach to the traditional divisions of labour has changed only slowly and the attitudes conveyed in the following statements were still quite prevalent in 1981:

We find that women are generally in the majority on courses on sales techniques, buying, sales promotion and display, and that men tend to predominate in courses on financial management and instructional techniques ... the only limitations to (women's) advancement in distribution are those arising from their own, and perhaps their employers', perception of the sort of work upon which they should be engaged. (Distributive Industry Training Board, 1975)

There is no bar to [women] joining any course. The only restriction is that many of them have domestic ties. In the main we are talking about training at craft and operative level, as many of the women are not career-minded and therefore not attracted to career courses. (Footwear, Leather and Fur Training Industry Board, 1975)

TABLE 2   LENGTH OF TRAINING RECEIVED BY GIRLS AND BOYS
ENTERING EMPLOYMENT, 1978

| Length of training | *Male* | | | *Female* | | |
|---|---|---|---|---|---|---|
| | *All* | *Apprentices* | *Others* | *All* | *Apprentices* | *Others* |
| No training | 36·4 | – | 57·7 | 48·2 | – | 52·3 |
| 1–2 weeks | 2·6 | – | 4·2 | 4·4 | – | 4·7 |
| 3–8 weeks | 7·5 | – | 11·9 | 19·1 | – | 20·7 |
| 9–26 weeks | 8·0 | – | 12·7 | 13·0 | – | 14·1 |
| 27–52 weeks | 3·3 | – | 5·2 | 3·5 | – | 3·8 |
| 53–104 weeks | 6·0 | 8·1 | 4·7 | 4·6 | 21·8 | 3·2 |
| 105 weeks or more | 36·2 | 91·9 | 3·6 | 7·2 | 78·2 | 1·3 |

Source: *Employment Gazette*, December 1980.

The Industrial Training Board for the hairdressing industry (which accounts for 75 per cent of female apprentices) has been abandoned: that industry depends heavily on the cheap labour of girls who spend most of their time washing hair and sweeping floors, and get very little proper training. There has never been a Training Board for clerical work – which is the largest single source of jobs for women, accounting for 40 per cent of full-time female employees.

However, since 1975 some of the Training Boards have set up special training courses for women. The Engineering Industry Training Board pays grants to firms that recruit women technicians, trainees, in addition to their normal intake. In 1980, 250 grants were made. The Engineering and Clothing Allied Products Industry Training Board gave scholarships to girls for degree courses in engineering. Others, including the Food, Drink and Tobacco Board, give grants to employers developing women employees as managers. The Clothing and Allied Products Board gives grants to employers offering training to women as clothing machine mechanics, work study practitioners, and for middle management. In 1980/81 eighteen 'Wider Opportunities for Women' courses were being set up throughout the U.K. by the Manpower Services Commission, for women who have not worked outside the home for some time (if at all) and who now want a job.

The Manpower Services Commission's Training Services Division (TSD) runs what are known as 'TOPS' (Training Opportunities Scheme) courses for women and men. One of their aims is to provide 'opportunities for women to train for traditionally male occupations'. The number of women on government training courses has increased dramatically – from 6,000 in 1972 to just over 32,000 in 1979, or 43 per cent of all TOPS trainees that year. The number of women taking non-traditional courses in craft subjects such as motor vehicle repair and carpentry has also increased, from 127 in 1975 to 785 in 1979; but the vast majority continue to train for traditional female occupations, mainly in clerical, secretarial and commercial fields. In 1980, 23,000 women completed TOPS courses in these subjects, about 70 per cent of all women TOPS trainees. However, the percentage is down since 1975, when 85 per cent of all female TOPS trainees took clerical/commercial courses.

A survey of 764 establishments, carried out in 1980 for the Department of Employment, showed that equal numbers of women and men take advantage of on-the-job training, but men get far more off-site and off-the-job training (17 per cent, compared with

7 per cent of women) which tends to be more expensive, as well as more significant as a means to promotion.

Women fill a high proportion of places in apprenticeships and training schemes for professional, intermediate and junior non-manual and personal service workers – but these account for only 15 per cent of all sorts of training. Women's participation in training for management (3 per cent) and for skilled manual jobs (45 per cent of all training, in which 2 per cent of trainees are female) is derisory. See p. 68 for training schemes for the unemployed.

One reason why women haven't fought harder for their right to proper training is that so many of them have been brought up to believe that their chief destination is marriage and motherhood – with employment as an insignificant phase between school and the first pregnancy. Of course, this is far from the truth. Nowadays, most families need two breadwinners. Allowing a ten-year interval for child-rearing, most women can anticipate thirty years of paid employment. Women make up 44 per cent of the labour force. Those aged between 40 and 49 account for the largest section (20 per cent) of female employees. Well over half the married women over 35 go out to work. One in six households depends on a woman as the sole or main breadwinner. Yet they still bear the main burden of domestic labour – shopping, washing, and generally looking after their husbands and children. So they do two jobs: paid work outside the home and unpaid work within. The husband's job takes priority. If *he* has to move, the wife goes too. Child-care facilities are so scarce that many women are forced into part-time or temporary work – usually the lowest paid, the least secure and offering the least potential. Forty per cent of women do part-time work, compared with 5 per cent of men. It is women, not men, who are expected to take time off work when their children are sick and to stop and start their jobs to fit in with school holidays. Domestic duties may leave them little time for trade-union activities, so they tend to be more vulnerable to low pay and redundancy.

People cling to the myth that 'workers' and 'women' are two separate species: a proper 'worker' does not have domestic com-mitments, while a proper 'woman' has home responsibilities and therefore is not a fully-fledged 'worker'. As a result, *all* women, regardless of their domestic situation, suffer from the generalized assumptions employers make about female workers: 'it's not worth training them, they'll only leave'; 'they're unreliable, always taking time off'; 'they only work for pin-money'. It's a vicious circle. It will not be broken until more people accept that women *and* men are workers with dual responsibilities – to earn money and to look after their homes and families; and that both need shorter and more flexible working hours to fulfil their commitments.

## What can be done to change the situation?

Of course, there are no simple remedies. In the first place, girls need real equality of opportunity at school (more about that on p. 335). When they start to think about training and jobs, they need full and unbiased information about the range of possibilities that are open to them, and good advice to help them choose what is best – according to their potential, not their limitations. It is not within the scope of our book to offer this kind of information and advice, but at the end of this section we have included a list of organizations, addresses and publications that we hope will be useful (p. 497).

The Sex Discrimination and Equal Pay Acts which came into force at the end of 1975 are supposed to give women equal rights at work. But as most women know by now, there won't be any miracles. The laws can be used to combat the more immediate and obvious forms of inequality – but they won't sweep away the underlying patterns of discrimination we have just described. They leave plenty of loopholes – so it's easy for employers to remain within the letter of the law, whilst defying the spirit of it.

JOIN A UNION

With or without the new Acts, women can achieve very little as isolated individuals. They need to organize in trade unions to fight for equal rights and for better pay and conditions for all workers.

But the unions will not fight effectively unless women themselves are actively involved and properly represented at every level.

Women are joining trade unions nearly twice as fast as men. One third of all women workers now belong to unions and they account for more than a quarter of the membership of all unions affiliated to the Trades Union Congress. But they are very poorly represented among trade-union officials and elected representatives. Only about 5 per cent of officials are female. At the 1980 meeting of the TUC there were more than 1,200 delegates, but only 120 were women.

### BE ACTIVE IN YOUR UNION

Try to attend union meetings regularly, take part in discussions, policy votes and elections. If your branch holds its meetings at a time or place which is inconvenient or off-putting for women, get together with other members and try to get this changed. Meetings held during work hours or at lunchtime and at your place of work may be more suitable than evening meetings at a pub. If your union holds weekend schools which you can't attend because there are no facilities for children, demand that they provide a crèche. You may find that your union takes a strong stand for women at a national level, but your local representatives and fellow members are behind the times. Don't be discouraged – find out what the official policy of your union is and make sure that it is carried out in your area. If you don't like the official policy, start organizing now to change it.

If you feel isolated because your branch meetings are dominated by men, and you want a chance to meet other women, find out whether your union provides any special women's committees, courses or conferences. Taking part in these should be a good way of planning campaigns for the future and generally building up confidence and experience. Some unions are now making big efforts to encourage women to join and be more active. Some still give the impression that women are acceptable as long as they behave like men. There is a continuing debate within trade unions about special provisions for women. Some members argue that if women want to be equal they shouldn't have any privileges or separate arrangements; that women's issues should not be hived off from the mainstream of union life; and that the best way to move towards equality is to treat women the same as men. However, if no positive steps are taken to encourage women to be more active in their unions, men will continue to have the first and last say; women will continue to feel intimidated or uninvolved in what they see as a man's world; and issues of particular concern to women will remain at the bottom of the pile of union business. So at this stage we need discrimination in favour of women, to encourage them to become more active and ensure that unions fight for the things women need – such as equal pay, child-care facilities and adequate maternity leave – so that in future special provisions will not be necessary.

In 1979 the TUC published a Charter for Equality for Women within Trade Unions. It is reproduced overleaf, and is the first official call for special provision for women within trade-union structures to ensure that their views are represented. Since its publication some large unions such as the General and Municipal Workers Union and the Transport and General Workers Union have taken steps to set up special women's committees in their regions to advise the union on what action they should be taking for women members. If you think your union isn't doing enough for women use the Charter to back up your argument that it should do more.

MAKE THE NEW LAWS WORK FOR YOU

The Sex Discrimination and Equal Pay Acts got off to a very poor start. In the first six months of 1976, only 20 complaints of sex discrimination were heard by industrial tribunals and only 5 of them succeeded; out of 110 equal pay claims, only 31 were won. During 1979, 61 complaints of sex discrimination were heard. Only 16 succeeded. The number of equal pay claims has dropped since 1976. In 1979, 78 claims were heard by a tribunal. Thirteen succeeded.

The fact that so few cases have been brought under the Sex Discrimination Act suggests that women have been put off by the

# A TUC CHARTER

## EQUALITY FOR WOMEN WITHIN TRADE UNIONS

**1** The National Executive Committee of the union should publicly declare to all its members the commitment of the union to involving women members in the activities of the union at all levels.

**2** The structure of the union should be examined to see whether it prevents women from reaching the decision-making bodies.

**3** Where there are large women's memberships but no women on the decision-making bodies special provision should be made to ensure that women's views are represented, either through the creation of additional seats or by co-option.

**4** The National Executive Committee of each union should consider the desirability of setting up advisory committees within its constitutional machinery to ensure that the special interests of its women members are protected.

**5** Similar committees at regional, divisional, and district level could also assist by encouraging the active involvement of women in the general activities of the union.

**6** Efforts should be made to include in collective agreements provision for time off without loss of pay to attend branch meetings during working hours where that is practicable.

**7** Where it is not practicable to hold meetings during working hours every effort should be made to provide child-care facilities for use by either parent.

**8** Child-care facilities, for use by either parent, should be provided at all district, divisional and regional meetings and particularly at the union's annual conference, and for training courses organized by the union.

**9** Although it may be open to any members of either sex to go to union training courses, special encouragement should be given to women to attend.

**10** The content of journals and other union publications should be presented in non-sexist terms.

complexity of the legislation and the low success rate. Legal aid is not available for tribunal hearings, and since most employers can afford to hire lawyers while individual women cannot, this obviously puts them in a much stronger position, particularly where the woman is not represented by a trade union. If the laws are to be put to women's advantage, it is important for individual workers and trade-union representatives to understand their provisions and how they can be enforced, and for legal aid to be extended to tribunal cases. The Act also needs improving (see p. 85).

## What the Sex Discrimination Act says

*The first chapter describes the general provisions of the Act. Since it is relevant to this section (which deals with employment and training only) we suggest you read it first.*

Under the Sex Discrimination Act it is illegal, in the field of employment, to treat a woman less favourably than a man would be treated in the same circumstances; or to treat a married woman less favourably than a single woman would be treated in the same circumstances. (Although we describe the Act as it applies to women, it is illegal to discriminate against either sex.)

The Act covers temporary and permanent employees; apprentices and trainees; partners in firms with six or more partners; and self-employed workers who are contracted to do a particular job (such as 'lump' building workers and contract cleaners).

IT APPLIES TO THE FOLLOWING ASPECTS OF WORK

Training; recruitment; considering applicants for jobs; hiring; additional benefits, such as extra time off, or help with housing; promotion or transfer to another job; putting workers on short time; redundancy or dismissal; *and* conditions of employment or money payments which are *not* included in your contract (see below: *What is a contract?*).

LINKS BETWEEN THE SEX DISCRIMINATION AND EQUAL PAY ACTS

1. Any provision for payment of money which is included in your contract of employment must be dealt with under the Equal Pay Act. This could cover wages, salaries, overtime pay, bonuses, sick pay, etc.
2. Any other conditions of employment which are included in your contract must also be dealt with under the Equal Pay Act. This could cover hours of work, length of holidays, etc.
3. Any provision for the payment of money or employment conditions which is *not* included in your contract of employment must be dealt with under the Sex Discrimination Act.
4. If an employer offers you a job on terms which infringe the Equal Pay Act, he is discriminating unlawfully. In this case, you must bring your complaint under the Sex Discrimination Act, not the Equal Pay Act.

*For a full account of your rights under the Equal Pay Act, see p. 72.*

### What is a contract?

Your contract of employment may be in writing or it may have been made verbally when you took on the job. So if, for instance, you start work as a shop assistant on Monday morning and you are simply told what hours you are expected to work and how much you will be paid, that constitutes a contract. However, if you have been in a job for at least thirteen weeks and working sixteen hours a week or more, your employer must give you a written contract or statement setting out the terms of your employment to include hours, pay, holidays, etc. If you find that the hours, rates of pay, or other terms and conditions are less favourable than those given to men doing similar work, you can make a claim under the Equal Pay Act.

## *Unlawful discrimination can be direct or indirect*

1. *Direct discrimination* is a straightforward matter of treating a woman less favourably than a man, or a married woman less favourably than a single woman.
2. *Indirect discrimination* means imposing certain conditions which can be met by more men than women or more single than married women. It is unlawful unless it can be shown to be justifiable. It is relatively easy for employers to avoid getting caught practising direct discrimination, so it's particularly important to watch out for indirect discrimination and take action against it wherever possible. It could make a big difference if this part of the law were properly enforced.

*Here are some examples to help you identify different kinds of unlawful discrimination:*

1. You apply for an apprenticeship in welding. You are refused. Only boys are taken on and their qualifications are no better than yours. This is *direct* discrimination.
2. You apply for a job. You have all the right qualifications but you are not given an interview. Only men are interviewed and a man is hired. No women have held the job before. This is *direct* discrimination.
3. You work for a building society, which offers cheap mortgages to some of its employees. When you apply for a mortgage you are told that you aren't eligible for one. You discover that all male and single female employees in your salary grade are eligible for cheap mortgages, while married women are not. This is *direct* discrimination against married women.
4. All women workers at your factory are put on short time. The employer argues that the women don't need a full week's wage as much as the men because they 'only work for pin-money'. This is *direct* discrimination.
5. You work as a secretary in a large company. You apply for a place on a course which the company offers in management training. Two male clerks in your office are allowed to go on the course, although their qualifications are no better than yours. Your boss says he 'can't manage without you' and refuses to let you go. This is *direct* discrimination.

6. You work as a tracer in an engineering company and you apply for promotion to become a draughtswoman. You are told that only those who have served apprenticeships on the shop floor are eligible for promotion. Neither you nor any other woman has ever served an apprenticeship with the company. This is *indirect* discrimination. Unless the employer could show that an apprenticeship was an essential qualification for a draughtswoman, he would be breaking the law.

7. A company recruits trainees from local schools. It insists that *all* applicants should have O-level physics and chemistry. The local schools are not co-educational. Both subjects are available at girls' schools, but very few girls take them as it is traditional for them to opt for biology. This is *indirect* discrimination. If the employer cannot show that it is justifiable because trainees need a knowledge of physics and chemistry to do the job he would be breaking the law.

8. Your employer issues redundancy notices to individual workers in three out of eight wage grades. All three grades are predominantly female. Nearly all male workers are in the other grades. This is *indirect* discrimination. The employer is breaking the law unless he can prove that he is justified in limiting redundancies to the three predominantly female grades.

## Discrimination is not always unlawful

The Act is full of loopholes – some more reasonable than others. It does not cover the following:

1. Treating a single woman less favourably than a married woman. For example, it would still be lawful for an employer to give extended maternity leave (beyond the provisions of the Employment Protection Act, p. 91) to married women, but to refuse it to single women.

2. Conditions relating to pregnancy or childbirth. It is still legal for an employer to give special treatment to a woman who is having a baby – this covers maternity pay and extra time off, and possibly also dismissal or similarly unfair treatment as explained on pp. 60–61.

3. Conditions relating to retirement and pensions. Female employees can still retire earlier than male employees and be given inferior pension rights. (More about pensions on pp. 154–69.)
4. Employment in private households.
5. Where an employer has less than six people working for him.
6. Employment in the army, navy or air force.
7. Mining: women were forbidden to work underground in mines before this law was passed. They are still barred from working in active mines, although they can work in mines which are disused, or hold jobs which involve only an insignificant amount of time in an active mine.
8. Working for a church which has a sex bar either because of its religious doctrine or in order to avoid 'offending the religious susceptibilities of a significant number of its followers'. So the Church of England can go on refusing to ordain women.
9. Only women are allowed to be midwives, except in certain colleges and hospitals approved by the Department of Health.
10. Where sex is a *Genuine Occupational Qualification* (GOQ) for all *or part* of a job. Like most of the Act's provisions, this applies to men as well as women. The Act says that sex can be a GOQ in the following situations:
(a) The 'essential nature' of the job calls for a man for reasons of 'physiology'. This would apply, for instance, to modelling. It could not be used to exclude women from a job where physical strength was needed, simply because of the general assumption that women are weaker than men; each applicant would have to be judged on her/his merit.
(b) The 'essential nature of the job calls for a man for reasons of authenticity'. This applies only to entertainment and dramatic performances and could cover actors, singers and dancers. As in the case above, it would be necessary to show that the 'essential nature' of the job would be 'materially different' if done by a woman.
(c) The job must be done by a man in order to preserve 'decency or privacy' because it involves physical contact with men in circumstances where men might reasonably object to having

women present. This could cover masseurs, friskers, and assistants in men's clothing shops who have to measure the inside leg. It cannot generally be used against women doctors, nurses or other medical attendants, since women are commonly employed in these jobs already, although there is an exception for single-sex hospitals, see below (f).

(d) The job must be done by a man to preserve 'decency or privacy' because men are likely to be undressed or using sanitary facilities and might reasonably object to a woman being present. This covers lavatory attendants and changing-room attendants, but in the latter case it applies only to attendants who help fit clothes, with access to changing cubicles – not to shop assistants who merely direct customers to changing rooms.

(e) The nature or location of the job would make it impractical for a female employee to live anywhere except in premises provided by the employer, where men are already living and where there is no separate sleeping accommodation for women, nor toilets or bathrooms which they could use in privacy. In a case like this, the employer can go on hiring men – but *only if* it would be unreasonable to expect him to provide separate facilities for women (if it were prohibitively expensive, or impossible to find extra room). This could only cover jobs on ships, some lighthouses and remote work sites.

(f) The job is in a single-sex hospital, prison, old people's home, children's home, mental home or any other place for people needing special care or supervision. But it must be 'reasonable', considering the 'essential character of the establishment' to insist that the particular job is held by a person of one sex only. This clause is very vague and it is hard to tell exactly what it could mean. It may, for instance, cover teachers and nurses in a children's home, but not gardeners, cooks and caretakers. The Act does not allow a man to be governor of a women's prison.

(g) The job provides individuals with personal welfare, education or a similar service and the service can 'most effectively' be provided by a man. This could cover personnel officers, probation officers, social workers and teachers. It is extremely vague.

One example given is where a man might respond better to a male welfare worker. But beyond that it is not clear which services, or in what circumstances, might be provided more effectively by members of one sex.

(h) The job must be done by a man because of the restrictions imposed by the protective laws (see p. 104 for details of the protective laws). There is a danger that this could be used by employers as a way to go on treating women less favourably than men.

(i) The job must be held by a man because it is likely to involve work outside the United Kingdom in a country 'whose laws or customs are such that the duties could not be performed effectively by a woman'. This allows discrimination in jobs such as salesmen travelling to Arab countries.

(j) The job is one of two to be held by a married couple (such as caretakers of an old people's home).

POINTS TO REMEMBER ABOUT THE 'GENUINE OCCUPATIONAL QUALIFICATION'

The GOQ clause could provide useful loopholes for employers trying to get around the Sex Discrimination Act. Watch out for attempts to rearrange jobs to take advantage of the clause. Here are some points worth remembering:

1. An employer cannot claim exemption under the GOQ clause for hiring new workers if he already has enough workers of one sex to do the job (for instance, if he already has enough men to fill the night shift, he cannot discriminate against women when he takes on more workers).

2. The GOQ clause can only be used on one job at a time. So if, for instance, a department store succeeded in its claim that it must hire a man to work in the men's underwear department, this doesn't mean that all underwear sales people in that store, or anywhere else, would automatically be exempted. It would have to be argued for each job that the GOQ applied.

3. The GOQ does not apply to any situations *not* described in (a) to (j) above. An employer cannot argue, for instance, that sex is a genuine occupational qualification because 'my customers prefer women'; or 'my men won't work with a woman in charge'; or 'I can't afford to build extra toilets'; or 'It's not a nice job for a woman'. None of these situations is mentioned in the GOQ clause.

*Note:* Employers can discriminate *in favour* of women in some circumstances, as explained on p. 50.

## Organizations which are covered by the Sex Discrimination Act

1. *Training bodies*, such as industrial training boards and the MSC's Training Services Division, and anyone else who has been recognized by the Department of Employment as providing job-training facilities. These must not treat women less favourably than men in selecting them for training courses or in the type of training given.

    Training bodies can discriminate in favour of women in some circumstances, see p. 50.

2. *Employment agencies.* It is unlawful for an employment agency to discriminate against you by the terms it offers; by the way it provides any of its services; or by deliberately omitting to provide services. So an employment agency cannot cater for men (or women) only; it cannot have separate lists of jobs for women and men or display separate advertisements. It cannot refuse to send you for an interview because it thinks the employer would prefer a man. It is very difficult to monitor the activities of employment agencies since so much of their business is done by telephone, without making any records. Their success depends on providing employers with the sort of workers they want, so they can act as a convenient buffer between discriminating bosses and the law.

If you have evidence that an employment agency is breaking the law, you can complain to an industrial tribunal (p. 488).

3. *Licensing bodies.* Organizations which give licences or other forms of authorization to enable a person to do a particular type of work must not discriminate against you by refusing to give you a licence; or giving it on inferior terms; or taking the licence away. This covers – among others – the Law Society, which issues certificates of practice to solicitors; the Director of Fair Trading, who licenses credit and hire businesses; magistrates, who license publicans and money lenders; the Jockey Club; and the police, who license taxi drivers.

Wherever a licensing body has to consider the 'good character' of an applicant, it must take into account whether he or she has previously discriminated unlawfully. So a magistrate reviewing a publican's licence would have to take account of any evidence that he had refused to serve women since the Sex Discrimination Act came into force.

Complaints against licensing bodies go to industrial tribunals (p. 488).

4. *The Government* must not discriminate against women in making public appointments. Every year, the Government appoints hundreds of people to public bodies such as the BBC and boards of nationalized industries. If you come across this kind of discrimination, report it to the Equal Opportunities Commission (p. 481). Only they can deal with it.

5. *Trade unions.* These must not discriminate in any of the ways we have already described when referring to employers generally. In addition they must not treat women less favourably in any of the following ways:

(a) In deciding whom to admit to membership;

(b) By refusing to let you join;

(c) In the terms on which they offer you membership;

(d) In the way they give you benefits, facilities or services (such as social facilities, legal services or representation at an industrial tribunal or during a strike);

(e) By expelling you or putting you at a disadvantage in some other way.

They cannot charge men and women different subscriptions or give them different rates of strike or sickness pay, or other benefits. However, retirement and death benefits are not covered by the Act. Complaints against trade unions, employers' or professional associations go to an industrial tribunal (p. 488). Trade unions can discriminate in favour of women in some circumstances (see below).

6. *Employers' and Professional Associations.* These must not discriminate in any of the ways described above for trade unions. Complaints go to an industrial tribunal. However, employers' and professional associations can discriminate in favour of women in some circumstances, see below.

## Positive discrimination in favour of one sex is allowed in some circumstances

Patterns of discrimination are so firmly rooted in some areas that they cannot be shaken just by ceasing to discriminate *against* women. Positive action *in favour* of women is vital. Since positive action involves discrimination against men, there is a special clause in the Sex Discrimination Act which makes it legal – but only in the circumstances outlined below.

1. Training bodies can take positive action in favour of women in some circumstances. This covers the Manpower Services Commission's Training and Employment Service Divisions and the industrial training boards. Other bodies may get special permission from the Department of Employment. Positive action may be taken to train women in areas of work where men are in a substantial majority – it can include limiting access to women only, giving them special encouragement to enrol in courses, and making special provision for training women who are returning to work after raising their families (see p. 67).
2. If an employer has no women or very few in a particular type of

work, he can encourage women to apply, without breaking the law. But once they have applied, he must treat male and female applicants equally. Employers can lay on special training courses for women in similar circumstances. A survey by the Equal Opportunities Commission published in September 1978 showed that only seven employers out of 441 had laid on special training for women, and most of these had been geared to encourage them to become managers.

3. Trade unions and professional associations can discriminate in favour of women. This is a particularly important provision in view of the need for women to become more actively involved in trade unions (see p. 38). There are four ways in which positive action can be taken:

(a) Organizing training to help women hold posts within the union (such as shop stewards' courses for women only).

(b) Encouraging women to take advantage of opportunities to hold posts within the organization (such as a special campaign to recruit female officials).

(c) Recruiting one sex only (such as a special campaign to recruit more women).

(d) Reserving a quota of seats on elected committees to ensure that a reasonable number of women are elected.

Trade unions can only discriminate in favour of one sex in order to redress the balance in areas where the other sex has been predominant. So a union cannot conduct a special campaign to recruit more women if it already has a substantial proportion of female members  only if women are in the minority.

4. Employers' organizations and professional associations can discriminate in favour of women in the same way as trade unions (see above). Unlike the U.S. affirmative action programmes, the British law does not oblige anyone to take positive action − it merely refrains from penalizing those who do. So it will be up to women themselves, and to trade unions, training bodies and other organizations that are allowed to discriminate in favour of women, to take the initiative.

*See p. 85 for more about positive action in the workplace.*

## Job advertisements

It is illegal to advertise a job in a way which indicates that the employer intends to discriminate unlawfully. So jobs cannot be advertised under headings such as 'Women's Appointments'. They must not use words which imply that the employer is looking for men (or women) only, such as 'girl Friday' or 'waiter' unless the advertisement specifically says that both sexes will be considered. Advertisements for jobs where discrimination is allowed (such as in private households, small firms or abroad) can state which sex is required. The following advertisement, found in a national newspaper before the Act came into force, would certainly be illegal now.

WHAT'S NEW IN LONDON, PUSSYCAT?

Could be a super new job with the boss of a five million pound company in sunny South Wimbledon. Young, married and a bit of a tiger at times, he's looking for a very special Secretary/P.A. who can also drive a Daimler or a sports car. Travel, top salary and a lot more besides are all waiting for the girl who makes him purr.

The next advertisement, found in a national newspaper on 16 June 1976, is probably also against the law:

We need the services of an experienced scaffolding designer/draughtsman to provide design/calculation service for all types of scaffolding applications. Familiarity with scaffold systems together with knowledge of the contracting side of the industry is essential . . .

It uses the word 'draughtsman' but nowhere does it mention that women will be considered for the job.

If you find an unlawful job advertisement, bring it to the attention of the Equal Opportunities Commission (p. 481). Alternatively, if you think the advertisement discriminates against you personally (by deterring you from applying for a job) you can complain to an industrial tribunal.

## *How to get your rights*

This section tells you how to take a complaint of sex discrimination to an industrial tribunal. But of course this isn't the only way of fighting discrimination against women workers. If you belong to a trade union, collective bargaining or, if necessary, industrial action may prove the most effective way of getting your rights. It may be best in your case to combine both means – using the legal procedure to back up your negotiations.

WHEN TO CLAIM

If you think someone has discriminated against you in any of the ways described in the first part of this chapter, you can make a complaint to an industrial tribunal within three months of the day on which the discrimination occurs. Get the complaint form from your local employment exchange or job centre.

*If your complaint is late* you will not be able to pursue it unless you can show the tribunal that it would be unreasonable to expect you to make the complaint in time. The tribunal could accept a late complaint if you were refused a job but the employer did not appoint another person until three months later – or for some other similar reason. Also, the tribunal could accept a late complaint if you had taken it first to the county court, by mistake.

WHAT CAN YOU CLAIM?

There are three things for which you are entitled to claim:

1. A decision that the employer has discriminated unlawfully, and a statement about your rights and those of the employer.
2. A recommendation (e.g. that you should be promoted or given the fringe benefit that you were previously refused).
3. An award of money as compensation.

It is up to you to decide what recommendations you want from the tribunal. You should make this decision in advance, so that you can tell the conciliation officer and (if it gets that far) the tribunal. For instance, if you were refused a job, you might want to ask to be given the next available vacancy. If you were refused a fringe benefit, you could ask to be given it on the same terms as male employees. If you want compensation, you must ask for it.

HOW MUCH COMPENSATION?

Work out carefully what you have lost, taking everything into consideration. If, for instance, you were refused a job, you may have been unemployed, or working at a lower wage than you would have been if you had been given the job. Estimate what you have lost in earnings. If the employer refuses to carry out a recommendation (e.g. to give you the next available job, if that is what you have asked for) the tribunal can award you extra compensation instead. But you will have to return to the tribunal for this.

Compensation can include money for 'injury to feelings'. So if, for instance, you were refused promotion, you should ask for a sum of money for the insult you have suffered. You don't have to decide on the sum in this case – the tribunal will decide.

Compensation for *indirect* discrimination can be awarded only if it is proved that the employer *intended* to break the law. If he discriminated unintentionally, he cannot be made to pay, but the tribunal can still make a recommendation that he stops discriminating.

There are special rules for working out compensation for dismissal or redundancy, whether the employer is guilty of sex discrimination or merely unfair dismissal. These rules are on pp. 101–2. The maximum compensation is £6,250.

GET HELP WITH YOUR CASE

If you belong to a *trade union*, ask your shop steward or union official to help you bring your case. She or he should be able to represent you at the conciliation stage if you have a meeting with representatives of the Advisory, Conciliation and Arbitration Service (ACAS), and at the tribunal hearing.

If you cannot get adequate help from your trade union, seek advice from a *solicitor*. You may be able to get this free or partly free under the 'green form procedure' described on p. 454. The solicitor should help you work out exactly what form your complaint should take, what ruling you should ask the tribunal to make, and what evidence you should collect to back up your case. The solicitor may also help you prepare a written statement setting out your case in detail to present to the tribunal.

If you are not sure whether you have proper grounds for a complaint, or you want guidance on which section of the Act applies to your case, you can inquire in writing to ACAS. Write to the regional manager, at the appropriate address listed at the end of this section (p. 63). Alternatively you could try writing to the Equal Opportunities Commission (address, p. 63). The Commission should advise you in a letter, but it may not be able to give you detailed, or even accurate, advice if it doesn't know the full facts of the case. Or write for advice to the Women's Rights Officer, National Council for Civil Liberties (address, p. 64).

PREPARE YOUR CASE CAREFULLY

Collect any documents and information that might back up your case. You have a right to put questions to your employer in order to gather evidence. There are special questionnaire forms which you can use for this purpose: official forms are available from the Equal Opportunities Commission and the National Council for Civil Liberties has produced a more detailed questionnaire, in our view more satisfactory. Alternatively, you can put your own questions to the employer in a letter (make sure you keep a copy). He is not obliged to answer your questions at all, but if he doesn't, or answers evasively, this could count against him when the case is heard.

The sort of information you need to collect depends on the

nature of your complaint. If, for instance, you were refused a job or a promotion, you should try to produce:

1. Details of the job you want, including the advertisement for it, if there was one.
2. Correspondence between you and the employer, including your letter applying for the job/promotion and any letters you received from him.
3. Evidence of your relevant qualifications and experience.
4. Evidence of whether the position you want has been held by other women in the past.
5. Evidence that the person who got the job (i.e. the man or single woman) was not better qualified for it than you.

*If you are complaining about indirect discrimination* you will need to show that significantly fewer women than men could meet whatever test or condition the employer has imposed. If, for instance, the employer limits a particular benefit to employees above a certain salary grade, you will need to know what proportion of those employees are women.

*In all discrimination cases* it is useful if you can get information about general patterns of discrimination within the company, both in the present and in the past. Statements from employees will help.

WHAT HAPPENS NEXT?

When you have sent your complaint form to the industrial tribunal (as explained on p. 53) a copy of it is sent to the employer and to the local officer of ACAS. The officer will contact you and will probably try to settle the matter by conciliation. This is important as a lot of cases are withdrawn at this stage. You may be asked to meet the conciliation officer and the employer to discuss the situation. Make sure you have your case fully prepared and your union representative (if you have one) with you. Don't withdraw your complaint unless you get what you want. ACAS has been criticized for putting too much pressure on women to settle out of court without getting their rights.

If there is no conciliation, your case goes to the tribunal. You will be told the hearing date. The procedure is explained on p. 488.

### IF YOU WIN, BUT YOU HAVE REASON TO THINK THE EMPLOYER WILL GO ON DISCRIMINATING

You can report the case to the Equal Opportunities Commission and ask it to apply for a court injunction ordering the employer to stop discriminating. If the Commission does this and the employer does not obey the injunction, he can be sent to prison. If you think the employer will go on discriminating against other female employees, you can ask the Commission to make an investigation and issue a Non-Discrimination Notice. The Commission's powers are described on p. 481.

## How has the act worked in practice?

### ONE SUCCESSFUL CASE

Three pack house workers, Kathleen Kidd, Ann Harris and Iris Morris, brought a complaint against their employer of fifteen years, John Spencer Scott, of Scott and Knowles Fruit Farm. In January 1976, Scott notified the three workers by letter that all women would cease to be full-time workers on a forty-hour week and would become casuals on a thirty-hour week. This enabled him to avoid giving them equal pay, by reducing their hourly rate from 91½p to 80p, the new casual rate.

The action followed the new Agricultural Wages Order of 1976, which abolished male and female rates of pay, but introduced a new differential between full-time staff doing thirty-one hours a week or more, and part-time staff doing thirty hours a week or less. The volume of work was not reduced – Mr Scott introduced overtime to make sure that all of it was done. But, as casual workers, the women had no security and could be laid off at any time.

The women were members of the National Union of Allied and Agricultural Workers. They pointed out to Scott that they had contracts stipulating a forty-hour week but he retorted that 'the union didn't run his farm'.

Their case was heard by an industrial tribunal in Ashford, Kent, on

3 May 1976. They asked for a return to the forty-hour week and compensation for the money they had lost since their conditions were changed.

Scott's lawyer claimed that the women were not full-time workers and that they were free under a special arrangement to have time off for family duties whenever they wanted. Ann Harris replied that she only took time off to take her daughter to hospital once a year and when she was sick. It was claimed that the women's job needed no intelligence and that they did different work from the men. The women told the tribunal that, although fruit grading was their main job, they did almost all other jobs in the pack house at some time or other. The tribunal decided that Scott had discriminated unlawfully and recommended that the women be restored to a forty-hour week and be awarded back pay.

But most cases have not been so successful. It has been very difficult to prove discrimination.

### DIRECT DISCRIMINATION CASES

You have to prove that you have been treated less favourably than a man has been, or would be, treated in similar circumstances, *and* that the reason for your treatment is because you are a woman or because you are unmarried. It is usually difficult to produce evidence showing the reason for your treatment. Very few employers admit that they do not select women for jobs, training, promotion or other benefits because of their sex. They nearly always produce another reason and you have to prove them wrong.

If an employer fails to produce a reason for treating you less favourably you should succeed in your claim. For example, in the case of Ms Smith who applied to be a 'fireman', all the men were considered after their references had been looked at, but she was rejected before hers were taken up. The Lothian and Borders Fire Board gave no explanation for treating her differently so the tribunal found in her favour.

But other decisions have shown that it is only too easy for employers to convince a tribunal that they are not discriminating.

Mrs Coleman was employed as a booking clerk at a travel agency. In March 1978 she became engaged to a man employed by a rival travel operator. She promised her employer she would not tell him confidential information. However her employer discussed the situation with her husband's firm and, as they thought he was the breadwinner, decided to dismiss her. They did not tell her of the decision until two days after the marriage in September when she got a letter of dismissal with two days' pay in lieu of notice.

Mrs Coleman succeeded in her claim to the Industrial Tribunal but her employers appealed and the Employment Appeal Tribunal said she had not been discriminated against on grounds of sex. There was no evidence to show that her employers would not have dismissed a man in similar circumstances. 'There is nothing to suggest other than that the Appellants decided to resolve the position in what they thought was the best interest of the couple.' As the dismissal was so abrupt Mrs Coleman got £555 compensation for unfair dismissal, but she got nothing for sex discrimination.

Even if an employer asks discriminatory questions when interviewing you for a job, this will not necessarily mean that you succeed in your claim.

Miss Saunders applied for a job as a golf professional with Richmond Borough Council. She failed in her complaint that she had not been selected because she was a woman, even though in her interview she had been asked such questions as whether she thought men would respond as well to a woman professional as to a man; whether the hours were too long for her; whether the job was too unglamorous; and whether she would be able to control troublesome male players. No clear reason was given by the Council for her non-selection, though it appeared that the Committee thought she was not available for a further interview. Miss Saunders appealed but the Employment Appeal Tribunal said that it is not necessarily unlawful to put special questions only to candidates of one sex: it depends whether the *intention* is to discriminate against the woman concerned.

Sometimes reasons which seem sex-related still do not mean that the woman succeeds with her complaint.

When three women complained that they had been unfairly selected for redundancy on sex grounds, the Court of Appeal held that the employer was entitled to select them for lighter tasks, as the decision to do so was not based on sex but on practical experience of organizing work in the warehouse. It followed that, if the need for this lighter work diminished, the employer could select the women for redundancy while the men kept their jobs. Lord Denning said it was like the Inns of Court: 'The heavy work is done by outside porters. They do the lifting and carrying and so forth. Inside at the tables, the waiting and serving meals is done by the women. There is no sex discrimination at all. It is a natural division which comes about because of the different physical qualities of the two sexes.'

If you are complaining that you have been treated unfavourably or, as the Act puts it, 'subjected to a detriment', not all forms of different treatment count.

In a 1977 case when a Mr Peake employed at Automotive Products complained that he was discriminated against because the women at the factory left five minutes early, the Court of Appeal said the treatment must involve 'an element of something inherently adverse or hostile to the interests of the person of the sex said to be discriminated against'. In this case the judges agreed that the arrangement allowing women to leave five minutes early was made in the interests of safety and good administration and was in fact a chivalrous gesture not detrimental treatment.

In similar vein when Miss Schmidt complained that her employers, Austicks Bookshop Ltd, would not allow her to wear trousers while serving customers, her claim failed. According to the court, it was not 'serious or important enough'; men also had instructions on what they could wear.

But in a more recent case it has been said the employer cannot avoid a finding of sex discrimination because he has good intentions.

Ms Greig was refused a job by Community Industry as a painter and decorator. The employer said it was in her own best interest and that of business, because she would be the only woman in the team. The Employment Appeal Tribunal said their motives might be good, but their action nevertheless amounted to unlawful discrimination on the grounds of sex.

*Dismissal because of pregnancy is not sex discrimination.*

If you are dismissed because you are pregnant after you have worked for your employer for a year your dismissal will be unfair and you can ask for your job back and compensation (see p. 101). The Sex Discrimination Act gives protection from dismissal along with other forms of less favourable treatment from the first day of employment. So if you have not been employed for one year you might think that you could claim protection under the Sex Discrimination Act, since being dismissed because of pregnancy would appear to be discrimination against women. At the time of writing, however, the law says otherwise.

Miss Hurley was employed by Arding and Hobbs at Clapham Junction in South London. Her employers, Allders Department Stores, dismissed her while she was pregnant. At the time she had not been employed for a year, so could not bring a claim for unfair dismissal. Instead she brought her claim under the Sex Discrimination Act. The majority of the Employment Appeal Tribunal decided her claim failed because 'in order to see if she had been treated less favourably than a man . . . you must compare like with like, and you cannot in this case. When she is pregnant a woman is no longer just a woman. She is a woman . . . with child, and there is no masculine equivalent.' The woman on the tribunal, Ms Pat Smith, disagreed. She said the 'like with like' comparison is not between women who are pregnant and men who cannot become pregnant. Rather, since pregnancy is a medical condition, the question is whether the employer applies different and less favourable criteria to a pregnant woman requiring time off than to a man requiring time off for a medical condition.

It will need another case and a better court to decide that Pat Smith had the sensible answer.

INDIRECT DISCRIMINATION CASES

As we explained on p. 43, to establish that you have suffered indirect discrimination, you must prove that there is a requirement or condition with which a considerably smaller proportion of women than men can comply. The key test case in this area is that of *Belinda Price vs Civil Service Commission:*

Belinda Price was barred from entering the Civil Service's Executive

Grade by an upper age limit of 28. At the time she applied she was in her early thirties and she had spent a number of years at home looking after her children. She alleged indirect discrimination on the ground that many more women than men are at home looking after their families during their twenties, and therefore cannot comply with the age requirement. Her case went to the Employment Appeal Tribunal, where it was decided that an age bar could constitute indirect discrimination; it was then referred back to the industrial tribunal to consider whether this particular age bar did so, and whether it was justifiable. The Tribunal decided in Belinda Price's favour, on the ground that the age bar discriminated against women and was not justifiable, because the desired aim of the Civil Service Commission – to achieve a certain balance of ages within the Service – could be reached by other means.

Key points emerge from this case which are important to note if you are considering taking a case of indirect discrimination:

1. The test of whether fewer women than men can comply with the condition (i.e. the age bar) was applied not to all women and men in the population, but only to suitably qualified women and men.
2. When it came to deciding who can or cannot *comply* with the condition, it was decided that this involved looking at currently usual behaviour, rather than what was theoretically possible. In other words, the fact that women with small children *can in theory* leave them with a child minder and go off to work in the Civil Service before they are twenty-eight does not count. What counts is that *in practice* many women find they *cannot* go out to work in their twenties while their children are young.
3. Once these points have been established, it is then necessary for the complainant herself to show that she cannot comply.
4. At this point, it is up to the employer to prove that the condition is justifiable on non-sex grounds if he is to avoid a finding of unlawful discrimination. In the Price case, the Employment Appeal Tribunal said that the employer must first prove that the requirement or condition is genuinely necessary; the need for it must then be weighed against its discriminatory effect to assess whether it is justifiable. If it is merely convenient and the same

result can be achieved by some other non-discriminatory method, then the employer fails to show that it is justifiable and therefore lawful.

It is perhaps because these indirect discrimination cases are so complicated to prove that very few of them have been brought to tribunals.

## Further information

Advisory, Conciliation and Arbitration Service (ACAS), for inquiries about the employment provisions of the Sex Discrimination Act. The head office is Cleland House, Page Street, London SW1 (01 211 3000). Write to the regional manager at your nearest regional office:

*Northern Region*, Westgate House, Westgate Street, Newcastle upon Tyne NE1 1TJ (0632 612191).

*Yorkshire and Humberside Region*, City House, Leeds LS1 4JH (0532 38232).

*North Western Region*, Boulton House, 17/21 Chorlton Street, Manchester M1 3HY (061 228 3222).

*Midlands Region*, Alpha Tower, Suffolk Street, Queensway, Birmingham B1 1TZ (021 643 9911).

*London Region* and *South Eastern Region*, Clifton House, 83–117 Euston Road, London NW1 2RB (01 388 5100).

*South Western Region*, 16 Park Place, Clifton, Bristol BS8 1JP (0272 211921).

*Advisory, Conciliation and Arbitration Office for Scotland*, Franborough House, 123–157 Bothwell Street, Glasgow G2 7JR (041 204 2677).

*Advisory, Conciliation and Arbitration Office for Wales*, Phas 1, Ty Glas Road, Llanishen, Cardiff CF4 5PH (0222 762636).

Equal Opportunities Commission, Overseas House, Quay Street,

Manchester M3 3HN (061 833 9244). The EOC publishes guides to the new law.

National Council for Civil Liberties, 23–5 Tabard Street, London SE1.

*Rights for Women*, by Patricia Hewitt, is the best guide to the Sex Discrimination Act and other new laws affecting women; from the National Council for Civil Liberties.

## Further suggestions on training

### CAREERS ADVICE

Make sure you get good careers advice. If you are at school or in full-time education you have a right to free advice with a careers officer who is provided through the Careers Service. Look up your nearest office in the telephone directory or ask your local education authority. It's worth taking advice as early as possible as certain forms of training require certain O- or A-Level passes, for which you will need to plan ahead.

For people over 18 who have left school or college, free 'occupational guidance' is provided through the government-run Employment Service. This can be especially helpful for women who want to go back to work in later life and don't know what to do. It's available at forty-four centres in Britain – you can arrange an interview through your local employment exchange.

Whether the careers advice you get is more helpful than telling you to become a sales assistant rather than a factory-hand will depend largely on the individual officer. Careers services are often understaffed, and the advice you are given in one quick interview may be rather superficial. If you feel you need more guidance, ask for further interviews. Remember to keep a critical attitude to what you are told: careers teachers or officers may have a sexist bias, causing them to channel you into a 'female' job, or an occupational bias – tending to give advice in terms of the labour needs of the area: if there is a shortage of office staff, for example, they may suggest you become a typist, which may not be the best thing for you.

## BOOKS ABOUT JOBS

*Equal Opportunities*, by Ruth Miller, Penguin Books, £2·95.

*Careers Guide*, published by HMSO, is revised annually. For more details about particular jobs see the HMSO *Choice of Careers* series, available from the Occupational Information Centre, 97 Tottenham Court Road, London W1.

## FURTHER EDUCATION AND TRAINING

There are several hundred further education colleges in Britain offering a wide range of courses – both academic and 'vocational' (designed to qualify you for a particular type of work). To find out what is available in your area or field of interest, write to the Department of Education and Science Further Education Information Service, Room 26, Elizabeth House, 39 York Road, London SE1 (01 928 9222). They send out useful booklets free of charge.

## HIGHER EDUCATION

You can study for a degree at a university or polytechnic. The minimum academic requirement is normally two A level passes, but exceptions are made for mature students and in some other cases. If you have at least two A Levels and have been accepted for a place at a university, polytechnic or college of education, you have a right to a grant from your local education authority; without two A Levels, you may still get a discretionary grant. Grants are means-tested on the income of your parents, yourself or your husband, depending on your circumstances. For more information, contact the National Union of Students Grants Adviser, 3 Endsleigh Street, London WC1 (01 387 1277).

*The Open University* is open to anyone over 21 and resident in the

U.K., regardless of qualifications; grants are not available. Teaching is done by a combination of radio and television programmes, weekly seminars and one-week residential summer schools. For details write to the Open University, P.O. Box 48, Milton Keynes, MK7 6AB.

*Which University?*, published by Cornmarket Press, is a complete guide to degree courses. It's expensive, so look for it in your local library.

*UCCA*, the Universities Central Council on Admissions, publishes a handbook on university admissions procedure, price 40p from UCCA, P.O. Box 28, Cheltenham, Glos GL50 1HY.

*The Compendium of Degree Courses*, published by the Council for National Academic Awards, 344–54 Gray's Inn Road, London WC1, is a free and annually revised guide to all first degree courses at polytechnics.

### ON-THE-JOB TRAINING

Your Careers Officer should have a complete list of apprenticeships and training schemes in your area. The *Personnel and Training Year Book*, published by Kogan Page, lists industrial training courses at every level: look for it at your local library as it's expensive. More information can be obtained from the Careers Occupation and Information Centre (COIC), The Pennine Centre, 20–22 Hawley Court, Sheffield.

As far as general opportunities for on-the-job training are concerned (rather than apprenticeships) it's worth choosing carefully where you start work. Some kinds of employment provide better opportunities than others. The civil service and local government are two examples where a wide variety of technical as well as commercial training may be available for women.

GOVERNMENT TRAINING SCHEMES

The government Training Opportunities Scheme (TOPS) is open to anyone over 19 and may be particularly helpful if you want to change your type of work or if you are returning to employment after raising a family. Most women currently on TOPS courses are learning to be secretaries and typists (see p. 35), but a far wider range of courses are available to women as well as men – in government 'skill centres', further education colleges and on-the-job. It's just a matter of finding out about them and applying. Don't be put off applying for a course because it is normally done by men: insist on taking the aptitude test (if there is one), which will be fairly basic. You get a tax-free allowance while you are on the course, with additional allowances for dependent children, unless you are married.

For a limited range of TOPS courses, higher age limits have been negotiated with the appropriate industry or professional body, in order to protect the position of existing schemes for training apprentices or other young entrants. These include building site management training (minimum age 25); clerk of works (22); commercial vehicle body building (20); men's hairdressing (19½); heating and ventilating fitting (23½); pipe fitting in the petrochemical industry (23); and plumbing (23). There is also a minimum age of 21 for heavy goods vehicle driving, in line with HGV licensing requirements. Applicants over 29 are not usually considered for driver training; nor are applicants over 50 considered for courses in domestic appliance servicing. There is an upper age limit of 35 for certain computer courses.

'Wider Opportunities for Women' courses are part of the TOPS scheme. There are no specific restrictions on entry, but they are aimed at women who have not been in paid employment for some time and who wish to return to work, but do not know what kind of work they want, or how to go about getting a job. They provide a chance to sample different types of work. Some are in traditionally male areas. They include advice on available employment and training opportunities. In 1980 about 400 women were taking these courses.

TRAINING FOR THE UNEMPLOYED

Between 1974 and 1978 the official rate of unemployment among women increased more than three times as fast as that of men. In 1980, the official unemployment figure for women was 660,700, out of a total of 2,039,500 unemployed. Only women registering for work at a Job Centre are counted as unemployed. The actual rate of female unemployment is probably more than twice as high.

In November 1979 a working group of the Manpower Services Commission reported on the need to use special training programmes for the unemployed as a means of introducing girls and women to areas of work usually dominated by men. As the report points out, women traditionally work in a narrow range of industries, many of which (e.g. footwear, clothing, textiles) are declining. The introduction of new technology was likely to diminish job opportunities for women, for example in the distributive trades, other service industries and clerical work. The working group recommended that women should train in areas where there was a shortage of suitable job applicants, and in areas where jobs were expanding – for example, certain skilled manual jobs, management and computers.

The report boldly states: 'The range of job-related abilities is roughly the same among girls as among boys . . . *there are practically no jobs which cannot be done by girls, given the opportunity and appropriate training*' (their italics). It calls for special programmes to be set up for this purpose. We list below the schemes for the unemployed which are available at the time of writing, in addition to the TOPS courses, listed above.

1. *Youth Opportunities Programme* (YOP). Most young people become eligible after six weeks of unemployment, but this is waived in certain cases (for example, for disabled young people). The YOP is intended for young unemployed people under 19; however, it is mainly focussed on the 16–17 age group and in some circumstances young people up to the age of 24 are considered eligible.
2. *Community Industry*. Run by the National Association of Youth

Clubs under the general aegis of the Manpower Services Commission. For unemployed young people aged 17–26.
3. *Community Enterprise Programme* (CEP). Aimed at the long-term unemployed, operating nation-wide, mainly on environmental improvement work being carried out by private firms. In 1981 there were 25,000 places in this programme.

WHERE TO APPLY

School leavers should apply for training schemes at their local careers office; others should apply at their local Job Centre. Addresses in the telephone directory.

## Equal pay

We have an Equal Pay Act but we don't have equal pay. Although the Act was passed in 1970 and came into force in December 1975, it has only slightly narrowed the gap between male and female wages. Since 1977, the gap has actually widened again.

| | *Pence per hour* | | | | | | |
| | 1970 | 1974 | 1975 | 1976 | 1977 | 1978 | 1979 |
| --- | --- | --- | --- | --- | --- | --- | --- |
| Men | 67·4 | 104·8 | 136·3 | 162·9 | 177·4 | 200·3 | 226·9 |
| Women | 42·5 | 70·6 | 98·3 | 122·4 | 133·9 | 145·0 | 185·7 |
| *Women's earnings as a percentage of men's* | 63·1 | 67·4 | 72·1 | 75·1 | 75·5 | 73·9 | 73·0 |

Women tend to work shorter hours than men because of their

responsibilities at home, but that doesn't explain why they earn so much less, as you can see from the figures above, which compare their average hourly earnings, excluding overtime.

It's true that many women have had equal pay for years – particularly in the civil service, nationalized industries and in local authority jobs. For the majority, however, the Equal Pay Act has meant nothing at all. This is because it is designed mainly to give women equal pay with men when they are doing the same or very similar jobs. Most women don't work alongside men, but in separate occupations where there are few or no men with whom they can compare. The only other way they can benefit directly from the Act is by having their work graded as equal in value by a job evaluation scheme. But these schemes are usually introduced by employers who have no wish to give their female workers more pay, so they often fail to put a fair price on women's jobs. (More about job evaluation on p. 74.)

Ever since the Act was passed employers have been busy working out ways of avoiding equal pay – by reducing the number of jobs done by both sexes; by introducing new wage structures which put most women in the lower grades; or by paying bonuses to men for merit, long service or willingness to work overtime. It's important

to watch out for these moves. You may be able to use the Sex Discrimination Act to put a stop to them (p. 41). Make sure your trade union resists any attempts to get round the Equal Pay Act. It's also important that employers shouldn't get away with paying less for a job just because it is usually done by a woman. One trade union, TASS (the white collar section of the engineering union) has been campaigning with the slogan 'Men's pay for women' to get this idea across.

The Equal Pay Act gives you certain basic rights and enables you to claim them by going to an industrial tribunal. It's not the only way of getting higher pay and better conditions. You may get more through collective bargaining with the help of your trade union. If all else fails, you may find that a strike or some other form of industrial action is the only way to achieve your demands.

At first many women were bitterly disappointed by tribunal decisions in equal pay cases – which often seemed to flout the spirit of the new law. The summer of 1976 saw the famous strike of women workers at the Trico-Folberth windscreen-wiper factory. They claimed equal pay with men doing identical work alongside them, but they had no faith in the tribunal procedure and decided collective bargaining and industrial action were the best means of achieving what they wanted. Their union, the Amalgamated Union of Engineering Workers, made the strike official. When the company applied to a tribunal for a ruling on equal pay, they took no part in the hearing. The tribunal ruled against them. It decided the men's pay originated from the time they worked the night shift; although there was no longer a night shift, the employer was entitled to draw a 'red circle' round the men, maintain their higher pay, and treat their cases as 'materially different' from the women and any new entrants to their jobs. The women continued their strike for five months and eventually won a new pay deal which incorporated the principle of equality.

By October 1976, things had taken a turn for the better. The Employment Appeals Tribunal (p. 491) had made its first decisions on how the Act should be interpreted. These were far more favourable to women than many tribunal decisions had been – and set a precedent for future cases.

### Your rights under the Equal Pay Act

You should be paid the same as a man:

1. When you are doing the same or broadly similar work; *or*
2. When your work has been given the same value as his by a job evaluation scheme.

In addition to equal pay, any other terms and conditions of employment which are contained in your contract should be equal. These might include holidays, shift work, premiums, bonuses, luncheon vouchers and other fringe benefits. (Your contract of employment may be in writing or it may have been made verbally; any terms or conditions which are not contained in your contract are covered by the Sex Discrimination Act, p. 41.)

Certain conditions are excluded, so they need not be equal:

1. Maternity leave.
2. Retirement age: you can still retire at 60, five years earlier than men.
3. The protective laws, which limit the hours of women factory workers (p. 104): employers can continue to pay men more and give them different terms and conditions for working hours which women cannot work because of the laws.
4. Private pension schemes: from April 1978, you must be allowed to join occupational schemes on the same terms as men with whom you can claim equal pay; but it will still be lawful for women to get inferior benefits, such as lower pensions or no benefit for widowers.

*Wages agreements* which have separate rates for women must be amended – at least to incorporate the women's rate into the lowest male rate. Wages agreements include collective agreements negotiated by trade unions; employers' wage structures drawn up without union involvement; wages regulation orders; and agricultural wages orders. More about these on p. 83.

*Men can claim* equal pay and conditions in the same way as women. Men in the police force successfully claimed a special shoe allowance, previously given to women only. But claims by men will be very rare, for obvious reasons.

## When can you claim equal pay?

1. You must be employed. Apprenticeships count as employment. Self-employment only counts if you are working under contract to someone else (e.g. as a contract cleaner, agency typist or 'lump' building worker).
2. There must be a man who has better wages or conditions than you with whom you can compare jobs. You and he must be working for the same employer or group of employers. If you are not at the same work place, you must both be employed on the same terms and conditions – for instance, you may be covered by the same collective agreement negotiated by your trade union. You can compare yourself with a man who was recently employed at the same work place but who has now left.
3. You and he must be doing work that is *either* the same or broadly similar, *or* rated as equivalent by a job evaluation scheme. If your jobs have different titles, it doesn't matter. It is the *content* of the job that counts. So if, for example, you are serving in a shop where you and other women are described as 'shop assistants' while the men are described as 'trainee managers' although they are getting no more management training than you, you can claim equal pay with them.

IS YOUR WORK THE SAME OR 'BROADLY SIMILAR'?

The Employment Appeals Tribunal has ruled that this decision should be taken in two stages. First: *Is there a broad similarity between your job and the man's?* This should be decided without a minute examination of the detailed differences between your jobs.

If it is found that there is a broad similarity, the next thing to be decided is this: *Are the differences between the things you do and the things he does of practical importance in relation to your terms and conditions of employment?* What counts is day-to-day practice, not what is written into your contracts. What is the nature of each difference? How often does it operate? Your claim should not be defeated by minor differences which occur often, nor by more important differences which occur only rarely. Here are some examples of differences considered of 'practical importance':

1. The man was doing heavier work than the woman for about 30 per cent of his time.
2. The man had unsupervised responsibility all the time, when the woman did not.
3. The man's work required greater training or skill.

Here are some examples of differences that have been considered '*not* of practical importance':

1. The man worked Sunday morning overtime and did a night shift one week in three; the woman was unable to do so because of the protective laws.
2. The man and woman operated in different departments.
3. The man had two to three years' extra experience.
4. The man performed an important duty which took only a few minutes per day.

*Note:* These examples are not entirely conclusive. We have quoted them to show how the law is *likely* to be interpreted.

HAS YOUR WORK BEEN 'RATED AS EQUIVALENT'
BY A JOB EVALUATION SCHEME?

Job evaluation is a way of grading jobs according to value. It is supposed to take account of the demand made on each worker under various headings – such as how much effort and skill they need for the job and how much responsibility. Each job is given a detailed description and is allotted a number of points, according to what its ingredients are. It is then placed in a certain grade. Each grade is given a different wage or range of wages within an upper and lower limit. If your job has been given the same number of points as a man's, you can claim equal pay. It may not be enough just to be in the same grade.

Some job evaluation schemes are unfair to women because they apply criteria which discriminate against them. For instance, some award fewer points for manual dexterity than for manual strength. Women's jobs often need nimble fingers and men's jobs often need brawn – but why should one be considered less valuable than the other? If your trade union or works committee has already agreed to a job evaluation scheme, you cannot normally ask a tribunal to award you equal pay with a man who has been awarded more points than you on the basis of the job evaluation – unless the scheme is blatantly discriminatory. If the tribunal decides that it is, it becomes unlawful and has to be amended (p. 83). If your employer imposed the scheme without agreement by the workers' representatives, then the tribunal may ignore it. If there is nothing fundamentally wrong with the scheme, the tribunal must abide by it. However, if you *are* doing broadly similar work to a man who is graded higher than you under a job evaluation scheme you can try claiming equal pay with him, by comparing the work you are both doing, rather than referring to the scheme. Such claims are not easy, as the employer is likely to use the scheme as evidence that your work was not broadly similar.

If a job evaluation exercise is about to take place where you work, find out how points are to be awarded. If the points system discriminates against women, you and other workers should challenge the basis of the scheme before it is introduced. If you already have a discriminatory scheme, get your trade union to renegotiate it.

THE NEXT STEP

The Equal Pay Act says that every woman has an *equality clause* in her contract of employment. If you succeed in proving to an industrial tribunal that you and a man are doing work that is the same or broadly similar, or 'rated as equivalent', the equality clause operates to give you pay and conditions not less favourable than the man's – *unless* your employer can prove there is a *material difference* between your case and his which justifies giving the man a better deal in spite of the equality clause. At this point, the burden of proof shifts from you to the employer: *you* had to prove that the equality clause should operate; *he* now has to prove that he is justified in treating you less favourably than the man. If he fails, you win your claim. If he succeeds, you lose.

## WHAT AMOUNTS TO A 'MATERIAL DIFFERENCE'?

Basically this is a genuine difference, other than sex, between your case and the man's, which the employer can prove is so important that it overrides your apparent entitlement to equal pay and conditions. It cannot be a straightforward difference between the things you do and the things he does – this has already been dealt with (see above, p. 74). Neither can it be because the man was paid more in his previous job. It must be some quality or qualification that he has, which deserves higher pay. Here are some examples of factors that *may* amount to a material difference:

1. Your employer pays service increments; the man is entitled to a higher increment because he has worked longer than you.
2. The man has a personal qualification, such as greater skills or potential than you, which the employer can prove is of practical use.
3. You are on different wage scales that have been negotiated nationally (or at least very widely) between trade unions and employers; the wage scales are not themselves discriminatory; the difference between them is not due to sex discrimination; nor is the fact that you are on a scale which pays you less than a man.
4. The man is paid more because he is in a 'red circle' and you are not; and the reasons for this are not due to past sex discrimination.

*What is a 'red circle'?* There has been a lot of argument and confusion about the 'red circle' and its relation to the Equal Pay Act. A red circle exists when an employer moves one or more

employees from higher-paid jobs to lower-paid jobs and maintains their higher rate of pay – for those individuals alone; or when he regrades a job to a lower grade allowing present job holders to retain their higher rate of pay while all newcomers go on the new lower rate: those who retain the higher rate are said to be within the red circle. In the crucial test case of *Snoxell vs Vauxhall* (which is described in more detail on p. 82) the Employment Appeals Tribunal decided that two women should have equal pay with men who were in a red circle. This was because the red circle grew out of a discriminatory situation: the higher wages preserved for the men originated in wage grades from which women were actually excluded. Had this not been so – and had female employees stood an equal chance of getting into the red circle in the first place – the women might have lost their claim.

## Making your claim to the industrial tribunal

1. *Victimization is illegal*, so don't be afraid to try. If you think you are being victimized as a result of your claim for equal pay, you can take a complaint to the tribunal (see p. 488).
2. *When to apply*: you can make your application to the tribunal at any time while you are in the job or, if you have left, within six months of the date you left. Get the application form from your local employment exchange or job centre.
3. *What can you claim?* Back pay, or cash compensation for loss of any benefits, for up to two years before the date on which you make your application.
4. *Get help with your case.* If you belong to a trade union, consult your union representative. If you do not, consider joining one. Your union should represent you at the tribunal hearing, or it may get higher wages for you by means of negotiations. A trade union can also protect you against victimization: if union organization is strong enough at your place of work, its protection may be more effective than the protection of the law. If you cannot get trade-union representation, you can, of course, bring your own case and you may well succeed. In 1979, most women who had taken equal pay claims to tribunals had done so with trade-union representation. But those who had represented themselves were no less successful.

It may be helpful to get advice from a solicitor, which is available free or partly free if your income is low (see p. 452). You can get advice on your rights under the Act from the Advisory, Conciliation and Arbitration Service (address, p. 63), or from the Equal Opportunities Commission (EOC) (p. 63). The EOC has power to help individuals with their cases and to arrange representation for them at tribunal hearings, but it does so very rarely and will only consider the possibility if you specifically ask for that kind of help.

5. *Prepare your case carefully.* Collect any relevant documents and information that might support your claim. If you have a written job description, make sure you have a copy of it. Find out whether it was prepared in collaboration with your trade union (if you belong to one). If it was, the tribunal will attach more importance to it. Find out how closely your job description tallies with that of the man. If you think your job description is inaccurate because it doesn't describe what you actually do, then you should make careful notes of the inaccuracies and, if necessary, get other people at your workplace to act as witnesses at the tribunal and support your own account. If what you actually do is more like the man's job than your job description says it is, it will be important for you to prove it to the tribunal. If you don't have a job description, write down what your job involves, task by task, saying how much time you spend on each. Write down what the man's job involves in the same way. If there are any differences, you should be able to argue that these are not of practical importance when it comes to pay or conditions.

6. *What happens next?* The procedure is described in the section on industrial tribunals, p. 488.

### If you win an equal pay claim

This will not necessarily help other women doing similar jobs at your place of work. In November 1976, six women at the Electrolux factory in Luton won equal pay. More than 100 other women had made claims to the tribunal, but these had been deferred for more than nine months by the tribunal chairman. Many of them went on working in jobs identical to those for which equal pay had been won, but the company still paid them at the lower rate. Their only legal remedy was to wait for each individual claim to come up before the tribunal, or to get the Equal Opportunities Commission to issue a Non-Discrimination Notice (p. 483). The Commission undertook a formal investigation at Electrolux (its first in the employment field) but announced in February 1977 that this would take at least four months. Meanwhile, the women were still waiting for equal pay. They were at a special disadvantage from the beginning because one of their local trade-union officials would not back them. The E O C did not complete the equal pay aspect of the investigation until 1979 and even then had not completed the investigation into sex discrimination. By then there had been a job evaluation scheme and the equal pay claim had been settled. This was clearly a case that should have been dealt with by means of collective bargaining, or by referring the existing wages agreement at Electrolux to the Central Arbitration Committee (p. 83).

## Cases showing how the Act has been working

*A claim that failed because there was no man with whom the woman could compare jobs:*

Mrs Pittam worked as a skilled 'site clerk' on a building site, doing typing and other clerical work. She claimed equal pay with the building labourers on the site, who were paid substantially more than her. The tribunal found that her work was not broadly similar to theirs; and there had been no job evaluation exercise to rate her work equal in value. She had no remedy for her low wages under the Act. Her claim was dismissed.

*A claim that failed because the women's jobs were not considered 'the same or broadly similar':*

Six women working in the herring industry in Great Yarmouth put in a claim for equal pay because they were getting 10p an hour less than the men at their factory. In the busy season, from August to December, their main job was 'rhiving' which involves putting herrings on to sticks before they are smoked. In the quiet season they spent most of their time filleting and packing the smoked fish. The men were chiefly responsible for loading and unloading herrings for salting, sousing and smoking, and then packing and loading them on to lorries. Most of the men's jobs were also done by the women from time to time – whenever the employer asked them. The tribunal chairman said that 'quite obviously one of the most skilled jobs in this business and the most essential part of this business is the women's work . . . it is every bit as important and skilled (if not more so) than the work of the men'. Nevertheless, it was decided that their jobs were not broadly similar to the men's, so the women lost their claim.

*A claim that was won on the grounds that the woman's work was 'broadly similar' to the man's:*

Barbara Lawton, a cook in the directors' kitchen at Capper Pass Ltd, claimed equal pay with two assistant chefs in the works canteen. There were a number of differences between their jobs. (1) Ms Lawton cooked one meal a day for up to 20 people in a quasi-domestic kitchen; the men cooked three meals a day for up to 350 people in an industrial kitchen. (2) She worked a 40-hour week; they worked a 45-hour week and one Sunday in three. (3) She was responsible to the catering manager; they were responsible to the head chef and sometimes deputised for him. The tribunal awarded Ms Lawton the same hourly rate as the assistant chefs. The employers appealed and the Employment Appeals Tribunal upheld the original decision.

*A claim that succeeded although the employers said differences were of practical importance:*

Ms Shields was employed as a counterhand in Coomes Bookmakers shop in London at an hourly rate of 92p. Mr Rolls was also employed as a counterhand but paid £1·06 an hour. Her employers said his extra pay was because he was expected to deter troublemakers and potential robbers and deal with them if the need arose. He also transported cash between branches. The Industrial Tribunal decided that the man's security role was a difference of practical importance and rejected Ms Shields's claim. Her case went to the Court of Appeal. The judges there said that she did the same job as Mr Rolls and should receive the same hourly rate. It was not as if Mr Rolls had been specially selected or trained to deal with troublemakers. He was only selected for that task because he was a man. He may have been a small nervous man, who could not say 'boo to a goose'. He only got the higher hourly rate because he was a man. Ms Shields should receive the same.

*A claim that failed because of a 'material difference':*

Robina Varlay was a clerical worker employed by the Navy, Army and Air

Force Institutes (NAAFI) in Nottingham. NAAFI staff in Nottingham worked a 37-hour week while the London staff worked a 36½-hour week. Ms Varlay claimed the right to work the same hours as her male counterparts in London under the Equal Pay Act. It was agreed that they were doing broadly similar work. NAAFI argued that women and men in Nottingham worked a 37-hour week, while women and men in London worked 36½ hours. There was a material difference between Ms Varlay's case and that of the men with whom she compared herself – namely that she worked in Nottingham and they worked in London. It was pointed out that shorter hours were common in London and not confined to NAAFI employees. The Employment Appeals Tribunal stressed that a material difference had to be a real difference and could only be established in the clearest possible case. Ms Varlay's claim failed.

*A claim that succeeded in spite of a plea of 'material difference':*

Ms Snoxell and Ms Davies, inspectors at Vauxhall Motors, Luton, claimed equal pay with male inspectors who had worked there as long as they had. In 1971 there had been a grading exercise at the factory. The men's jobs had been regraded and put in a lower grade, but the men who were there at the time were 'red circled', which meant they kept the higher rate of pay. All new male inspectors were put on the lower rate. When equal pay was introduced at Vauxhall, female inspectors including Ms Snoxell and Ms Davies were paid the lower rate along with the men who had started the job after 1971. Since they had been working as inspectors before that, they claimed equal pay with the red-circle inspectors and took their case to an industrial tribunal with the help of a male shop steward. Their union, the Transport and General Workers' Union, did not give them official backing, perhaps because it negotiated the 1971 agreement. The tribunal dismissed the women's claim, accepting Vauxhall's argument that the difference in pay was due to a 'material difference' – namely the red circle which had been drawn around the men before the Equal Pay Act came into force. The Equal Opportunities Commission recognized that this was an important test case and represented the women at their appeal. The Employment Appeals Tribunal upheld the appeal, ruling that a present pay differential which originated in a discriminatory practice before the Equal Pay Act came into force could count as a 'material difference': the red circle at Vauxhall had always excluded women, so it could not be defined as a 'material difference other than sex'.

*Another claim that succeeded in spite of a 'material difference' plea:*

Ms Fletcher was employed as a clerk in a sales office by Clay Cross (Quarry Services) Ltd. She claimed equal pay with Mr Tunnecliffe who had recently been employed on the same job and was paid £8 a week more. Her employers agreed that they did the same job but said that it was not because Mr Tunnecliffe was a man but because he was receiving a higher wage in his previous job and would not come for less.

The industrial tribunal and the Employment Appeal Tribunal turned down Ms Fletcher's claim because they said Mr Tunnecliffe's higher previous salary was a 'material difference' and was not sex-based since the employer was indifferent as to whether they employed a man or a woman. The Court of Appeal disagreed. They said a material difference had to be a personal difference between the man and the woman which related to their jobs. It could not be a factor not related to their qualities or jobs such as what he had been paid before. It did not help the employer to argue that he did not intend to discriminate.

## Wages agreements

The following agreements are all covered by the Act:

1. *Collective agreements.* These are agreements made voluntarily by employers and unions through collective bargaining. They cover the great majority of workers.
2. *Employers' pay structures.* These are drawn up without any union involvement, and tend to apply particularly to office workers and other non-manual workers in private firms.
3. *Wages regulation orders or agricultural wages orders.* These are orders made by a wages council or agricultural wages board. They are legally binding on employers. About 3½ million workers are covered by wages councils and are generally found in industries where union organization is weak, particularly hotel and catering, clothing industries, shops, laundries and hairdressers. Most wages council industry workers are low paid.

A wages agreement can be amended by the Central Arbitration Committee if it contains any provisions which apply to one sex only. You, as an individual, can't make a referral to the Board. –

this must be done through a trade union. The following people can make referrals:

| Type of agreement | Those who can make referrals |
|---|---|
| collective agreement | trade union, employer or Secretary of State for Employment |
| employers' pay structure | Secretary of State or employer (but unions need to watch these) |
| wages council order or agricultural wages order | Secretary of State, either on his own initiative or if requested by a member of the wages council/agricultural wages board concerned. |

In the first few years of the Act many women received equal pay rises as a result of their wages agreement being amended to raise the female rate to the lowest male rate. This process has now been completed but women are still usually in the lowest grades. The Act needs amending to allow the Central Arbitration Committee to deal with less open cases of discrimination against women.

## Equal pay and opportunity under European law

Since Britain joined the Common Market in 1973 British law has been subject to the Rome Treaty, Article 119 of which says women must receive equal pay for the same work.

If a woman considers that a decision in the British Courts is in breach of Article 119 of the Rome Treaty she can complain to the European Commission which in turn can refer a case to the European Court for a decision. The European Commission itself looks at the laws of member countries to see if they comply with the Rome Treaty and if not satisfied can start enforcement proceedings against countries to make them change their laws.

The Rome Treaty is supplemented by 'Directives' which say in more detail what laws the countries should have and how they should be enforced. There is one directive on equal pay which extends the requirement of equal pay to *work of equal value*; one on sex discrimination, and one (not yet in force) on equal treatment of men and women in social security schemes.

In 1979 the Commission decided that a number of countries were not complying with Article 119 or the directives on equal pay. They said that the British Equal Pay Act was too restrictive in that it only gave equal pay to work of equal value if there had been a job evaluation scheme. This may require our Equal Pay Act to be amended.

There have been a number of equal pay cases which have gone to Europe. In one, it was decided that a woman could compare her pay with that of a man who recently did the same job even if he had now left the firm. In another, it was ruled that paying part-time women workers less than full-timers would be contrary to Article 119, if it was disguised discrimination against women which the employer could not justify on economic grounds. In what amounted to a very unhelpful judgement in the case of *Jenkins vs Kingsgate Clothing Ltd*, the European Court said that if a U.K. tribunal were to accept the employer's claim that he had good reason for paying part-timers less, then an equal pay claim would not succeed.

In a third case the European Court ruled that U.K. law was in breach of Article 119 in excluding discrimination in occupational pensions if employers pay the employees' contributions by increasing their gross pay. The women claimants work for Lloyds Bank. All women below the age of 25 enjoyed a non-contributory pension scheme but received no benefit if they resigned or retired before the age of 25. The men had to contribute but the amount of their contribution was paid as extra salary and if they left before the age of 25 the amount contributed was refunded to them. The scheme must now be amended.

## Positive action in the workplace

The Sex Discrimination Act has done little to break down job segregation or to widen opportunities for women. Women's groups and trade unions are increasingly taking an interest in the idea of 'positive action' as a means of promoting equal opportunity at work. This goes beyond the prohibition of unequal treatment, and involves taking special, positive measures to counteract the effects of past discrimination and enable women to compete for jobs, training and promotion on genuinely equal terms with men. It does *not* involve discrimination against men at the point of selection.

'Positive action' has been practised in the United States since the early 1970s. It is known there as 'affirmative action'. Under U.S. law, employers can be obliged to introduce 'affirmative action programmes' for a number of reasons. Employers holding government contracts must show *either* that they already employ women and members of ethnic minority groups at all levels in sufficient numbers (i.e. in proportion to the numbers available for work in the locality); *or* that they are making a 'good faith' effort to do so, by means of affirmative action. Likewise, employers who are accused of unlawful discrimination on grounds of race or sex can be obliged by the courts to introduce an affirmative action programme. Under U.S. law, it is possible to take legal action on behalf of a group (or 'class') of people, and this can make it easier to put legal pressure on employers.

Under U.K. law, this kind of 'class action' is not possible; nor can employers be obliged to introduce positive action programmes – either because they hold government contracts, or because they are found guilty of unlawful discrimination. The Sex Discrimination Act allows certain kinds of positive action and these are outlined on pp. 50–51. It does not in any way advocate or promote positive action; it simply says that in some circumstances it is not against the law.

Unless and until the law is amended, the only way to get positive action introduced into the workplace is through negotiations between workers and employers, instigated by women and by unions (and possibly even by management). There are only a few cases where this has actually been done in the U.K., but by 1980 the idea was growing in popularity. The Trades Union Congress in September 1980 passed a resolution in favour of positive action and in November that year it held a special consultative conference on the subject.

The following basic steps are necessary for the successful introduction of a positive action programme:

1. Analyse the workforce. Find out how many women and men are employed by the organization in question, and at what levels of pay and seniority.
2. Where they are not employed in approximately equal numbers and on equal terms, identify the causes of inequality (e.g. If women don't apply for certain jobs, what are the factors that deter them? If they are not thought to be adequately qualified for certain jobs, why is this?).
3. Work out what steps are necessary for overcoming the obstacles identified in (2). Some suggestions are outlined below.
4. Establish goals for employing more women which can reasonably be attained, using the steps in (3); and set timetables for attaining them. For example, it might be decided to aim for the employment of women in 25 per cent of engineers' jobs within five years.
5. Set out the agreed 'positive action' measures, with goals and timetables, in every detail, in a written agreement.
6. Establish a joint employee/management group to monitor the progress of the programme. Ensure that women are adequately represented in this group.
7. Monitor progress closely. If goals seem unlikely to be attained, or are not attained, adjust the programme to make it more effective.

SOME MEASURES WHICH MIGHT BE INCLUDED
IN A POSITIVE ACTION PROGRAMME

These are taken from a consultative paper prepared by the TUC in March 1980. They may not be appropriate in every workplace, and they may not be sufficient on their own to promote genuine equal opportunity. We present them as suggestions, which may be used as a starting point for devising a positive action programme.

1. Publicly a union should press an employer to commit himself to being

an Equal Opportunities employer. This could involve insisting on the TUC 'Equal Opportunities Clause' (see below) in all agreements, and the employer informing the local Job Centre of his policy, giving the local press the information in the form of an article or letter and, most important of all, including an appropriate statement on all job adverts both internal and external.

2. Evaluation schemes that decide the grading of the job should be based on the level of skill, training and responsibility needed and not on differentials between male and female 'skills' (e.g., does the scheme say it is more skilful to be able to solder intricately or to lift heavy boxes?).

3. Ensuring that the job description is an exact description of the duties of the job and does not imply sex stereotyping; e.g., does a receptionist have to be 'attractive' or a sales representative an 'active executive type'? The job description should be drawn up after research into what the job requires, not based on assumptions such as that all fork-lift drivers carry heavy weights.

4. As with job evaluation schemes and job descriptions, criteria for promotion should be laid down enumerating the skills that need to be developed; such things as formal qualifications should be looked at carefully, in terms of their necessity, their desirability or whether they could be gained after promotion.

5. Actions in the recruitment stage should include making adverts attractive and available to women (this can be done with recourse to the Equal Opportunities Clause); including a picture of a woman as well as a man in the advert; making sure the wording does not put women off (e.g., a re-introduction of the use of 'female wanted' might be a positive encouragement); advertising in women's magazines (though to do so exclusively is discriminatory); contacting local women's groups, school teachers and careers officers dealing with girls to inform them of the vacancy; ensuring all vacancies are advertised internally and to all people, and using an employment noticeboard to display vacancies.

6. Personnel staff, including receptionists, should be made aware of the implications of an Equal Opportunities (EO) policy, and have available a full job description, so that women seeking jobs are not put off when making their initial approach.

7. At the interviewing stage, the application form should declare the employer has an EO policy and state any relevant grievance procedure. It should also only ask questions relevant to the job applied for and not ask for unnecessary personal details.

(a) In a large concern more than one interviewer should be used, preferably with a mix of sexes.

(b) Interviewers should be trained in interview and assessment techniques to eliminate unconscious bias.

(c) It should be agreed previously what skills the interviewers are looking for; there should be an interview report form to ensure a common standard, and discussion afterwards between interviewers.

(d) Any testing process should be job-related, and have a direct correlation between test and job performance; for instance, if a mechanical comprehension test is used, is it really indicative of future performance?

(e) Questions should be aimed at assessing the person's skills and abilities, and should not include questions which are only put to women, on home circumstances, future plans, etc.

(f) It is good employment practice to explain why a person did not get the job, and what improvements would make them acceptable. This enables the person to understand and assess their performance at interviews, and ensures that interviewers are fair.

8. In promotion, the advertised commitment to an EO policy is most important, and should be made by the chief executive.

(a) All promotions should be circulated internally; the use of an employment noticeboard as a focal point would be an advantage.

(b) These vacancy notices should include job descriptions and candidate requirements, not just job titles, and should be checked for indirect discrimination such as a requirement of continuous service.

(c) The possibility of promoting part-time workers should be investigated.

(d) An annual review system should be used to discuss with staff their progress and future plans in employment terms, and any training or job opportunities that might benefit them.

(e) Seminars should be held for supervisory staff on how to evaluate personnel performance free of discrimination.

(f) Staff suitably qualified for promotion should be personally alerted to the vacancy.

(g) All staff should be encouraged to take training courses that will help in their promotion prospects.

(h) In-service seminars, courses and discussions on issues relevant to management development should be held. These should be non-residential, wherever possible, and in working hours.

(i) The same criteria used for a recruitment interview should be used for a promotion interview.

(j) The creation of recognized grievance procedures should be established, preferably in the form of a committee with management and workers represented.

9. The working conditions should be examined to see if they could be made more attractive to women; for instance, the provision of crèches or paying for places in a local nursery where local authority provisions do not meet their needs.

(a) Extensive use should be made of flexible working time, flexible holiday times and the right to carry over leave from one year to the next.

(b) The improvement of maternity provisions to allow more flexibility than the statutory requirements.

## THE TUC'S MODEL EQUAL OPPORTUNITIES CLAUSE

The parties to this agreement are committed to the development of positive policies to promote equal opportunity in employment regardless of workers' sex, marital status, creed, colour, race or ethnic origins. This principle will apply in respect of all conditions of work including pay, hours of work, holiday entitlement, overtime and shiftwork, work allocation, guaranteed earnings, sick pay, pensions, recruitment, training, promotion and redundancy.

The management undertake to draw opportunities for training and promotion to the attention of all eligible employees, and to inform all employees of this agreement on equal opportunity.

The parties agree that they will review from time to time, through their joint machinery, the operation of this equal opportunity policy.

If any employee considers that he or she is suffering from unequal treatment on the grounds of sex, marital status, creed, colour, race or ethnic origins he or she may make a complaint which will be dealt with through the agreed procedures for dealing with grievances.

### FURTHER INFORMATION

*Positive Action for Women*, by Sadie Robarts, with Elizabeth Ball and Anna Coote, published 1981, from NCCL, 23–5 Tabard Street, London SE1.

# Maternity leave

Working women who become pregnant have a right – on certain conditions – to six weeks' paid maternity leave at 90 per cent of their basic weekly wage, and reinstatement in their job twenty-nine weeks after the baby's birth. These are minimal rights, established under the Employment Protection Act 1975.

The Employment Act 1980 made the legal procedure for telling your employer you are going on maternity leave and want to return to your job more complicated. It also allowed small employers not to give women their jobs back in certain circumstances and larger employers to give them different jobs. This is explained below, p. 97. The only good part of the 1980 Act introduced the right to paid time off work for ante-natal visits.

Neither the pay nor the length of leave is sufficient. The provisions fall short of the TUC's demand for thirty weeks' paid leave, as well as a number of private agreements that are already in operation. Child-care facilities are in such short supply that many women are unable to take advantage of the provisions because they have no one to look after their babies when the twenty-nine-week period comes to an end. British women are still in a worse position than their European counterparts. In France, women get fourteen weeks' leave with 90 per cent of their basic wage; in Italy, they get twenty weeks with 80 per cent of their basic wage. Hungarian women are entitled to five months' leave on full pay and a further three years with monthly cash allowances, followed by reinstatement without loss of seniority or pension rights.

## *To qualify for these minimal rights, you must satisfy the following conditions*

1. You must have been working for the same employer for at least two years at the beginning of the eleventh week before the baby is due. (So you should have been with the employer for about eighteen months before you get pregnant.) This condition excludes a great many women. There is a very high turnover in

female employment, especially among women of child-bearing age. Some women have to change jobs because their husbands are posted to different parts of the country. Others, who already have children, are forced to stop and start work several times during the year because of school holidays and the shortage of child-care facilities.

2. You must work more than sixteen hours a week; *or* more than eight hours a week if you have been with your employer at least five years.

3. You must stay in your job at least until the beginning of the eleventh week before the week in which the baby is due. If you cannot work until then because of your health, go on sick leave but do not resign from your job.

4. You must tell your employer in writing that you intend to exercise your right to claim maternity pay and return to work. You must do this on two occasions: first, at least three weeks before you leave work, when you must tell him the expected date of confinement (or, if you find you have to leave sooner than you expected, as soon as possible); and second, you must tell him the date you intend to return to work at least three weeks in advance of that date. It's best to keep a copy of your letter in case you have any difficulty obtaining your rights.

5. If your employer writes to you while you are on maternity leave asking you to confirm that you intend to return to your job, you must reply in writing within fourteen days.

*If you have been dismissed because of your pregnancy* you still have a right to reinstatement twenty-nine weeks after the baby's birth, provided that:

1. You have fulfilled all the conditions outlined above (except the one which says you must carry on working until the eleventh week before the baby is due).

2. You have been *fairly* dismissed because you are incapable of 'adequately doing the work' (e.g. you are constantly lifting heavy weights) or because it is illegal for your job to be done by a pregnant women (e.g. you are a radiologist); *or*

3. You have been *unfairly* dismissed and you have succeeded in bringing a complaint against the employer to an industrial tribunal. In this case, you have a right to six weeks' maternity pay as well.

More details about fair and unfair dismissal on p. 100.

*Fathers cannot legally qualify* for leave or pay when their babies are born. Men should be encouraged to share responsibility for their children and some families may find it more convenient for the man, rather than the woman, to take extended leave. They should be allowed that choice. Some unions have negotiated paternity leave arrangements for fathers, giving them a week or more of leave at the time of their babies' birth.

## How much maternity pay?

Your employer must pay you 90 per cent of your *basic* weekly pay. (This means that women who rely on overtime, bonuses or tips will be at a great disadvantage.) Before you get your maternity pay, the basic rate of the state maternity allowance (currently £20·65 a week) is deducted – whether or not you are actually entitled to claim it.

You will probably be able to claim maternity allowance if you have been paying full National Insurance contributions. If you are single, you may get additional allowances for dependent children; and whether you are single or married, you may also get an earnings-related supplement (extra money based on the level of your earnings) which is being phased out and will finish in January 1982 (see p. 148): none of this is deducted from your maternity pay. Nor is the £25 maternity grant which you can claim if you or your husband have been paying full National Insurance contributions. (See p. 149 for details.)

TWO EXAMPLES SHOWING HOW MATERNITY PAY IS WORKED OUT

Judy Carter's basic weekly pay is £70 a week. She has been paying full National Insurance contributions and is entitled to maternity allowance. She has no dependent children.

*Her employer pays*
| | |
|---|---|
| 90 per cent of £70 | £63·00 |
| Minus maternity allowance | £22·50 |
| Total | £40·50 |

*In addition, she gets from the state*
| | |
|---|---|
| Maternity allowance | £22·50 |

*Altogether she gets:*   £63·00

*Note:* Until January 1982, she will also get a small extra 'earnings-related supplement', see p. 148.

Doreen Thompson's basic weekly pay is £50. She has taken the married women's option to pay reduced National Insurance contributions, so she is not entitled to maternity allowance.

*Her employer pays*
| | |
|---|---|
| 90 per cent of £50 | £45 |
| Minus maternity allowance | £22·50 |
| Total | £22·50 |

You can ask your employer to give you your maternity pay in a lump sum at the beginning of the six weeks, if you want to. Otherwise it will be paid weekly or monthly, depending on how you are normally paid. Your employer may run a maternity pay scheme which gives different benefits. If so, you will get *either* the benefits of your employer's scheme, *or* those you are entitled to by law, whichever are better. You won't get both.

## WHERE DOES MATERNITY PAY COME FROM?

A Maternity Pay Fund has been set up by the government. It is financed by National Insurance contributions from all employers (*not* from employees). Your employer will be responsible for handing over the cash to you; but he can then claim it back in full from the Fund.

## IF YOUR EMPLOYER DOES NOT PAY YOU

If in exceptional circumstances your employer can't afford to pay you the money in the first place (if he has been declared insolvent, for instance), you can claim your maternity pay directly from the Fund. Your chances of getting it are at the discretion of the Secretary of State for Health and Social Security. If your employer simply refuses to give you maternity pay, for no good reason, you can claim payment directly from the Fund. But the Secretary of State will grant it only if he is satisfied (a) that you are entitled to maternity pay; *and* (b) that you have made every reasonable effort to persuade your employer to pay you.

## HOW CAN YOU PERSUADE YOUR EMPLOYER TO PAY?

Make sure he knows what the law says. If you belong to a trade union, get your shop steward or union official to put your case to him. If that doesn't work, bring a complaint against him to an industrial tribunal, within three months of the last day on which the pay was due – i.e. before your baby is eight weeks old. You will need to show the tribunal that you have worked for the employer for two years; that you worked up to the eleventh week before the baby was due; and that you told the employer within the proper time limit that you intended to claim maternity pay. So keep copies of all relevant correspondence. (See p. 488 for how to complain to an industrial tribunal.)

It seems that, if your employer refuses to give you maternity pay for no good reason, you cannot claim it directly from the Fund until you have complained to an industrial tribunal. It seems an unfair burden on a woman who has just had a baby to have to go through all this. It would be better if she could claim directly from the Maternity Pay Fund, with the Secretary of State being responsible for bringing a complaint against the employer.

### Getting your job back

If you fulfil the conditions outlined above, pp. 91–2, you have a right to reinstatement in your job twenty-nine weeks after your baby is born. The law says that you must normally return to the same job as the one you left, *according to your contract of employment.* (The exceptions to this rule are described below.) So obviously a lot depends on how your job is described in your contract. If the description is vague, you may have to return to a job which bears little resemblance to your old job. For instance, if your contract just says that you are a 'shorthand typist', and doesn't specify the department or person you are working for, you may have to work in a different part of the company when you go back. If you are a teacher employed by a Local Education Authority, you could, in theory, be placed in a different school when you go back to work, if your contract merely says that you are a teacher with a certain LEA. Check up on your contract *well* before you take maternity leave. If you think the terms are too vague, try to get them changed.

The law also says that you must return to work 'on terms and conditions not less favourable' than those which would have applied if you had never been away. So if others doing the same job have received a pay rise in your absence, then you should automatically get the new rate when you return. Your period of maternity leave should not count as an interruption in your employment in terms of seniority, access to pension schemes, promotion prospects, and so on.

The exceptions to this part of the law are:

1. Your employer had only five or fewer employees including yourself immediately before you went on maternity leave. He does not then have to give you your job back if it is not 'reasonably practicable' to do so; nor does he have to offer you a suitable alternative job. In these circumstances you lose all rights to go back to work and your employer does not have to give you any compensation.

2. Your employer has more than five employees but does not find it reasonably practicable to give you back the job you were employed to do. In this case he can offer you an alternative job. The job must be suitable for you, and the kind of job, the place where you work and your terms and conditions of employment must not be substantially less favourable to you than your original job. These exceptions were introduced in October 1980 so at the time of writing it is too early to say how they will work in practice. If you belong to a trade union, ask your union to make sure your employer gives you your original job back. No woman should be moved to a less satisfactory job while on maternity leave. It is hard enough having a baby and arranging to come back to work without worrying about what job you are going to get.

THE TWENTY-NINE-WEEK LIMIT ON MATERNITY LEAVE CAN BE EXTENDED IN THE FOLLOWING SITUATIONS

1. If you are ill, you can delay your return to work for up to four weeks. You must have a doctor's statement to prove that you are ill and you must tell your employer before the first twenty-nine weeks are up. You can only have one four-week extension.

2. If there is some interruption of work, such as a strike, on the day you are due to go back to work, you can delay your return until the interruption is over.

3. Your employer can delay your return to work for up to four weeks. He must tell you he intends to do this before the first twenty-nine weeks are up. He must also give a reason for the delay and tell you the date on which you can return. (The law doesn't say that the employer can only do this once – a worrying omission.)

*If your employer refuses to let you return,* or keeps extending your period of leave for no good reason, you can bring a complaint against him to an industrial tribunal within three months of the date you intended to return to work. You will need to show the tribunal that you have worked for the employer for at least two years; that you worked until the eleventh week before the baby was due; and that you told the employer, within the proper time limits, that you intended to return to work. So keep copies of all relevant correspondence. (See p. 488 for how to complain to an industrial tribunal.)

*You are credited with National Insurance contributions* while you are receiving maternity allowance, but not for the rest of the time that you are on maternity leave. However, if you were paying full contributions before you stopped work, your pension rights will be protected during the time you are at home, as explained on p. 134.

*If you want to have more children*, you don't have to wait another two years before you can claim maternity leave and pay. You can, in theory come back to work when your baby is six or seven months old, get pregnant again quickly and, as long as you work up to the eleventh week before the second baby is due, you can claim all the same rights again.

## How your maternity rights could be improved

Don't be content with the provisions of the Employment Protection Act – try to negotiate better terms through your trade union. Several organizations have 'union negotiated agreements' for maternity leave and pay. This does not mean that all their members are getting what they are claiming; simply that these are recommended as negotiating terms. Does your organization have an agreement? Is it implemented? Here are some examples:

| | Qualifying service | Maximum leave | Maternity pay | Conditions | Other notes |
|---|---|---|---|---|---|
| London and Manchester Assurance | 2 years | 40 weeks | 24 weeks 90% pay | None | Must normally work 35 hours pw |
| Times Newspapers (clerical) | 2 years | 1 year | 18 weeks full pay | None | |
| BPC | 1 year | 8 weeks | 8 weeks full pay | None | |
| | 1 year | 40 weeks | 16 weeks full pay | Return to work for 3 months | |
| Roadchef | 1 year | 40 weeks | 2 weeks full pay | None | |
| | 2 years | ,, | 10 weeks full pay | | |
| | 3 years | ,, | 12 weeks full pay | | |
| | 4 years | ,, | 14 weeks full pay | | |
| | 5 years | ,, | 16 weeks full pay | | |
| | 6 years | ,, | 18 weeks full pay | | |
| | over 7 | ,, | 20 weeks full pay | | |
| Local Education Authorities (teachers) | 1 year | 18 weeks | 4 weeks full pay | Return to work for 13 weeks | 6 weeks post-natal leave if child dies |
| | 2 years | 40 weeks | 2 weeks 90% pay +12 weeks ½ pay | | Post-natal leave for adoptive parents |
| Local authorities | 1 year | 18 weeks | 6 weeks 90% pay | Return to work for 3 months | Further unpaid leave at employer's discretion |
| | 2 years | 40 weeks | +12 weeks ½ pay | | 1 month post-natal leave if child dies (less than 2 years' service) |
| London Borough of Camden | 1 year | 40 weeks | 16 weeks full pay +24 weeks ½ pay | Return to work | 1 month post-natal leave if child dies |
| Post Office | 1 year | 40 weeks | 13 weeks full pay | Return to work for 13 weeks | |

Source: Labour Research, Bargaining Report.

## Unfair dismissal and redundancy

If you are unfairly dismissed from your job, you have a right to your job back, or cash compensation.

### When can you claim that you have been unfairly dismissed?

1. You have worked for the employer for at least twelve months, and for at least sixteen hours a week; *or* you have worked for the employer for at least five years, and for between eight and sixteen hours a week; *and*
2. Your employer sacked you; *or* you were employed for a fixed period and your contract wasn't renewed; *or* you gave in your notice because the employer changed an important term of your contract without your agreement. You did not simply leave of your own accord; *and*
3. The industrial tribunal decides that he has not dismissed you for any of the following reasons:
(a) You are incapable of doing the job properly, or your qualifications are unsuitable.
(b) You deserved to be sacked because of your conduct.
(c) You are redundant.
(d) You cannot stay in the job without either you or your employer breaking the law (e.g. your job involves driving and your licence has been suspended).
(e) You are pregnant and your pregnancy makes you incapable of doing the job properly (e.g. it involves modelling, dancing or lifting heavy weights).
(f) You are pregnant and the law forbids pregnant women to do your job (e.g. because it involves radioactive material).

*If you are pregnant* and your employer dismisses you for none of the reasons listed above, you can claim unfair dismissal. If he dismisses you because of reason (e) or (f) he must try to find you a suitable alternative job. If there isn't one available, the dismissal is fair; but if there is and he doesn't offer it to you, the dismissal is unfair. In any case, you may be eligible for maternity pay or maternity leave, as explained on p. 91. But if you are dismissed while pregnant and you have not been employed for 12 months, it appears that you do not have a claim under the Sex Discrimination Act (see pp. 60–61).

### How to get your rights

Complain to an industrial tribunal within three months of the date of your dismissal. (See p. 488 for how to do this.)

Get help from your trade union. It may also help to get advice from a solicitor (particularly if you don't belong to a union). You may be able to get legal advice free or partly free, under the 'green form' procedure (p. 454). Your complaint will first be referred to the Advisory, Conciliation and Arbitration Service (ACAS). Make sure that your union representative is with you if you are invited to meet the conciliation officer: don't agree to a conciliation unless you get what you want at this stage. If you don't agree, your complaint goes to the tribunal.

If the tribunal accepts that you have, in fact, been dismissed unfairly, then it is up to the employer to prove that the dismissal was fair. In other words, he will have to prove that he dismissed you for one of the reasons listed under (3) above.

If the tribunal decides that you have been unfairly dismissed it can order one of three things:

1. *Reinstatement* in your old job, with all rights and benefits restored, as though you had never been sacked. So you get any back pay due to you (*minus* any money your employer has paid to you since your dismissal, and any wages or social security you received in the meantime). Your seniority and pension rights are preserved; and you are given any improvements in your terms and conditions which you would have had if you hadn't been dismissed (such as a pay rise).

2. *Re-engagement* in a job which is comparable to the one you had before, or another suitable job, with back pay and employment rights preserved (as for reinstatement). (If the tribunal decides you were partly to blame for your dismissal, it may order that you be re-engaged on less favourable terms, for instance, without back pay.) Reinstatement and re-engagement orders are very rare. If you want one, make sure you say so on your application form.

3. *Cash compensation* in which the amount you get is worked out in two parts: a 'basic' award and a 'compensatory' award. You may also get an 'additional' award.

(a) The basic award depends on your age. You get one and half weeks' pay for each year that you worked for the employer when you were over 41. You get one week's pay for each year's service when you were aged 22–41. You get half a week's pay for each year's service aged 18–21. No more than twenty years' work can be counted. No pay above £130 a week can be counted. If you are over 59 (over 64 for men) when dismissed, the award is reduced.

(b) The compensatory award depends on the financial loss you have suffered as a result of being dismissed; the maximum total is £6,250. In working out how much to claim, you should calculate:

(i) The wages you have lost, based on your take-home pay minus tax and National Insurance.

(ii) Any fringe benefits you have lost, such as accommodation, meals or transport.

(iii) Any seniority or long-service rights you have lost: this could include money to compensate you for losing promotion prospects or the right to maternity leave (it will take you two years to build up that entitlement).

(iv) The cost of looking for another job, such as travelling or moving house.

(v) The cost of continuing unemployment – the tribunal can estimate how long you are likely to be unemployed and award you lost wages for that period.

(vi) If you were dismissed on grounds of sex or race discrimination, or victimization for trade-union activities, you can claim extra compensation for 'injury to feelings'.

(c) You may get an additional award if the employer refuses to obey an order to give you your job back. This can amount to between thirteen and twenty-six weeks' pay; or between twenty-six and fifty-two weeks' pay if the dismissal was because of sex or race discrimination, or victimization for trade-union activities.

## How does the tribunal come to its decision?

It will take the following things into account:

1. Whether or not you want your job back.
2. Whether or not it is 'practicable' for the employer to take you back. The employer may claim that it is not practicable: the word is not defined by law. There is a danger that the tribunal may simply accept the employer's word without really trying to find out whether he could give you your job back.
3. Whether or not you were partly to blame for your dismissal – for instance, whether you were slightly inefficient at your job, or inclined to arrive late most mornings.
4. Whether or not a permanent replacement has been taken on to do your job. This will only stop you getting your job back if the employer can prove that there was no other way of getting the job done, or that you delayed in bringing your complaint and it wasn't reasonable for the employer to go on coping without a permanent replacement.

You should decide in advance what you want the tribunal to order. If you don't want to return to work for the employer, work out how much compensation you think should be paid to you. If you disagree with the tribunal's decision, or if you think the tribunal has made a mistake, you can appeal. (See pp. 491–2 for how to do this.)

### If you are dismissed because of redundancy

This will count as unfair dismissal only if you can show that you have been unfairly selected for redundancy, or that your employer had no justification for calling your dismissal a redundancy. Otherwise, redundancy does *not* count as unfair dismissal. If it does not, you cannot get your job back, nor can you get a compensatory award. But you can claim redundancy payment, provided you have worked for the employer for at least two years, and for at least sixteen hours a week (or for between eight and sixteen hours a week, if you have worked for the employer for at least five years). Redundancy payment is worked out in the same way as the 'basic' award for unfair dismissal. You claim it by going to an industrial tribunal.

## Women workers and the protective laws

In the nineteenth century women, children and men all worked between twelve and fourteen hours a day. The only difference was that women were paid less than men, and children were paid less than women. The first reform came when the 'ten-hour day' was introduced for women and children. Then children were taken out of the factories and put into schools. Eventually, certain restrictions were placed on working hours and conditions for women – partly out of concern that they might damage their own health and their children's if they were forced to work long hours in factories as well as run their homes, and partly because male workers were afraid that if women continued to compete for jobs on equal terms they would bring unemployment and threaten their pay and conditions. The same restrictions were placed on young people under eighteen. They are known as the protective laws. They are still in force.

The terms of these laws apply only to factories: that is, places where people are employed in manual labour, making, breaking up, altering, repairing, finishing, cleaning, or washing anything, or adapting anything for sale. A lot of places that you wouldn't normally think of as factories fit this description – for instance, slaughter-houses and film studios. The terms of the laws do not apply to women in management jobs who are not doing manual labour.

*The Sex Discrimination Act does not affect the protective laws.*

## What do the protective laws say?

The laws are too complex to be explained in full here, largely because there are so many exceptions to the rules. Here are the main restrictions. They are set out in Part 6 of the Factories Act 1961 and the Hours of Employment (Conventions) Act 1936.

1. Women cannot work for more than forty-eight hours a week.
2. Women cannot start work before 7 a.m. or go on working after 8 p.m. (1 p.m. on Saturdays).
3. No work on Sundays, bank holidays, Christmas day or Good Friday without a weekday in lieu.
4. Women are not allowed to clean machinery if this would expose them to risk of injury.
5. There are also limited regulations preventing women working with certain toxic materials, or where they may be exposed to dangerous radiation.
6. Overtime is limited to six hours a week and 100 hours a year. It cannot be worked during more than twenty-five weeks in one calendar year.
7. *In factories working a six-day week:*
(a) Women must not work for more than nine hours a day without overtime.
(b) They must have a half-hour rest period after four and a half hours of continuous work; or after five hours if they have a ten-minute break at some point during the five-hour stretch.
(c) The total hours actually worked in a day, including overtime, should not be more than ten (five and a half on Saturdays).
8. *In factories where all women work a basic five-day week:*

(a) Women can work for ten hours a day without overtime, or ten and a half hours including overtime (these time limits do not include meal breaks and tea breaks).

(b) If a woman is then employed on a sixth day in the week, she can work for only four and a half hours on that day and it must all be counted as overtime; she may do no other overtime in that week.

*Night work:*

One of the main effects of the protective laws is to prevent women working at night, unless there is an exemption order in force (see below, p. 107). However, women employed solely in cleaning, including night cleaners, are not covered by the laws.

## What are the main exceptions to the laws?

1. *Shift work.* An employer may get permission from the Health and Safety Executive to employ women on a double day-shift system (that is, a system with two day-time shifts), provided the shifts do not begin before 6 a.m. nor end after 10 p.m. (2 p.m. on Saturdays) and the hours of each shift do not exceed an average of eight hours a day. Before permission is given, the workers concerned must be informed of the proposed shift system; a secret ballot must be held to see if they agree and a majority must be in favour. If the factory is a new one, however, a ballot may not be required.

2. *Specialized processes.* Laundries may make women work a total of ten hours a day on two days a week other than Saturday, starting no sooner than 6 a.m. and ending no later than 9 p.m. The same applies to factories making bread, flour, confectionery or sausages. Women employed in the preserving, curing or canning of fruit or vegetables during June, July, August or September are exempt from the restrictions on working hours and subject only to conditions laid down in the Fruit and Vegetable Preserving (Hours of Women and Young Persons) Regulations 1939.

3. *White collar women*. The rules on hours of work do not cover women holding 'responsible management positions' who do not normally do manual work.

## How can a factory be exempted from the laws?

If an employer wants to employ women during hours that are forbidden by the protective laws (and which are not covered by the exceptions listed above) he can apply to the Health and Safety Executive for an exemption order. It is then up to the Executive to make whatever consultations it thinks appropriate. It will grant an order if satisfied that 'it is desirable in the public interest to do so for the purposes of maintaining or increasing the efficiency of industry or transport'. It will not grant an order simply on the grounds that women want to work during hours that are forbidden by the protective laws. So exemptions can be granted for the benefit of industry, but not for the benefit of workers. This should be changed so that workers, too, can ask for exemption orders. There are two kinds of exemptions, 'special' and 'general':

1. *Special exemption orders* apply to individual factories and need to be renewed every year. The employer applies to the local Factory Inspector who then consults the management and the workers. It is not necessary for the workers to agree before an order is made, but they may be able to stop it by negotiating through their trade union or by industrial action. When the order is granted, details of permitted hours must be posted in the factory.
2. *General exemption regulations* cover industry as a whole, or sections of industry. They have no time limit. Applications for one of these orders should be made by a joint industrial council, a wages council, a conciliation board or another organization representing employers or workers. If the application comes from one side of industry alone, the Health and Safety Executive must consult the other side before granting an order. So far, there are only two which affect women: one is the Cotton Factories (Length of Spell) Exemption Order, 1947, which

permits women in cotton factories to work up to five hours without any break at all.

## How many women are involved?

There are approximately two million women working in factories. At present 223,100 are covered by exemption orders; 65,500 are specifically exempted for night work.

## Recent moves to repeal the laws

Nowadays, many people say that the protective laws are old-fashioned and unnecessary. It is argued that they prevent women from competing with men for better-paid jobs; that they help employers to avoid carrying out the Equal Pay Act; and that women should not enjoy special protection if they want to be equal with men. The Equal Opportunities Commission, set up in 1975, has a duty to review the protective laws, in consultation with the Health and Safety Commission, and to report what changes it considers necessary. In a report published in March 1979, it recommended that nearly all the protective laws should be repealed. The Health and Safety at Work, etc., Act, 1974, makes it possible for the protective laws to be repealed gradually and replaced by regulations. This means that they could be weakened significantly, or abolished altogether, without proper debate in parliament.

## Why should the laws be kept?

There are many compelling arguments in favour of repealing the protective laws, but most women workers and trade unions have resisted any attempts to do so. There is a strong case for granting exemptions which are requested by the women themselves, for social reasons (e.g. there are particular reasons why it would be more convenient for them to work certain hours forbidden by the laws). But beyond that, there are plenty of strong arguments for keeping the laws. For example:

1. Most women have two jobs to do. They work to earn money and they work in the home – shopping, cooking, cleaning and looking after their families. Shift workers often go short of sleep and are forced to keep hours which clash with the normal routine of other members of their family. Most women find it hard to combine their home responsibilities with shift work. Until men take an equal share of work in the home, repealing the laws will not reduce discrimination, but merely increase the pressures on women with families and on the families themselves, particularly the children.

2. The shift system is an unsatisfactory way of working for women *and* men. Rotating shifts are bad for the health. In his book *The Hazards of Work: How to Fight Them* (Pluto Press), Patrick Kinnersley writes: 'Your body clock is the key to the most harmful effects of shift work. It is set to a certain programme when you are a child and you cannot reset it completely unless you change to a different living/sleeping routine and *stick to it.*' He quotes several surveys of shift workers. In one, '75 per cent of the men interviewed said they felt physically below par. They blamed this mainly on the fact that they found it difficult to sleep during the day and lost their appetites . . . A German survey found that the ulcer rate among rotating shift workers was eight times as high as for the fixed shift group'. Continuous night work is less disturbing physically, but it is socially disruptive. As Kinnersley writes: 'You have to go off to work just at the time when life for most people is beginning, when families and communities are getting together after the divisions of the day . . .'

3. People who favour repeal argue that the protective laws restrict women's freedom of choice. But it is unlikely that they would have any real choice if the laws were repealed. If jobs were scarce and the only work available involved shift work, they would be forced to take it. When unemployment is high, this is

a very real threat. It would be truer to say that the laws protect women's freedom to choose to work an ordinary day-time shift.

4. The only advantage of shift work is that it pays better. But *nobody* should have to work long, unhealthy, unsocial hours to get adequate wages. While the protective laws remain in force, women have the opportunity of negotiating wages equivalent to the basic male rates and management cannot argue that they must do shift work and long hours of overtime as a precondition. Women, who are generally more concerned than men about conditions at work, don't want to pay the price for 'equality' by transferring the worst features of men's lives to their own. If equality is the goal, what is needed is not to abolish the laws but to work out ways of extending their protection to men – and to all occupations where there are no strong reasons for work to be done at night. Meanwhile, the protective laws should be recognized as a form of positive discrimination in favour of women, helping to right the social imbalance which has built up over centuries and they should be used by women to their best advantage. Wherever possible they should be extended to protect men too.

5. There is no guarantee that women would benefit financially from shift work. Women are badly paid, and always have been, because they are badly organized. Less than one third of working women belong to trade unions and only a tiny number of them are officials. They would be in a far weaker position than men when it came to bargaining for the higher wages which are the only compensation for working long and unsocial hours.

6. At first there was a fear that employers would use the protective laws to avoid equal pay. But it has now been established that men and women doing similar work on different shifts should be paid the same *basic* rate. Women should certainly not be blackmailed into giving up their legal rights as the price for equal pay. Repealing the laws would not prevent employers from trying to dodge the Equal Pay Act. They have been busy segregating male and female jobs and devising many ingenious schemes for avoiding the Act ever since it was passed in 1970.

They will continue to do so, whether or not legal restrictions on women's employment are lifted.

7. A survey of 764 establishments was carried out for the Department of Employment in 1980 and was reported in the *Employment Gazette*, November 1980. Among other things, it looked at the effect of shift working on equal pay and opportunities, and concluded: 'Shift working, which is commonly cited as a reason for discrimination . . . only affects 24 per cent of jobs studied, and only 21 per cent regularly. The jobs concerned are mainly intermediate non-manual, and skilled and semi-skilled manual . . . it does not appear that shift working is a major obstacle to women's employment opportunities, nor that it has a great effect on differential earnings between men and women.'

## Part-time workers

Two out of every five female employees work less than thirty hours a week; one in four works less than sixteen hours a week. Part-timers are disadvantaged in a number of ways. They are usually concentrated in lower-paid jobs: in 1979, 79·5 per cent of part-time women workers (i.e. nearly 2¾ million) were earning less than £1·50 an hour, compared with 47·8 per cent of full-time women and 12·5 per cent of full-time men. They are seldom considered for promotion. They are often the first victims of redundancy. They are rarely able to play as much part in union activities as full-timers. When they are unemployed they cannot register for work unless they are prepared to say they are available for full-time work. And those who work less than sixteen hours a week do not qualify for a range of statutory rights which cover full-time workers. The table below summarizes the rights of part-timers under the Employment Protection (Consolidation) Act 1978. See also p. 85 for the decision of the European Court in relation to part-time workers.

| Rights | Qualifying period of continuous employment |
| --- | --- |

*Rights which are not dependent on how many hours you work each week*

| | |
| --- | --- |
| Protection from victimization for trade-union activities | None |
| Time off for trade-union duties and activity | None |
| Dismissal for trade-union activity | None |
| Protection from race discrimination | None |
| Protection from sex discrimination | None |

*Rights which you have only if you work sixteen hours or more each week, (or if you work eight hours or more* and *have been at the same workplace for five years or more)*

| | |
| --- | --- |
| Unfair dismissal | 52 weeks qualifying period |
| Unfair dismissal for pregnancy | 52 weeks qualifying period |
| Written reasons for dismissal | 52 weeks qualifying period |
| Minimum period of notice | 4 weeks qualifying period |
| Written statement of contract (terms and conditions) | 13 weeks qualifying period |
| Maternity pay | 2 years by the 11th week before confinement |
| Right to reinstatement after birth | 2 years by the 11th week before confinement |
| Redundancy pay | 2 years qualifying period |
| Time off to look for work | 2 years qualifying period |
| Written statement of redundancy pay calculation | 2 years qualifying period |
| Guarantee pay | 4 weeks qualifying period |
| Medical suspension pay | 4 weeks qualifying period |
| Itemized pay statement | First pay day |

**FURTHER INFORMATION**

*Part-time Workers Need Full-time Rights*, by Anne Sedley, 75p from NCCL, 23–5 Tabard Street, London SE1.

# Homeworkers

There are between 100,000 and 150,000 'homeworkers' in Britain. They sew, knit, pack, assemble and paint goods, usually for 'piece' rates, in their own homes. Isolated from their fellow workers, they are almost entirely unorganized. Less than 1 per cent are male.

A homeworker has no legal protection – against sacking, redundancy or the hazards of her work – unless she fights to be recognized as an employee before an industrial tribunal. This is no easy matter. A handful have fought and won. But the great majority neither know that the opportunity is open to them, nor dare to risk their livelihood by taking action against their employer. They are often badly exploited. A 1979 survey found that nearly two-thirds of homeworkers earned under 60p an hour (less than a third of the national average hourly earnings); and as many as a third of homeworkers earned 20p an hour – a *tenth* of the national average.

The case has been argued for a special Homeworkers' Protection Bill to extend employee status to homeworkers, and so to include them in the provisions of the 1970 Equal Pay Act, the 1972 Contracts of Employment Act, the 1974 Trade Union and Labour Relations Act, the 1975 Sex Discrimination Act, the 1976 Race Relations Act, and the 1978 Employment Protection (Consolidation) Act. Such a bill would mean that homeworkers would automatically have rights to itemized pay slips, to a proper statement of the conditions of employment, to maternity pay and to claim redundancy pay and fight unfair dismissal. At the time of writing, efforts to get a Homeworkers Bill through Parliament have not been successful.

However, it is possible for homeworkers to go to industrial tribunals and gain 'employee' status, if their cases are strong enough. Here is one example:

Mrs Cope worked for seven years for Airfix Footwear Ltd, assembling shoe parts which required company tools and equipment. The glue she and the other homeworkers used had been rejected by employees who worked on the company premises. Mrs Cope's work was delivered and collected daily by the company van. She was paid weekly but neither income tax nor

National Insurance contributions were deducted from her pay packet. In 1977 she found herself dismissed by Airfix – without warning and without compensation, on the grounds that she was a self-employed person and an independent contractor.

Mrs Cope decided to fight for recognition of her status as an employee and so for compensation for unfair dismissal. The industrial tribunal in Sheffield decided in her favour on the ground that she was basically the 'servant' in a master–servant relationship. She could not be seen as an independent contractor because her only skill was that which she had learnt from her work, and anyway she did not have the time to work for anyone else. It was clear that her work could satisfactorily have been done in the factory – the work location was interchangeable from Airfix's point of view. Lastly, the 'control' test clearly showed that Mrs Cope was under the company's discipline and was by no means free to do as she wished from day to day or week to week.

Airfix chose to appeal to the Employment Appeal Tribunal on two main grounds: first, that there was only a general contract between the company and Mrs Cope over the work, and second, even if one went as far as describing it as a contract of employment, it could only justly be seen as a daily one. The Employment Appeal Tribunal disagreed and confirmed that Mrs Cope was an employee. She won her compensation – but at the price of hefty lawyers' fees.

FURTHER INFORMATION

*The Hidden Army*, by Simon Crine, 90p from the Low Pay Unit, 9 Poland Street, London W1.

# 3. Money

## Tax

Tax is a complete mystery to most people. If you work for an employer your tax is probably deducted before you get your take-home pay, so you may never think about how much you are paying or why. It's worth knowing how your tax is calculated – you may even find that you are paying too much.

### Basically what happens is this

1. You earn a certain amount of money each year.
2. You get what are called 'allowances', which means that some of the money you earn is tax-free and you get all of it.
3. You can get extra tax-free personal allowances for a number of different reasons – for instance, if you are paying off a mortgage.
4. The rest of your income is taxable. This means that you pay a certain percentage of it in tax, depending on the rates set by each annual budget.
5. What's left after that is yours to spend.

The government department which deals with tax is the Inland Revenue. Normally your tax will be dealt with by the local Inspector of Taxes. The system of having your tax deducted before you get your take-home pay is known as PAYE (Pay As You Earn). Most people who work for an employer pay tax through PAYE.

As you might expect, the Inland Revenue does not go out of its way to see that everyone pays as little tax as possible. You won't get any extra tax-free allowances unless you claim them. You do this by filling in your 'income tax return' form from the Inland Revenue. If you pay tax through PAYE, the Inland Revenue will send you a tax form every one to three years, depending on how stable they think your financial circumstances are. You should also receive a 'coding notice' – this explains what your tax allowances are and gives you what is called a 'code number', indicating the amount of those allowances. If your code is changed, you should be sent a new coding notice. If you don't pay through PAYE (for instance, if you are self-employed) you will probably be sent a tax form regularly each year.

### Are you paying too much tax?

There are several reasons why you may be paying too much tax. You may not have filled in a tax return form since you became eligible for certain allowances. You may have changed jobs and your employer does not know what your code number is. You may have been given the wrong code number (a survey showed that 25 per cent of all code numbers were incorrect). Don't rely on your employer to sort out your tax for you.

If you think you are paying too much tax, the first thing to do is to find out the address of the local tax office which deals with your tax. It will be the one which covers the area where you *work* (not the area where you live, if the two are different). You can ask the accounts department at your place of work for the address of the tax office, or look it up in the phone book, where it is listed under 'Inland Revenue'. Once you have the address, write to the Inspector of Taxes: tell him the name and address of your new employer and his tax reference (which you can find out from the accounts department) and ask to be sent a tax return form. You must then fill in the tax return form, claiming all the tax allowances you think you should have, and supplying the relevant information. Don't be intimidated by the formality of it – the form is really quite simple to complete, if you take it slowly and read the notes that go with it. If you don't understand something, or can't remember details that you are asked to supply, write to the Inspector of Taxes before you fill in the form, explaining your situation in your own words; or phone them up – they can be quite helpful.

If you move around from job to job and you think you may be paying too much tax, keep a list of all your employers and their addresses, and how much you were paid by each one. If you can't remember what you were paid, you can always write to your previous employers and ask for the dates of your employment and the amount you were paid: they will probably have records of this.

You get any excess tax back in the form of a 'tax rebate'. If you don't claim it back soon after you have paid it, it isn't lost. You can reclaim tax up to six years after you have paid it, and it will be paid back to you eventually.

*If you start a new job* where you pay tax through PAYE, the wages department will ask you for your form P45. This is a form which you should have been given when you left your last job: it says how much you earned, how much tax you paid and what your code number is. It is very important to keep your form P45 between jobs. (If you leave it behind when you change jobs, you should contact the wages department at your last place of work and ask them to send it to you.) If you then give it to the wages department at your new place of work, they should continue to deduct tax at the rate you were paying before (unless the wages clerk makes a mistake, which sometimes happens, so check when you get your pay packet).

If you have lost your P45, or you don't have one because this is your first job, your new employer is obliged to tell the Inland Revenue that you have started working for him; you will have tax deducted at the 'emergency' rate until you have filled in a tax return form and the Inland Revenue has worked out how much tax you should be paying. Emergency tax is the same as the rate of tax paid by a single person who has no extra tax-free allowances – it is fairly high, so that if you go down to a lower rate when you get coded you will get a tax rebate. You will probably be sent a tax return form shortly after you start your new job. If not, write to the local tax office and ask to be sent one.

### How much tax will you have to pay?*

As is the habit of most government departments, the Inland Revenue treats single women and married women as two completely different species. They treat single women like single men and married women like inanimate objects attached to their husbands. If you are separated from your husband, see p. 124.

### Single women

As a single woman, your tax position is the same as a single man's. You don't pay tax on the first £1,375 you earn each year. This is your 'personal allowance' and you usually get it automatically without having to claim. There are extra tax-free allowances you

* The figures quoted in this chapter are for 1980–81.

may be able to claim, depending on your circumstances. Allowances usually go up each year, so check the latest rates with your local tax office. Here are the main ones:

1. *Additional personal allowance.* If you are bringing up a child or children single-handed, whether or not you are getting mainten-ance payments from their father, you can claim an 'additional personal allowance' of £770 a year.
2. *Housekeeper allowance.* If you are widowed and you have a woman living with you who acts as a housekeeper, you may be able to claim an allowance of £100 a year. But you cannot claim this as well as the additional personal allowance. You can only claim one of the two.
3. *Son's or daughter's services allowance.* If you have a daughter or son living with you for whom you are financially responsible and on whom you are dependent for 'services' due to your own infirmity or old age, you may claim an allowance of £55 a year.
4. *Dependent relative allowance.* If you have any relatives whose income is not more than the basic National Insurance retirement pension (see p. 139) and to whom you are giving some sort of financial help, you may be able to claim a 'dependent relative allowance' of up to £100 a year or £145 if you are unmarried, or if you are married but not living with your husband – the exact amount depending on how much you are helping them. (The help may be in the form of goods, not just money.) There is no limit to the number of dependent relatives you may have.
5. *Life assurance relief.* If you have a life assurance policy you will probably get tax relief on it, but this is normally deducted from the premium before you pay it.
6. *Tax relief on occupational pension contributions.* If you are paying into an approved occupational pension scheme (i.e. run by a private company, not the state), your contributions are deducted before your earnings are assessed for tax.
7. *Other tax allowances.* You can claim tax relief on interest you are paying on a mortgage or, in certain circumstances, on a loan from a bank or finance company. Write to the company to whom

you are paying the interest and ask for a 'certificate of interest', which you then forward to the Inland Revenue. You can also claim tax relief on any expenses you have incurred 'wholly, necessarily and exclusively' in the course of your employment, which have not been reimbursed by your employer.

## IF YOU ARE RECEIVING MAINTENANCE FROM A FORMER HUSBAND OR THE FATHER OF YOUR CHILDREN

*Where the maintenance is for you:*

If the man is making payments to you under a legal separation agreement, the rule is that he should deduct the basic rate of income tax from all payments. He must account to the Inland Revenue for the tax he deducts. You may claim any tax allowances you are eligible for (for example, an additional personal allowance), and (depending on your total income) you may receive a tax rebate. The tax deducted by the man will be looked upon by the Inland Revenue as though it had been paid by you.

If the man is paying a small amount of maintenance under a court order, the rule is that he doesn't have to pay tax on it at all but pays it gross. *You* may have to pay tax on it if your total income is high enough to be taxable. This rule applies if the payments are no more than £33 a week or £143 a month for the benefit of a spouse; or £18 a week or £78 a month for the benefit of a child under 21.

*Where the maintenance is for your children:*

If the maintenance order says that the maintenance is to be paid to the child, the money will not be added to your income for tax purposes, so you will not have to pay tax on it. In effect, what this means is that the child has an independent income, although the money is paid to you to administer for the child.

### Child tax allowance

If you are resident in Britain and have dependent children living abroad for whom you receive no child benefit (see p. 185) or equivalent allowance in the country where they are living, you may be able to claim tax allowance for them until 1982/3. Consult your local tax office (in the telephone directory under 'Inland Revenue') or an accountant.

### Married women

For tax purposes, your income is treated as part of your husband's. This means that your husband has to fill in the tax form with details of your income and his. He is responsible for paying any tax that either of you owes to the Inland Revenue. If you are paying tax through PAYE, your husband will only be responsible for paying tax on your unearned income – if you have any. He gets a married man's allowance of £2,145 a year (*check with your local tax office for current rate*). In addition, if you are in paid work, you can earn up to £1,375 before paying tax. If you help your husband with his business, you cannot claim this relief unless he pays you proper wages.

Married couples have a slight tax advantage over two single people if the wife is earning because her husband will still get his married man's allowance. That means they will get £770 more in tax allowance than two single people. They would lose the financial advantage of this if their joint income were large enough to be liable for a higher rate of tax (say, more than £17,000 a year). But in that case they would be able to opt for separate taxation of the wife's earnings.

#### THE MARRIED MAN'S ALLOWANCE MAY SOON BE ABOLISHED

At the end of 1980, the government published a Green Paper which proposed, among other things, to abolish the married man's tax allowance, and to give men and women the same personal allowance, whether they are married or single. Several options were put forward as alternatives. In the political climate of the time, it seemed most likely that some arrangement would be made to give an extra tax allowance to an employed person whose spouse was at home with domestic responsibilities. In most cases, this would go to men with non-employed wives, and it would amount to a tax incentive for married women to stay at home. A better alternative would be to use the money saved by abolishing the married man's allowance to increase child benefit.

### YOU MAY WANT YOUR TAX TO BE DEALT WITH SEPARATELY FROM YOUR HUSBAND'S

This can be an advantage if you want to handle your own tax affairs and retain a degree of privacy. It may also give you a financial advantage, as you will see if you read on. The systems that have been devised for separating married women's tax are absurdly complex. There are three different systems, which we explain below, giving the advantages of each.

1. *Separate assessment.* This system enables the Inland Revenue to treat you as a separate 'unit' from your husband – up to a point. Between you, you pay as much tax as you would have done without separate assessment. Most tax allowances, including the married man's and married woman's earned income allowances, will be divided between you in proportion with your earnings (although in any circumstances you will not get *less* than the wife's earned income allowance). Some allowances are divided according to how much money each of you is paying out. For example, tax allowances for dependent relatives go to the one who is paying the maintenance, but if you both are, they will be divided according to how much you each pay. If you are paying interest on a loan which is in your name, the tax relief will go to you, not your husband.

   Without separate assessment, all tax allowances except the wife's earned-income allowance go to the husband, so this system would mean that you yourself pay less tax.

It also enables you to fill in your own tax return form, if you want to, *but not automatically*. The Inland Revenue is still only obliged to send one form to your husband. However, if he does not give adequate details of your income and expenditure on this form, the Inland Revenue will send another one for you to fill in and it will normally make a habit of sending one for each of you from then on. To get separate assessment, write to your local Inspector of Taxes between 6 January and 6 July in the year you want to be separately assessed. You will be sent a special form which one of you has to sign.

2. *Separate taxation of wife's earnings.* This can only be an advantage if your joint earnings are well over £17,000 a year. It means that you and your husband each get a single person's tax allowance of £1,375 a year. So, between you, you get £770 *less* in personal tax allowances. You do not fill in a separate tax return form – you and your husband are still treated as a single 'unit' by the Inland Revenue. If you have any unearned income, it is still assessed as part of your husband's income.

The advantage is that your earnings are taxed entirely separately from your husband's. Each of you, therefore, pays tax at the basic rate of 30 per cent on the first £11,250 of your respective taxable earnings (according to rates set for the year 1980–81). For example: You earn £6,500 a year and your husband earns £12,000 a year, so your joint earnings are £18,500. *Without* separate taxation of wife's earnings, higher rates of tax would have to be paid on £3,730. *With* separate taxation of wife's earnings a higher rate would not have to be paid on any of it.

Separate taxation is only worth doing if it means a reduction in the total amount of tax you and your husband pay which offsets the reduction in your personal tax allowances. If in doubt, seek an accountant's advice, or ask your local tax office. To get separate taxation of wife's earnings, write to your local tax inspector. You will be sent a special form, which you and your husband must sign.

3. *Separate assessment and separate taxation of wife's earnings.* This

gives you the advantages of both systems, if your combined earnings are well over £17,000. Apply to your local tax inspector in writing that you want separate assessment *and* separate taxation of wife's earnings. You will be sent two forms to sign, one for each system.

None of these alternatives gives you complete privacy, since your husband can still find out whether your income is above the level that would make it an advantage to elect for separate taxation of wife's earnings.

## *If you are separated*

If you separate from your husband and he stops supporting you, notify the Inland Revenue: you should become eligible for the same tax allowances as a single person. If your husband continues to claim a married man's tax allowance while not supporting you, he could find himself in serious trouble. Write to the local Inland Revenue office and tell them (a) that you and your husband have separated; and (b) that you want to complete an income tax return form.

---

TAX EXAMPLE ONE

Sarah is an unsupported mother with two children aged 6 and 9. She works as a computer punch-card operator and earns £80 a week (£4,160 a year). She also receives child benefit of £15·50 a week (£806 a year).

| | |
|---|---:|
| Her total annual income, minus child benefit is | £4,160 |
| She has the following tax allowances: | |
| 1. personal allowance | 1,375 |
| 2. additional personal allowance | 770 |
| These add up to | £2,145 |
| So her total taxable income is £4,160 minus £2,145 which comes to | 2,015 |
| Tax at 30 per cent of £2,015 amounts to | 604·50 |
| So her net income after tax is £4,160 minus tax of £604·50, plus child benefit of £806 which comes to | £4,361·50 |

TAX EXAMPLE TWO

Carol and Fred are married with no children. They have not applied for separate taxation of wife's earnings as their incomes are not high enough to benefit from it. Carol works as a quality supervisor in a sweet factory and earns £5,500 a year. Fred is an apprentice engineer and earns £4,000. They are paying £600 interest on their mortgage this year, which qualifies for tax relief.

| | |
|---|---|
| Their total earnings are | £9,500 |

They have the following tax allowances:

| | |
|---|---|
| 1. married man's allowance | 2,145 |
| 2. wife's earned-income allowance | 1,375 |
| 3. mortgage interest | 600 |
| Their total tax allowance is | £4,120 |

| | |
|---|---|
| So their total taxable income is £9,500 minus £4,120 which comes to | £5,380 |
| Tax at 30 per cent of £5,380 amounts to | £1,614 |
| So their net income after tax is £9,500−£1,614 which comes to | £7,886 |

---

## If you are self-employed

You can claim the same tax allowances as an employed person. You do not normally pay tax through PAYE, but through the 'Schedule D' system. You can claim tax relief on all sorts of expenses incurred in your work – heating, phone, rent, equipment, etc. It's often worth getting help from an accountant – if she or he is efficient and you don't earn a great deal, you may end up paying very little tax, or none at all. Get a written estimate first; some of them charge extortionate rates.

FURTHER INFORMATION

*Income Tax and Sex Discrimination*, by Patricia Hewitt, from NCCL, 23–5 Tabard Street, London SE1.

## National Insurance

The National Insurance scheme is a bureaucrat's dream. It's so complicated that no one really knows why they are paying money into it each week, what they are getting in return, or what they might be missing if they don't pay. (Do you?)

### *How the National Insurance system works*

The basic idea is that you pay National Insurance contributions while you are working and in return you get money to live on while you are prevented from working – for instance, while you are unemployed, sick, having a baby or retired.

Some important changes, which have made the scheme fairer to women, were introduced by the 1975 Social Security Pensions Act. Previously, the scheme was based on the idea that women were bound to be financially dependent on men and provisions varied according to whether you were single, married, separated, divorced or widowed. The new scheme aims to give women and men a greater degree of equality – particularly as it enables women to earn a good pension even when they have taken several years off

work to raise a family. The new scheme started in April 1978, but will take twenty years to come into full effect.

Every woman aged between 16 and 60 should have a National Insurance number. This is the number of your personal 'account' which is held at a central office in Newcastle upon Tyne. Your account shows how much you have paid in contributions and what benefits you can claim. Let your employer know your National Insurance number. If you don't know it, ask your local Social Security office.

We have divided the section on National Insurance into two main parts:

1. *Contributions*, pp. 128–37. This deals with the money you pay into the National Insurance scheme – which varies according to whether you are employed, self-employed or non-employed. It may also vary according to whether you are single or married, as explained on p. 133.

2. *Benefits*, pp. 137–53. This deals with the money you receive in return for your contributions. In different circumstances you get different benefits and we deal with them each in turn. The main ones are unemployment benefit, sickness benefit and maternity allowance. Sometimes, your right to benefit may be affected by whether you are single, married, divorced or separated. Where appropriate we point this out. (Pensions are also part of the National Insurance scheme. But because the subject is so complex – and so important – we have dealt with it separately on pp. 154–70.)

*Please read the first part first! Otherwise you may find the second part (on benefits) even more confusing.*

**Important!** All the figures quoted in this chapter were accurate in November 1981 but they are likely to change since the rates for National Insurance contributions and benefits normally go up each year. If you want the latest figures check with your local Social Security office. **Even more important!** At the time of writing, the government was planning changes to the National Insurance scheme, which in particular would affect your rights when sick and off work. We have described these changes in the appropriate sections.

## Contributions

There are three main types of National Insurance contribution. These are called Class 1, Class 2 and Class 3. The type you pay depends on your work situation. There is also a Class 4 contribution for self-employed people which is different from the rest because it doesn't earn any benefits (see p. 131).

### CLASS I CONTRIBUTIONS

*If you work for an employer* you must pay these. You and your employer both make regular payments into your account. The size of your contribution depends on the level of your earnings. Each year *you* must pay 7·75 per cent of your earnings and *your employer* must make a contribution worth 10·2 per cent of your earnings. For example, if you earn £70 a week your contribution is £5·42 a week and your employer's is £7·14. (Your employer also pays a National Insurance surcharge worth 3·5 per cent of your earnings. But this is a 'payroll tax', i.e. it does *not* go towards paying for your benefits.)

However, there is an *upper limit* to the earnings on which these percentages are calculated – it is currently £200 a week (equivalent to £10,400 a year). If you are lucky enough to earn more than £200 a week, neither you nor your employer need pay any proportion of what you earn above that level. The most you need pay in contributions, therefore, whether you earn £200 or £350 a week, is £15·50 a week, which is 7·75 per cent of £200.

If you earn less than £27 a week (which is currently the 'lower earnings limit') no contributions need be paid.

If you are over 60 and still in employment you needn't pay any contributions, but your employer has to go on contributing at the same rate.

If you are employed through an agency – as a cleaner or a temporary secretary, for instance – you and the agency (officially your employer) must pay Class 1 contributions into your account.

Class 1 contributions are collected through the 'Pay As You Earn' (PAYE) system, which means they are deducted from your earnings before they reach you (PAYE is explained on p. 116).

Under the new pension scheme which started in April 1978 there are different contribution rates for people 'contracted in' and 'contracted out' of the state pension scheme. If you are contracted in, you will pay the rates as explained above.

If you belong to an occupational pension scheme which meets the government's minimum requirements, you will probably have been 'contracted out' by your employer. (Occupational pensions are explained on p. 170.) This means that you will contribute less towards the state pension scheme. If you are contracted out *you* pay:

1. 7·75 per cent of your earnings up to the 'lower earnings limit'. (The 'lower earnings limit' is currently £27 a week. If you earn less than £27 you won't pay any contributions; if you earn more than £27 a week you will pay 7·75 per cent of the first £27 of your weekly earnings); *and*

2. 5·25 per cent of your earnings above the 'lower earnings limit' up to the 'upper limit' (which is currently £200 a week). So if you earn £70 a week, you will pay 7·75 per cent of £27, plus 5·25 per cent of £43 (which is the difference between £27 and £70). That will come to a total of £4·35 a week.

Meanwhile, *your employer* will pay:

1. 10·2 per cent of your earnings up to the 'lower earnings limit' (currently £27 a week); *and*

2. 5·7 per cent of your earnings above the 'lower earnings limit' and below the 'upper limit' (currently £200 a week).

So, if you earn £70 a week your employer will pay 10·2 per cent of £27 and 5·7 per cent of £43 which will come to a total of £5·20 a week. (He will also pay the National Insurance surcharge of 3·5 per cent.)

See pp. 163–6 for what you get from the state pension scheme if you are 'contracted out'.

CLASS 2 CONTRIBUTIONS

You must pay these *if you are self-employed*. The rate is £3·40 a week. If your *net* earnings (that is, your total 'gross' earnings minus the expenses you have incurred in the course of your work) come to more than £3,150 a year, you must also pay *Class 4* contributions which are earnings-related. This means you must pay, in addition to the flat-rate contribution of £3·40 a week, 5·75 per cent of your net earnings between £3,150 and £10,000 a year. So if, for example, your accounts for the year show that you have made a 'profit' of £4,500 you will have to pay £77·62 in Class 4 contributions.

You can arrange to pay your Class 2 contributions directly

through your bank or National Giro account, by filling in the form at the back of Leaflet N I 41, which you can get at your local Social Security office. Otherwise, you must get a contribution card from your local Social Security office and buy a stamp each week from the Post Office, which you stick on the card. The card lasts for a year: at the end of the year you return it to the Social Security office and collect another one. Class 4 contributions are assessed and collected by the Inland Revenue, along with your tax. (More about Schedule D tax for the self-employed on p. 125.) If your self-employed earnings are below a certain level you can apply for a certificate of 'exception' which means you will not have to pay any contributions at all. The level above which you must pay contributions is currently £1,475, but you are allowed to deduct certain expenses from your earnings before arriving at that figure. Leaflet N I 27A, available from your Social Security office, gives fuller details. Leaflet N I 208 tells you what the 'exception limit' is for the current year.

CLASS 3 CONTRIBUTIONS

*You can pay these if you are neither employed nor self-employed.* You may be in this situation if you are at home looking after your family; if you are claiming supplementary benefit or living abroad; or if you are a student. In this case you do not *have* to pay contributions. But if you don't, you may lose your right to claim some of the benefits which are available under the National Insurance scheme. So you can, if you wish, pay Class 3 contributions on a voluntary basis. You pay £3·30 a week, either by standing order through your bank or National Giro account, or by buying stamps each week to stick on a card. However, you *cannot* choose to pay Class 3 contributions if:

1. You are being 'credited' with contributions, as explained immediately below; *or*
2. You have 'opted out' of paying full contributions as explained on p. 133 and you want to remain opted out. If you have opted

out and you want to pay Class 3 contributions you will have to opt back into the National Insurance scheme. Once you have done this you will have to pay full Class 1 or 2 contributions as soon as you become employed or self-employed again.

*You can use Class 3 contributions to make up your insurance record if it is incomplete.*

If, in any one tax year, you have paid Class 1 or 2 contributions for part of the year, but not for the whole of it, that year will not count towards your pension. (Tax years are reckoned from April to April.) In this case, you can complete your record with Class 3 contributions. How will you know? You should receive a statement of your National Insurance 'account' for each tax year before the end of the following tax year: if your record for the year is incomplete, it will tell you how many Class 3 contributions you need to pay to complete it. You can then pay by sending a lump sum (by postal order, Giro or cheque) to your Social Security office.

*You must pay Class 2 and 3 contributions within a certain time limit* – that is, before the end of the second tax year after the year in which they are due. So your contributions for the 1981–2 tax year must be paid by 5 April 1984.

SOMETIMES YOU GET CONTRIBUTIONS 'CREDITED' TO YOU WITHOUT HAVING TO PAY FOR THEM

If you are receiving unemployment benefit, you will normally be 'credited' with Class 1 contributions, which means you get them without having to pay. The same is true if you are receiving sickness or industrial injury benefit, maternity allowance, invalidity pension or invalid care allowance. If you are unemployed or sick and you don't qualify for benefit (for instance, when you stop being eligible for unemployment benefit at the end of a year out of work) you may still be credited with Class 1 contributions. If you are aged between 16 and 18 and in full-time education or training, you will be credited with Class 3 contributions. You may also be credited with contributions if you have interrupted your employment to go on a training course; for more information see Leaflet NI 125.

### THE MARRIED WOMAN'S OPTION

Until 11 May 1977 married women had a choice about paying National Insurance contributions. They could either:

1. Pay full contributions like single women; *or*
2. 'Opt out' of the National Insurance scheme and pay reduced contributions – relying instead on their husbands' insurance, which covered them for limited benefits only.

*The married woman's option is being phased out.* So it only affects women who opted out before 11 May 1977. If you opted out and were still paying reduced contributions on that date, you can continue to do so until you retire – *unless:*

1. You decide to opt in and pay full contributions – Class 1, 2 or 3 – in which case you can't change your mind and opt out again; *or*
2. You have a break from employment which lasts for more than two consecutive tax years (tax years being reckoned from April to April). In this case you must start paying full contributions when you go back to work.

If you were not 'opted out' on 11 May 1977 you cannot choose to be so.

### HOW MUCH DO YOU PAY IF YOU HAVE 'OPTED OUT'?

*If you are employed* you pay nothing if your earnings are below £27 a week, but if you earn more than £27 a week you pay 2·75 per cent of your earnings up to the 'upper limit' of £200.

*If you are self-employed* you pay nothing if you earn less than

£3,150 a year and Class 4 contributions if you earn more than
£3,150.

### PROTECTION OF PENSION RIGHTS
### FOR PEOPLE WITH 'HOME RESPONSIBILITY'

This is a new provision which started in April 1978. It applies to
women and, in certain circumstances, to men.

*If you stay at home to look after children* you are not expected to
pay contributions of any class and you cannot qualify for most
National Insurance benefits. (Both these points were also true
before April 1978.) However, since April 1978 your right to a
pension is protected. This means that when you retire your basic
pension will be worked out as if you had paid contributions during
those years at home. This protection lasts until your youngest child
reaches 16. You can earn up to £27 a week doing part-time work
and still be covered. But you must fulfil the conditions below for a
*complete* tax year, in order for your pension rights to be protected.
Part of a tax year is not enough.

*If you stay at home to look after a sick or elderly relative* your
pension rights are protected in the same way if you are taking care
of someone (who is getting one of the attendance allowances,
pp. 206–7) for at least thirty-five hours a week, or if you are allowed
to receive supplementary benefit without 'signing on' for work
because you are looking after an invalid.

*Men are also covered* for 'home responsibility' if they are single. If
they are married and looking after children at home, they should
be named by their wives to have the right to receive Child Benefit
each week, in order to be covered.

*If you have taken the married woman's option*, and you were paying
reduced contributions when you left employment to take on 'home
responsibility', your pension rights are not protected for the first
two years that you are at home. After two years, your 'married
woman's option' is automatically revoked. As a result, your pension

rights are protected for the rest of the period in which you have home responsibility. When you return to employment (or self-employment) you have to pay full contributions.

So if you have opted out and you can foresee a time when you might have to leave employment to take on home responsibility, it's worth opting back into the National Insurance scheme if you want your pension rights protected for those first two years. You become eligible for protection of pension rights as soon as you cancel the married woman's option, without having to pay any contributions at the full rate.

*Important note:* Having your pension rights *protected* while you have 'home responsibility' is not the same as being *credited* with contributions. When your basic pension is being worked out, the 'home responsibility protection' will only come into force if you have already paid or been credited with twenty years of full contributions.

Make sure you notify your local Social Security office when you first leave employment to take on 'home responsibility'. This will ensure that your pension rights are protected.

DECIDING WHETHER TO OPT IN

If you have taken the married woman's option and you are still paying reduced contributions, you may be wondering whether it's worth opting *in* to the National Scheme and paying contributions at the full rate. Here are some points worth considering:

1. *If you stay opted out:*
(a) You get no unemployment benefit, sickness benefit or maternity allowance.
(b) You are entitled to limited benefits only – and these are dependent on your husband's insurance. You can get a maternity grant and a lower rate of retirement pension, but only if he has paid the appropriate number of contributions. Do you know what his insurance record is like? Does he know? If you can't find out from him ask your local Social Security office. They

can tell you how much benefit is due to you on the basis of his record as it stands, but they will not give you any more details about his insurance.

(c) You get a lower rate of pension than you would if you had paid full contributions throughout your working life.

(d) If you have 'home responsibility' your pension rights are not protected for the first two years, as explained above, p. 134.

(e) Of course you save money by paying reduced contributions – but is it worth it?

2. *If you opt in:*

You can claim the full range of benefits in your own right. And you get more for your money under the new system than you did under the old:

(a) From April 1978 married women who pay full contributions get the same rate of unemployment and sickness benefit as single women. Under the old system, they got less.

(b) Your pension rights are protected if you have 'home responsibility', as explained above, p. 134. Under the new system you can stay at home looking after children or sick or elderly relatives for a long time and still earn a good pension in your own right.

(c) National Insurance contributions get more and more expensive – but are they worth it?

*Note:* Since the new scheme takes twenty years to come into full effect, older women may not reap the full benefits. See pp. 161–5 for more details of the new pension arrangements and how your pension can be affected by the married woman's option.

HOW TO OPT IN – OR OUT

If you got married or started work after April 1978, you will be expected to pay full contributions. If you have opted out in the past and want to remain opted out, you don't have to do anything. But if you have opted out in the past, and now want to opt in, ask for form NI 1 at your local Social Security office, complete Declaration A on Form CF 9 at the back of the form, and return it to them. But you will not start having full contributions deducted until the beginning of the next tax year.

DIVORCED WOMEN

There are special arrangements to help you qualify for certain benefits if you were paying reduced contributions before your divorce (see p. 142).

## *Benefits*

To avoid unnecessary confusion we advise you to read the previous section on contributions before you tackle this. We've tried to make it as clear as possible, but it hasn't been easy!

The benefits you can claim under the National Insurance scheme depend on which class of contributions you have been paying.

| *If you have Class 1 contributions you can claim* | *If you have Class 2 contributions you can claim* | *If you have Class 3 contributions you can claim* |
| --- | --- | --- |
| unemployment benefit | – | – |
| sickness benefit | sickness benefit | – |
| invalidity benefit | invalidity benefit | – |
| maternity grant* | maternity grant* | maternity grant* |
| maternity allowance | maternity allowance | – |
| retirement pension | retirement pension | retirement pension |
| death grant | death grant | death grant |

These are the benefits you can claim on the basis of your own contributions.

If you are married you can claim the *maternity grant* (p. 149), *death grant* (p. 181) and a lower rate of *retirement pension* (p. 160) on the basis of your husband's contributions if you have opted out or haven't paid enough contributions to claim them in your own

* For babies expected on or after 4 July 1982, you won't have to have paid contributions to get a maternity grant.

right. *Widow's benefits* are also based on your husband's contribution record.

If you are divorced you may, in certain circumstances, be able to claim a *child's special allowance* (p. 152) on the basis of your ex-husband's contributions.

If you are self-employed and have been paying Class 4 contributions, you don't get any more benefits than you do if you are paying only Class 2 contributions: it's really just a surcharge, like the extra 3·5 per cent that your employer has to pay if you are employed.

Claiming benefits is no simple matter. You must have a certain number of the right class of contributions paid or credited to you over a certain period of time. If you don't have enough contributions, the amount paid to you will be smaller. If you have less than a minimum number of contributions you won't get anything, but you may be able to claim supplementary benefit (see p. 189). Sometimes the number of contributions you have to pay and the amount of money you get varies according to whether you are single, married or divorced. The exact requirements vary from one benefit to another.

We shall now deal with the different benefits in turn.

## Unemployment benefit

This is 'the dole'. You claim it when you're out of work.

HOW MANY CONTRIBUTIONS DO YOU NEED AND WHAT DO YOU GET IN RETURN?

*If you are single:*
You should get the standard rate of unemployment benefit if you satisfy the following conditions:

1. During the twelve months which ended in April the year *before* you claim, you paid or were credited with Class 1 contributions on earnings of at least fifty times the lower earnings limit (£23 per week from April 1980 to April 1981). So if, for example, you

want to claim unemployment benefit at any time during the year beginning with the first Sunday in January 1982, you must have paid or been credited with contributions on at least £1,150 (fifty times £23) during the tax year ending April 1981; *and*

2. If you were paying National Insurance contributions before 6 April 1975 you must, in addition, have *paid* at least twenty-six Class 1 contributions during your working life; *or*

3. If you started paying National Insurance after 6 April 1975 you must have *paid* contributions on at least twenty-five times the lower earnings limit in any one tax year since 6 April 1975 (which is £27 per week from April 1981 to April 1982).

If you don't satisfy condition 1 because you have paid or been credited with Class 1 contributions on earnings of *less* than fifty times the lower earnings limit in the relevant tax year, you will get a lower rate of benefit provided that: (a) you have paid or been credited with Class 1 contributions on earnings of at least twenty-five times the lower earnings limit during that year; *and* (b) you satisfy condition 2 or 3. The more contributions you have paid, the more benefit you will get. If you cannot meet these two minimum provisions, you will get no benefit at all.

*If you recently left school and you are unemployed* you should be able to claim unemployment benefit if you have paid Class 1 contributions on earnings of up to twenty-five times the lower earnings limit. If you wish you can register for work at your Local Authority Careers Office (you can do this up to the age of 20 if you finished full-time education within the last 2 years). Otherwise, register for work at your employment office or job centre. Claim benefit in the same way as those over 18.

*How much do you get?*

The standard rate is £22·50 per week for a single person from November 1981. You can get extra money if you have dependants. The weekly rates are:

for a child 80p (plus Child Benefit)
for an adult dependant £13·90

*Who can be an adult dependant?*

You can claim extra benefit for *one* person who falls into one of the following categories:

1. *A male relative.* He must be your father, stepfather, father-in-law, grandfather, brother, stepbrother, half-brother, son, stepson or grandson. He must be living in your home and an invalid, incapable of supporting himself. You must be paying at least half the cost of his support.
2. *A female relative.* She must be your mother, stepmother, mother-in-law, grandmother, sister, stepsister, half-sister, daughter, stepdaughter or granddaughter. She must be living in your home and earning no more than £13·90 a week. You must be paying at least half the cost of her support. If she is married she must be living apart from her husband or he must be an invalid, incapable of supporting himself or giving her any financial help.

   *Note:* A female relative, unlike a male relative, need not be an invalid and incapable of self-support in order to qualify as your dependant. This did not change when the new scheme was introduced, so it is one glaring inequality which persists within the National Insurance Scheme.
3. *A woman looking after your dependent children.* She must be *either* living in your home *or* employed by you and having expenses of not less than £13·90 a week; *and* not earning more than £13·90 a week except from looking after the children. You must also be claiming extra benefit for the children. You cannot claim this benefit for a *man* looking after your dependent children.

*You may get extra money which is related to the level of your earnings.* This is explained on p. 148. (After January 1982 you won't be able to start getting this any more.)

IF YOU ARE MARRIED

*If you have opted out* of paying contributions you cannot claim unemployment benefit. If your husband is unemployed and has paid the right number of contributions (as described above) he can claim extra money for you as his dependent wife. The rate is £13·90 a week. If you are earning more than that amount, he cannot claim extra benefit for you.

*If you have not opted out* you must meet the same conditions as a single woman to qualify for unemployment benefit.

### How much do you get?

You get the same as a single woman. You cannot claim extra for your husband and children unless your husband is an invalid and incapable of supporting himself. If you are not getting extra benefit for your husband you may be able to claim extra benefit for another adult dependant, in the same way as a single woman can (see p. 140). This will change in stages in 1983 and 1984. By 1984 married men and married women will be able to claim increases for a spouse on the same conditions.

IF YOU ARE SEPARATED BUT NOT DIVORCED

*If you have opted out* you are in the same position as any other married woman who has opted out. If your husband is getting unemployment benefit he can only claim extra for you if he is supporting you and you are earning less than £13·90 a week.

*If you haven't opted out* you must have paid the same contributions as a single woman in order to claim unemployment benefit. You can claim extra benefit for your dependent children in the same way as a single woman.

IF YOU ARE DIVORCED

There are special rules which may help you to qualify for unemployment benefit if you have not paid the right number of contributions during the relevant tax year. You may be able to claim the dole if you have *paid* Class 1 contributions equal to twenty-five times the lower earnings limit in any one tax year *after* April 1975, and *before* the beginning of the tax year in which your marriage ends. So if, for example, your marriage ends in July 1982, you must meet this condition in any one tax year between 6 April 1975 and 5 April 1981. See leaflet NI 95 to help you.

*How much do you get?*
The same rate as a single woman.

YOU CAN BE DISQUALIFIED FROM CLAIMING
UNEMPLOYMENT BENEFIT

In certain circumstances, you are not allowed unemployment benefit, no matter how many contributions you have paid:

1. You get no unemployment benefit for the first three days you are out of work, unless you have been unemployed or sick during the previous 8 weeks.
2. You get no unemployment benefit for any day you are on holiday or abroad (unless you are looking for work in the Common Market); or when you have done a normal week's work, paid or unpaid. However, a recent test case showed that you *might* be able to do voluntary work for a charitable organization without losing your right to unemployment benefit.
3. You will probably lose your right to benefit in the following circumstances:
(a) You were paid for a period of 'notice' at the end of a job but you didn't have to work during that time, in which case you will not get benefit until the period of notice comes to an end.
(b) They find out that you have a part-time job.

(c) You are so choosy about the sort of work you are prepared to do that you have no reasonable chance of getting a suitable job.

(d) You are awarded a sum of money by an Industrial Tribunal under the provisions of the Employment Protection Act to cover payment you should have received after you left your last job. (This could happen if you made a complaint of unfair dismissal.) If the award you receive covers a period for which you have already been paid unemployment benefit and it was *not* for redundancy payment the amount of the benefit may be deducted from your award.

4. You may be disqualified for up to 6 weeks in the following circumstances:

(a) If you turn down a job without a good reason; *or*

(b) If you left your last job voluntarily, 'without good cause'; *or*

(c) If you lost your last job through 'misconduct'.

5. If you are out of work because of a trade dispute, you will not get unemployment benefit – whether it is a strike or a lock-out – as long as the trade dispute lasts. The only exception to this rule is by proving that you are not 'participating in, or directly interested in the outcome of' the trade dispute.

6. You stop getting unemployment benefit after you have been claiming it for a full year. If you continue registering for work and 'signing on' at your Unemployment Benefit Office, they will go on crediting you with Class 1 contributions. If you get work for at least thirteen weeks and you work at least sixteen hours each of those weeks, and if you then become unemployed again, you should be able to claim benefit for as long as another year.

If you are disqualified from claiming unemployment benefit, you can claim supplementary benefit, as explained below, p. 189. But the amount can be reduced under certain circumstances for up to six weeks.

## HOW TO CLAIM UNEMPLOYMENT BENEFIT

It's important to go to your local Employment Office as soon as you find yourself out of work. (It may be called a Job Centre and it is officially known as the local office of the Manpower Services Commission.) If you delay you may not get any money for the period before your first visit. Take with you your form P45: this is the income tax form which should have been given to you by your last employer. If you haven't got a P45 form, tell them your National Insurance number. If you don't know your National Insurance number, inquire at your local Social Security office. But *don't delay*. You can find your number later.

You register for work at the Employment Office. Then go to the Unemployment Benefit Office to 'sign on' and fill in a form to claim benefit. You will then be told to come back to the office each fortnight to sign on. They make you do this every fortnight that you want to claim benefit. It's their way of getting proof that you are available for work and therefore eligible for unemployment benefit. Try not to miss any fortnight. If you do, you will have to go through the whole form-filling process again before you sign on the following fortnight. (You may be allowed to go away for two weeks if you let them know well in advance; tell them where you are going and explain that you are still eligible for work.) If you want to 'sign on' and get your benefit every week instead of every fortnight, ask the manager of the local office. They *must* let you do this if you ask.

In all this you will need a lot of patience and perseverance. You may have to put up with hours of waiting and being shuttled from one department to another. The system seems designed to discourage anyone who is not absolutely desperate for money. Don't expect to get paid as soon as you register for work. They have to check up on your record first.

When your money finally arrives, it will either be sent to you through the post in the form of a Giro order which you can cash at any Post Office, or you will be told that you can collect it when you go to sign on. The government is shortly going to tax unemployment benefit and supplementary benefit for the unemployed. Tax will not be levied on the benefit before you receive it, but you will no longer get a tax rebate when unemployed. Any adjustments will be made at the end of the tax year or when you get another job.

*If you are unemployed and not eligible for unemployment benefit*, or if the benefit you are getting is not enough to live on, you can claim supplementary benefit. If you are getting less than £21·30 unemployment benefit a week (as a single person) you should get supplementary benefit to make it up to that level. You should also get extra to cover rent and rates. Ask for Form B1 at your Employment Office and take it to your Social Security office. If you are married it's more complicated, because your right to supplementary benefit depends on whether your husband is working and how much he is earning. If you are eligible for supplementary benefit and your joint income is less than £34·60 a week, the claim must be made by your husband. Supplementary benefit is explained in detail on pp. 189–205. After 1983, the person in the couple who is the 'main breadwinner' will be able to claim.

## Sickness benefit

This is what you claim when you are off work because of illness, rather than unemployed. Sickness benefit is almost identical to unemployment benefit. You must have the same number of contributions during the same 'contribution year' in order to claim. The rates paid are exactly the same. The conditions that apply to single, married, separated and divorced women are the same as for unemployment benefit. The only difference is that you can claim sickness benefit if you have Class 1 or Class 2 contributions. (You can only claim unemployment benefit with Class 1 contributions.)

### HOW TO CLAIM SICKNESS BENEFIT

Get your doctor to give you a signed statement about your illness; send it to your local Social Security office within six days of your becoming too ill to work. Your doctor will have the necessary form

It stands for
**Desperate Hours of Sitting
& Self control**

and should be familiar with the procedure. Just tell her you want to claim sickness benefit.

From September 1980, new National Insurance rules mean that you will not get any sickness benefit if you are off work sick for three days or less. Usually you will only get benefit from the fourth day of illness. But, if you are off work for four days or more, you can claim for the first three days as well if you have been off work sick or unemployed during the previous eight weeks. If you can't get a statement from your doctor within six days write to your local Social Security office, say that you are claiming sickness benefit and tell them your full name and address, date of birth and, if you can, your National Insurance number. If you don't know your number, write to them anyway. The important thing is to let them know that you are claiming benefit before the six days are up. Tell them you will be forwarding a doctor's statement and do so as soon as possible afterwards. (Obviously, this course of action would not be appropriate if your doctor has *refused* to give you a statement – but only if you could not get to her in time.) The money will be sent to you by post in the form of a Giro order which you can cash at any post office.

You can go on claiming sickness benefit for twenty-eight weeks. After that, if you are still too ill to work, you become eligible for invalidity benefit. From April 1983 the way you get money when you are off work sick, and how much you get, will probably be changed. The government set out proposals in a Green Paper in April 1980 to make *employers* pay their workers for the first eight weeks of sickness; after that, the sickness benefit would be paid by the DHSS as described above. The employer will probably have to pay one flat rate to everyone, regardless of what family responsibilities you have. You will probably have to pay income tax and National Insurance contributions on the money each week, too. For more details, ask your local Social Security office or your employer. (Married women who have 'opted out' – see p. 133 – would not be covered.)

### Invalidity benefit

You can claim invalidity benefit if you are still too ill to work after you have been claiming sickness benefit for twenty-eight weeks. It is paid at a higher rate than sickness benefit. The rate for a single person is £28·35 a week, with more for dependent children. From April 1979 additional benefit is given (depending on your level of earnings since that date) in the same way as for the additional pension. See p. 157. If you are under 55 when you first claim it you get an extra allowance which varies according to your age. If you do not qualify because your insurance record is incomplete, there is a new 'non-contributory' invalidity pension you can claim. See p. 206.

### Industrial injuries benefit

You may be able to claim this if you are injured at work or you contract what is known as a 'prescribed industrial disease'. This benefit does not depend on your National Insurance contributions (see p. 205). But your rights to industrial injuries benefit, at least for the first eight weeks off work, may be affected by the changes in sickness benefit (see above) from 1982.

### Earnings-related supplement – up to January 1982

The earnings-related supplement is extra money you may get if you are receiving unemployment or sickness benefit, industrial injuries benefit or maternity allowance. This depends on what you were earning before you stopped working.

The amount of money you get depends on your *reckonable earnings* during the tax year before the calendar year in which you claim benefit. What are your reckonable earnings? They are the total of your earnings as indicated by the amount you paid in National Insurance contributions during the relevant tax year (remember, National Insurance contributions may not indicate your total *real* earnings, as shown on p. 132). This figure is divided by fifty to establish your reckonable earnings. There goes another dreaming bureaucrat . . .

*How much do you get?*

1. You get one third of the amount by which your reckonable earnings exceed the 'lower earnings limit' (£23 a week to April 1981), up to £30; *and*
2. If you earn more than £30 a week you get 10 per cent of the amount by which your reckonable earnings exceed £30, up to the 'upper earnings limit' (£165 to April 1981).

*For example:*

If your reckonable earnings are £83 a week you get one third of £7 (£2·33), plus 10 per cent of £53 (£5·30) which comes to a total of £7·63. Got that? There's just one catch. When your flat-rate benefit and your earnings-related supplement are added together, they must not exceed 85 per cent of your reckonable earnings. It's possible that they might if you were claiming extra benefit for dependants. If this happens, there's simply a cut-off point where your total benefit reaches 85 per cent of your reckonable earnings in the relevant tax year.

The earnings-related supplement is paid from the thirteenth day after you had to stop work and continues for up to 156 days after that, not including Sundays. It then stops.

*You will not get an earnings-related supplement:*

1. If you are married and you have opted out of paying full National Insurance contributions.
2. If you are self-employed.
3. *After January 1982.* The government is abolishing earnings-related supplement for new claims after 3 January 1982.

## Maternity benefits

### MATERNITY GRANT

This is a sum of £25 to help with the immediate costs of having a baby. You can claim it whether you are single or married if you satisfy the following conditions. (If you're married you can claim it if your husband satisfies the same conditions.)

1. You must have *paid* Class 1, 2 or 3 contributions on earnings equal to twenty-five times the lower earnings limit in any one tax year (April to April) since you first began to contribute; *and*
2. You must have paid or been credited with the same amount of Class 1, 2 or 3 contributions in the tax year which ended the April before the calendar year in which your baby is due. So if your baby is due in February 1982, the tax year which counts is April 1980 to April 1981.

If you are not married, you cannot claim the maternity grant on the contribution record of the baby's father.

You can claim the grant if your baby is stillborn, provided your pregnancy lasted at least twenty-eight weeks. If you have more than one baby at a time, you get an extra £25 for each baby that survives.

Get the claim form BM4 from your local Social Security office or from your maternity or child welfare clinic. You can apply at any time from fourteen weeks before the baby is due to three months after it is born. For babies expected on or after 4 July 1982, you don't have to have paid any contributions to get the grant.

MATERNITY ALLOWANCE

This is a weekly allowance that you can get for several weeks before and after your baby is born. You can claim it whether you are single or married, but you can only claim it on your *own* contribution record, and if you satisfy the following conditions:

1. You must have *paid* Class 1 contributions on earnings equal to twenty-five times the lower earnings limit, or twenty-five Class 2 contributions in any one tax year since you began to contribute; *and*
2. You must have paid or been credited with Class 1 contributions on earnings equal to fifty times the lower earnings limit, or fifty Class 2 contributions, in the tax year which ended the April before the calendar year in which the first payment of the allowance is due.

Maternity allowance is not paid while you are doing paid work. If you are not working it is normally paid for eleven weeks before your baby is due and for seven weeks after it is actually born. The least it is paid for is eighteen weeks. If your baby is born later than expected you will get maternity allowance for longer.

*How much do you get?*

The standard rate is £20·65 a week. If you don't have the full number of contributions, you will get less. You can claim additional allowances for your dependent children, but if you are married you cannot claim for your children unless your husband is disabled and incapable of work or you are living apart. You might also get an earnings-related supplement as you do with unemployment benefit. This is explained on p. 148.

Get the claim form BM4 from your local Social Security office or from a maternity or child welfare clinic. You can put your claim in at the beginning of the fourteenth week – and not later than the eleventh week – before the baby is due.

*You are credited with National Insurance contributions* while you are receiving maternity allowance, but not for the rest of your maternity leave. You are entitled to twenty-nine weeks' leave, as explained on p. 91. You can, if you wish, pay voluntary Class 3 contributions during this period (p. 131).

MOTHERS UNDER 16 CANNOT CLAIM MATERNITY ALLOWANCE

Withholding money does not stop babies being born. A mother under 16 obviously cannot meet the contribution requirements for maternity allowance. But she cannot even claim supplementary benefit in her own right. The only way to get money is for her parent or guardian to claim supplementary benefit for her as a dependent child. She *can* claim Child Benefit and Child Benefit Increase (see p. 185) and a maternity grant (see p. 149).

Local councils have power to give financial help to mothers under 16 under Section 1 of the Children and Young Persons Act (1963). But it is a purely discretionary power and few councils use it.

If you have a baby when you are under 16 – or if you know someone who has – it might be worth approaching the social services department of your local council and asking for help. You may have to remind them of the relevant Act. If you get no help there, contact the National Council for One-Parent Families (address, p. 153).

This section was accurate in November 1980. But the government has discussed the possibility of changing to a new system in which employers paid flat-rate maternity pay, instead of the above benefits being available. So check at your local Social Security office and with your employer.

### Child's special allowance

This is an allowance you can claim in the following circumstances:

1. You are divorced, but not remarried, or living with a man 'as husband and wife'; *and*
2. Your former husband has died; *and*
3. You are looking after a child; *and*
4. Your husband was supposed to be paying at least 25p a week towards the support of the child and, if he wasn't, you had taken reasonable steps to get him to pay.

The rate is £7·70 for each child. If you want to know more about this, inquire at your local Social Security office. Or get leaflet N I 93 and claim form CS 1 from your Post Office or Social Security office.

### Death grant

You can claim this on your contribution record or your husband's (pp. 81–2).

### Your right to appeal

If you disagree with a decision which has been made about your right to any National Insurance benefit, you can appeal to the National Insurance local tribunal. The procedure for appealing is described on p. 492.

### Further information

The Department of Health and Social Security publishes leaflets on most aspects of the National Insurance scheme. They are often difficult to understand since they are full of jargon and have a rather pompous turn of phrase. But if you have the patience to plough through them, you should find most of the details you need. Make sure you get the most up-to-date leaflets: they are regularly revised. Ask for them at your nearest Post Office, Citizens' Advice Bureau or Social Security office and if you can't get them there, write to Department of Health and Social Security, P.O. Box 21, Stanmore, Middlesex HA7 1AY. The following are relevant to this section:

FB 2: *Which Benefit?*
NI 1: *National Insurance Guide for Married Women*
NI 2: *Prescribed Industrial Diseases*
NI 5: *Injury Benefit for Accidents at Work*
NI 12: *Unemployment Benefit*
NI 16: *Sickness Benefit*
NI 16A: *Invalidity Benefit*
NI 17A: *Maternity Benefits*
NI 27A: *Self-employed People with Small Earnings (National Insurance Contributions)*
NI 41: *Guidance for the Self-Employed*
NI 42: *Voluntary Contributions*
NI 93: *Child's Special Allowance*
NI 95: *Guidance for Women Whose Marriage is ended by Divorce or Annulment*
NI 125: *Training for Further Employment*
NI 155A: *How your Earnings-Related Benefit is Worked Out*
NI 192: *People Employed Through Agencies*
NI 196: *Benefit Rates*
NI 208: *Contribution Rates*
NP 12: *National Insurance Guide for Students and Apprentices*
SB 9: *After You Have Claimed Supplementary Benefit (When You're Unemployed)*

The National Council for One-Parent Families is at 255 Kentish Town Road, London NW5 (01 267 1361).

Claimants' unions and the Child Poverty Action Group may be able to help you claim National Insurance benefits (see pp. 196–7).

## Pensions

Most women retire at 60. Do you know what you will live on when you reach that age? Will you have a pension of your own? Will you be able to draw a pension on your husband's insurance? Or will you have to live on supplementary benefit?

The size of your pension is determined by how much money is paid towards it during your working life. So it's important to think about it when you are young and to understand how the pension system works. You may find that you can take a decision now which will make your old age financially more secure.

In the past, women have had a far worse deal than men where pensions are concerned. Many still do. Seventy-three per cent of all pensioners who receive supplementary benefit are women. This means that they have no pensions, or pensions that leave them below the bread-line.

### *The new pension scheme*

A new scheme which aims to give women equal pension rights was introduced by the Social Security Pensions Act 1975. It started in April 1978 and will take twenty years to come into full operation. How much it affects you depends on your age:

1. If you were under 40 in 1978 your pension will be based almost entirely on the new scheme.
2. If you were aged between 40 and 60 your pension will be based partly on the old scheme and partly on the new.
3. If you were over 60 your pension will, of course, be based entirely on the old scheme.

*Your marital status may affect your pension. Under the old pension scheme there were different conditions for single, married, separated and divorced women. These will continue to affect many women until the new scheme becomes fully operative. So we have divided this chapter into four main parts – for single, married, separated and divorced women, in that order.*

### If you are single

This section deals with:

1. Your pension rights under the new scheme.
2. Your pension rights under the old scheme and how you are affected by the changeover.

HOW THE NEW PENSION SCHEME WORKS

Your basic pension is in two parts. You get:

1. A basic pension. The current rate is £29·60 a week; it will probably go up each year; *and*
2. An additional pension which is related to the level of your earnings. This part of your pension represents 25 per cent of your average earnings above the level of the lower earnings limit (currently £27 a week), up to a limit which is seven times the lower earnings limit (currently £200). The average is based on your twenty highest-earning years after April 1978, whether they are early or late in your working life; and they needn't be consecutive. For example:

If your average earnings in your twenty highest-earning years are £79 per week, your additional pension – at today's rates – will be 25 per cent of £52 (which is the difference between £27 and £79), that is £13 per week.

Before the average is worked out, your earnings during those twenty years are revalued to offset the effects of inflation – so they are worth the same when your pension is worked out as they were when you earned them.

HOW DO YOU QUALIFY FOR THE BASIC PENSION?

1. *To get any pension at all* you must fulfil one of two conditions: *either* before 6 April 1975 you must have *paid* fifty Class 1, 2 or 3 National Insurance contributions, at any time; *or* after 6 April 1975 you must have paid Class 1, 2 or 3 contributions in any one

tax year on earnings which add up to at least fifty times the weekly 'lower earnings limit' (currently £27).

2. *To get the full basic pension* you must have paid or been credited with the right amount of contributions per year for the right number of years. Be brave, read on . . .

(a) You have *the right amount of contributions* in one year if you have paid or been credited with contributions equal in value to Class 1 contributions on fifty times the weekly 'lower earnings limit'.

(b) *The right number of years* usually means thirty-nine years (as a minimum). As a general rule you should pay the right amount of contributions – as described above – for nine tenths of your working life. What is officially considered to be your 'working life' may bear no relation to the number of years you have actually worked. Your 'working life' is usually forty-four years (from 16 to 60). *However*, if you were over 16 in 1948 your official 'working life' may be shorter, according to certain rules of mind-boggling complexity. If you feel strong enough, turn to p. 168 for fuller details.

3. *Your pension rights are protected if you stay at home to look after children*, since the new scheme started in April 1978. Your pension rights are protected until your youngest child is 16. You need not pay contributions but your basic pension does not suffer. It is worked out as though you had paid contributions during those years. The same is true if you stay at home to look after an invalid who gets an attendance allowance, or if you are getting supplementary benefit and do not have to 'sign on' for work, because you are looking after an invalid or elderly person. This is known as protection of pension rights for those with *home responsibility*. It applies to women and (in certain circumstances) to men (more details are on p. 134).

Having your pension rights protected during a period of home responsibility is *not* the same as being 'credited' with contributions. (Credits are explained on p. 132.) In order to get the full basic pension, you must have actually paid or been credited with contributions for at least twenty years. The rest of the time can be made up with years in which your pension rights are protected because of home responsibility.

*If you fail to accumulate the right number of contributions for the right number of years* and you do not qualify for the special protection given to people with home responsibility (for instance, if you spend some time living abroad or living on social security and not paying or being credited with contributions) your basic pension is reduced. The amount by which it is reduced depends on your contribution record. It is worked out on a sliding scale. If you have paid or been credited with contributions for half your working life (approximately twenty years) you will get half the basic pension.

HOW DO YOU QUALIFY FOR THE ADDITIONAL PENSION?

To get the maximum additional pension you must pay contributions equal in value to Class 1 contributions on fifty times the 'lower-earnings limit' each year for at least twenty years after 6 April 1978. Class 1 contributions are explained on p. 128. If you have paid these contributions for less than twenty years, your additional pension is reduced. It is worked out at 1¼ per cent of your average earnings above the lower earnings limit for each year that you pay regular Class 1 contributions after 6 April 1978. And remember, when your additional pension is worked out, each year's average earnings are revalued to offset the effects of inflation. If your average earnings exceed seven times the lower earnings limit, what you earn above that level will *not* count towards your additional pension. It's possible to qualify for an additional pension even though you fail to qualify for the full basic pension.

Class 2, 3 and 4 contributions do not count towards your additional pension. Nor do the years in which your pension rights are protected because you have home responsibility: this protection extends only to the basic pension.

*If you belong to an occupational pension scheme* which meets the government's minimum requirements, you may be 'contracted out' of the state pension scheme, which means you pay reduced contributions (as explained on p. 129). You still get the basic pension but you do not get an additional pension from the state. Instead you get an earnings-related pension from your occupational scheme – and if it's a reasonably good scheme you'll get more than you would from the state. (More about occupational pensions on p. 170.)

### WHAT ABOUT THE CONTRIBUTIONS YOU PAID UNDER THE OLD PENSION SCHEME?

Any Class 1, 2 or 3 contributions you paid before the start of the new scheme in 1978 count towards your basic pension, but they do not count towards your additional pension.

If you spent some time at home looking after children or sick or elderly relatives *before* the scheme started, your pension rights are not protected during those years. If you did not pay contributions while you were at home, that counts as a gap in your insurance record. If you have paid contributions for less than thirty-nine years your basic pension will probably be reduced, as explained above, pp. 155–7.

*Under the old pension scheme, you may have paid contributions towards a graduated pension.* The graduated pension was the earnings-related scheme run by the state as part of the old pension system. It was wound up in 1975. If you paid contributions to a graduated pension before then you will be paid whatever you earned from your contributions between 1961 and 1975. The amount will be very small – the average graduated pension being paid in 1975 was 27p a week – but from April 1978 it has been revalued to keep in line with the cost of living.

If you belonged to an occupational pension scheme you would probably have been 'contracted out' of the graduated scheme and therefore you would have been paying reduced contributions towards it. In this case you will get a (very small) graduated pension from your contributions to your occupational scheme.

*Will your whole pension be protected against inflation?* Once you have retired and have been awarded your pension it will be increased regularly. The basic pension used to be increased in line with earnings or with prices, whichever was greater. From November 1980 the basic pension and the additional pension are increased in line with prices.

*Two examples showing how single women are affected by the new pension scheme*

1. Pauline was 16 when the new scheme started. She left school and went to work as a shop assistant. At 22 she stops work and has a child. She stays at home with the child for three years and then returns to work. When she is 30 her mother dies and she has to stop work again to look after her father who is an invalid. Meanwhile she studies at night school and takes accountancy exams. Her father dies when she is 40 and she gets a job as an accountant/book-keeper. She stays in this job until she retires at 60. Pauline gets the full basic pension (£29·60 per week) because her pension rights were protected during her two spells of 'home responsibility'. She also gets an additional pension. Her highest-earning years were between 40 and 60 when her earnings were worth, on average, £79 a week. So her additional pension is one quarter of the difference between £27 and £79 (£52) which is £13. Her total weekly pension, reckoned in today's terms, is £42·60. It should, of course, be increased in line with inflation.

2. Freda was 45 when the new scheme started. She has worked in a food-processing factory ever since she left school, except for about eight years when her mother was ill and she had to stay at home to look after her. She goes on working in the factory until she retires at 60. Freda's basic pension is reduced because of the gap in her contribution record while she was looking after her mother: that happened before the scheme started, so her pension rights were not protected.

   She gets a basic pension of approximately £27 a week. She also gets an additional pension based on the last fifteen years of her working life (from the date the new scheme started to the date of her retirement). It is worked out at 1¼ per cent of her average earnings above the lower earnings limit, for each year since the scheme began. For the first ten years her earnings were worth £79 a week; for the last five she was put on short time and the value of her earnings was reduced to £67 a week.

So her additional pension is worked out like this: (1¼ % of £52) × 10 *plus* (1¼ % of £40) × 5. This comes to £9 a week. So her total pension in today's terms is approximately £36 a week.

## *If you are married*

This section shows:

1. How you can get a pension on your own contribution record.
2. How you can get a pension on your husband's contribution record.
3. How the 'married woman's option' affects your pension.

There are two ways you can get a pension when you retire:

1. *On your own contribution record*, in the same way as a single woman. If you have paid or been credited with full National Insurance contributions (or have had your pension rights protected because of home responsibility) regularly for approximately nine tenths of your working life you can qualify for a full pension in your own right. You get the same as a single woman. If you have less than the required number of contributions, your pension will be proportionately lower.
2. *On your husband's contributions*. You may get a married woman's pension on the basis of your husband's contributions. The rate is £17·75 a week – so it's less than you would get if you earned a full pension on the basis of your own contributions. You get your own pension book and draw the full married woman's pension in the following circumstances:

(a) Your husband has paid or been credited with Class 1, 2 or 3 contributions for nine tenths of his working life.
(b) You yourself have paid or been credited with full contributions (or have had your pension rights protected because of home responsibility) for *less* than nine tenths of your working life – for example, less than thirty-nine years.
(c) The basic pension you have earned from your own contribution

record is *lower* than the married woman's pension you would get from your husband's insurance.

(d) Your husband has reached 65.

(e) You have retired.

You only get *one* pension – from your own contributions or your husband's, whichever is higher. If your husband has paid or been credited with contributions for less than nine tenths of his working life, the married woman's pension is reduced. If you are less than five years younger than your husband (if he is under 65 when you retire at 60), you have to wait until he is 65 and retired before you draw the married woman's pension. But until then you can draw whatever pension (if any) you have earned from your own contributions.

If you are more than five years younger than your husband (if he reaches 65 before you reach 60), he gets an increase in his own pension equivalent to the married woman's pension, until you retire. But if you are earning more than £45 a week, this increase is reduced and the more you are earning the less of it he gets. Once you retire, he stops drawing the increase and you start drawing a pension, either on the basis of your own contributions, or on the basis of his, whichever is higher.

## HOW THE MARRIED WOMAN'S OPTION AFFECTS YOUR PENSION

As a married woman you may have been paying reduced contributions. If so, this will probably affect your pension.

*Under the old scheme* all married women could choose not to pay full contributions and to rely instead on getting a married woman's pension on the basis of their husband's contribution record. This is known as taking the 'married woman's option' and is explained on p. 133.

*Under the new scheme* you cannot choose to opt out of paying full contributions while you are working. The last date on which you could do so was 11 May 1977, and then only if you were married before 6 April 1977. However, if you were already paying reduced contributions in May 1977 because you opted out before that, you can continue to do so until you retire, unless:

1. You decide to opt in and start paying full contributions, in which case you can't change your mind and opt out again; *or*
2. You have a break in your employment after 5 April 1978 which lasts for more than two consecutive tax years (tax years being reckoned from April to April), in which case you must start paying full contributions when you return to employment.

How much pension you get depends on whether you have taken up the married woman's option and, if so, when and for how long.

*If you have not opted out* and you were paying full contributions in May 1977 you must continue to do so while you are employed or self-employed. You are in the same position as a single woman, with two exceptions:

1. You may have taken up the married woman's option for a limited period before 1977. If so, that period *does not count* towards your pension: it counts as a gap in your contribution record and if the gap is longer than four years your basic pension is likely to be reduced.
2. If your basic pension is reduced below the level of the married woman's pension, you may get that instead, as explained above, p. 160.

If you have stayed at home to look after children or sick or elderly relatives since the new scheme started in April 1978, your pension rights are protected in the same way as a single woman's.

You can earn an additional pension in the same way as a single woman – on the basis of your own contributions. You cannot get an additional pension on your husband's contribution record. If you qualify for the married woman's pension and do not receive a basic pension from your own contributions, you may still get an additional pension, based on your contributions after the new scheme began.

*If you have opted out* and you were paying reduced contributions in May 1977, you can continue to do so; or you can choose to opt in and start paying full contributions at any time. If you continue to opt out, you do not get the same pension as a single woman. You may qualify for a married woman's pension on your husband's insurance, as explained above, p. 160, but if he has not paid or been credited with the right number of contributions, your married woman's pension is reduced. You get no additional pension. If you have 'home responsibility' (if you take time off work to look after children or sick or elderly relatives at home) your pension rights are not protected for the first two years. After that, your option is automatically revoked: you start getting protection of pension rights and as soon as you return to employment you have to start paying full contributions.

If you opted in when the new scheme started you can qualify for an additional pension in the same way as a single woman. You may also qualify for a basic pension on your own contributions. (As a rough guide: if you opted out for more than ten years and your husband's record is complete, you will probably not get a pension on your own contributions because the amount would be less than £17·75 which is the full married woman's pension. If you opted out for less than ten years or your husband's record is incomplete, you may get a pension on your own contribution record.) Once you have started paying full contributions your pension rights are protected immediately you leave employment to take on home responsibility, in the same way as a single woman.

DECIDING WHETHER TO OPT IN

On p. 135 we describe the pros and cons of opting in – with reference to pensions and other National Insurance benefits. Here are some further points to consider, which concern pensions only:

1. If you were under 40 when the new scheme started, you can earn the maximum additional pension (that is, one quarter of your average earnings during your twenty highest-earning years,

above the lower earnings limit, currently £27, and below the upper limit, currently £200 a week). The younger you are, the more you can benefit from opting in.

2. If you have a break from employment in the future to look after children or sick or elderly relatives, the first two years of that period will *not* count towards your basic pension if you have opted out and are paying reduced contributions immediately before you stop working outside the home. They *will* count if you were paying full contributions at that time.

3. If your husband has not paid contributions regularly throughout his working life and you are relying on him for your pension, your married woman's pension may well be very small.

4. If you pay full contributions for no more than 30 years altogether, the basic pension you earn from your own contributions will be lower than the married woman's pension (as long as your husband has a good contribution record). So if you can earn only a small additional pension because your earnings are low, it may not be worth your while to opt in.

5. If you are self-employed, your contributions are much more expensive and you get no additional pension from them. So there is less to be said for opting in.

It's up to you to decide in the light of your own circumstances. Our recommendation is that it's best to opt in, especially if you are under 40, employed and you expect to have 'home responsibility' in the future; or if your husband has a poor contribution record. It's important to know what your husband's record is like – particularly if you want to remain opted out. Your local National Insurance office should tell you what pension you are entitled to on your husband's contributions, although they won't give you full details of his record.

*Two examples showing how the married woman's option could affect your pension:*

1. Joan was 30 when the new scheme started. She started work at 16, paying full contributions, but she opted out when she married at 26.

Now, at 30, she decides to opt in. When she is 32 she has a child and stays at home for five years until the child goes to school. Then she returns to work and pays full contributions until she retires at 60. She qualifies for a full pension (£29·60 a week) on her own contributions because she opted out for only four years; and since she opted in before leaving employment to look after her child, her pension rights were protected for the whole of that period. Her highest-earning years were between 49 and 60 when her earnings were worth, on average, £87 a week. She therefore gets an additional pension of £15 a week, which is one quarter of the difference between £27 and £87. Her total weekly pension is £42.

2. Sally was 41 when the new scheme started. She opted out when she married at 20 but before that she had been paying full contributions since she started work at 16. When she was 28 she started a family and left employment for fifteen years. At 43 she returns to work and is obliged to pay full contributions – and goes on doing so until she retires at 60. She gets no basic pension from her own contributions because she has a twenty-three-year gap in her insurance record. Her pension rights were not protected during her period of home responsibility before the new scheme started; nor are they protected for the first two years after it starts because she has taken the married woman's option. Two years

JOAN          SALLY

after the scheme starts Sally's option to pay reduced contributions is automatically revoked, but in her case it happens too late to bring her a basic pension of her own. Instead she qualifies for a married woman's pension of £17·75 a week on her husband's contribution record. She gets an additional pension of her own, based on her contributions between the ages of 43 and 60. Worked out at 1¼ per cent of her average earnings above the lower earnings limit, for each of those 17 years, her additional pension comes to £4·95 a week. Her total weekly pension is £22·70.

## If you separate from your husband

You are in the same position as a married woman as far as your pension is concerned. If you are under 60 when your husband retires, he can still draw extra pension for you (which *he* can keep), provided he can show the National Insurance officials that he is supporting you financially. But there is one difference: a married woman who is not separated can earn up to £45 a week without causing a reduction in her husband's pension. As a separated woman, if you earn over £17·75 a week, your husband will not be able to draw any extra pension for you.

If you are over 60 when your husband retires and you don't qualify for a pension of your own, you can draw a pension on your husband's contribution record, but at the married woman's rate only. If this is not enough to live on (which it generally isn't) you can claim supplementary benefit, as explained on p. 190. You would obviously be in a better position if you had your own pension through your own contributions, or if you were divorced.

## If you get divorced

If, at the time of your divorce, your husband has paid more contributions than you (both before and after the date of your marriage), you can 'adopt' his National Insurance record to help you qualify for a single person's pension. This means that all the contributions he has paid, from the date of his sixteenth birthday up to the date of your divorce, are counted as though they were your own – and it makes no difference if he remarries. From the date of your divorce, you have to pay like a single woman and when you reach 60 your pension is worked out in the same way as a single woman's. Your pension does not alter if you remarry when you are over 60.

Here is an example of how the rule works:

You left school at 16, but you did not go out to work until you were 20. You married at 24 and opted out of paying contributions when you were 25 because you started a family. (This was before the new scheme started.) You did not start paying contributions again when you went back to work at 35. You divorced at 40. Up to the date of your divorce, you had therefore paid contributions for only ten years. Your husband started work at 16 and paid his contributions regularly right up to the divorce. His contribution record is obviously a great deal better than yours so you are able to adopt it as your own. You will get a pension as though you had paid contributions all the way from 16 to 40. If you pay contributions as a single person regularly for another twenty years until you are 60, you will get a full single person's pension.

However, if you divorce and then remarry *before* you are 60, you cannot count your former husband's contributions towards your pension. Instead, you will draw a married woman's pension on your second husband's contribution record in the same way as any other married woman – unless you happen to qualify for a higher pension on your own contributions.

If you divorce when you are over 60, you will get a single person's pension based on the number of contributions your husband has paid – unless you qualify for a higher pension on your own contributions – and you will get this even if you and your former husband are both still working. (It will be reduced if you earn over a certain amount, though.)

### If you are widowed

Your pension rights are explained in the section on widows' benefits, p. 180.

### Special notes for women who were over 16 in 1948

The amount of basic pension you receive depends on the number of years in which you are expected to have paid regular insurance contributions, as explained on p. 155. This period is known as your 'working life' although it may have nothing to do with the number of years you actually worked. Here's how the length of your 'working life' is calculated:

1. If you started paying contributions before 5 July 1948, your pension will be calculated as if your working life started at the beginning of the tax year in which you started paying contributions, or 6 April 1936, whichever is later. So if, for example, you were 35 on 5 July 1948 and you started paying contributions when you were 30, your pension will be worked out as if your working life began on 5 April 1943. If you retire at 60 your pension will be calculated as if you had a working life of thirty years.

2. If you were over 16 on 5 July 1948 but you did not start paying insurance contributions until after that, your pension will be calculated as if your working life began on 6 April 1948. (You will be credited with contributions for any weeks between 5 July 1948 and *either* 6 April 1948 *or* your sixteenth birthday, whichever happened later.) So if, for example, you were 25 on 5 July 1948, your pension will be worked out as though your working life began on 6 April 1948.

    You will be credited with contributions between 6 April and 5 July 1948. If you retire at 60 your pension will be calculated as though you had a working life of thirty-five years.

*To get a full basic pension*, you must have paid regular contributions for at least the number of years indicated by this table:

| *If your working life* | |
| :--- | :--- |
| *is this long . . .* | *. . . you must have paid regular contributions for at least this number of years:* |
| 21–30 | The length of your working life, minus 3 years. |
| 31–40 | The length of your working life, minus 4 years. |
| 41 years or more | The length of your working life, minus 5 years. |

Anyone who can make head or tail of that deserves to get a pension! If in doubt, inquire at your local Social Security office.

### If you go on working after you are 60

You can claim your pension, stop paying National Insurance contributions and then earn a further £52 a week without your pension being reduced.

Alternatively, you can *increase* your pension if you do the following things:

1. you work between the ages of 60 and 65; *and*
2. during that time you give up your right to any pension or widow's benefit you might be getting.

THIS IS HOW YOUR PENSION WILL BE INCREASED

For every week between 6 April 1975 and 6 April 1979 that you

1. worked without drawing pension; *and*
2. didn't draw any other benefit; *and*
3. kept paying contributions;

you get an extra 1 per cent of your pension for every eight weeks that you go on working. From 6 April 1979 this was increased so that the gain is 1 per cent for every seven weeks, and you no longer have to pay contributions when you reach 60.

## If you go on working after you are 65

You get your pension whether you work or not; you cannot earn any further increase in it; but you can earn as much as you like without it being reduced.

## If your pension doesn't leave you enough to live on

You have a right to supplementary benefit.

If you are single and your weekly income is less than £29·60 a week, you can claim supplementary benefit to bring it up to this level, plus extra for rent, rates and certain special needs.

If you are married your right to claim supplementary benefit depends on the joint income of you and your husband. If it is less than £47·35 a week your husband can make a claim for supplementary benefit. But you yourself cannot claim unless you are living apart from him. Each of you can earn £4 a week without any reduction in your benefit.

If you are 80, you can claim an extra 25p a week in supplementary benefit. If you are over 70, an extra £1·65 a week is automatically added to your benefit as a heating allowance.

You can claim an additional allowance if you need extra heating, or if you are blind. You can also get extra help with baths, diet, hospital fares and special wear and tear of clothing for a child. But if you get extra payments for anything other than age, blindness or heating, you will only get the difference between what you claim and 50p.

Full details about supplementary benefit on p. 189.

## Occupational pensions

An occupational pension is one paid by a private pension scheme provided by your employer. If you belong to an occupational scheme which meets certain minimum requirements laid down by law you are probably 'contracted out' of the state pension scheme. This means that you and your employer pay reduced National

Insurance contributions (as shown on p. 129) and instead you both contribute to the occupational scheme. (A few private schemes provide pensions without requiring contributions from employees, but these are rare.)

## What do you get?

1. Your basic pension from the state (see p. 155); *and*
2. A pension provided by the private scheme which is related to your earnings; *and, perhaps*
3. You may also get other benefits from your occupational scheme, such as a lump sum on retirement or benefits for your dependants when you die.

## There are minimum standards for all occupational schemes

Some occupational schemes provide better benefits than others. But a scheme must meet certain minimum requirements in order for its members to be 'contracted out' of the state scheme. From April 1978 the minimum requirements include the following:

1. The rules of your pension scheme *must* allow for 'equal access' to the scheme for men and women. This means that the age of entry must be the same, the length of qualifying service must be the same, and the scheme must be either voluntary or compulsory for both sexes. There is one exception: older women can be barred from joining a scheme five years earlier than men (at 55, say, compared with 60 for men) because they retire five years earlier.
2. An occupational scheme must provide you with a pension which is no less than the 'additional' pension you would have received from the state if you had not joined a private scheme. This is known as the *guaranteed minimum pension*. The level is pegged to inflation. 'Additional' state pensions are explained on p. 157.
3. When a man belonging to a contracted out scheme dies his widow must be provided with a pension worth at least half the

guaranteed minimum pension that would have been due to him at the time of his death. The other half is paid to her by the state. Widows' pensions are explained in detail on p. 180. (A few schemes provide widowers' pensions, but these are not compulsory.)

4. If you leave a job where you belonged to a contracted out scheme, your right to a guaranteed minimum pension must be preserved, provided that:

(a) You have been in that scheme for at least five years since 6 April 1975; *and*

(b) You are over 26 when you leave the job.

THERE ARE THREE WAYS IN WHICH YOUR PENSION RIGHTS CAN BE PRESERVED

1. You can arrange for the pension you have accumulated so far to be transferred to another occupational scheme, if there is one at your next place of work, and your next employer agrees.

2. Your employer keeps whatever pension you have earned up to the date of leaving the job; he must then protect it against inflation and pay it to you in regular instalments when you retire.

3. Your employer can transfer your pension rights back into the state scheme. He does this by paying to the state what would have been paid towards your 'additional' state pension if you hadn't belonged to an occupational scheme. He can choose to do this only partially, so that you do not get the guaranteed minimum pension from the state. If so, he is responsible for paying you the difference.

### *Check up on your occupational scheme!*

A lot of people belong to private pension schemes without knowing what benefits they provide or under what conditions. If you belong to one, make sure you know the details. If you are married, find out about your husband's scheme, as well. You should both ask your trade union representatives or go straight to the pensions manager of your place of work. If you don't like what you find, try to negotiate better terms. Here are some points to look out for:

### HOW IS YOUR PENSION WORKED OUT?

Some occupational pensions are worked out on a more generous basis than others. Here are the three main ways in which they are calculated:

1. You get a fixed amount for each year of belonging to the scheme. For instance you might get £15 for each year. If you have belonged to the scheme for twenty years, you will get a pension of £300 a year, which is approximately £5·80 a week. (Of course, you get your basic state pension as well.) These schemes are now quite rare, and would not be of a high enough standard to 'contract out' of the new state pension scheme.
2. Your pension is based on your average earnings throughout the years you have belonged to the scheme. This means you get a proportion of what you earned each year, added together to make up your pension.

I'm trying to draw my pension

3. Your pension is based on your final salary. For each year that you have belonged to the scheme, you get a proportion of your final salary. 'Final salary' could mean *either* your earnings in the year before you retire *or* your average earnings over the last few years before you retire. Make sure you know which – it could make a big difference.

As you can imagine, a pension which is based on your final salary is likely to be larger than one which is calculated by methods (1) or (2). Method (3) is now in fact the most common.

## DOES YOUR SCHEME PROVIDE BENEFITS FOR YOUR DEPENDANTS?

All schemes must provide for widows, but some also provide for widowers and other dependants.

## IS YOUR PENSION PROTECTED AGAINST INFLATION?

Occupational schemes are obliged to pay you a guaranteed minimum, which must be increased regularly in line with state pensions, to take account of inflation. But they are not legally bound to maintain the value of any pension you receive above that level. In fact, some pension schemes use any pension *above* the guaranteed minimum to inflation-proof the guaranteed minimum itself! By what means, if any, does your scheme propose to maintain the value of your pension? Vague promises about 'making adjustments' or 'paying bonuses' are not good enough. Some schemes increase pension values by as little as 3½ per cent a year. Few pension schemes increase pensions by the current inflation rate; but you should insist upon a minimum guaranteed percentage rise each year, plus a commitment to a regular review to see whether they can be increased by more.

## DOES YOUR SCHEME DISCRIMINATE AGAINST WOMEN?

The law gives 'equal access' to pension schemes to men and women (see p. 171). But it is still quite legal for women, once they have joined a scheme, to be given inferior benefits to men. It is very common for occupational schemes to discriminate against women in the following ways:

1. Women's pensions may be calculated in a way which gives them less money than men. For instance, their pensions may be based on a smaller fraction of their earnings. The excuse commonly given is that women retire earlier and live longer (according to national statistics) and therefore their pension has to be stretched over a longer period. Since women normally have no option about retiring at 60, and since they can't help living longer and have to pay the same for food and housing as men, this sort of discrimination should not be tolerated.
2. A scheme may provide benefits for a man's dependants, but not a woman's.
3. It is quite common for employers to exclude certain groups of employees – who just 'happen' to be mainly female – from the pension scheme (e.g. part-time workers or workers earning below a certain amount per year).
4. A scheme may provide additional benefits   such as pensions for other dependants – for men but not for women.

DOES YOUR SCHEME DISCRIMINATE AGAINST WOMEN INDIRECTLY?

Women tend to have different employment patterns from men, and as a result they may be unable to reap equal benefits from their pension scheme. A good scheme should take these factors into account. Many do not, and so discriminate indirectly – for instance:

1. A lot of women work part-time. Does your scheme exclude part-time workers?
2. A lot of women have a break from employment while they have maternity leave. Does your scheme preserve the pension rights of women during this period?

CAN YOU NEGOTIATE BETTER TERMS?

If you negotiate through your trade union you may be able to eliminate direct and indirect discrimination and generally improve the provisions of your pension scheme. So find out what the terms are and fight for a better deal.

### For further information

The Occupational Pensions Board, Apex Tower, High Street, New Malden, Surrey KT3 4DN: set up by the government to monitor occupational pension schemes.

The Company Pensions Information Centre, 7 Old Park Lane, London WIY 3LJ: a source of general information – but not individual advice – on occupational pension schemes. It has published three booklets, *Pensions for Women, How to Understand Your Pension Scheme* and *How Changing Jobs Affects Your Pension*; all are free but provide only rudimentary advice.

Age Concern, 60 Pitcairn Road, Mitcham, Surrey CR4 3LL (01 640 5431): information and campaigning centre for old people's welfare rights.

## Widows' benefits

If your husband dies, you will probably be entitled to widow's benefit. The amount you get and the type of benefit you receive will depend on:

1. How old you are when he dies; *and*
2. How much he has paid in National Insurance contributions.

If you remarry or live with a man 'as husband and wife' you lose your right to widow's benefit.

### If you are under 60 when your husband dies

You may get one or more of the following benefits:

1. Widow's allowance.
2. Widowed mother's allowance.
3. Widow's pension.

We shall deal with these in turn.

#### WIDOW'S ALLOWANCE

This is paid for the first twenty-six weeks after your husband's death.

*How do you qualify?*
You get widow's allowance if your husband has *either*

1. Paid twenty-five National Insurance contributions of any class before 6 April 1975; *or*
2. Paid contributions in any one tax year after 6 April 1975, on earnings worth at least twenty-five times the weekly 'lower earnings' limit. Currently, the 'lower earnings limit' is £27 a week so he would have had to pay contributions on at least £675 in the tax year April 1981 to April 1982, for example.

*How much do you get?*
1. The standard rate is £41·40 a week.
2. You get more if you have children under 16 or under 19 and in full-time training or education. The rate is £7·70 for each child. You get this in addition to Child Benefit which is explained on p. 185.
3. You may get more money, based on your husband's earnings. This is known as the *widow's earnings-related addition*. You get an amount based on your husband's National Insurance contributions in the tax year before he died. The amount you get is worked out in the same way as the earnings-related supplement,

described on p. 148. (However, this will be abolished from January 1982.)

## WIDOWED MOTHER'S ALLOWANCE

You should get this when your widow's allowance runs out after twenty-six weeks, if you have dependent children. The standard rate is £29·60 a week, and you get additional sums for your children, at the same rates as you got with your widow's allowance. The widowed mother's allowance ceases when you no longer have any children under 16, or under 19 and still in full-time training or education.

## WIDOW'S PENSION

You will get this if:

1. You are over 40 when your widowed mother's allowance ends;
   *or*
2. You are over 40 when your husband dies and you have no dependent children: in this case you get a widow's pension when your widow's allowance ends.

If you are 50 you get the standard rate (currently £29·60 a week). The younger you are, the less you get, as Table 3 shows.

## WILL YOUR BENEFITS BE REDUCED IF YOU ARE WORKING?

There is no limit to the amount of money you can earn while you are getting widow's benefit; your benefit will not be reduced. Widow's benefits are assessed for tax and you must declare them to the Inland Revenue. (Don't worry – if you are only getting widow's benefit, you probably won't have to pay any tax on it.) However, if you are receiving a state grant for education or training, your benefit will be either reduced or withdrawn until the grant ceases.

TABLE 3

| Your age when your husband died or when your widowed mother's allowance ends | Percentage of standard weekly widow's pension |
|---|---|
| 40 | 30 |
| 41 | 37 |
| 42 | 44 |
| 43 | 51 |
| 44 | 58 |
| 45 | 65 |
| 46 | 72 |
| 47 | 79 |
| 48 | 86 |
| 49 | 93 |
| 50 or over | 100 |

## DOES A WIDOW HAVE TO PAY NATIONAL INSURANCE CONTRIBUTIONS?

You can pay reduced contributions, like a married woman who has opted out (see p. 133), from the time of your husband's death *either* until the end of the tax year in which he died, if his death was before 1 October, *or* until the end of the tax year following the one in which he died, if his death was after 1 October.

If you are self-employed or non-employed during this period, you need pay no contributions at all. After this period has come to an end, you must pay full contributions while you are employed or self-employed, *unless* you are not working because you have 'home responsibility', as described on p. 134. In this case, you need not pay National Insurance contributions, but your pension rights are protected. You don't have to pay full contributions if you are getting a widow's benefit.

## CLAIMING SICKNESS AND UNEMPLOYMENT BENEFIT

There are special provisions to help widows to qualify for sickness and unemployment benefit. Inquire at your local Social Security office. But if you qualify for unemployment or sickness benefit whilst receiving a widow's benefit, you will get the *higher* of the two benefits only (under rules called the 'overlapping benefits regulations'). This is likely to be your widow's benefit.

WHAT HAPPENS WHEN YOU REACH 60

At 60, or later if you go on working, your widow's pension will be changed to a retirement pension. You get it automatically at 65, even if you continue to work.

If you are still entitled to a widowed mother's allowance or widow's allowance and the rate is higher than your pension would be, you can go on receiving that allowance until you cease to be eligible for it.

### If you are 60 or over when your husband dies

1. If your husband is *not* entitled to a retirement pension when he dies (for instance, if he is too young), you will get the widow's allowance for twenty-six weeks. After that you will get a retirement pension.
2. If you are receiving a married woman's retirement pension when your husband dies, it will be increased to the single person's rate. If you are getting the standard pension, this will mean an increase from £17·75 to £29·60.
3. If you are receiving a retirement pension on your own contribution record and your husband is entitled to a retirement pension when he dies, your pension will be based on your husband's contribution record, or your own, or a combination of both, depending on which gives you the highest pension.

*Under the new pension scheme* which started in April 1978, you are entitled to whatever 'additional' pension your husband had earned up to the time of his death. Additional pensions are explained on p. 157.

If he belonged to a contracted out pension scheme, the law says the scheme must pay you a widow's pension worth at least half the additional pension he would have earned from the state if he had not belonged to an occupational scheme. (In other words, the scheme must pay you at least half the *guaranteed minimum pension*, as explained on p. 171.) The state then pays you the other half. However, the scheme may make more generous provisions for widows. It may, for instance, pay you the full amount of the occupational pension your husband had earned, which would probably be more than an additional pension from the state. (More about occupational pension schemes on pp. 170–76.) You get the additional pension or occupational pension *as well as* any widow's benefit or retirement pension you may receive. (You pay income tax on an occupational pension, too.)

GRADUATED PENSIONS

The graduated pension scheme was wound up in 1975 but you or your husband may have paid graduated contributions before that. If so, when you retire you will receive half the graduated pension he has earned, plus any graduated pension you have earned from your own contributions. The rates are very low, but the government is now inflation-proofing them every year. More about graduated pensions on p. 158.

IF YOU GO ON WORKING AFTER YOU ARE 60

If you are getting a retirement pension, you can earn up to £52 a week without it being reduced. If you are over 65, or if you are still getting widow's benefit, you can earn as much as you like without the pension or benefit being reduced.

You can increase your pension by working after 60, as explained on p. 169.

## Death grant

This is a lump sum which you claim if either you or your husband has been paying National Insurance contributions. It will probably be £30, but if the contribution record is incomplete, you may get less. Full details are given in leaflet NI 49, which you can get from your local Social Security office.

### How to claim all widows' benefits

Fill in the form on the back of the death certificate and send it to your local Social Security office, or visit the office and make your claim in person. Be sure to make your claim within three months of your husband's death. The widow's benefit you get after widow's allowance for the first twenty-six weeks should be sent to you automatically.

IF YOU THINK YOU ARE GETTING THE WRONG AMOUNT

You can appeal to the National Insurance local tribunal, as explained on p. 492.

### If you haven't got enough to live on

claim supplementary benefit (see p. 190).

## Widows' inheritance

### If your husband has made a will

his money and belongings will go to whomever he has named in the will. Most married couples – if they make wills at all – make 'mutual' wills, so that the husband has one will leaving everything to the wife and the wife has another leaving everything to the husband. There is normally an arrangement to leave everything to the children if husband and wife die together. A will can also appoint a guardian to look after the children.

It's best if you and your husband do make wills, because it can save a lot of anxiety when either of you dies. A will is not valid unless it is properly drawn up, so it's advisable not to rely on a home-made one, but to get a solicitor to do it for you. They normally charge between £25 and £50 for a straightforward will. If you have a low income you should be able to get legal advice free or partly free under the 'green form' procedure, p. 454.

## If your husband has made a will but leaves little or nothing to you or your children

you and your children can apply to court for a share in his estate (the money and property he left behind). Consult a solicitor straight away: you must make your application to court within six months of the court releasing the Grant of Probate (explained below, p. 184). You can do this even if you were not married or living with him when he died, provided he was paying a substantial amount towards your needs. So if, for example, you were divorced from him and remarried, but he was still paying you a regular allowance, you could make a claim on his estate. The same is true if you were living with him, but not married to him.

HOW MUCH WILL YOU GET?

Whatever your relationship with him at the time of his death, the court must consider the following:

1. Your present and future financial needs;
2. Any physical or mental disability you have;
3. The financial resources and needs of all other people making a claim on his estate;
4. His obligations towards all other people who have a claim on his estate;
5. The size of the estate;
6. Your conduct;
7. Where a child is applying, the court must consider
(a) The child's educational or training expectations; *and*
(b) If it is not the man's own child, how far he has taken responsibility for it in the past.

If you were married to the man, or divorced from him at the time of his death, the court must also consider:

1. Your age;
2. How long your marriage lasted;
3. The contribution you made to the welfare of the family, by looking after the home and caring for the husband and children.

If you were married to him and living with him at the time of his death, you can expect no less than you would receive in a divorce settlement (see p. 375). If you were not, then you may get less.

### If your husband dies without leaving a will

and you have no children between you, you will get everything. If you have children by him, you will be entitled to his personal belongings and to the rest of his property up to the value of £40,000, free of death duty and legal costs. If his property is worth more than that, you are entitled to interest from half of the balance, after death duties and legal costs have been deducted. The children will get the rest when they reach the age of 18.

If you have no children but other surviving relatives, you take everything up to £85,000 and the interest on half of the balance.

Whatever your relationship with the man, you can apply for a share in his estate in the same way, and on the same conditions, as you can if he leaves a will (see above).

### Before you can take over your inheritance

you will probably have to get a 'Grant of Probate' (if he left a will) or 'Letters of Administration' (if he didn't leave a will). Both are obtainable from the Probate Registry in the High Court. If you've inherited a large amount, it's best to instruct a solicitor to deal with this side of affairs. Your bank may also advise you. Otherwise, you can make your own application to the Probate Registry. The address for the London area is the Personal Applications Department, Principal Registry of the Family Division, Room 3, South

West Wing, Bush House, London WC2. If you live outside the London area, ask your Citizen's Advice Bureau for the appropriate address.

### Further information

National Insurance leaflets N I 51, *Guide for Widows*; N P 35, *Your Benefit as a Widow for the First 26 Weeks*; and N P 36, *Your Benefit as a Widow after the First 26 Weeks*, from your local Social Security office.

National Organization for the Widowed and their Children, Cruse House, 126 Sheen Road, Richmond, Surrey TW9 1UR (01 940 4818), offers information and advice for widows, and produces some useful fact sheets and a book called *Begin Again* by Margaret Torrie.

## Child benefit

This is a new benefit introduced in April 1977 to replace 'family allowance' and child tax allowances (which were gradually phased out). You can claim it if you have one or more children, whether you are single or married. It is the only money that a mother has an automatic right to receive. You don't need National Insurance contributions to claim it. You don't have to fill in any complicated forms or answer questions about your financial resources.

You get £5·25 for each child. If you are a single parent or other person bringing up a child alone you can claim an extra £3·30 for the first child (this is called One Parent Benefit). You go on getting Child Benefit as long as you have a child who is:

1. Under 16, or under 19 and in full-time education or training; doing a 'non-advanced course'; *and*
2. Living at home with you or being financially supported by you. You may be able to claim Child Benefit for a child who is not your own but who is living with you and being supported by you.

To get Child Benefit you have to fill in a simple claim form, which you can get from your local Social Security office. You will be sent a book of money orders which you can cash every week at your local Post Office. The order book is always sent to the mother, except where she is not living with the children and the father is looking after them and supporting them on a permanent basis.

Unlike family allowance, Child Benefit is tax free. It is not counted when your income is assessed for tax. However, to compensate for the loss in revenue, the government has abolished child-tax allowances.

## Family income supplement

The family income supplement (FIS) is a weekly allowance intended for poor families. In order to get it you have to have the right family circumstances and a low enough income to qualify; and fill in a claim form with details of your income and circumstances.

Despite massive advertising campaigns, many people do not know of the existence of FIS or, if they do, have difficulty in claiming it. So it is hardly surprising that less than 75 per cent of people eligible for FIS actually claim it. Moreover, FIS encourages people to stay in low-paid employment. It is payable to families (including one-parent families) that have at least one dependent child and a total gross income which falls below a prescribed level; it can only be claimed by families where the 'head of the household' is in full-time work. (In two-parent families this *must* be the man until November 1983.) In November 1981, the prescribed level was £74 for a family with one child, plus £8 for each child after that.

### When can you claim FIS?

You can claim FIS if you have at least one dependent child living with you *and*:

1. You are single, working at least twenty-four hours a week, and have an income below the prescribed level; *or*
2. You are married or living with a man 'as man and wife', he is working at least thirty hours a week, and the total family income is below the prescribed level.

If you are married or living with a man you cannot claim FIS in your own right, since the man is considered to be 'head of the household'. You must both sign the claim form, but you can only do so if *he* is in full-time work. You cannot claim FIS when you are employed and the man is not. In this situation, if you haven't enough to live on, the man will have to claim supplementary benefit, as explained on p. 190. From November 1983 onwards you will be able to claim FIS whether the man or the woman is working full time.

Any children who are under 16, or over 16 and still at school, can be counted as part of your family as long as they are living with you. But you cannot include your own children if they are living away from home. Child Benefit will not be included when your gross income is being worked out.

## How much FIS will you get?

This will depend on how little you are earning. It is worked out at *half* the amount by which your total family income falls short of the prescribed level, but not everything is included. For example, Child Benefit and attendance or mobility allowances are ignored. The maximum you can get is £18·50 if you have one child, plus £1·50 for each other child. Here are two examples:

1. You are married with two children. Your husband is earning £72 a week. You are not working and the family has no other source of income. Your total income is £72 a week, which falls short of the prescribed level (£82) by £10. You will therefore get £5 FIS a week.
2. You are single with one child. You are earning £25 a week and receiving maintenance for yourself of £12 a week. Your total income is £37, which

falls short of the prescribed level by £37. You get the maximum of £18·50 a week.

## How to claim

Get the claim form (FIS 1) from your local Post Office. If they don't have it, get it from your local Social Security office. You should also make sure that they give you the prepaid envelope for sending it off. Fill in the form with details of your income. You should enclose your pay-slips for the last five weeks, if you have them. If you are paid by the month, you should enclose the last two monthly pay-slips. But don't delay in sending off the form if you haven't kept them. If you are single, only you need sign the form, but if you are married, or making a joint claim with the man you are living with, you must *both* sign the form. Send it off to the Department of Health and Social Security, Family Income Supplement, Poulton-le-Fylde, Blackpool FY6 8NW.

*If they decide you are eligible*, you will be sent a book of orders which can be cashed at your local Post Office every week. You will be able to draw FIS for fifty-two weeks, and it will not be affected if your circumstances change during that time. After fifty-two weeks you must renew your claim.

*If they decide you are not eligible* and you think the decision is wrong, you can appeal against it. Write to the Blackpool address and tell them you intend to appeal.

*Note:* While you are receiving FIS, you are automatically entitled to free prescriptions, free dental treatment and glasses under the National Health Service; free welfare milk and food for children under school age and expectant mothers; free school meals for schoolchildren; and fares refunded for any members of your family going to hospital for treatment. Your FIS book acts as a passport to these benefits, but you must still claim them; they will then be given to you without further inquiries about your income, etc.

## Supplementary benefit

Supplementary benefit is money you can claim from the state if you haven't enough to live on. It says a lot about the position of women in Britain that over 61 per cent of all people who receive supplementary benefits are women. They include single women who aren't eligible for full National Insurance benefits, unsupported mothers, wives of men claiming supplementary benefit, prisoners' wives, divorced and separated women, widows and women pensioners.

Benefits are very low indeed – scarcely enough to keep you above the bread-line. If you are going to make a claim, you need even more patience and perseverance than you would if you were claiming unemployment benefit. It helps if you also have a thick skin, a stubborn disposition and an equally determined friend to back you up when you go to the Social Security office – preferably a member of a claimants' union or the Child Poverty Action Group (more about these at the end of the section, p. 196).

There are detailed regulations which say how much money should be given out, to whom and in what circumstances. The Supplementary Benefits Officers often make all kinds of personal judgements about people without any justification before deciding whether they need benefits. Their judgement is guided by an official handbook called the 'Supplementary Benefits Handbook', and guidelines from the Chief Supplementary Benefits Officer. They seldom if ever tell you how to get the maximum amount that you are entitled to. Since November 1980, supplementary benefits have been made more like the National Insurance system. There are regulations made by Parliament, which lay down the outlines of your rights. And if one of the Social Security Commissioners (judges) makes a judgement about a borderline case, other similar cases will also be judged on the basis of that one.

However, you have a *right* to supplementary benefit if you haven't enough to live on. So don't be put off. First you must know *how much* you have a right to – including the basic allowance and all the possible extras. Then claim for as much as you can get. When you get your benefit, you should get a statement of how it had been worked put (form A 14 N). If you are not given one, insist that they give you one. It will help you work out your rights.

(Supplementary benefit is called 'supplementary allowance' when paid to people under 60 and 'supplementary pension' when paid to people over 60. For the sake of simplicity, we have called it 'supplementary benefit' throughout.)

### When can you claim supplementary benefit?

*You can claim* if you are single, separated, divorced or widowed, and if your financial resources are very low.

*You cannot claim* if you are married and living with your husband or if you are living with a man 'as husband and wife'. If you are, it is the man who must make the claim. He will receive the rate for a married couple, which is less than the rate for two single people. This particular rule gives rise to a great deal of hardship and confusion when it is applied to single women who are living with men but want to remain financially independent. It used to be known as the 'cohabitation rule' and is explained in more detail on p. 199. From November 1983, the person in the couple who is the 'main breadwinner' will be allowed to claim for both of them, and any children they have. But the rate for a 'married couple' will still be lower than for two single people.

*Under 18.* You cannot claim supplementary benefit if you are under 16. You cannot claim if you are 16 and still at school unless you are 'head of a household'. If your parents are claiming supplementary benefit, they can claim extra for you as their dependant. When you have left school, you will not be able to claim until the end of the holiday. Then you have the same right to claim supplementary benefit as anyone else, although you get a lower rate if you are not a 'householder' (as explained below).

*You may have to register for employment before you can claim.* If you have a child under 16 who is living with you; if you are looking after a sick or aged relative; or if you are sick, recently widowed or over 60, you can go straight to the Social Security office and make your claim. Otherwise you are supposed to go to your local Employment Office or Job Centre and register for work before you claim supplementary benefit. They don't normally make you do this if you are over 45, although they might if you have no children under 16.

## How much do you get?

The amount of supplementary benefit you get depends on how much you can claim and how much other income you have (if any). It is paid in the form of a weekly allowance to cover regular living expenses, with additional payments (if and when you claim them) to cover extra expenses that crop up. From 24 November 1980 onwards, you cannot get any supplementary benefit if you have 'capital' (savings) of £2,000 or over. And it is much more difficult to get additional ('single') payments for extra expenses. But claim for these anyway; you have nothing to lose.

HERE IS THE MAXIMUM AMOUNT OF MONEY THAT CAN BE CLAIMED AS A WEEKLY ALLOWANCE:

1. *If you're under 60 and you have been on supplementary benefit for less than a year, or are required to register for work before claiming:*
(a) A basic allowance to cover day-to-day living expenses for yourself. This is £23·25 for a single person who is a householder (which means someone who is directly responsible for household necessities and rent); £18·60 for a single person who is not a householder, or £14·30 for a non-householder aged between 16 and 18; and £37·75 for a married couple.
(b) Additional weekly allowances for any dependants you have. The rates are:

for a dependant aged 18 or over      £18·60
16 or 17      £14·30
11 to 15      £11·90
10 and under      £7·90

(c) An amount to cover your rent and rates. These will usually be paid in full, unless the Supplementary Benefits Officer decides that they are unreasonably high, in which case they will pay a contribution towards them.

(d) You can claim further weekly allowances if you have 'additional requirements', for instance if you need special food or if you have heavy laundry expenses.

(e) If extra heating is a special need, you can get an allowance for this as well. But there is already a weekly amount of £1·65 added to the allowances above for families with a child or children under 5.

2. *If you are over 60* OR *if you have been claiming supplementary benefit for over a year and you don't have to register for work:*

(a) The basic allowance is higher – £29·60 for a single person, £47·35 for a married couple and £23·65 for a non-householder. You get the same allowances as a person under 60 for dependants, rent and rates.

(b) If you are over 80 you get an extra 25p a week.

(c) You can claim an additional allowance if you need extra heating, or if you are blind.

(d) If you claim any other allowance to cover special needs, you will get only the difference between what you claim and 50p.

YOU MAY GET LESS SUPPLEMENTARY BENEFIT
IF YOU HAVE OTHER MONEY COMING IN

1. If you are receiving Child Benefit, FIS, National Insurance benefits or maintenance payments, the amount of these will be deducted in full.

2. You and your husband, or the man you are living with, can each earn up to £4 net a week, which will be ignored when working out

your benefit. All other net earnings for married couples, or couples living as 'husband and wife', are deducted. 'Net' means *after* tax, National Insurance and work expenses have been paid.

3. If you are a single parent, the same rule applies for the first £4 earned (i.e. they will be ignored). But *half* your weekly earnings, above £4 and up to £20 a week, will also be ignored. Any earnings above £20 a week will be taken into account.

4. In addition, income of up to £4 a week from all other sources (e.g. tax rebates) will be ignored.

## What about savings?

If you own the house you live in, its value will be completely ignored. But apart from that, if you have savings (or 'capital') of more than £2,000, you will be refused supplementary benefit altogether. If you have £2,000 or less you can claim the full benefits and your savings will not be taken into account.

If you get a redundancy payment of £2,500, for example, you won't get supplementary benefit. You will be expected to live off this money until it is less than £2,000; and *you* are expected to tell the local Social Security office when this happens. But if they think you have spent the money unreasonably (e.g. if you spent it on a luxury cruise) they may refuse to give you any benefit.

*Note:* The rule about savings (or capital) *only* affects supplementary benefit. It does *not* affect National Insurance benefits like unemployment benefit, or FIS or any of the others.

### HOW TO WORK OUT HOW MUCH SUPPLEMENTARY BENEFIT YOU SHOULD GET EACH WEEK

1. Add up the total amount of money you can claim as a weekly allowance.

2. Add up the total amount of other income you have which must be deducted.

3. Subtract (2) from (1). The amount that is left is approximately what you should get as supplementary benefit.

## What else can you claim?

You can claim extra payments for clothes, footwear, prams, pushchairs, floorcoverings, bedding, furniture, cooker, heaters and similar essentials (although the weekly allowance is supposed to cover normal repair and replacement of clothing, footwear and normal heating costs). Extra payments are *meant* to be for 'exceptional needs' only. For example, you will not get a single payment to replace clothes or footwear if they have worn out through 'normal wear and tear' – although you will if there has been 'excessive weight gain', for example! You can also claim financial help with fares to visit relatives in hospital or your husband if he is in prison. Inquire about this at your local Social Security office.

If you are receiving supplementary benefit, you are also automatically entitled to free medical prescriptions, help with National Health dental and optical charges, welfare milk and vitamins, and free school meals for your children. You must claim for these benefits, but you will then get them automatically, with no further inquiries about your income, etc. You may also be able to claim further grants to help support your children while they are at school, if you apply to your local education authority.

### RENT AND RATE REBATES

If your income is low or you have a large family, you may be able to get rebates from your local council for your rent and rates. This is different from getting extra supplementary benefit to pay for them. If you get a rebate from the council, you don't get extra supplementary benefit to cover rent and rates as well. If you are entitled to only a small amount of supplementary benefit (for instance, to 'top up' maintenance payments or widow's benefit) you may be better off just claiming rent and rate rebates and not claiming supplementary benefit at all. To find out which is best for you, ask the local Social Security office. They will not work it out unless you ask them to specifically.

### If your husband is off work because of a trade dispute

He is disqualified from claiming supplementary benefit for himself. However, he can still claim benefit for you, at the rate for an adult non-householder, which is higher than the extra for a wife. He can claim the normal amount for rent and for any children you have. If he gets any money, e.g. tax rebates while he is off work, all but the first £4 of the total (including money from other sources, as shown on p. 192) will be deducted from the supplementary benefit. But fairly soon he will receive no tax rebates (see p. 145). New rules from 24 November 1980 mean that *£12 a week* will be deducted from the supplementary benefit that anyone involved in a trade dispute gets for his/her dependants. (This is in addition to any other income that the person gets, and regardless of other deductions.) Up to £13 a week strike pay is ignored, however.

### If you are off work because of a strike or other trade dispute

You can claim for the rent and for any children you have, unless, of course, you are married or living with a man, in which case only the man can claim. The same rule, which means that £13 a week is deducted from the benefit you get (see previous paragraph), would apply to you too. If you have no dependants, you will not be able to get any weekly benefit. You *may* be able to get an 'urgent needs payment' if you have very little money to live on, but only in a real emergency.

### How to claim

First of all, look at p. 190 to see if you have to register for employment before you can claim supplementary benefit.

1. If you do not have to register for employment, you should get Form SB 1 from your local Post Office and ask for the prepaid envelope to go with it. You then fill it in and send it to your local Social Security office.
2. Alternatively you can go straight to your Social Security office and make your claim in person.

3. If you have to register for employment, ask for Form B 1 at your Unemployment Benefit Office, fill it in, and take it or send it to your Social Security office.

When they get your form the Social Security office will want to interview you and ask you questions about your income and needs. A Supplementary Benefits Officer will probably visit your home. If they decide to give you supplementary benefit it will be paid by means of an order book, or by Giro order, which you can cash each week at a Post Office. But if you are in urgent need, you can ask for a Giro order 'over the counter' at the Social Security office.

You will find yourself in a much stronger position in getting your claim if you have someone to help you. Contact your local claimants' union, or the local branch of the Child Poverty Action Group if there is one in your area. If there isn't and you are having difficulty with your claim, go to your Citizens' Advice Bureau, or get help from a social worker: if you are not already in touch with one, contact the social services department of your local council. (The addresses of your local CAB and social services department are both in the telephone directory.)

### Your right to appeal

You can appeal to the supplementary benefits appeals tribunal if you don't agree with a decision taken by the Social Security office about how much supplementary benefit you should get. The appeals procedure is explained on p. 493.

### Further information

A *claimants' union* is a group of people claiming supplementary benefits or National Insurance benefits who get together to help each other with their claims and to spread information about available benefits. They accumulate experience of how to get the most out of the system and take collective action if Social Security officials prove to be particularly obstructive. There are no formal links between the local unions, no structure and no headquarters. If you want to know if there is one in your area, ask the other people waiting in the Social Security office. If there isn't one, you can always start one.

The *Child Poverty Action Group* (CPAG) is an organization which fights poverty for adults and children alike. It is a good source of information on all aspects of welfare rights and publishes some useful pamphlets and an invaluable booklet called *National Welfare Benefits Handbook*, price £1·50 from CPAG, 1 Macklin Street, London WC2 (01 242 3225/9149). Contact the London office to find out if there is a CPAG branch near you. There are sixty local branches.

The *Citizens' Rights Office* concentrates on helping people with specific claims and with appeals to tribunals. Also at 1 Macklin Street, London WC2 (01 405 5942/4517).

*The Penguin Guide to Supplementary Benefits* by Tony Lynes. A detailed description of how the supplementary benefits system works, which is as lucid as it can be, considering the complexity of the subject.

---

EXAMPLE ONE

Mavis and Bill Jones have three children aged 14, 11 and 6. Bill works as a self-employed house painter, but he is often out of work during the winter. As he is not entitled to unemployment benefit, he has to claim supplementary benefit. This is a summary of what they get, showing how their various sources of income are deducted from the money they receive as benefit.

*Benefit before deductions*

| | |
|---|---|
| Basic weekly allowance for a married couple | £34·60 |
| for a child aged 14 | £10·90 |
| for a child aged 11 | £10·90 |
| for a child aged 6 | £7·30 |
| Rent per week | £15·00 |
| Weekly HP payments on a cooker | £4·00 |
| | |
| Total before deductions | £82·70 |

*Deductions*

| | |
|---|---:|
| Child benefit for three children | £15·75 |
| Mavis works part-time and earns £16 a week, of which she is allowed the first £4 (after deductions) | £12·00 |
| | |
| Total deductions | £27·75 |
| | |
| Total weekly benefit is £96·65 minus £27·75 = | £68·90 |

EXAMPLE TWO

Judy is a single mother with two children aged 3 and 5. She has been living on supplementary benefit since the birth of her first child. As she is looking after children, she does not have to register for work before claiming benefit. Her rent and rates are £16 a week. She receives a small amount of maintenance from the children's father. This is what she gets.

*Benefit before deductions*

| | |
|---|---:|
| Basic weekly allowance for a single person who has been living on supplementary benefit for more than a year, who is not required to register for work | £29·60 |
| Allowance for a child aged 5 | £7·90 |
| Allowance for a child aged 3 | £7·90 |
| Rent and rates per week | £16·00 |
| | |
| Total before deductions | £61·40 |

*Deductions*

| | |
|---|---:|
| Child benefit and One Parent Benefit | £13·80 |
| Maintenance from the children's father | £15·00 |
| | |
| Total deductions | £28·80 |
| | |
| Total weekly benefit is £61·40 minus £28·80 = | £32·60 |

## 'Living together as husband and wife' (the 'cohabitation rule')

There is a rule which says that a woman who is living with a man 'as husband and wife' should be treated as the man's wife, even though she is not married to him. (This used to be called the 'cohabitation rule' until the official terminology was altered in 1976.) It means that a woman who is thought to be living with a man cannot claim supplementary benefit, widows' benefits or benefits for any of her children. She is expected to rely on the man to support her and her children from his earnings, or claim supplementary benefit for her as his dependent 'wife'. Supplementary benefit paid for a woman as a man's wife (£14·50 a week) is considerably less than that paid to a single woman (£23·25 or £18·60 if she is not a householder).

What often happens is that a woman loses her right to claim benefit because she is thought to be living with a man, even when she is receiving no money from the man, and when she has no wish to be financially dependent on him – and even, in some cases, when she is not actually living *with* him at all. There appear to be two main assumptions behind this rule:

1. A woman who is married to or living with a man and sleeping with him should be supported by the man.
2. A woman who is married to or living with a man and sleeping with him needs less money to live on than a woman who is living alone, with another woman, or with a man who does not share her bed.

The official justification is that an unmarried couple who live together should not get more money than a married couple. From November 1983 onwards, whoever is 'the main breadwinner' will be the one who can claim. But you will still get less money than two single people.

*You may be affected by the rule* if:

1. You are single, separated, divorced, or widowed; *and*

2. You are claiming supplementary benefit, widows' benefit, child's special allowance or One Parent Benefit; *and*
3. You are suspected of living with a man 'as husband and wife'.

### How do social security officials decide whether you are 'living together as husband and wife'?

Special investigators are employed to check up on women who are suspected of this. There are rules for them to follow. New ones were issued in 1980, in the *Supplementary Benefits Handbook* and in guidelines from the Chief Supplementary Benefits Officer. But the 1976 Act covering supplementary benefits also has rules dealing with 'cohabitation'. They say that, before a woman's benefit is withdrawn, her case should be judged in the light of these considerations:

1. *The woman and man must be members of the same household.* This would be so if the man normally lives under the same roof, that is to say in the same house, flat or apartment as the claimant and, usually, that he has no other home where he normally lives. It implies he lives there regularly, apart from absences necessary for his employment, visits to relatives, etc., and not merely occasionally. This factor is described as indispensable.
2. *The relationship must be more than an occasional or very brief association* – although there is no guidance as to how much more it should be. If they have just started to live together, they may be given time (weeks, rather than months) for their relationship to develop, before it is officially regarded as living together as husband and wife.
3. *Is the man bearing a major share of household expenses as distinct from paying rent or for board and lodging?* If so, this will normally be taken as evidence that the woman and man are living together as husband and wife, but is not in itself conclusive evidence. But if, on the other hand, the man is *not* providing any financial support, this is *not* evidence that they are not living together as husband and wife.

4. *Is there a sexual relationship between them?* A sexual relationship is not in itself regarded as evidence that they are living together as husband and wife. The rules say that if a couple are living together in circumstances in which a sexual relationship is as likely to exist as it would be in a marriage, it is unnecessary to prove that they actually have a sexual relationship. In this case, it will be assumed that they are living together as husband and wife and benefit will be withdrawn. Officers are instructed not to question claimants on this point. However, if a woman can prove that she does not have a sexual relationship with the man, her benefit will not be withdrawn. In other words, if it looks as if they are living together, it will be assumed that they are sleeping together unless the woman can prove otherwise – and if she can prove otherwise it will be assumed that they are not living together as husband and wife.

5. *Are there any children from the union?* If the woman is caring for children that she has had by the man, there will be a strong presumption that they are living together as husband and wife. But if the man doesn't act as a father towards her children, this should be very carefully considered.

6. *Are they publicly acknowledged as a married couple?* If they represent themselves to others as husband and wife (e.g. by visiting relatives or going on holidays together), this is evidence that they are living together as husband and wife. But if they don't represent themselves as married, this is not evidence that they are not living together as husband and wife.

7. *As general guidance*, the rules say that what has to be decided is whether the relationship, as a whole, of a couple living together in the same household has the character of that of a husband and wife.

The special investigators may call at your home and ask to look around. They will be searching for evidence that a man is living with you. If they call at an inconvenient hour – like early in the morning or late at night – you have every right to turn them away or ask them to come back another time. If you refuse them entry altogether, there is a danger that they will take that as evidence that you are 'guilty'. On the other hand, if they look around and find nothing, this will weaken their case. They may spy on your home to see if they can catch a man leaving it several mornings a week; and they may question your neighbours. The rules say they can do this in cases where there is no reasonable alternative. They are instructed not to question children: if they do, report them.

Evidence they collect may not amount to proof that you are living with a man as husband and wife. You are not 'guilty', for instance, if you have a boyfriend who stays with you occasionally, or if you are simply sharing accommodation with a male flat-mate, lodger or landlord without sharing the same bed. Nevertheless, women often have their benefit withdrawn when they are not living with a man 'as husband and wife'.

*If they decide that you are 'living together as husband and wife'*, your book of money orders will be taken away. But if you have children whose father is not the man you are living with, they should go on paying an allowance for you and them for four weeks. If they decide that your case justifies extra help, they may extend or increase the allowance for the children and give extra lump sums for urgent necessities (but only if you claim them).

*If you dispute their decision*, they will give you a leaflet explaining *their* interpretation of the law (do not accept this as final). When your benefit is stopped you will also be sent the reasons for their decision in writing and a copy of your own statement to them, plus details of any information on which the decision is based which was not contained in your statement.

### What to do if your benefit is stopped

Whatever the circumstances, it is almost certainly worth appealing against the decision.

1. Make a fresh claim for benefit at once to your local Social Security office. If you tell them you are in urgent need, you may

be able to get some money while you are waiting for your appeal to be heard.

2. Make an appeal at once and ask for it to be heard urgently. If you were getting supplementary benefit, appeal to the supplementary benefits appeals tribunal. If you were getting widows' benefits or child's special allowance, appeal to the National Insurance local tribunal. You can appeal to both if necessary. Do this – at the latest – before the twenty-eighth day after your benefit is stopped. If you don't you will have to explain why you haven't appealed sooner and the tribunal may refuse to hear your appeal. But if twenty-eight days have already gone by, it is still worth trying to appeal. Get the address of the appeals tribunal from your local Social Security office and see p. 493.

3. Try to get someone who knows about supplementary benefit appeals to represent you at the tribunal hearing. Contact the Child Poverty Action Group (address, p. 197) and find out if they have a branch near your home; or get in touch with a claimants' union or neighbourhood advice centre, if there is one in your area. If you can spare £1·50, it would be worth investing in the CPAG *National Welfare Benefits Handbook*, which gives a clear and detailed explanation of how to make an appeal.

4. The Clerk of the tribunal will let you know when and where the hearing will be held. He/she will send you copies of the papers which are to be presented to the tribunal, including details of the 'case against you'. This should give you a chance to prepare your defence. It is important to attend the tribunal yourself and, if possible, to have someone to represent you who has experience of cases like this. You are allowed to take two people with you. Collect together all the evidence you can find that might convince the tribunal that you are not cohabiting – such as rent book, wage-slips, and letters. Get witnesses to support your case – such as neighbours, your boyfriend or a social worker. It is particularly useful if you can produce evidence that your boyfriend is living somewhere else; or supporting another family; or that the man in question is in fact your lodger or your landlord. Don't be intimidated by the tribunal. Remember it is

up to them to prove that you are cohabiting and the evidence collected by the 'special investigators' can be very flimsy. You should be allowed to cross-question them.
5. If you can't prove that you are not cohabiting, you may be able to plead 'exceptional circumstances'. The tribunal is more likely to accept a plea of 'exceptional circumstances' if you are supporting the children of another man and the man you are living with refuses to support them or can't afford to – for instance, if he is already supporting another family.

## Other non-contributory benefits

Like supplementary benefit, the following benefits do not depend on your National Insurance contributions. That's why they are called 'non-contributory'.

### *Industrial injuries benefit*

You can claim this benefit even if you haven't been paying National Insurance contributions, in the following circumstances:

1. You were employed, rather than self-employed; *and*
2. You were injured at work or contracted what is known as a 'prescribed industrial disease'; *and*
3. As a result, you are unable to work.

The short-term 'injury' rate, £25·25 a week for a single person, is higher than sickness benefit. You cannot claim sickness benefit at the same time, but if you are eligible for sickness benefit you may get an earnings-related supplement. After six months if you are assessed as disabled as a result of industrial injury, you will get more money in the form of disablement benefit, and this varies according to how disabled you are. If you want to know more about either of these benefits, ask your doctor, your trade union branch official or your local Social Security office.

### Non-contributory invalidity pension

If you are single, you can claim this if you have been incapable of work – through disability – for at least twenty-eight weeks and you are not entitled to the National Insurance invalidity benefit described on p. 147. The rate is £17·75 a week, with extra for dependants. You can earn up to £16·50 a week in 'therapeutic earnings' which must be approved by your doctor, before the pension is reduced. If your husband is receiving an invalidity pension, he can claim £10·65 a week extra for you and you can earn up to £45 a week before the amount is reduced. To claim, get leaflet NI 210 from your Social Security office. If you have no other income, you should claim rent and rate rebates from your local council, or supplementary benefit to cover your rent and rates and to 'top up' your income to the supplementary benefit level, see p. 190.

Married women and unmarried women who are living with a man 'as husband and wife' cannot claim this invalidity pension unless they are considered incapable of performing 'normal household duties'. See leaflet NI 214 for more details, and *appeal* against the decision if you are refused benefit.

### Attendance allowance

You can claim this if
1. You are severely disabled, physically or mentally; *and*
2. For at least six months before you claim you have needed constant attention – and continue to need it.

The amount you get depends on how much attention you need. To claim, get leaflet NI 205 from your Social Security office.

### Invalid care allowance

This is a new benefit. You can claim it if you are unable to work to earn your living because you are at home acting as unpaid attendant to someone who is severely disabled and who is receiving an attendance allowance. You must be attending the person for at least thirty-five hours a week and earning no more than £6 a week (not counting work expenses). You cannot claim it if you are married and living with your husband or supported by him – even if he is the person you are looking after. Nor can you claim if you are living with a man. Your pension rights are protected while you are receiving this benefit (see p. 132). Invalid care allowance is paid at the rate of £17·75 a week.

### Mobility allowance

If you are severely disabled, virtually unable to walk and likely to remain handicapped for at least a year, you can claim £16·50 a week mobility allowance. How you spend the allowance is up to you.

### Guardian's allowance

You may be able to claim this if you are looking after an orphan child. The rate is £7·70 a week. Normally both parents of the child must be dead before you can claim, but you can sometimes claim if only one parent is dead, for instance, if the parents were divorced, if the surviving parent is missing or serving a long term in prison. More details in leaflet NI 14, from your Social Security office.

### Further information

See p. 197.

## Student grants

*You get the standard rate of grant*, whether you are single, married, widowed, divorced or separated. The maximum standard grant (for the year 1980–81) is £1,695 a year if you're a student in London, or

£1,430 if you're a student anywhere else in the U.K.; but it is reduced to £1,125 if you're living at home with your parents.

The grant is assessed on your parents' income (even if you are married) unless:

1. You are over 25; *or*
2. You have worked for three years between leaving school and going to college (looking after your children counts as work but only if you're married); *or*
3. There are special circumstances – e.g. your parents can't be found.

If you fulfil one of these conditions, your grant is *not* assessed on your parents' income, so you get the maximum grant, unless you are married, in which case your grant is assessed on your husband's income.

*You may get a higher-value 'mature student's' grant* if you start your course when you are over 26 and have been in full-time remunerative employment for three out of six years immediately before the start of the course.

### *Extra grants for dependent children and adults*

*If your grant is not assessed on your parents' income* because you fulfil one of the conditions outlined above, *and* you were married before you started your course, you can claim allowances for any dependent children you have and for your husband if he is financially dependent on you. The rates per year are:

| | |
|---|---|
| Spouse, or other adult dependant (or first child if no spouse) | £885 |
| Children: under 11 | £135 |
| 11–16 | £340 |
| 17 and over | £500 |

*If your grant is assessed on your parents' income*, or you are unmarried or you got married during your course, you may be able to claim dependants' allowances for your dependent children and husband from a special Hardship Scheme administered by the Department of Health and Social Security. The weekly rates are:

| | |
|---|---:|
| Spouse (or first child if no spouse) | £17·02 |
| Children: under 11 | £2·60 |
| 11–16 | £6·54 |
| 17 and over | £10·29 |

You will get these allowances during term time only, unless you are a single parent, in which case you will get them throughout the year.

*If your husband is a student*, he can claim grants and dependants' allowances in the same way as a female student.

*If you are working while your husband is a student* you can arrange for part or all of his married man's tax allowance to be transferred to you, if he agrees. If he has any earnings or unearned income (other than a grant or scholarship) during the year, you can only transfer the difference between this amount and the current level of the married man's allowance. You get your own earned income allowance as well. See p. 119 for details of tax allowance.

*If you're in any doubt about what your grant should be*, you can get more information by writing to your local education authority; the Department of Education and Science, Elizabeth House, York Road, London SE1; or the Grants Adviser, National Union of Students, 3 Endsleigh Street, London WC1 (or phone 01 387 1277).

# 4. Sex

## Sex under 18

Most of the legal restrictions on your sex life are lifted on your sixteenth birthday. But until your eighteenth birthday, there are still some things you cannot do without getting into trouble with the law. Once you are 18 you have reached the 'age of majority' and you can officially do what you like.

*Sixteen is the 'age of consent'.* This means that you can't legally have sexual intercourse until you are 16. The law does not seem very realistic in these days of earlier puberty and greater sexual freedom, but in fact it was not so long ago that the age of consent was 12.

The age of consent was raised to 16 in 1885. The reason was not to stop 15-year-old girls sleeping with their boyfriends, but to make it illegal to procure young girls for prostitution and the White Slave Trade – both flourishing businesses in the mid-nineteenth century.

The scandal of procuring young girls was brought to the public notice by Mrs Josephine Butler. She persuaded a Mr Stead, then editor of the *Pall Mall Gazette*, to illustrate the situation dramatically. With the help of the Salvation Army, he bought a 13-year-old girl for £5, kept her (suitably protected) in a brothel overnight and sent her to Paris the next day. He then published details of the transaction, pointing out that it was all entirely legal, under the title 'The Maiden Tribute of Modern Babylon'. The article caused a tremendous sensation and five days later a Criminal Law

Amendment Bill was rushed through Parliament, raising the age of consent to 16. Mr Stead got three months in prison.

The age of consent has stuck at 16 ever since. But some of the effects it has today are not at all what Josephine Butler would have envisaged in 1885. For example:

1. *You may find it difficult to get birth control under 16* (although withholding birth control never stopped anyone having sex). Girls under 16 are less likely to want children than older girls, but while it is possible for them to get contraceptives from some clinics in a rather 'under-the-counter' way it is not their right.
2. *If you are pregnant and under 16*, the only financial help you can get from the state is a maternity grant. You cannot get a maternity allowance, nor can you claim supplementary benefit in your own right. (We explain what you can do in these circumstances on p. 151.)
3. *You may find yourself in court if you are under 17 and having sexual intercourse or 'in danger' of having it*. This will only happen if your parents are not looking after you or if they feel they can't cope with you. You can be taken to court if

Birth control advice, eh? Well, **abortions** now and **contraceptives** later... when you're **16**

your parents, the police, or the social services department of your local council think that you are in 'moral danger'. 'Moral danger' in the eyes of the law can mean: that you are under 16 and likely to be having sexual intercourse; *or* that you are under 17 and away from home and likely to be having sexual intercourse.

(Incidentally, boys are not taken to court for the same reasons.)

If you are taken to court and it is decided that you are in need of 'care and control', the court will place you under a supervision order or under a care order. There is a full explanation of this, or what to do if it happens to you, on p. 369.

You are *less* likely to get into this kind of trouble if you are living in conventional surroundings and leading a fairly 'normal' life, even if you are having sex. You are *more* likely to if you mix with an unconventional crowd of people; if you have dropped out of school; if you leave home without your parents' consent; or if you are living with a man or in a mixed flat or commune, even if you are not having sex.

4. *A boy or man with whom you have sexual intercourse may be prosecuted.* The laws were designed to protect young girls from seduction. Unfortunately, they may also be used against a boyfriend you cared for and wanted to sleep with. Here is a list of the things a man cannot (legally) do with you if you are under 18.

(a) It is a very serious offence for a man to have sexual intercourse with a girl under 13. He cannot normally defend himself by claiming that she consented or that he thought she was older.

(b) It is an offence for a man to have sexual intercourse with a girl aged between 13 and 16. But if he is under 24, he may avoid being convicted if he can show that he thought she was over 16, unless he has been charged with the same offence before. It is assumed in law that a boy under 14 cannot be found guilty of illegal sexual intercourse.

(c) It is an offence to make an assault, indecent or otherwise, on anyone, but an indecent assault on a girl under 16 is more serious and carries a higher penalty.

(d) It is an offence for a person to let a girl under 16 use premises for sexual intercourse; or to encourage prostitution or illegal sexual intercourse.

(e) It is an offence to take a girl under 16 away from her parents without their consent. This could mean that a boy of 17 (or a man of any age, for that matter) might be prosecuted if he encouraged a girl of 15 to run away with him, even if he didn't have sexual intercourse with her.

(f) It is an offence for a man to take an unmarried girl under 18 away from her parents without their consent if he is taking her 'with intent to have unlawful sexual intercourse'. ('Unlawful' in this case means sex outside marriage.) The only way he can avoid conviction is by claiming that he thought the girl was over 18. So if you leave home and go to live with a boyfriend when you are 17, he may be prosecuted if he encouraged you to leave, even though it is perfectly legal for you to have sex.

## WHERE TO GET HELP WITH SEXUAL PROBLEMS IF YOU ARE UNDER 18

The Brook Advisory Centres specialize in helping young people with all sexual problems. There are six Brook centres in London, three in Bristol, five in Birmingham and one in Coventry, Cambridge, Liverpool and Edinburgh. If you live in one of these areas, you can find the address in the telephone directory. The head office is at 153a East Street, London SE17 (01 708 1234).

Many of the bigger towns and cities now have youth advisory centres. If there is one in your area, the Citizens' Advice Bureau will give you the address. Otherwise if you have a serious problem, try talking to your teacher (if you are at school) or go to the social services department of your local council (address in the telephone directory) and ask to see a social worker. Community Health Councils can also help. See p. 222 for details.

## Contraception

### *If you are under 16*

Although the law says that you should not have sexual intercourse until your sixteenth birthday, it is not illegal to use birth control. However, some family planning clinics may refuse to prescribe the Pill, or to fit you with a cap or coil.

The legal position is this: it is not illegal for a doctor to give you *advice* about contraception and probably not to prescribe the Pill. In most cases it is illegal for a doctor to give you a medical examination or treatment without your parents' consent: this would include fitting the cap or coil. However, the Department of Health and Social Security has made it clear to doctors that they can decide for themselves whether to provide contraceptive advice and treatment for girls under 16. It has pointed out that they would not be acting unlawfully if they did so 'in good faith' to protect a girl 'against the potentially harmful effect of intercourse' (i.e. unwanted pregnancy) – and without telling the parents. The DHSS suggests that doctors should ask the girl's permission to tell her parents, but advises them not to do so without her consent.

The result is that your chances of getting contraception depend on the prejudices of your doctor. Some will help you without any hesitation; some will insist that you get your parents' consent first; others will refuse to help you at all. (Some family doctors have been known to tell a girl's parents against her wishes.) A lot of girls get round the problem by saying they are 16 and they usually find that clinics don't check up on them. (Their own general practitioners could of course check their age on their medical cards.)

The Brook Advisory Centres specialize in helping young girls and boys on all sexual matters. They charge a small initial fee. The addresses are given at the end of the section (p. 232). You can rely on them to be sympathetic. They will encourage you to tell your parents, but they will not insist if you don't want to.

Likewise, it is the official policy of most family planning clinics not to turn anyone away. They are also likely to ask you to get your parents' consent, but they will not tell them if you don't want them to. Whether or not they let you have birth control supplies will depend on the attitude of the doctor at your local clinic. Don't be afraid to approach them. They have young people's advisory services attached to some clinics: ask if there is one in your area.

## If you are over 16

Whether you are single or married, you can get birth control advice and supplies from your local family planning clinic. Birth control advice and supplies of contraceptives are free.

### HOW TO FIND OUT WHERE TO GO

You can find the address of your local family planning clinic in the telephone directory under 'Family Planning'. It is best to ring first, or drop in to make an appointment. But some clinics will see you immediately. If you don't find it convenient to go to the clinic, try your family doctor. Other useful addresses are listed later in the chapter.

WHAT IF YOU CAN'T GET TO THE CLINIC?

If you are homebound because you are ill, or you have small children, or you live a long way from the clinic and have no transport, someone from the clinic may be able to visit you at your home. This is known as the 'domiciliary service'. It can only be arranged if you are referred to the service by a social worker or health visitor, but if you're in touch with one you can always ask to be referred. You can also order by mail contraceptives such as sheaths and spermicidal creams and pessaries from the Family Planning Association and Brook Advisory Centres (addresses, p. 222).

WILL THEY ASK A LOT OF INTERFERING QUESTIONS?

They are not supposed to and they probably won't. If they do, you don't have to answer. The only thing they have to know is your name, address and medical history. They may also ask you your age, your occupation, your partner's occupation and your marital status, but you don't have to tell them if you don't want to.

IS YOUR HUSBAND'S CONSENT NEEDED?

It is still the policy of most clinics to ask for your husband's consent if you are having a coil fitted or an operation for sterilization. Their excuse is that the doctor must be protected from being sued by an irate husband who might demand compensation for loss of his ability to have children. However, there are no known cases to indicate that this is necessary. Early in 1973, Lord Aberdare, Minister of State for Health and Social Security, replying to a question from Baroness Wootton in the Lords, stated: 'There is no legal requirement either under English or Scottish law that the consent of the spouse must be obtained for the sterilization of the partner.' Some women simply sign their husband's name for them. More and more doctors are prepared to fit coils or sterilize without the husband's consent. If you're single, there's no problem.

## What are the most effective forms of birth control?

THE PILL

There are two types of pill – the *combined pill* which contains the hormones oestrogen and progesterone, and the *mini-pill* which contains progesterone only.

The *combined pill* is taken daily on a monthly cycle of 21–22 days with a 7-day break.

| | |
|---|---|
| How it works | It prevents or reduces the release of eggs from the ovaries and alters the lining of the womb, making it impossible for an egg to implant successfully. It also changes the chemistry of the neck of the womb to prevent sperm getting through. |
| Advantages | Ninety-nine per cent safe if taken regularly. Periods are light – can ease pre-menstrual tension. |
| Disadvantages | You have to remember to take it every day. Can make you feel as if in the early stages of pregnancy with nausea, weight increase, lessening of sexual interest, depression. Sometimes leads to aggravation of migraine and vaginal infection. Switching types of pill may help. |
| | You should have a medical check up before taking this pill. It should not be prescribed for women with a medical history of thrombosis, blood vessel damage, heart disease, liver complaints or cancer. Not recommended for over-35s, particularly if smokers, or for breast-feeders. It can lead to a delay of up to a year or more in becoming pregnant after you have stopped taking it, but does not lead to infertility. |

The *mini-pill* is marginally less effective than the combined pill, probably because ovulation is not prevented.

| | |
|---|---|
| Advantages | Reliability – better than all other methods except the combined pill. Suitable for the older woman or if you are breast-feeding. At present long-term side-effects seem to be negligible. |
| Disadvantages | Pill must be taken every day at the same time. Periods can be irregular and scant (though this can be an advantage). Has fewer side-effects than the combined pill, but breast tenderness and depression can be aggravated. |

## THE COIL (IUD)

| | |
|---|---|
| What is it? | A small flexible coil or loop of plastic or copper which is inserted into the womb, without anaesthetic. If done skilfully, the insertion isn't painful. |
| How it works | Stops any fertilized egg from being implanted in the wall of the womb. No one knows exactly how. |
| Advantages | Once it's in you can forget about it except for yearly check-ups. You control your own fertility. It's usually very effective, though not quite as safe as the Pill. It is attached to a piece of string which you can feel to check whether it is properly in position. |
| Disadvantages | No good if you haven't been pregnant. (But see below: 'Copper-Seven coil'.) Can be uncomfortable at first and can cause irritation. In some women it causes backache and heavy menstrual and intermittent bleeding. |

| Where to get it? | It must be inserted by a doctor. You can get it from your local family planning clinic or family doctor. |

### COPPER-SEVEN OR COPPER-T COIL

| What is it? | A small plastic intra-uterine device, shaped like a '7' or a 'T', with a copper tail. |
| How does it work? | It causes a chemical reaction which prevents conception. |
| Advantages | It can be used by women who haven't yet been pregnant and is as effective as a conventional coil. More comfortable, because it is smaller. |
| Disadvantages | The long-term effects of the absorption of copper by the body are not yet known. Can be very painful at first if you have never had a child. Has been known to slip out unnoticed, although this is rare. All forms of IUD increase the risk of pelvic infections. |

### THE CAP

| What is it? | A rubber cap or dome that fits over the entrance to the womb. |
| How it works | It prevents the male sperm from entering the womb. |
| Advantages | You shouldn't be able to feel it once it's in. You control it. There are no side-effects. The cap is becoming more popular as many women become more worried by the immediate and long-term side-effects of the Pill and IUD. If used carefully, it is as safe as the IUD and *completely harmless.* |

Disadvantages      You have to remember to put it in before you
                   have intercourse. To be safe you must use
                   spermicide cream with it, and it can be messy
                   and awkward to insert. Even used with cream,
                   it is not as safe as the Pill. It's possible to put
                   it in wrongly, or to push it out of place. If you
                   have intercourse more than once a night you
                   should put more cream in. You have to leave it
                   in for six hours after intercourse, and it's a bit
                   of a performance taking it out: you have to
                   wash it, dry it and powder it before you put it
                   away.

Where to get it?   It must be fitted by a doctor. You can get it at
                   your local family planning clinic or from your
                   family doctor.

## SHEATH (FRENCH LETTER OR CONDOM)

What is it?        A thin covering of rubber which is fitted over
                   the penis.

How it works       It prevents the sperm from reaching the
                   womb.

Advantages         Anyone can buy it. Fairly straightforward to
                   use. You know if the man's got one on. It
                   offers some protection against venereal
                   disease. If used properly, it can be quite
                   effective.

Disadvantages      You have to rely on the man to use it. Some
                   men resent having to wear it. Must be put on
                   to an erect penis, so it can cause an
                   unwelcome interruption. It can decrease
                   sensitivity and lessen the enjoyment. Has been
                   known to slip off. The man has to withdraw
                   soon after ejaculation or it may leak. Now
                   only considered properly effective if used with
                   spermicidal pessaries.

Where to get it?     Most chemists, 'surgical supply' shops, family
planning clinics.


FEMALE STERILIZATION

What is it?     A surgical operation.

How does it work? There are two methods. The first is called
laparotomy, which ties off the Fallopian tubes
so that the eggs can't get to the womb. The
second, laparoscopy, is a newer method which
requires only two tiny cuts in the abdomen.

Advantages     Normally, it is completely effective, so once
it's done, there's nothing more to worry about.
It doesn't interfere with your sex life.

Disadvantages     You can't change your mind: the operation
isn't reversible. It's more complicated to
arrange than other methods of contraception.
Involves a stay in hospital of eight or nine days
for a laparotomy, or forty-eight hours for a
laparoscopy. Doctors will seldom operate on
women who haven't had at least one child.
Some women who have had laparoscopies
have later become pregnant – so this method
can't be regarded as 100 per cent effective.

Where to get it?     You can arrange it through your family doctor
or the doctor at your family planning clinic.
The doctor will have to refer you to a hospital.
It is then at the discretion of the surgeon at
the hospital whether to sterilize you or not.
Relatively cheap private sterilizations can be
arranged through the British Pregnancy
Advisory Service (address, p. 232).

MALE STERILIZATION (VASECTOMY)

What is it?    A minor surgical operation which can be done under local anaesthetic.

How does it work? Ties ducts from the testicles to prevent sperm being ejaculated.

Advantages    Completely effective. Doesn't affect the man's sex life or yours. If you have a steady relationship with him, you can let your own body function normally without any worries.

Disadvantages  You have to rely on the man to get it done. You only benefit if you have a steady relationship with him. The man can't change his mind about having children. Some men feel (wrongly) that it lessens their virility if they can't sire any more children. Doctors will seldom give vasectomies to men who haven't had at least one child.

Where to get it? The man can arrange it through his family doctor or family planning clinic. Relatively cheap private vasectomies can be arranged through BPAS and the Marie Stopes House (addresses, p. 233).

## For further information and help

*The Family Planning Association* head office is at 27–35 Mortimer Street, London W1 (01 636 7866). Family planning clinics are now part of the N.H.S.

*Brook Advisory Centres:* there are six of them in London, three in Bristol, five in Birmingham and one in Coventry, Cambridge, Liverpool and Edinburgh. Addresses in local telephone directories, and see p. 232.

*Community Health Councils (CHCs):* These exist to represent your interests in relation to the National Health Service. Many CHCs run shopfront advice centres and almost all will have detailed information on local health services, family planning clinics, sympathetic GPs, etc. If you cannot find the telephone number of your local CHC in the phone book, ring the national CHC information service on 01 388 4943.

## Abortion

The law still fails to recognize that it is every woman's right to control her own body. It does not allow a woman to have an abortion without the consent of two doctors. These doctors are usually men, they do not necessarily know what is best for the woman, and they themselves are not suffering from the unwanted pregnancy. Yet they make the decision. The woman cannot have an abortion just because she wants one.

Despite these legal obstacles, it *is* possible for most women to get an abortion if they know where to go for it. It helps if you are no more than twelve weeks pregnant and can spend *at least* £90 on the operation. Otherwise you may need to be very persistent and strong-willed if you are to avoid being depressed and discouraged. The more advanced the pregnancy, the harder it is to get an abortion: it is virtually impossible after six months.

*Some facts and figures:* about 147,000 legal abortions are carried out every year. (At the time of writing, the number was falling rapidly.) Under half of them are on the National Health; just over half the women are single. More married women get National Health abortions than single women. By far the most common reason for abortion is risk to the woman's physical or mental health. Over 80 per cent of abortions take place before the twelfth week of pregnancy.

This section is divided into three parts. The first explains the relevant law and how it works in practice. The second tells you what to do if you think you are pregnant. The third describes recent moves to restrict the right to abortion.

### What the 1967 Abortion Act says

The Act says that you may get an abortion under the following conditions:

1. Two doctors must sign a form saying that they genuinely believe:
(a) that continuing the pregnancy would involve a risk to your life or to the physical or mental health of you or any children you already have (taking into account your present and foreseeable circumstances); and that this risk would be greater than the risk involved in ending the pregnancy; *or*
(b) that there is a substantial risk that if the child were born it would suffer a serious handicap from a physical or mental abnormality – for example, if you had German measles in the early stages of pregnancy.
2. The abortion must be carried out in a National Health hospital or a clinic licensed by the Department of Health. This is so that the government can control the way private abortions are handled – some clinics have had their licences taken away because they don't meet required standards.
3. If these conditions are not met, abortion is legal if it is carried out by a doctor who genuinely believes that it must be done immediately in order to save your life or prevent serious permanent injury to your physical or mental health.

### How the Act works in practice

*As you can see, the law gives you no automatic right to an abortion.*
It is left to the 'discretion' of the doctor, and doctors are free to interpret the law as they see fit. In fact, a doctor could now authorize *any* abortion, because statistics show that abortion is safer than childbirth (there are two deaths for every 100,000 abortions and eighteen deaths for every 100,000 births) – so condition 1(a) is automatically fulfilled. But a doctor who believes that abortion is morally wrong would not see things that way. So we are left with a ridiculous situation whereby a woman who wants

an abortion is at the mercy of a doctor's personal prejudices and beliefs.

*But if you have money you can almost always get an abortion.* Some private clinics are very expensive (between £150 and £200 for early abortions, more for later ones), but you can get a relatively cheap abortion (about £105) through one of the non-profit-making agencies we have listed at the end of the section (pp. 232–3). Again, a late abortion will cost more.

*Getting an abortion on the National Health can be more difficult,* for two reasons:

1. You may not be able to find a National Health doctor who approves of abortion and is prepared to sign the form. In some parts of the country, very few doctors will. In 1977 a woman's chances of getting an abortion on the National Health were seven times greater in Newcastle than in Birmingham.
2. There are often long waiting lists and you may not be able to get a hospital bed before your pregnancy is too far advanced.

*The time factor is very important:* When you are less than twelve weeks pregnant it is easier and a lot safer to get an abortion. It can be very difficult (though not impossible) if you are more than twenty weeks pregnant, even if you are prepared to pay. This is because the foetus is bigger, making the operation more complex and more open to risk.

### What to do if you think you're pregnant (when you hadn't planned it)

1. Don't stop using contraceptives – you might be wrong.
2. When your period is two weeks overdue, have a pregnancy test (the test is not usually reliable until then). Don't wait any longer, hoping for the best. Abortion is simple and safe if it's done early. The sooner you find out whether you are pregnant, the longer you will have to decide what to do and to make the necessary arrangements. You can either go to your doctor for

the test, or to a private pregnancy testing clinic. Addresses of non-profit-making services are listed at the end of the section (pp. 232–3); commercial services (which charge about £5) are usually listed in the Yellow Pages of the telephone directory (under 'Pregnancy test services') and advertised in newspapers and magazines. Alternatively, you can buy a do-it-yourself kit, but these are not very reliable. A 'positive' result means you are pregnant; a 'negative' result usually means you're not.

3. If the result says you're not pregnant and your period still doesn't come, it may well have been wrong. It's best to have another test or see a doctor. If you miss two periods, you should definitely see a doctor. A positive result is very unlikely to be wrong.

4. If you find you are pregnant, don't panic or make any hasty decisions. Think about it carefully. If you are not absolutely sure what you want to do, try and talk it over with sympathetic people – perhaps with women who have had similar experiences. If you approach one of the organizations listed at the end of this section, they will help you make your decision: they won't push you into having an abortion if you are uncertain.

5. You don't have to have an abortion if you don't want one. If you are pregnant and single and you want to have the baby, you can contact the National Council for One-Parent Families (address on p. 233). It will put you in touch with people who can help while you are pregnant and after the baby is born.

6. You may want to have the child adopted: more about this on p. 358.

7. If you want an abortion, don't try and do it yourself. It can be very dangerous and it hardly ever works. 'Back-street' abortions, carried out by people who aren't doctors, are also dangerous.

8. If you want to try for a National Health abortion (that is, a free one) go to see your doctor. Try to get your own thoughts on the subject clear before you go, otherwise you may meet with hostile attitudes which could distress you or cause you to change your mind for no good reason. (Don't be alarmed! Not

all National Health doctors are uncooperative and yours may be very sympathetic.) If your doctor agrees to help you get an abortion, he will refer you to a gynaecologist for a second opinion. You may still have to wait some time before an abortion can be arranged. Remember that delay can be dangerous. If you are ten weeks pregnant and you don't have a National Health abortion lined up, it would be wiser to arrange a private abortion.

9. If you can't get a National Health abortion, or if you would rather pay and avoid the delay and complications you may encounter if you go through the National Health, go to one of the non-profit-making pregnancy advisory services. They may be able to help you get a National Health abortion even if you have been turned down; otherwise they will arrange a private abortion as cheaply as possible. They can usually help you out if you can't afford to pay, although they will ask you to try to raise the money first. Commercial pregnancy advisory services are in it to make money, so they charge a lot more. Addresses of non-profit-making services are listed at the end of this section (pp. 232–3).

10. If you are under 16 you can usually get an abortion through the National Health, although the doctor may insist on consulting your parents, even when you don't want them to know about it. If there is a Brook Advisory Centre in your area, try consulting them (address on p. 232).

11. If you are married, the doctor may ask for your husband's consent, but this may not be necessary, particularly if you have a private abortion. It is not required by law.

12. After you've had the abortion, make sure you have efficient contraception, so you don't run the same risk again – women often fail to do this. You should be able to get help from your doctor if you have a National Health abortion, or from the pregnancy advisory service (if it is a good one), or from your local family planning clinic. (See the section on contraception, p. 222.)

13. It's wise to go for a medical check-up a few months after you

have had the abortion. If you later decide that you want to have a baby, make sure that your doctor knows that you have had an abortion, as this can – very occasionally – cause complications.

## What are the different methods of abortion?

1. *Vacuum aspiration.* This is nearly always used if you are less than twelve weeks pregnant. The neck of the womb is usually dilated to take a small hollow tube of plastic or metal. The tube leads to a container from which the air has been removed, so that the contents of the womb are sucked out into the container. The procedure is simple, results in little blood loss, and can be carried out under a light general anaesthetic or local anaesthetic.
2. *Menstrual aspiration.* This is the term used for vacuum aspiration performed within six weeks of the last period and before a pregnancy test has been made; it is also known as menstrual evacuation or regulation. It is not yet in general use.
3. *Dilation and Curettage* (D and C). The cervix (neck of the womb) is dilated and the contents of the womb are scraped out with a small instrument called a 'curette'. The more advanced the pregnancy, the more the cervix needs to be stretched. The use of 'D and C' is declining, while vacuum aspiration is becoming more popular. 'D and C' needs a general anaesthetic.
4. *Prostaglandin induction.* For pregnancies over fourteen weeks a small catheter is inserted into the neck of the womb and a prostaglandin solution is fed into the uterus. This causes you to go into a minor form of labour. For later pregnancies the prostaglandin may be injected directly into the womb.
5. *Late terminations – over eighteen weeks.* These can be done by inserting a larger catheter into the neck of the womb and later, under a general anaesthetic, injecting adrenalin into the neck of the womb so that it has the effect of labour. Forceps are then used to evacuate the womb. The later the abortion, the greater the risk to your immediate health and of damage to the neck of the womb which can cause miscarriages in later pregnancies.

## Outpatient abortions

A few National Health hospitals and charitable agencies now provide out-patient facilities, so that women can have abortions in the first twelve weeks of pregnancy without staying in hospital overnight. There are many advantages: it can be far more convenient for the woman; it's cheaper; and it doesn't use up hospital beds. If it were more widespread there would be shorter waiting lists and more women could have early National Health abortions. Some London hospitals provide out-patient facilities (including the South London Hospital for Women, Kingston, King's College, Lewisham, the Samaritan Hospital for Women, and St Mary's, Paddington; one in Nottingham and another in Leeds). The British Pregnancy Advisory Service and the Pregnancy Advisory Service provide out-patient abortions.

## After the operation

Expect vaginal bleeding for a few days. It shouldn't be heavier than a period and it changes into a slight brown discharge. Mild period pains may be felt within the first few days. High temperatures, heavy bleeding and severe or persistent pains are signs that something is wrong – so make sure you see a doctor.

## Is abortion dangerous?

Since 1967 when abortion was made legal, the number of deaths from abortion has declined each year, even though the number of abortions has risen. In 1974 out of 163,000 legal abortions there were only six deaths, and mortality figures continue to fall.

As a general rule, abortion is entirely safe if carried out before the twelfth week of pregnancy, in clinical conditions. The vacuum aspiration method, with local anaesthetic, is safest of all. To minimize the danger, early abortion should be available to all women and to make this possible many more hospitals should provide out-patient facilities, and the law should be extended to give every woman the right to choose to end unwanted pregnancies.

### Sterilization with abortion

It is quite common for women who have abortions under the National Health Service to be sterilized at the same time. This happened to half the married women who had National Health abortions in 1971. If you have several children already, the doctor may try to persuade you to agree to be sterilized before he signs the form authorizing the abortion. Don't be blackmailed into it. You are quite free to refuse if you are in any doubt at all. You can't be sterilized unless you give your consent.

It may be more dangerous to be aborted and sterilized at the same time than to have either operation separately. If you want to be sterilized you can arrange to have it done later when you have had time to think it over. With modern techniques, it involves only a very small cut and forty-eight hours in hospital.

However, if you are paying to have a private abortion and you definitely want to be sterilized, it is usually cheaper to have both done at the same time. The British Pregnancy Advisory Service charges £104·50 for an abortion, £103 for separate sterilization, and £156·50 to have both done together. This may be worth considering if you live in an area where it is difficult to get sterilization on the National Health, either because of doctors' attitudes or because there is a long waiting list.
(More about sterilization on p. 221.)

### Recent moves to restrict women's rights to abortion

Since 1975 there have been five unsuccessful attempts to go back on the advances made in the 1967 Abortion Act – all by MPs introducing Private Members' Bills. James White's bill in 1975 was followed by William Benyon in 1977 and Sir Bernard Brain in 1978. In 1980 John Corrie introduced his Abortion Amendment Bill. The main points in these bills concerned:

1. The upper time limit for legal abortion, at present twenty-eight weeks. It was proposed that this be lowered to twenty weeks.
2. The status of charitable pregnancy advisory agencies in abortion counselling services. The bills threatened to get rid of these valuable services.
3. More delaying factors in seeking abortion. For example, James White's bill proposed that the two doctors who consent to the abortion should each have been in practice for at least five years and should not be in practice together.
4. Making it easier for doctors and nurses who object to abortion to opt out. It was not proposed, however, to help women affected by doctors and nurses opting out. For example, it could have been suggested that conscientious objectors referred women to other medical practitioners who would provide them with the services they needed.

These proposals may sound fairly innocuous, but their effect is bound to be restrictive. If any of them have been put into practice by the time you read this, your rights to abortion, described in this chapter, will be diminished. And Britain will have taken a backward step while the rest of Europe is moving forward. Even Roman Catholic countries such as Italy, where the traditional opposition to abortion has been far stronger than in Britain, are passing relatively liberal abortion laws.

The bills were supported by large and highly organized campaigns run by the Society for the Protection of Unborn Children and other organizations such as *Life*, which are backed by the Roman Catholic Church. The aim of the campaigns was to persuade MPs and the public that the 1967 Act was being abused and should therefore be tightened up. There were allegations of widespread profiteering, late abortions, women being forced to have abortions against their will, foetal material being sold to manufacturers of soap and other products, and live foetuses being used for experiments. These allegations have been exposed as false.

To defend and extend women's right to abortion in the face of these attacks the National Abortion Campaign rallied the support of many thousands of men and women against the bills in 1975, 1977 and 1978. The opposition to John Corrie's bill was even more wide-ranging, including groups as varied as the BMA, Doctors for a Woman's Choice on Abortion, the Methodist Board of Social Responsibility, Christians for Free Choice, Tories for Free Choice – and the TUC, which sponsored a massive demonstration supported by the other organizations in October 1979. This was followed in February 1980 with a lobby of Parliament of some 20,000 women and men opposed to the Corrie bill. The bill was finally defeated on 14 March 1980. David Alton, a Roman Catholic MP, then attempted to introduce a 10-minute rule bill to reduce the time limit for abortions to twenty-four weeks. This attempt failed even to get support for a vote at its first reading in the House of Commons. However, few women doubted that further attempts would be made to restrict their abortion rights.

### Useful addresses

(In 1980, prices for abortion ranged from about £100 to £200, late operations being more expensive, and a vasectomy cost around £50. *Check current prices*.)

*British Pregnancy Advisory Service*, headquarters at Austy Manor, Wootton Wawen, Solihull, West Midlands B95 6DA (05642 3225). Runs thirteen full-time and eleven part-time advisory clinics, and four nursing homes. Main telephone numbers: London – 01 222 0985; Brighton – 0273 509726; Birmingham – 021 643 1461; Cardiff – 0222 372389. Charitable organization for counselling, pregnancy testing, abortion, sterilization, vasectomy, artificial insemination.

*Pregnancy Advisory Service*, 40 Margaret Street, London W1 (01 409 1281). Charitable organization for pregnancy testing, counselling, abortion.

*Brook Advisory Centres*: London headquarters at 153a East Street, London SE17 (01 708 1234). Other Brook Centres at 233 Tottenham Court Road, London W1, and in Coventry, Bristol, Birmingham, Cambridge, Liverpool and Edinburgh – addresses in local telephone directories. Charitable organization funded by the NHS, for contraceptive advice, counselling, pregnancy testing and abortion referrals.

*Marie Stopes House, 'The Well Woman Centre'*, 108 Whitfield Street, London W1 (01 388 0662). Charitable organization for contraception, pregnancy testing, counselling, abortion, sterilization, vasectomy, help with minor gynaecological problems, psychosexual therapy.

*Release*, 1 Elgin Avenue, London W9 (01 289 1123). Arranges reasonably priced private abortions.

*Family Planning Association*: headquarters at 27–35 Mortimer Street, London W1 (01 636 7866); eleven regional branches. General birth control information service.

*National Council for One-Parent Families*, 255 Kentish Town Road, London NW5 (01 267 1361). Practical help and counselling for single parents and single pregnant women.

*National Abortion Campaign*, 374 Gray's Inn Road, London WC1 (01 278 0153). Campaigns for a woman's right to choose when to have children.

*CO-ORD, The Co-ordinating Committee in Defence of the 1967 Abortion Act*, 27–35 Mortimer Street, London W1 (01 580 9360).

# Rape

## *When is rape a crime?*

A man commits rape if he has sexual intercourse with a woman who is not his wife; and the woman does not at the time consent to it; and he knows at the time that she does not consent or he doesn't care whether she consents or not. Rape can take place without overt violence. Penetration, however slight, with or without ejaculation, counts as sexual intercourse.

*Boys under 14* are assumed in law to be incapable of sexual intercourse, so they cannot be convicted of rape. They may, however, be found guilty of attempted rape.

### Can a man rape his wife?

If a man has sexual intercourse with his wife without her consent he is not guilty of rape. The law assumes that 'in marriage she hath given up her body to her husband'. The only circumstances where you might be able to prove to a court that your husband raped you are:

1. You have obtained a separation order from a magistrates' court which contains a non-cohabitation clause. This means you no longer have a legal duty to live with your husband.
2. You and your husband have decided to separate and you have both signed a separation agreement in which he undertakes not to molest you.
3. You have started divorce proceedings and have been granted an injunction which forbids your husband to molest you. However, if you have filed a divorce petition and your case has not yet been heard, and you have not been granted an injunction, your husband cannot be guilty of rape.
4. You have been granted a decree nisi in divorce proceedings.

If your husband forces you to have sexual intercourse against your will and injures you, he may be guilty of assault. If you want a divorce, you should be able to use this as evidence of his 'unreasonable behaviour'.

A man may be found guilty of aiding and abetting another man to rape his wife – even if the other man is acquitted.

### Can a woman commit rape?

A woman cannot be found guilty of raping a man or a woman. She can, however, be found guilty of indecent assault, or of aiding and abetting a man to commit rape.

### How often does rape occur?

The incidence of rape has increased considerably over recent years, although no faster than the rate of violent crime generally. Between 1969 and 1973, the total number of violent crimes in Britain increased from 20,855 to 33,041. During the same period, the total number of rapes known to the police in the Metropolitan area increased from 869 to 998. More recent figures show that in 1978 there were 1,243 indictable offences of rape recorded by the police, compared with 1,015 in 1977 and 1,094 in 1976. People who have studied rape in the United States and Britain estimate that actual incidence of rape – including those that are not reported – is far higher.

### What must be proved to the court?

Before a guilty verdict can be reached in a rape trial, the prosecution – for which you are the chief witness – must convince the jury of four things:

1. That sexual intercourse took place.
2. That the man you accused of rape was the one who did it.
3. That you did not consent at the time of the rape.
4. That the man knew at the time of the rape that you did not consent, or didn't care whether you consented or not.

If it is clear that you had sexual intercourse with the accused man at the time you claim you were raped, the prosecution will still have to persuade the jury that you did not consent. In a case of this kind, the defence will normally try to prove *either* that you did consent, *or* that the man mistakenly believed you consented. The question of consent in rape trials can be extremely difficult to settle. Neutral witnesses and indisputable evidence are seldom available, so it becomes a matter of your word against the man's.

*The man's belief in your consent need not be reasonable, as long as it is genuine.* In the now famous case of *D.P.P. vs Morgan* which came before the House of Lords in 1975, the Law Lords decided that a man should not be found guilty of rape if he *honestly* believed the woman consented, no matter how unreasonable his belief might have been. The decision sparked off a fierce controversy and was the subject of much misunderstanding, so it requires further explanation. The facts of the case were these:

An RAF Sergeant, William Morgan, had invited three junior aircraftsmen to his house to have intercourse with his wife. He told them she might struggle but that they should not take her seriously, since she only pretended to resist in order to increase her own excitement. Mrs Morgan was not, in fact, a willing party to the attack, but the aircraftsmen claimed they believed she was. They were convicted of rape and sentenced to three years' imprisonment. Sergeant Morgan got seven years for aiding and abetting. They appealed and the case went to the House of Lords because it involved an important point of law. The Law Lords ruled that it was a proper defence to claim honest but unreasonable belief in the woman's consent, but upheld the convictions of the four men on the ground that no jury would have accepted their story in preference to that of Mrs Morgan.

Many people feared that it would become possible for any man to get away with rape just by telling the court that he believed the woman consented. However, this defence could only be used in a small minority of exceptional cases.

In fact, the Law Lords' decision upholds an important legal principle: that no person should be convicted of a serious crime which he or she did not *intend* to commit. In very exceptional circumstances, it might be possible for a man to hold a genuine belief, based on unreasonable grounds, that the woman consented to sexual intercourse. It would be very difficult to persuade the court that this was so: he would have to admit that the woman *did not* consent and then show that he believed at the time – without good reason – that she *did*. But if his belief was genuine and he

Furthermore, my client pleads that he was grossly provoked by his imagination

convinces a jury of this, he should be acquitted, since it would be unjust to convict a man who did not knowingly commit a rape. Of course, it would be of little consolation to any woman to know that her attacker had made a mistake.

The controversy which followed the *Morgan* decision concerned other issues as well. Women were rightly angry about the way rape cases were conducted. At the time, the law on rape had many unpleasant and unjust aspects, including:

1. During a trial where the woman's consent was the crucial issue, it was common for the barrister defending the man to ask the woman detailed questions about her previous sexual experiences and to make all sorts of allegations about her morals and life-style – with a view to persuading the jury that she was the sort of person who might have provoked, invited or imagined the attack.
2. It was also common for the victim's name and details of her personal life to be published in the press – often in a style which suggested that *she* was the one on trial.
3. The way rape trials were conducted and reported perpetuated certain myths about women, for instance:

- that women who were not virgins or faithful wives deserved what they got;
- that women who went out alone, hitch-hiked or wore revealing clothes invited attack;
- that men couldn't help themselves if they were 'provoked': they simply had to give vent to their natural virility;
- that women often imagined they had been raped, because secretly they longed for it to happen to them.

4. All this could make the process of reporting rape to the police and going to court an extremely gruelling and humiliating experience for the victim. As a result, many were deterred from coming forward and reporting the incident.

## The new law concerning rape

As a result of strong protests from women's organizations and some MPs, the Home Secretary appointed an advisory group, headed by Rose Heilbron, the High Court judge, to look into the law on rape. When the group reported in November 1975, it supported the Law Lords' decision in *D.P.P. vs Morgan* and recommended a number of changes in the law. Most of these were presented to Parliament by Robin Corbett, MP, in a Private Member's Bill, which had Home Office support. It became law in 1976. The main provisions of the Sexual Offences (Amendment) Act are these:

1. The new legal definition of rape makes it clear that the crime can take place without overt violence, or when the man does not care whether the woman consented or not.

2. Once a woman has told the police that she has been raped, it is illegal to publish her name in connection with the complaint, or other information likely to identify her. The only possible exception is where the man's lawyer gets permission from the judge to publish the woman's name to encourage essential defence witnesses to come forward.

3. The name of the accused man cannot be published until he is found guilty.

4. The woman may not be questioned in court about her sexual reputation or sexual experience with men other than the accused; nor may the accused man give evidence about this. There are two exceptions:

(a) When the man's lawyer can persuade the judge that he has evidence to show that the woman has previously behaved in a way that is similar to the way she behaved at the time of the alleged rape and that this evidence is crucial because it shows that the woman has particular sexual habits that are relevant to the defence. (For instance, that she went to a pub every Friday night and picked up a different man and took him back to her room to have sex with him, as she did at the time of the alleged rape.)

(b) If the woman or another prosecution witness claims that she (the alleged victim) is 'of good character' in sexual matters, the man's lawyer can then bring evidence to show that this is not true. In the eyes of the court, a woman is 'of good character' if she is a virgin, celibate or an indisputably faithful wife.

### What happens when you report a rape?

If you are raped and you report it to the police you will probably be asked to go straight to the police station to make a statement. You may have to spend several hours answering detailed questions about the attack and the circumstances which led to it – even if you are still in a distressed state. The police may be kind and helpful; on the other hand, you may find that they treat you in an unsympathetic manner. *Their* priority is to establish the facts of the case to decide whether it is worth prosecuting the man. They are not primarily concerned with helping you, the victim, overcome your distress.

You will be examined by a doctor, to find out whether intercourse or other sexual acts have taken place and whether there are any signs that the man used force or that you struggled to resist. The doctor will probably ask you questions about your medical history and he may also ask about your sex life. One London doctor who examines rape victims for the police explains why: 'We always ask the woman how often she has had intercourse, whether she has had an abortion, if she has had a child, when her last period was due. All these factors are important because they have a bearing on what shows up during in internal examination. For instance, if she has had "violent" sex recently, or an abortion, this may have caused bruising.' If you delay in reporting to the police, it may be more difficult to establish medical evidence of rape, particularly if you have had a bath since the attack occurred.

The police will probably not prosecute the man unless one or more of the following kinds of evidence are available:

1. A witness, other than yourself, who heard or saw the attack, or heard or saw evidence of it;
2. Medical evidence;
3. A recent complaint, i.e. you must have complained of rape soon after the attack occurred, either to the police or to another person who can act as a witness in court.

If the police decide to go ahead with the prosecution, they will send your written statement and the results of your medical examination to the man's lawyers before the trial. You will probably be cross-examined on this evidence in court.

You will not have to give oral evidence in court if the man pleads guilty. If he does not, you may have to give evidence (a) at the preliminary hearing in the magistrates' court; and (b) at the jury trial in the crown court. If you decide you don't want to appear, the police have power to issue a witness summons ordering you to come to court; if you fail to do so, you may be fined or imprisoned for contempt of court. Or, as often happens in practice, the case may be dropped.

### Deciding whether to report to the police

If rape victims don't report to the police, the result will be to encourage those rapists who get away with it to do it again and to encourage a general attitude that rape is a crime which the law does not reach. But considering the ordeal that many victims have gone through once they have reported the crime, it is not surprising that some women prefer to remain silent. Under the new law, rape trials should be a less gruelling experience for the victim and, hopefully, more now feel able to approach the police. In any event it's up to *you* to decide. If you feel it would be too distressing remember that you have no legal obligation to report the attack.

### How rape victims should be helped

Almost all rape victims need help which the legal authorities do not provide: help to deal with the sense of fear and degradation which so often follows the experience of rape; sympathetic medical and legal advice; and someone to talk to who has a real understanding of their predicament. There is evidence that women who do not have a chance to talk about their experience may sustain lasting mental damage, particularly in the area of their relationships with men. There are few professionals with much experience of helping rape victims in this country, and indeed many victims find it more helpful to talk to a woman friend or to another woman who has been raped. The problem is that they often don't know how to get this kind of help.

Social services departments should make proper provision for helping rape victims, by giving special training to social workers and by ensuring that counselling is available in an emergency. Women who have sexual problems resulting from being raped should be referred to a 'psychosexual specialist', i.e. a doctor who has special experience in helping with sexual problems.

When a woman reports rape to the police, she should be questioned by a woman officer. Policewomen should refer victims to local social services departments which should, in turn, provide them with help and support in overcoming their distress, and with practical advice.

### The Rape Crisis Centre

A group of women called the Rape Counselling and Research Group set up the Rape Crisis Centre in London in 1976. Following the example of women in the United States, who have set up similar centres in most major U.S. cities, they provide counselling, medical and legal advice, a 24-hour phone service, and support for women who go through the legal process. They also give talks to schools and other groups, with the aim of 'de-mythologizing and de-glamorizing' the subject of rape. Between March 1976 and October 1980 they gave help to more than 1,900 women who had been raped or sexually assaulted. In 1981 they had two full-time workers and three part-timers, with a support collective of about thirty members. Rape Crisis Centres have also been set up in Edinburgh (031 556 9437), Glasgow (041 331 2811), Nottingham (0602 410440), Leeds (0532 440058), Tyneside (0632 29858), Birmingham (021 233 2122), Coventry (0203 57709), Canterbury (0227 50400), (Oxford (0865 726295), Liverpool (051 709 1938) and Manchester (061 228 33602).

To contact the Rape Crisis Centre, telephone 01 340 6145 (24-hour phone) or 01 340 6913 during office hours; or write to them c/o P.O. Box 42, London N6 5BU.

### Further reading

*Against Our Will*, Susan Brownmiller, Penguin Books.

*The Facts of Rape*, Barbara Toner, Hutchinson.

## Lesbianism

There are no laws against lesbianism between women over 16. Male homosexuality, on the other hand, was strictly against the law until 1967, when it was made legal, but only if practised between two consenting men over 21 in private. The story goes that Queen Victoria, in whose reign male homosexuality was outlawed, could not believe that women indulged in such practices and therefore refused to consider a law against it. So it may be thanks to her that gay women are not penalized for their sexual preferences. However, this doesn't prevent them meeting discrimination in employment and housing. The Sex Discrimination Act does not outlaw discrimination on grounds of sexual orientation.

A man can divorce his wife for 'unreasonable behaviour' if he finds that she is lesbian.

### Lesbian mothers

The courts are very unlikely to grant custody of children to a homosexual parent. So if you are a lesbian mother and you are separated or divorced from the father of your children, it is best to try to reach an agreement with him that the children should stay with you and that he should have access (if that is what you want). If you cannot agree and have to go to court over it, you face a serious problem. Judges think homosexuality is a bad thing and should be discouraged as far as possible. Most of them also appear to know little about it and have absurd misconceptions – believing, for instance, that true lesbian women do not really love their children. They have irrational fears that children will be 'harmed' if they are brought up in a homosexual household, by learning to accept homosexuality as normal or (worse still) by becoming homosexual or otherwise sexually 'deviant'. They fear, too, that children might be teased or ostracized at school.

A typical case was reported in the *Guardian* (7 August 1975):

Last January, Pamela Bingham applied for custody of her 8-year-old daughter, Sally. Her former husband, David, contested her application. Pamela had been looking after Sally since the marriage broke up. The judge accepted that she had cared for her well and would treat her kindly; and that she and David were equally capable of providing a suitable home. A psychiatrist was called as an expert witness and recommended that Sally should remain with Pamela. Sally herself said she wanted to stay with her mother.

Since she parted from David, Pamela has been living with a woman in a lesbian relationship. David had also been living with a woman – he had remarried. The view from the Bench was that Pamela lacked 'femininity'; had a strong personality and a certain ruthlessness; and would not 'sacrifice her lesbian proclivities' for the sake of the child. Lesbianism, according to the judge, was unnatural and would give Sally an unhealthy attitude; her school friends might find out and taunt her with it. David was noted to be 'less intelligent' than Pamela, but to have 'hard-working habits'. His new wife made a very favourable impression.

The judge concluded that Sally would have a healthier and happier life with her father. Custody, care and control were duly awarded to David.

Eighteen months later, Sally was clearly miserable living with her father and the case was returned to the same judge who (with great reluctance) awarded custody to the mother. At around the same time (late 1976) another lesbian woman won custody of her children in a disputed case. These two cases can be taken as a sign that some judges' attitudes may be changing. But the odds are still heavily against any homosexual parents being thought fit to look after their own children. None of the fears which judges entertain about lesbian mothers has any reasonable foundation, since there has been no research which proves that children brought up in homosexual households are more likely to be sexually deviant or unhappy than any other children. If it were not generally believed in our society that heterosexuality is better than homosexuality because it is more widespread, there would be no reason for courts to treat homosexual parents differently from others. (More about custody on pp. 314–23.)

## Prostitution

Prostitution itself is not illegal. That is, it is not against the law for a woman over 16 to have sexual intercourse with a man in return for payment. Some marriages amount to little more than that.

But it *is* illegal to pick up a man in a street or public place for the purposes of prostitution. Call-girls, whose appointments are arranged by phone, cannot be touched by law, although those responsible for procuring girls for the business or living on their earnings can be prosecuted. Meanwhile, the call-girl's poorer sister who relies on casual pickups in Piccadilly or on Tooting Bec Common is likely to be hauled off to the magistrates' court if she is spotted by a policeman. What the eye doesn't see the heart doesn't grieve over.

A policeman can arrest a woman, without a warrant, if he reasonably suspects her of *both* of the following:

1. Being a 'common prostitute', that is, someone who has previously been cautioned for soliciting, but has persisted in doing so; *and*
2. Loitering or soliciting in a street or public place for the purposes of prostitution.

The first time a policeman sees you 'loitering or soliciting', he cannot arrest you, but he can caution you. The caution can be written down in the police records and quoted against you. If you are cautioned and you do not accept the accusation, you should apply to your nearest magistrates' court within fourteen days to have your record cleared. At the hearing, which is in private, the police have to prove that you were 'loitering or soliciting' at the time, and unless the court is satisfied that you were, it will order the caution to be struck from the record.

If the caution stays on your record, you are labelled a 'common prostitute' and a policeman can arrest you if he sees you 'loitering or soliciting' again. On a first arrest, the fine is likely to be small. But if you come before the court again and again, you may eventually be imprisoned. About 12 per cent of the prisoners in Holloway are there for charges connected with prostitution.

The laws against prostitution are often used by managers of hotels, cafés and restaurants as a pretext for not serving women late at night if they are unaccompanied by men. However, now that the Sex Discrimination Act has been passed, it is illegal to refuse to serve any woman in these circumstances, unless there are very good reasons for suspecting that she herself is a prostitute (see p. 402).

It is *not* a crime for a man to hire a woman for prostitution. It is *not* a crime for a man to solicit a woman in a street or public place, for instance by 'kerb crawling'. However, it is an offence for a man to solicit another man, either on his own behalf or on behalf of a woman.

You can be accused of soliciting if you are not actually in a street or public place, as long as you can be seen from there, as this case shows:

A woman called Alfrida Burridge was charged with soliciting by the Southampton police, who said they had seen her sitting for about fifty minutes on a high stool in a bay window, dressed in a mini-skirt and low-cut top and illuminated by a red light. During that time she hadn't spoken or gestured to anyone in the street. She had previously been cautioned and convicted for soliciting and therefore labelled as a 'common prostitute'. She was acquitted at first but her case went to the Court of Appeal in 1975, when she was found guilty on the ground that there was evidence that she had been 'tempting and alluring prospective customers'.

**FURTHER INFORMATION**

English Collective of Prostitutes, P.O. Box 287, London NW6.

# 5. Marriage

## Getting married or living together: the pros and cons

Obviously nothing we say will stop you doing whatever you feel like doing, but we thought it might help to point out some of the practical advantages and disadvantages of both. The 'unmarried' column assumes you are living with one man on a fairly permanent basis.

| *Advantages of being married* | *Disadvantages of being unmarried* |
|---|---|
| Most people still do it this way. If you are a conformist by nature, you may find it simpler. | This is more unusual. There are social pressures towards getting married. And what do you call him? Man? Husband? Lover? There isn't a word which describes the relationship adequately and many couples end up referring to each other as 'husband' and 'wife', with the woman adopting the man's name. |
| If you have children, the law assumes that your husband is their father, and he is responsible for supporting them, even if you get divorced. | If you want to claim maintenance from the father of your children, you must either take affiliation proceedings within three years of the birth, or prove that he has paid maintenance during that time. |

## Advantages of being married

If you divorce or separate, you can claim maintenance for yourself and your children.

Some landlords insist that couples should be married before they rent accommodation.

If you get divorced, you have certain rights to stay in the home until you are divorced as well as a claim on the family home.

## Disadvantages of being unmarried

If you separate, you can claim maintenance for your children but not for yourself.

You may have to pretend that you are married in order to get accommodation, unless you can find a sympathetic landlord.

You have few legal rights to occupy the home if it is in the man's name. If you separate, you will probably have to leave. (But if you have made a financial contribution or helped improve the home, or if you have children, you may be able to claim a share of its value.)

*Advantages of being married*

The tax position is more favourable if you are married. Your husband can claim a married man's tax allowance, and if you are working you get earned-income relief, which amounts to a single person's tax allowance. So between you, you can earn an extra £770 before tax. (You can't do this if you are very rich, but instead you can be taxed as single people so you don't lose out.)

If your own National Insurance record is incomplete you may be able to draw a pension based on your husband's record, which is higher than the pension you could get from your own contributions.

If you cannot get a maternity grant on your own insurance, you may be able to get one on your husband's. (But you will get one anyway after July 1982.)

*Disadvantages of being unmarried*

The man only gets a single person's tax allowance, unless you are looking after his children, in which case he can claim an allowance for you as an 'adult dependant' but then you would not be in a position to get earned-income relief.

You cannot claim a pension on the man's insurance.

You can only get a maternity grant on your own insurance – until July 1982, when you get one anyway.

Even though you are single, you cannot claim supplementary benefit as a single person if you are found to be living with a man. You are supposed to rely on him to support you.

*Advantages of being married*

If your husband dies, you inherit most or all of his property (if he has any).

You are entitled to widow's benefits.

In employment and training, the Sex Discrimination Act makes it illegal to treat a married woman less favourably than a single woman.

*Disadvantages of being unmarried*

You may find you have no claim to the man's property when he dies, unless he has left you something in a will or he has been supporting you and you make a claim to court.

You get no widow's benefits.

The Sex Discrimination Act does *not* make it illegal to treat a single woman less favourably than a married woman in any circumstances.

*Disadvantages of being married*

You have to pay £13 for a marriage licence.

In order to be unmarried, you have to go through a divorce.

If you go out to work, you may find it difficult to get a suitable job or promotion because employers will assume that you are going to have children – although in theory this would be unlawful under the Sex Discrimination Act.

*Advantages of being unmarried*

You save £13.

If you want to separate, you don't need a divorce.

Employers do not automatically assume that you are going to leave to have children (although they may assume that you're going to get married).

## Disadvantages of being married

Unless you have money (in which case you can buy most things), or unless you know a sympathetic doctor, you will probably need your husband's consent before you can get a coil fitted or have an abortion or sterilization.

If you and your husband have a serious dispute over your children you will have to go to court to settle the matter.

Until you get a divorce, you cannot normally get your husband to leave your home, even if you own it.

Your income is treated as part of your husband's for tax purposes. You cannot easily conceal your earnings from him. Tax allowances for mortgage payments will normally go to him and he will get your tax rebates, unless you apply for a separate assessment.

You cannot claim extra sickness or unemployment benefits for your husband or children (unless your husband

## Advantages of being unmarried

Your body is your own. You will not need the man's consent in order to get a coil or have an abortion or sterilization.

If you have children, you have sole parental rights over them. The man cannot legally overrule any decisions you make concerning them, unless he has a court order giving him access or custody.

If you own the home, you can throw the man out at any time.

You are taxed as a single person and you have complete control over your financial affairs. You can normally get a tax allowance for your children, unless you are receiving maintenance for them.

You have full rights under the National Insurance scheme and get full sickness and unemployment benefit. If you

*Disadvantages of being married*

is disabled and incapable of earning a living). If you have been relying on your husband's insurance because you took the married woman's option before May 1977, you cannot draw a pension until he retires and then you get less than a single person; and you are not entitled to any sickness or unemployment benefit.

You cannot claim supplementary benefit in your own right. Your husband has to claim the married couple's rate and you get less than a single person.

*Advantages of being unmarried*

have children, you can claim extra benefits for them.

You can claim supplementary benefit in your own right and you are entitled to the full single person's rate, as long as they don't find out you are living with a man.

### Legal status of a common law wife or cohabitee

The law in England and Wales does not recognize the 'common law wife' (although it does in Scotland, as explained on p. 506). Either a woman is legally wed with all the advantages or disadvantages that it entails or she is a 'spinster' living in an unlawful union with a man, in which case the law affords her little protection. Recently, however, there have been signs that the law is a little more favourably inclined towards 'mistresses' or 'concubines', as some judges.call them. (The case described on p. 385 is evidence of this.)

## Getting married under 18

You can't get married until you are 16.

If you are under 18, you can't get married without your parents' consent. If you are a ward of court you will need the consent of the court. You will need the consent of both your parents except in the following circumstances:

1. Your parents are divorced or separated: in this case you will need the consent of the parent who has been awarded custody of you.
2. One of your parents has deserted the other: you will need the consent of the parent who has been deserted.
3. You have been placed in the care of the local authority: you will need the local authority's consent.
4. You are adopted: you will need the consent of your adoptive parents.
5. One of your parents cannot give consent (e.g. because she or he cannot be traced or is mentally disabled): the Superintendent Registrar or the Church authority can let you get married with the consent of the other parent only. But if the consent of that parent is not needed for another reason (because of divorce, for instance), you will need special permission from a higher authority – from the Registrar-General if you are getting married in a registry office; or from the Master of Faculties, if you want a church wedding. Your Citizens' Advice Bureau will tell you where the nearest registry office is. Ask your local vicar how to contact the appropriate Church authorities.
6. If you have been married already and widowed, you can marry without your parents' consent, even if you're still under 18.

IF YOUR PARENTS REFUSE CONSENT

You may apply to the magistrates' court, the county court or the High Court for consent. It is easiest to apply to the magistrates' court. You can go along any morning at ten o'clock and tell the magistrates that you want to marry. A date will be fixed for your case to be heard and it will take place in private, although your parents can be present.

GETTING MARRIED IN SCOTLAND

If you are 16 or over you can get married without your parents' consent anywhere in Scotland. Gretna Green is close to the border, which is why it has become so famous. At least one of you must stay in Scotland for fifteen days to meet the residence qualification, and the Registrar will publish notice of your intended marriage. If you want to know more there's a useful leaflet, *Marriage in Scotland*, available from the Scottish Office, Dover House, Whitehall, London SW1 (01 233 3000).

IF YOU LIE ABOUT YOUR AGE

in order to get married without your parents' consent, you may be prosecuted for making a false statement, but this will not invalidate the marriage (as long as you are 16 or over).

IF YOU MANAGE TO GET MARRIED WITHOUT YOUR PARENTS' CONSENT,

your marriage is valid anyway, provided you are 16 or over.

ONCE YOU ARE 18

you are free to marry without your parents' consent.

## Outline of a married woman's rights
### *The Sex Discrimination Act*

It is illegal to treat a married person less favourably than a single person, in employment and training. It is also illegal to treat a married woman less favourably than a married man (see p. 41 for details).

### Changing your name

Most women adopt their husband's surname when they marry. In fact, there is nothing in law that says you have to (nor, incidentally, that you have to wear a wedding ring at any time). It is entirely up to you. You can keep your own name or you can combine it with your husband's in a double-barrelled name – although if this idea catches on in a big way one could imagine difficulties for future generations.

If you take your husband's name you can keep it after you get divorced and even after you remarry, if you want to.

You can change your name at any time, just by calling yourself by your new name. But there are times when you might need official-looking proof of your new name, to show your bank or the Passport Office, for instance. You can get this by swearing a statement before a Commissioner of Oaths. A solicitor can prepare the statement for you. This should not cost more than £20. It is known as a 'statutory declaration'. You can also change your name by deed poll, a more complex procedure. Some professional bodies require this as proof of a name change. You'll need your husband's written consent, 'unless good cause is shown to the contrary' and you must reveal your marital status. A man need not do so; he can even change his wife's name without her consent.

Afternoon Mrs Bloggs-Brown-Smith

If you and your husband have children, they will be given his name and you won't be able to change that without his consent, even when you have separated or divorced him, unless the court gives you permission – which it very rarely does.

If you dislike being asked your marital status on official forms, where men are not asked the same question, there is no reason why you should reply – unless you can see that the information is absolutely relevant. It may help to write a note by the question, explaining that your marital status is not relevant in the circumstances.

The title 'Ms' is gradually becoming more acceptable in official circles.

## Sex

When the Sexual Offences (Amendment) Bill was first introduced to Parliament, it made rape within marriage illegal in the same circumstances as rape outside marriage. But this part of the bill was deleted before it became law. However, in 1980 the Criminal Law Revision Committee recommended that rape within the marriage should be made illegal. At present your husband cannot normally be prosecuted for rape if he forces you to have sexual intercourse against your will, unless you are divorced or have a separation order which includes a 'non-cohabitation' clause – because, as far as the law is concerned, when you marry a man you consent to have sexual intercourse with him while you are married. But if he makes unreasonable sexual demands on you (or none at all, for that matter), you may be able to use this as grounds for divorce (see pp. 285–6).

## The family home and other possessions

Since 1882, married women have been allowed to own property. But while you are married you have no right to a share of any of your husband's property. You can only claim a share when you get divorced. If your husband buys a house, you would be better off if it were purchased in both your names and not in his name alone. But whether it is in your name or not, you have a right to stay in the home for as long as your marriage lasts, and possibly longer. A married woman's rights to the family home are explained in detail on p. 371.

If you and your husband disagree about who owns what, you have a legal right to the following:

1. Anything you own at the date of your marriage and anything you buy with your money during the marriage.
2. Anything your husband buys and gives to you or puts in your name, such as a house or a car, unless he can prove that he didn't give it to you. If he disputed your claim, you would have to present some proof that he gave it to you, such as an entry in a diary, a note that went with the gift, or evidence from someone else who saw him give it to you.
3. Any money, stocks or shares that have been deposited into a bank in your name – or into a joint account with your husband, in which case you may be entitled to half.
4. You would normally be joint owner of anything purchased from a joint bank account or other pooled resources.

You would not have a right to money paid by your husband as a guarantee against your overdraft, or as a surety for a mortgage you are paying.

Your husband does not usually have a right to money, stocks or shares you have deposited into a bank in his name, except where you are being maintained by him and he is receiving an income from your property with your knowledge and consent.

### Money matters

As a married woman, you have a right to your own income and your own bank account. But when it comes to tax, your income is treated as though it belonged to your husband, unless you apply for separate assessment (more about that on p. 122).

During the time that you are married, you have no right to any part of your husband's income and capital, beyond the fact that he has a duty to maintain you (and you him). You can only claim a share when you get a divorce or decree of judicial separation.

### BANK ACCOUNTS

On the whole, it's best to have a joint bank account with your husband if you are dependent on him; and best to have your own bank account if you have an independent income. If you have your own bank account, the money in it belongs to you. If you have a joint bank account and you and your husband disagree about who has a right to the money in it, your claim will depend on the following factors:

1. If you have been paying in sums from time to time, you will normally be entitled to half the money in the account, even if you've paid in less than half. Likewise, your husband will be entitled to half, even if you have paid in more than him.
2. If you haven't paid anything into the account and you have simply been drawing out money to cover household expenses, it could be decided that your husband had opened the account as a convenient method of managing his household affairs and had not intended to give half the money to you – in which case you would not be entitled to any of the money.
3. If you have paid all the money into the account and your husband contributed nothing, it will probably be decided that all the money belongs to you.

### HOUSEKEEPING MONEY

There was a time when anything a married woman bought or saved out of her housekeeping money actually belonged to her husband. Back in 1949, a woman called Mrs Hoddenott won some money on a football pool which she had paid for with savings from her housekeeping money. She bought some furniture with the winnings and it was later decided in court that her husband owned that furniture. But the law was changed in 1964. You now have a right to *half* of anything you save, buy, or win out of your housekeeping money, unless you and your husband agree to the contrary. This ruling does not apply to money your husband gives you for other purposes, such as a dress allowance, nor does it apply to money you give him (which is all his).

NATIONAL INSURANCE

As a married woman you may have opted out of paying National Insurance contributions, as explained on p. 133.

## Children

You and your husband have equal custody of your children and you are equally responsible for maintaining them. If you have a dispute over them, the matter will have to be decided in court. The court's decision will rest on what is best for the welfare of the children. More about children on p. 314.

## Entering into contracts

You have as much right as a single woman to make contracts where and when you please (although this wasn't always so). However, you may find that the people you are most likely to want to make contracts with, such as hire purchase companies and landlords, still ask for your husband's signature. If they do this just because you are a woman and not because you have little or no income of your own, they are breaking the law (see p. 402).

If your husband *does* sign a contract for you, he is responsible for paying any debts that you might incur as a result.

If you come to an agreement with your husband in the normal course of domestic events – say for example that he promised to pay you a certain amount of housekeeping money each week – the agreement probably won't be legally binding. The only way you could make it legally binding would be to draw up a contract (you would need a solicitor's advice), and this might make it possible to sue for breach of contract.

### Leaving the country

You can get a passport without your husband's consent, even if you were previously on his passport. If you are on your husband's passport, you must submit his passport with your application form to the passport office. If you can't get hold of it, you must give the passport office your husband's name and last known address and they will have to write to him and ask for it.

You can put your children on your passport, or get them separate passports without your husband's consent. More about that on p. 320.

You can use the title 'Ms' on your passport.

### 'Domicile'

'Domicile' does not have anything to do with citizenship or nationality: it is a legal term which implies that a person intends to settle permanently in a particular country. It only becomes important if you want to take legal action, as it determines where the case can be tried. Before the law was changed in 1973, a married woman automatically had the same 'domicile' as her husband, even if she was living in another country. Therefore, a woman living in England could not start divorce proceedings against her husband if he was living abroad, except in special circumstances.

A married woman now has a right to her own domicile. She can start divorce proceedings in England or Wales if she has her permanent home there or if she has lived there for one year immediately before she starts proceedings – no matter where her husband is.

## Citizenship

If you are not a citizen of the United Kingdom and you marry a man who is, you can apply for U.K. citizenship. If you are a U.K. citizen permanently settled in the U.K., and you marry a foreigner, he has a right to settle in Britain with you, but he cannot automatically register as a U.K. citizen on marriage. More details of immigration rules on p. 421.

# Domestic violence

This section tells you how the law can help if your husband or the man you live with is violent towards you or your children.

The law is not the only means of protection. If you are forced to leave your home to escape attack, you may be able to take refuge in one of Britain's women's aid centres (contact address, p. 277). The first of these was set up in Chiswick in 1972. Its founder, Erin Pizzey, succeeded in focusing public attention for the first time upon the age-old custom of woman battering. By 1979, there were 150 women's aid centres in towns and cities throughout the country, with grants from local authorities, urban aid programmes and charitable trusts. They provide a temporary home and invaluable moral support for battered women and their children. But funds are always in short supply so they can be rather cramped and they seldom provide more than short-term, emergency shelter. Some women move on to share accommodation with others who are in a similar situation. Many would prefer to return to their own homes if they could be sure their men would not attack them again.

Until recently, women were able to get little or no protection from the law. The police normally refused to intervene in what they called 'domestic disputes'. The procedure for obtaining court injunctions ordering the man not to attack was far too complex and lengthy. Married women had to start proceedings for judicial separation or divorce – which for many seemed too drastic a step at a time when they needed immediate protection and a breathing space to consider the future of their relationship. Single women had to start county court proceedings to claim cash compensation for injury or damage to property. And when injunctions were issued, many women found they weren't worth the paper they were written on, as their men continued to assault them.

In 1975, a Select Committee of the House of Commons was set up to consider violence in marriage. It heard evidence from (among other sources) organizers of the women's aid centres and women who had taken refuge in them. It found the relevant law to be very weak and recommended certain changes. These were incorporated in the Domestic Violence Act, which went through Parliament in 1976 and came into force in June 1977. In 1978, the Domestic Proceedings and Magistrates' Courts Act was passed; the sections offering protection to battered women came into force in November 1979. The law is potentially much stronger now, but a lot of women don't know about the protection it offers and most solicitors are reluctant to take on cases of this kind because they are not as lucrative as others.

Even when it becomes better known and more accessible, the law will scarcely begin to provide a remedy. The problem of battered women is a social one, deeply rooted in the way men and women have been brought up to regard themselves and each other, and in the links our society fosters between marriage and property, sex and violence. So other remedies are needed. The battering won't end until men and women change their attitudes and women learn to defend themselves and to assert their right to freedom from assault. At its best, the law is a cumbersome and inappropriate means of dealing with a failure in human communication. The most it can do to protect a woman from being beaten by a man is to send the man to prison. Clearly, imprisonment is not a satisfactory solution to any social problem. In its own way it is as oppressive as the practice of wife beating. But when men refuse to obey court orders, it is the only solution available under the present system.

In some cases, men are not deterred by the threat of imprisonment and the women feel it is safer to hide in a women's aid centre than to go to court and reveal their whereabouts. In addition to stronger legal protection for battered women we need more public funds to provide refuges. The Select Committee recommended that a women's aid or 'family crisis' centre be set up in every fair-sized town. Predictably, however, these recommendations haven't been carried out because of restrictions on public spending. Instead, some refuges have been closed down because of lack of funds.

## Protection in the county court (or High Court)

The details that follow apply whether you are married or living with a man in the same household, or were living with him until he assaulted you. For the sake of simplicity, we have used the word 'husband' to apply to the man in either circumstance. (See p. 273 for the procedure in the magistrates' courts.)

*If your husband is physically violent towards you or your children, you can apply to court for an injunction.*

### WHAT IS AN INJUNCTION?

It is an order from the court which requires a person to behave in a particular way. You can ask for the injunction to order different things, according to the circumstances of your case. For instance, you might need an injunction which orders your husband to do one or more of the following:

1. Not to assault you;
2. Not to assault your children;
3. To leave your home and not return;
4. To keep a certain distance from your home, e.g. outside a half-mile radius;
5. To let you into the home.

It is generally more difficult to get an injunction which orders your husband to leave the home, as shown on p. 271.

The injunction is written out by a court official. On the back is a notice addressed to your husband which tells him that if he disobeys the order he is liable to be sent to prison for contempt of court. It must be delivered into his hands – it can't just be left at an address where he is likely to collect it.

*An injunction may be 'backed' by power of arrest.* This gives the police power to arrest your husband if he disobeys the order. A special request has to be made for it, as explained on p. 268. If the injunction is not 'backed' by power of arrest and your husband disobeys the order, your solicitor will have to take steps to have him brought to court and committed to prison. See p. 269.

### HOW DO YOU GET AN INJUNCTION?

You can apply to the county court for an injunction under the Domestic Violence Act. You can also apply to the High Court, but this is very rarely done. Unless you feel confident about tackling it yourself, it's best to apply for legal aid and get a solicitor to make the application for you (see p. 452 for how to do this). If you can't get legal aid and you cannot afford to have a solicitor represent you in court, it would probably be helpful to pay for one to advise you and help you complete the necessary forms.

Your solicitor (or you yourself if you make the application on your own) will need to take the steps outlined below, *unless* you are applying for a divorce or judicial separation, in which case the procedure is slightly different.

1. *Prepare the form of Originating Application*, with two copies. There is no standard form, so have it prepared by a solicitor or ask at the county court for help. It should set out the names and addresses of you and your husband and state briefly what you are asking for and why (attach two copies). If you want the injunction to contain a power of arrest, the Application should say so (see p. 268).

2. *Prepare your affidavit,* with two copies. This is a sworn statement which must be signed before a solicitor (at a cost of £2 plus 50p extra for each exhibit), or before one of the clerks at the county court, which is free. It should describe the date, place and nature of any assaults or threats of assault your husband has made upon

you. If you are asking for an injunction which orders your husband to leave the home the affidavit should explain why you cannot continue living in the same house as him and, if possible, what other accommodation he can go to. It should also say whether your home is owned or rented in both your names, in his name, or in yours. If you have witnesses they should also make affidavits.

3. Take the Originating Application, the affidavit, your legal aid certificate, and a draft of the order you are asking for to the county court covering the district where you or your husband lives. If you are not legally aided you will have to pay a fee of £15. If you tell the court official that you are receiving legal advice under the 'green form' procedure (p. 454) or that you are on supplementary benefit, you will not have to pay.

4. Ask for your case to be heard urgently. Unless your case is *extremely* urgent (i.e. unless you are in immediate danger of serious assault) your husband should be notified of your application by being personally handed a copy of the application, the affidavit and a notice of the court hearing. He should normally have at least four days' notice of the hearing. The court bailiff will do this if you ask, for an extra fee, or your solicitor can arrange it. If you do not have a solicitor, check how quickly the bailiff will serve the notice, as you may find a private inquiry agent will do it more quickly. Look them up under 'detective agencies' in the Yellow Pages; you will, of course, have to pay.

*Here is a summary of the short cuts you can take if your case is urgent:*

1. In most cases of urgency you can apply for emergency legal aid. You should be granted this almost immediately without a very detailed assessment being made of your financial resources.

2. *If your case is extremely urgent:* you may be able to apply for an injunction without swearing an affidavit.

3. If it seems too dangerous to tell your husband or he cannot be found in order to give him notice of what you are doing, you can make an *ex parte* application for an injunction which can then

be granted in his absence and without his having any prior warning. Normally you can only get an injunction preventing him assaulting you this way; you cannot get one which orders him to leave home. An injunction granted without your husband being present will only last for a few days and within the time set there will be another hearing so that your husband can be present.

4. Even if your husband is given notice of your application, he does not have to be allowed two days' grace before the hearing.
5. You can ask for a court hearing on the day that all the necessary forms are delivered to court, instead of waiting two days. There is always a judge 'on duty', even at weekends and during the court vacations, although you may have to travel to find one.
6. If you are applying for an injunction in the course of divorce proceedings, you can do so before you file the divorce petition, if you promise the court that you will file it as soon as possible. Taking all these short cuts, you might be able to get an injunction within twenty-four hours, or at least within a few days.

IF YOU ARE APPLYING FOR A DIVORCE OR JUDICIAL SEPARATION

You can get an injunction in the course of these proceedings (see p. 278 for how to obtain a divorce or separation). If you are at all uncertain about wanting a divorce, it's best to apply for an injunction in the way we have described above, so that you can think about ending your marriage later. The same is true if your case is very urgent and you have not yet started proceedings for divorce or judicial separation: it usually takes some time to prepare divorce or separation papers and this could delay your injunction.

However, once the proceedings for divorce or judicial separation are under way, you can go at any time to the court which is dealing with the case and ask for an injunction. A date for the hearing will be fixed at the court and, unless your case is very urgent, a written notice of your application must be handed personally to your husband, telling him the date of the hearing. He must be allowed two clear weekdays' notice before the hearing. This means that if he receives notice of the application on a Monday you can go to court on the Thursday of that week.

If your husband cannot be contacted in time to give him notice, then you can make what is called an *ex parte* application for an injunction to be granted in his absence (see above, p. 265). The judge may postpone the hearing to allow more time for him to be found, but he is unlikely to do so if your case is urgent.

You will need to prepare an affidavit in the same way as you would if you were applying for an injunction in the county court (see above, p. 264). It can be very difficult to apply for an injunction in this way if you are not represented by a solicitor. If you are doing your own divorce (as on p. 290) and your husband assaults you, you should consider going to a solicitor and applying for legal aid (see p. 452).

AT THE HEARING

The hearing will be similar whether you are applying for an injunction in the county court or in the course of divorce or separation proceedings. It will normally be in private with only your husband, your representatives and witnesses allowed to be present. Only if it has got to the stage of your asking that your husband be sent to prison will the public be admitted. You must attend the hearing. If you have a solicitor, he or she will conduct the hearing and you will just have to answer questions when asked.

The judge reads your affidavit and you will probably have to give evidence. It helps if you have something to back up your story, such as a doctor's letter confirming that you have been injured, or a witness who saw you being attacked or heard your husband threaten you after a previous attack. Failing that, friends who saw you shortly after an attack when you were upset or bruised can act as witnesses. Your witnesses should, if possible, complete affidavits, but if there is not time they should attend the hearing to tell the court what they know. If the judge is satisfied that your case is sufficiently serious, he will grant an injunction which orders your husband not to assault you; he may include in the injunction an order for your husband to leave the home. At this stage, you can ask the judge to attach power of arrest to the injunction. He can do this if he is satisfied that your husband's assault has caused you 'actual bodily harm' (i.e. some physical injury such as a bruise or cut). He must also be satisfied that your husband is likely to assault you again.

The period for which a power of arrest is attached to the injunction will not normally exceed three months. Many judges do not like granting powers of arrest and will only do so in very serious cases. In a High Court case the judges said it should be seen as 'exceptional', though this is not what the Act says.

If the judge agrees to attach a power of arrest, a copy of the injunction is delivered by the court bailiff to your local police station and to your husband. If you think the court bailiff may be slow in doing this, or may be unable to find your husband, send a telegram telling your husband what the injunction says. If you can show that he knows what it says, it may be possible to enforce it, even if he hasn't received a copy. If the judge does not attach power of arrest, the court bailiff will not usually serve the injunction on your husband. Your solicitor should arrange it or you could use an inquiry agent. The injunction does not become binding until it has been delivered into his hands – although a judge may be prepared to enforce it if you can prove he knows of it by other means, e.g., by being at the court hearing or receiving a telegram. If it contains a power of arrest, this operates even if your husband has not received a copy of the injunction.

WHAT HAPPENS IF YOUR HUSBAND DISOBEYS THE INJUNCTION?

1. *If the injunction is backed with power of arrest*, notify your local police station and they should arrest your husband and bring him before the judge within twenty-four hours. Sometimes the police are reluctant to use their powers and you may need to persuade them. Make sure your solicitor has explained exactly what the injunction says and when the police can arrest your husband, so that you are in no doubt. You should attend the

court hearing with your solicitor. A further hearing may be arranged before the judge decides what action to take: if so, you will have to prepare an affidavit, giving details of how your husband disobeyed the injunction. Try to get a witness or a doctor's statement to back up your story. It may be that the police officer who made the arrest can give evidence on your behalf. If the judge thinks your husband's disobedience is sufficiently serious, he may send him to prison.

2. *If the injunction is not backed with power of arrest*, your solicitor will have to go to court to fix a hearing date and have notice of the hearing delivered personally to your husband. The hearing will normally take place at least two days later, so all in all you must expect about a week to elapse between your husband's disobeying the injunction and the court hearing at which you can ask for him to be sent to prison. However, if your husband has seriously assaulted you and you are in immediate danger of further assault, your solicitor should be able to arrange a hearing more quickly. In cases of this kind, you would obviously be in a safer position if the injunction originally gave the police power to arrest your husband.

*If your husband is sent to prison*, he is not given an ordinary prison sentence. He is jailed for 'contempt of court' which means that he can apply to be released at any time by 'purging his contempt'. In other words, if he says he's sorry and promises not to disobey the injunction again, he will probably be let out. You will be given a chance to turn up in court and oppose his release, but it is up to the judge to decide. Most judges are keen to let the men out of prison as soon as possible. There is no minimum time limit on the length of time the man must stay in prison before he can be released; it may be a few days or a few weeks and it may bear no relation to the seriousness of the assault. You have no way of knowing how long you will be safe.

*When he comes out of prison*, the injunction is still effective, so if he assaults you again you will have to make another application to the court to have him committed to prison; then he can be released again by 'purging his contempt'. Some men are in and out of prison quite regularly.

*If you decide that you want to be reconciled* with your husband while he is in prison, tell your solicitor. If you have started divorce proceedings, these can be stopped without any difficulty and he will be released.

*If you get a divorce*, the injunction can continue in force if necessary. If you do not already have an injunction and your ex-husband assaults you, you can apply for an injunction by going to the county court, as described above. Alternatively you can apply to the divorce court, provided it is not more than about two years after the divorce hearing.

IF YOU HAVE CHILDREN

*If you are not married* you have sole custody of your children unless the court awards custody to the father, which happens very rarely. The father has a right of access to the children (which may be curtailed if he is violent towards them) and a liability to maintain them.

*If you are married*, under the Guardianship of Minors Act you and your husband have equal rights and responsibilities towards your children until a court decides otherwise. If you get a divorce on the grounds of your husband's 'unreasonable behaviour' and there is a dispute over the custody of the children, the court will have to decide who will have custody.

*If you have to leave your home to avoid being attacked try to take your children with you if you want them to live with you. If you leave them for more than a few days you may endanger your claim for custody when it comes to court.*

(More about custody on p. 320.)

*If your husband threatens to take your children away*

1. If there are no divorce proceedings you can have them made wards of court as explained on p. 320.
2. If you are engaged in divorce proceedings, apply immediately to the divorce court for an injunction (see p. 263).

## WHEN CAN YOU GET AN INJUNCTION WHICH ORDERS YOUR HUSBAND TO LEAVE THE HOME?

*If you are not married* and the home is in your name, you should get the order without any difficulty. If the home is in the man's name or joint names, the judge has the power to order the man to leave. In reaching his decision, he should use the same tests as in the case of a married woman. In practice, it may be difficult to persuade the judge to order the man out. See the case of *Davis vs Johnson* below for an example of a woman who succeeded. Even if the house is in the man's name you may be entitled to a share in it (see p. 385).

The case of *Davis vs Johnson*, 1977, shows how the Domestic Violence Act applies to unmarried women. Jennifer Davis had a daughter aged two and a half by Mr Johnson and they lived together in a council flat. The flat was in their joint names, although she paid the rent. He beat her frequently. Eventually she fled to Chiswick women's aid refuge, then went to the county court and asked for Johnson to be turned out so that she could return to the flat. The judge first granted her application, but then withdrew the injunction when he heard of two Court of Appeal decisions which implied that an order of that kind could not be made when the woman was unmarried and the home was not in her name alone. Ms Davis appealed to the Court of Appeal which convened a special court with five judges to give a ruling. Three of the judges – a majority – came down on the side of Ms Davis, saying the intention of the Act was clearly to give unmarried women the same protection as their married sisters. It is worth recalling the words of Sir George Baker, the President of the Family Division of the High Court, who was one of these: 'Was this provision only a tiny miserable mouse incapable of even a nibble at the end of domestic hooliganism?' (His Lordship did not think so.) 'The Act was plain as a pikestaff . . . and enabled the county court to provide immediately for the urgent and pressing need of a wife and child for a roof excluding a violent husband from what had been the matrimonial home.'

*If you are married* and not yet divorced, it is not easy to obtain an order for your husband to leave, unless the home is in your name alone. Judges are very reluctant to evict any husband from a home which is owned or rented in his name or jointly with his wife. The attitudes of different judges are not consistent and even the Court of Appeal seems to make contradictory decisions.

The general test is whether it is impossible for you to live in the same house as your husband. When considering this the judge looks at your husband's conduct: the degree of violence he has used and how often; whether he says that he will not assault you in the future and whether he appears to be sincere about this. The judge also considers what accommodation is available for you both. If you have a large house which could enable you and your husband to live virtually apart whilst under the same roof, he is less likely to be evicted than if you live in a very small house and with children so that you are always at close quarters. The court also considers whether you or your children are likely to be injured physically or mentally if you continue to live with your husband. If he has promised not to assault you in future and you have not given him a chance to keep his promise the court may say that you ought to test his good faith by living with him before they will agree to order him out. The court also considers where your husband could live if he were evicted. These are all points that you should consider when you are making your application so that you can give your evidence on each of them.

*A case where the husband was ordered to leave the home during divorce proceedings – Bassett vs Bassett, Court of Appeal, 1974:*

Mr and Mrs Bassett lived in a small flat with a teenage son by Mr Bassett's previous marriage and a young child of their own marriage. Mrs Bassett told the court that she had twice been assaulted seriously. She had left the home with her young child and had gone to live with her mother in very overcrowded conditions; she had also filed a petition for divorce. She said it was impossible for her to return to her own home while her husband was there. The Court of Appeal agreed and said that they had to reconsider the children's need for a home and the relative hardship suffered by husband and wife. They agreed that the marriage had broken down and that Mr Bassett might well have to leave the home anyway. The court took account of the very overcrowded conditions in which Mrs Bassett was living and the effect it was having on the young child of the marriage. It was decided that she should be able to return to the family home and that it was therefore right to order Mr Bassett to leave, even though the flat was in his name.

*A case where the husband was not ordered to leave – Parris vs Parris, Court of Appeal, 21 November 1975:*

Mr and Mrs Parris had been married for eleven years and had three children aged 5, 4 and 1. Mr Parris owned the home which had 4 rooms, plus kitchen and bathroom. Mrs Parris said that her husband was moody, that he stayed away from home for nights on end and that he had been violent towards her on two occasions. She had left the home and was living in cramped accommodation at a women's aid refuge. Mr Parris denied his wife's allegations and proposed that she should come back so that they could live separately under the same roof. Mrs Parris said she couldn't return until her husband had left. The Court of Appeal decided that until the couple were divorced it was impossible for them to decide who was telling the truth and that Mrs Parris should therefore return home and try out her husband's suggestion. They refused to order Mr Parris to leave.

## Taking legal action in the magistrates' court

Most women find that magistrates' courts are nearer to their homes, more familiar to them and less intimidating than the county court or High Court. Therefore it makes a difference whether magistrates have power to protect women from domestic violence. Until the 1978 Domestic Proceedings and Magistrates' Court Act they could give no effective protection. When a wife was able to prove a 'matrimonial offence' such as adultery, desertion or persistent cruelty, she could, provided she was 'not guilty' of adultery, apply for a maintenance order: if she was in danger of physical violence the magistrates could then add a 'non-cohabitation' order. This had a very limited effect. It did not mean that the husband was ordered to leave the home. Indeed, many magistrates would not make a 'non-cohabitation' order if the wife was still living with her husband. Nor did it mean her husband was ordered not to molest or assault her. Legally it ended her duty to cohabit, but its only practical effect was that many councils would transfer a tenancy from husband to wife when there was a non-cohabitation clause. Often it took several weeks to get a hearing at a magistrates' court. Certainly in London it was a slower business than applying for an injunction.

Under the 1978 Act married women are offered some real protection. (This does not apply to unmarried women.) It gives a magistrates' court power to order your husband:

1. Not to use or threaten violence against you or a child of the family. (Called a personal protection order);
2. To leave the matrimonial home;
3. If he has already left the home, not to re-enter;
4. If you have left and want to return, to allow you to enter and stay in your home.

The magistrates can make order (1) if they are satisfied that your husband has threatened violence or been violent towards you or a child of the family. They can make orders (2) and (3) if they are satisfied that your husband has been violent towards you or a child of the family; or that he has threatened to be violent towards you or a child of the family and has been violent towards someone else, and that you are in danger of being physically injured by him. They can order (4) when making an order under (2) or (3).

Power of arrest can be attached to the order if the magistrates are satisfied that your husband has injured you or your child and that he is likely to do it again. (It cannot be attached to an order that your husband leave the home or to an order that he should not enter the home.) This enables the police to arrest your husband when they have reasonable suspicion that he has broken the order. The police can keep him in custody for up to twenty-four hours and must in that time bring him back before a magistrate to be dealt with. Christmas Day, Good Friday and Sundays do not count when calculating the twenty-four hours.

If the order does not have a power of arrest attached to it and your husband breaks the order, you have to go back to the court to apply for the issue of a warrant of arrest – see below for how to go about this.

The drawbacks to using a magistrates' court as compared to the county court are:

1. The atmosphere of magistrates' courts is usually more hurried than county courts. They still too often seem like the police courts they originally were. Unless you are lucky your hearing may be rushed through without time to explain it in detail.
2. There is no procedure for writing out your case beforehand in affidavit form. While this makes preparation easier it means the court does not have the details of your case and can lead to a decision being taken on inadequate information.
3. You have to tell the magistrates all the details of your marriage, which you may find distressing.
4. Orders can only be made at the court, so it may be impossible to get an emergency order on a Sunday. County court judges can make orders outside court (e.g. at their home) in an emergency.
5. The power of magistrates' courts is more limited than county courts. As well as not being able to protect unmarried women:
(a) They can only protect 'children of the family' which means children of both you and your husband, or children you have treated as being one of the family, e.g. by accepting financial responsibility. It may be that you have a foster child living with you, or a child born prior to your marriage for whom your husband has refused to take financial responsibility. Neither will be protected.
(b) They can only make an order protecting you from violence, while the county court can protect you from 'molesting' which includes 'pestering' as well as violence and threats of violence and would include mental cruelty.

On the other hand you may find it easier to go to a magistrates' court, for the reasons stated above. If so, the broad outline of the procedure is as follows (the details were not clear at the time of writing, because the regulations for the new Act had not yet been made):

1. You will need to 'apply for a summons' against your husband. You should seek advice from a solicitor who will normally be able to represent you under the legal advice and assistance scheme at little or no cost (see p. 454). She or he will help you make the application. If you do not have a solicitor, inquire at or telephone the local court to find out when they hear applications. These are heard in private. Just say why you need protection and what kind of order you want and explain why it is urgent. No fee has to be paid to the court. You may want to apply for maintenance at the same time, in which case you will have to satisfy the court that your husband has failed to provide reasonable maintenance for you or a child of the family; that he has behaved in such a way that you cannot reasonably be expected to live with him; or that he has deserted you. The court can then order that he pay a weekly sum for you and any children, or a lump sum. Even if the court does not find your husband has been guilty of unreasonable behaviour, failing to maintain, or desertion, it can order that he gives you custody of the children and order maintenance for the children though not for you.

2. When your application is granted, the summons will be issued and a date fixed for the hearing. The hearing may be in a few weeks' time.

3. If it is urgent, the magistrates can make an 'expedited' personal protection order. Other orders such as that your husband should leave the home cannot be expedited. If you want an expedited order, you must take a written statement, explaining why you (or your child) are in immediate danger of assault from your husband, to the court when you ask for the summons. Ask your solicitor to prepare this for you. An expedited order can be made even if your husband has not been served with the summons, if

the hearing is at very short notice, or even if it is at a date earlier than the one stated on the summons. An expedited order cannot last longer than twenty-eight days. Then there will be another full hearing of your case before the order expires to decide whether it should continue. If necessary the twenty-eight-day period can be extended. The order will not take effect until it is served on your husband.

4. At the hearing your solicitor (if you have one) will prepare the case and conduct the case and you will just have to answer questions.

5. If you are conducting your own case make sure you have all your witnesses in court. It is not enough to produce letters from them. Also bring any relevant documents, such as a medical report. The Clerk of the Court will explain the procedure to you and help you give your evidence and cross-examine your husband.

## Further information

For the address of your nearest women's aid centre, contact the National Women's Aid Federation, 374 Gray's Inn Road, London WC1 (01 837 9316).

# 6. Divorce and Separation

## How to go about getting a divorce or separation

If you want to be legally separated from your husband, the two most common ways of doing it are:

### 1. By getting a divorce

This ends the marriage altogether so that you and your husband become single people again (see p. 280).

### 2. By getting a matrimonial order from a magistrates' court

This does not end the marriage, but it means that you can make firm arrangements for maintenance and custody of the children (see p. 301).

WHICH TO CHOOSE

There is no point in going to a magistrates' court for an order unless:

(a) you don't want to end the marriage because you think that there is a chance of a reconciliation; *or*

(b) you are waiting to apply for a divorce (for instance, because

you have been married for less than three years or because you
have lived apart for less than two years) and in the meantime
you need money; *or*

(c) you and your husband cannot reach an agreement about who
should look after the children.

Proceedings in a magistrates' court can be just as lengthy as
divorce proceedings, and the amount you are likely to get in
maintenance from a magistrates' court is usually less than the
amount you would get in a divorce court. Despite recent changes
in the law, the powers of a magistrate are still more limited than
those of a divorce judge and he cannot make any arrangements
concerning your home (see p. 304 for details).

Divorce proceedings are usually fairly straightforward these days
and divorce courts have far wider powers to make financial and
other arrangements. So unless you need to wait for a divorce or you
believe that you and your husband can settle your differences, don't
bother with a magistrates' court order, but start divorce proceedings. All in all, there are five different ways of becoming legally
separated from your husband. The others are:

### 3. You can come to a voluntary agreement with your husband

Get a solicitor to draw up a legal document so that the terms of
your agreement can be enforced in a court of law. This has the
same effect as a separation order, but it means you don't have to go
to court. Obviously this is only appropriate if you and your husband
are on reasonably good terms. It is often used by couples who are
waiting to get a divorce on the basis of a two-year separation; or
who have agreed on a trial separation (see p. 310).

### 4. You can get a judicial separation

This means going through the same proceedings as you would if you were getting a divorce, but it does not end the marriage. It is rarely done these days except by people who have religious objections to divorce. Judicial separation is explained on p. 311.

### 5. You may be able to have the marriage annulled

This has the same effect as a divorce but it requires proof that your marriage is not valid. This would only be appropriate in certain circumstances, which are described on p. 311.

### Of course, it could happen the other way round

Your husband could start proceedings against you (although men seldom, if ever, apply for separation orders, since they are rarely in a position to claim money from their wives). We hope the information given here will be equally useful if you are on the receiving end, but for the sake of simplicity we have written it as though you were taking legal action against your husband. It would apply in reverse if he were taking action against you.

## Divorce

### When can you apply?

As a general rule, you can't get a divorce until you have been married for three years. But you may be able to get one sooner if you have suffered 'exceptional hardship' because of the marriage, or if your husband is 'exceptionally depraved'. It was said in a recent case that the judge can take into account not only the hardship you have suffered because of your husband's conduct but also the hardship you will suffer if you have to wait for your divorce. The judge must also consider the welfare of your children and whether there is any possibility of a reconciliation. You can apply even if you are still living with your husband.

## What do you have to prove?

You must prove to the court that your marriage has broken down *'irretrievably'* for one of five reasons:

1. You and your husband both want a divorce and you have been living apart for at least two years.
2. You have been living apart for five years and you want a divorce, even if your husband doesn't.
3. Your husband has deserted you for at least two years.
4. Your husband has committed adultery and you find it intolerable to live with him.
5. Your husband has behaved in a way that makes it unreasonable to expect you to live with him.

## Living apart for two years

This is the easiest way to get a divorce. If you and your husband have lived apart for two years and both agree to a divorce, you don't have to present any other reason to the court. Your husband must give his consent by filling in a special form and sending it to the court. He can withdraw his consent at any time up to the granting of the divorce – so can you.

'Living apart' means living in separate households. It is just possible to claim a divorce if you and your husband have been living under the same roof. This is explained under the heading of 'Desertion' (p. 283).

The two years of living apart are supposed to be continuous, but if you have lived together occasionally during that time for a total of not more than six months, you can still get a divorce after you have lived apart for a total of two years. So if you tried a reconciliation and it lasted three months, you can apply for a divorce two years and three months after the date when you first started living apart.

The judge can postpone the final granting of the divorce if he thinks that adequate financial provision has not been made for you (or your husband).

### Living apart for five years

This is the simplest way of getting a divorce if your husband does not give his consent. (And it's the simplest way for him to divorce you if you don't consent.) When the Divorce Reform Act was passed in 1969, it was this provision that led to its being called the Casanova's Charter by some who feared the wholesale desertion of ageing and blameless wives by randy and irresponsible husbands. Nothing of the sort has happened – although it is almost impossible to stop a divorce being granted. In certain cases the Act offers some protection:

1. A judge can refuse to grant a divorce which has been sought under the five-year ruling if he thinks it would cause grave hardship (financial or otherwise) to the wife (or husband) who refused consent. He might do this if the husband had refused to pay maintenance to the wife or if the wife would suffer from losing her pension rights under the husband's insurance. In deciding, the judge must consider how the husband and wife have behaved and what would be in the best interests of the children. So far there have been a few cases where the wife has succeeded in this defence. As a general rule, a divorce will be granted if the woman will receive no less from supplementary benefit or National Insurance than she would have received if she had remained married. This is illustrated by the case of *Reiterbund vs Reiterbund*, which went to the Court of Appeal in October 1974.

Bessie and Solomon Reiterbund were married in 1942. They had two children, now grown up, and they had separated in 1956. When the case was heard, she was 52 and he was 54. Mrs Reiterbund opposed the divorce on the grounds that she would not be entitled to a widow's pension if her husband died before she was 60; nor would she get a married woman's pension when she retired. When the case was heard Mr Reiterbund was not paying her any maintenance. She was living on supplementary benefit of £7·75 a week; he was disabled because of chronic bronchitis and received invalidity benefit of £8·25 a week. The Appeal Court decided that Mrs Reiterbund would receive no less from supplementary benefit if she were divorced than she would receive from her husband's insurance if she remained married; either way, she would be living off 'public funds'. Her appeal was dismissed and the divorce granted.

2. A judge can grant a decree nisi but refuse to make it absolute until he is sure that adequate financial provision has been made for the wife (or husband).

## Desertion

This means you can apply for a divorce if:

1. Your husband has left you; *and*
2. He has stayed away for at least two years; *and*
3. He has done so intentionally.

YOU CAN ALSO GET A DIVORCE FOR DESERTION
UNDER THE FOLLOWING CIRCUMSTANCES

1. You go on living under the same roof with your husband, but he refuses to have anything to do with you. In one case, a wife withdrew to a separate bedroom which she kept locked, refused to cook for her husband or do any household duties for him and only communicated with him by notes: it was decided that she had deserted him. But in another case, a wife refused to have any sex with her husband and hardly ever spoke to him, but occasionally cooked him a meal and did some household chores: it was decided that, although it was an unhappy household, it was one household rather than two and therefore it was *not* a case of desertion; *or*

2. You split up because you could not agree on where to live. If this is so, the one who has acted 'unreasonably' can be divorced for desertion. It used to be the case that the husband had the right to say where the home should be and if the wife disagreed she was guilty of desertion. This is still true today, but only if the husband is the breadwinner and the wife isn't working. If you and your husband both work, you have equal rights to say where your home should be. So unless one of you has obviously acted more unreasonably than the other, the law does not make it clear how the divorce should be granted and it will be left to the judge to decide on the facts of the particular case.

In fact, desertion is rarely used as a reason for applying for a divorce, except where a wife has been hoping her husband might return. If your husband deserts you and you don't want to wait two years, you may be able to divorce him for 'unreasonable behaviour' as described on p. 285.

### YOU WILL NOT BE ABLE TO GET A DIVORCE FOR DESERTION IN THE FOLLOWING CIRCUMSTANCES

1. Your husband left you because you behaved unreasonably. (A fuller explanation of this is given under the heading 'Unreasonable behaviour', on p. 285.)
2. Your husband has been imprisoned or mentally ill and therefore had no choice about living apart from you.
3. Your husband made a genuine offer to return and you refused.
4. You and your husband have lived together for a total of six months or more since the time he deserted you. You are allowed up to six months' attempted reconciliation, as explained under the heading 'Living apart for two years' (p. 281).
5. You have sexual intercourse with another man and the court decides that this was the reason why your husband deserted you: or you have intercourse with another man after your husband has deserted you – since this ends his duty to return to you.
6. You and your husband have been legally separated by a decree

of judicial separation. In this case you will be able to get a divorce under the two-year ruling.

### Adultery

You can get a divorce for this reason if you can prove to the court

1. *That your husband had sexual intercourse with another woman.* This is normally done by the husband and the woman involved making written statements to an inquiry agent (private detective) or solicitor admitting their adultery. Alternatively, there should be evidence of a familiar relationship between them, indicating that they were likely to have intercourse. Proof that they have spent a night in the same bedroom is normally taken as evidence of adultery. Direct evidence from an eye witness is not necessary. *And*

2. *That you find it intolerable to live with your husband.* Usually, all you have to do is to say that you find it intolerable to live with him. If asked to explain why, the reason you give need not be the adultery. If you go on sleeping with your husband for a long time after you discover that he has slept with another woman, you will not be able to get a divorce on the ground of adultery. But you are allowed up to six months' attempted reconciliation, as explained under the heading 'Living apart for two years' (p. 281).

### Unreasonable behaviour

This part of the law is very vague and it would be impossible to list all the kinds of behaviour that might be called unreasonable. Each case must be decided on its own particular facts, but the following guidelines may be useful:

1. According to the law, the behaviour complained of must be 'grave and weighty'.
2. Your husband's behaviour would be 'unreasonable' if it were clear that he knew that it would result in your leaving him, and

*... grave and weighty behaviour ...*

that any normal woman in your position would have done the same.

3. Physical or mental cruelty, if sufficiently 'grave and weighty', would be unreasonable. You can claim physical cruelty by saying that he has knocked you around with kicks and blows; but the odd blow struck in a temper may not be considered unreasonable. Persistent nagging, insults, slights or unkindness might amount to mental cruelty. If your husband completely ignored you, that might be counted as mental cruelty.

4. Sodomy or bestiality would be considered unreasonable; so would:

5. Mentally unbalanced behaviour;

6. Drunkenness (depending on how often it happened and what effect it had on him);

7. Unreasonable sexual demands;

8. Refusing to have children – by insisting on coitus interruptus or contraceptives, or by having a vasectomy without your consent;

9. Refusing to have sexual intercourse.

*Here is a typical account by a woman whose husband's behaviour would be accepted as 'unreasonable' by the court:*

My husband stopped being interested in me sexually or any other way. I became suspicious and when I questioned him he admitted he had another woman. He said he was in love with her but didn't want to leave me and the children. He suggested I might find another man. He used to come home from work, spruce himself up and go out again. He would come back at one or two o'clock in the morning. This happened several times a week.

*To give you an idea of what does not amount to unreasonable behaviour in the eyes of the law, the case of Buchler vs Buchler (1947) is still cited as an example. The judge pronounced:*

It may no doubt be galling – or in some sense of the word humiliating – for the wife to find that the husband prefers the company of his men-friends, his Club, his newspapers, his games, his hobbies or indeed his own society, to association with her, and a husband may have similar grievances regarding his wife. But this may be called the reasonable wear and tear of married life.

*The more recent case of Stringfellow vs Stringfellow (25 February 1976) gives another example of what is not considered unreasonable behaviour:*

Mrs Stringfellow was married in 1969 and had two children aged 5 and 4. The marriage was happy enough until 1975 when, she said, her husband suddenly lost interest and ceased to respond to her sexually. He started going out in the evenings without her and apparently had no feelings for her or the children. In February 1975 he told her to go to her parents for a week so that he could sort out his feelings, as he no longer loved her and wanted to regain his freedom. She felt shocked and rejected but agreed to go and when she returned he insisted that he wanted to leave her, and did so in March. She thought that her husband's behaviour might have been caused by depression or overwork and tried to persuade him to go to a Marriage Guidance Counsellor. He refused. A few months after her husband left she filed a petition for divorce. This was refused and she appealed. The Court of Appeal said her husband had done nothing more than indicate his attitude had changed towards her and that he could not show affection or have sexual intercourse. The Court said that a wife could not obtain a divorce on the ground of 'unreasonable behaviour' simply because her husband had deserted her; Mrs Stringfellow would have to wait until her husband had deserted her for two years and then apply for a divorce on the ground of desertion.

## How to get a divorce

### THERE IS NO LEGAL AID FOR UNDEFENDED CASES

As from 1977 you cannot get legal aid to be represented in court for a straightforward undefended divorce. This means that most women will have to conduct their own cases as they will be unable to afford solicitors' fees. But you can still obtain legal advice and assistance under the 'green form' procedure (see p. 454). Under this procedure your solicitor can prepare your divorce petition and other necessary forms and letters. Your solicitors' name and address can be put on the petition so that documents sent by the court in reply to the petition, and giving information about the hearing date etc., will go to them, and they will tell you what to do next. Most petitions now are dealt with by post so you probably won't have to go to court. You will have to go to court, however, to tell the judge about the arrangements you have made for your children (see p. 321).

### FULL LEGAL AID IS AVAILABLE IN SOME CASES

You can still get legal aid in the following circumstances:

1. You cannot proceed without legal aid because of a physical or mental disability.
2. Your divorce has to be heard in court. (Almost all undefended cases are now conducted by post.)
3. Your application for divorce is opposed by your husband; or you wish to oppose his and have reasonable grounds for doing so.
4. You have been married for less than three years and are asking the court's permission to start divorce proceedings (see p. 280).
5. You need an injunction (see p. 264).
6. You are making a claim for money – for example, for mainten-

ance or a share in the family property – and your husband disputes your claim.

7. You are claiming custody or access to the children and your husband disputes your claim or disagrees with any arrangements you are proposing for the children.

8. You oppose any claim your husband makes under 4–7 above.

9. There is some other complicated matter for which the court decides you should have legal aid.

*Defended divorces* are usually very expensive. They can also take a very long time and can be most disheartening. Some divorces are defended only at the beginning while disagreements over children and property are sorted out. Only one in a hundred continue to a defended hearing: these can last several days and cost more than most people can afford unless they are getting legal aid.

### WHERE TO FIND A SOLICITOR

If you don't know how to get hold of a solicitor, ask your local Citizens' Advice Bureau (address in the telephone directory) or go to the magistrates' court and ask the officials there to tell you where you can find one. Read the section on 'Going to a solicitor', p. 449.

### WHAT WILL IT COST IF YOU PAY A SOLICITOR?

If all is agreed between you and your husband and there are no complications, the actual divorce will probably cost at least £150, although all solicitors fix their own fees, so it could be more or less. If there are complications over maintenance and custody of children (and you are not eligible for legal aid because your income is not low enough) it could cost you a great deal more. If your husband is defending the divorce it may be very expensive indeed. Make sure that your solicitor gives you an estimate of the cost before you start and tells you if anything happens to put the price up during the proceedings. If you apply for a divorce – and get one – on the grounds of adultery, desertion, or unreasonable behaviour, your husband will be ordered to pay your legal costs. But this may not help if he doesn't have the money to pay, or disappears.

## How to conduct your own divorce

(What follows applies to undefended divorces. If a solicitor is acting on your behalf, she or he will take the same steps – except, of course, the first!)

### GET LEGAL ADVICE

It is always wise to get legal advice before you start, even if you have to pay for it. If your income is low, you should get it free or partly free under the 'green form' procedure described on p. 454. The solicitor who advises you can discuss any problems you have; help fill in the necessary forms; and try to reach an agreement with your husband over custody and access to the children, division of property and payment of maintenance.

At the time of writing, the 'green form' procedure allows solicitors to do only £75 worth of work; they have to get permission from the Law Society before they can do any more without charging their clients. Many women need even more than £75 worth of help if they are to be sure of getting a settlement which is in the best interests of themselves and their children. However, if you aren't able to agree about financial matters or the children you can then apply for legal aid.

Get a copy of the official booklet, *Undefended Divorce*, available free from the Divorce Registry, Somerset House, Strand, London WC2. This gives detailed advice on the procedure.

### PREPARE YOUR PETITION

Get three copies of the petition form from your nearest divorce county court or, if you live in London, from the Divorce Registry. They are free. There are explanatory notes accompanying the petition to help you answer the questions.

When you complete the form, be sure to ask for everything you want from the settlement. For instance, you must say that you want custody or access to the children; that you want maintenance payments while the divorce is going through; that you want periodical payments for you and the children after the divorce, a lump sum and an order to transfer property to your name (see p. 297). You don't have to pursue all the claims listed in your petition, but if you don't list them at this stage you may find it difficult to claim them later on. Consult a solicitor if you are in any doubt about what you should claim.

If you have children you will also need three copies of the form 'Statement of Arrangements for Children', available free from the court.

### TAKE THE FORMS TO COURT

Take two copies of the completed petition form and two copies of the 'Statement of Arrangements for Children' to the court at Somerset House if you live in London, or to your nearest divorce county court. You must also take your marriage certificate. Get the address from the telephone directory under 'county court', or ask your Citizens' Advice Bureau where it is. You have to pay a £35 filing fee if you are not legally aided, but if you tell the court that you are receiving legal advice under the 'green form' procedure or that you are receiving supplementary benefit, you need not pay it. You will be given a reference number. Keep a third copy of each form for your own use.

### NOTIFY YOUR HUSBAND

The court sends your husband a copy of the petition, the 'Statement of Arrangements for Children' and an 'Acknowledgement of Service' form which he has to complete and return to the court. You will be sent a copy. If he does not return the 'Acknowledgement of Service', the documents will have to be handed to him personally.

You can ask the court to arrange for the county court bailiff to do this for you.

### PUTTING IN FURTHER EVIDENCE

Get two copies of a form called 'Affidavit by Petitioner in support of Petition'. There is a different version of this form for each of the grounds for divorce (two years' separation, adultery, etc.) so specify which one you want. Also get a form called 'Application for Directions for Trial'. Both forms are available from the court and should be sent directly to you when the court receives the signed 'Acknowledgement of Service' from your husband. Complete the Affidavit and 'Directions for Trial' forms. Take them to a solicitor with your copy of the 'Acknowledgement of Service' form completed by your husband, and any other documents you need to support your case. (*This solicitor cannot be the one who gave you legal advice.*) If you are divorcing after two years' separation by mutual agreement, or after five years, you don't need any other documents and you probably won't need any if you are divorcing because of your husband's desertion. But if you are divorcing because of your husband's adultery, you need a signed statement from him (preferably witnessed by a solicitor or inquiry agent) admitting adultery, giving the date and place where it first happened and saying when and where it happened again, if it did. He should also confirm that he is making the statement voluntarily and that he knows it is for divorce proceedings. There is a place on your 'Affidavit by Petitioner' form where you say that you are submitting this document and any others. If you are divorcing because of your husband's unreasonable behaviour, you may have a medical report from your doctor (saying, for example, that you have been injured); if so, submit this too.

You then make a statement to the solicitor – either swearing by God, or affirming if you are not religious – confirming that the Affidavit is signed by you and the information in it is correct. The solicitor signs the Affidavit and you pay him £2 plus 50p for each other document attached to it. Send all the papers to the court.

## THE COURT MAY RAISE A QUERY

The judge may have a query about your divorce application. It's unlikely that this will happen if your divorce is straightforward. If there is a query, the papers may be sent back to you with a request for more information, or a date may be fixed for your case to be heard in open court. If this happens, consult a solicitor: you should be able to get legal aid for the solicitor to represent you in court.

## THE DECREE NISI IS GRANTED

Normally this is done in your absence and you are notified by post. If the divorce is brought after two years' separation, or five years' separation, and you have asked the court to consider your financial position, the decree cannot be made absolute until the court is satisfied that adequate financial provision has been made for you.

## IF YOU HAVE CHILDREN

The decree cannot be made absolute until the court is satisfied that proper arrangements have been made for the welfare of the children. An appointment will be made for you to go to court to tell the judge what arrangements have been made for them. Your husband will also be notified and can go if he wishes. This happens even though you both agree about the arrangements. The hearing is in private and if there are no complications you shouldn't need a solicitor. If you have a social worker who is in contact with the children, you could ask her to go with you to help tell the judge about them. If the judge is satisfied about the arrangements, he says so. If he is worried about something – for instance, that there is no one to look after the children during school holidays while you are at work – he may ask you to go away and make alternative arrangements and come back to explain them at a later date. If your husband does not agree with your proposals for looking after the children, or is asking for custody himself, no appointment will be fixed. In this case, you will need a solicitor.

THE DIVORCE IS MADE ABSOLUTE

Six weeks after your decree nisi is granted (whether by post or not) you can apply for your decree absolute. Do this by getting a small form called 'Application for Decree Absolute' from the court, filling it in and sending it back to the court. Your decree will be sent to you in the post. The divorce is then complete and you and your husband are single people again.

### If your husband disputes any claim you make in the course of divorce proceedings

He may send an 'Answer' to the court stating his disagreement. If this happens, your case becomes a defended divorce and is dealt with in the High Court. You should definitely see a solicitor as it becomes very much more complicated. You can apply for legal aid, as shown on p. 452.

If your husband disputes any claim you make in relation to maintenance or custody, you should also make sure you get a solicitor's help and apply for legal aid.

### How can you stop your husband divorcing you?

It isn't easy. You would have to show that the reason presented as grounds for divorce was not true, and that your marriage had not broken down 'irretrievably'. If your husband is divorcing you on the grounds of adultery, unreasonable behaviour or desertion, you may be able to prove that these are not true. But if he applies for a divorce after five years' separation there is nothing you can do about it, unless you can prove that you would suffer grave hardship as a result. This is very difficult, as shown on p. 282.

## How to get a divorce if you have married a man from abroad

IF YOU MARRIED UNDER LAWS THAT PERMIT POLYGAMY

(i.e. marriage where the husband can have more than one wife), your marriage may not be recognized by the English courts. The legal position is very complicated and you should consult a solicitor.

IF YOUR HUSBAND LIVES ABROAD

Before the law was changed in 1973 a woman could not get a divorce in Britain if her husband was permanently resident ('domiciled') in another country. However, if your permanent home is in Britain you can now get a divorce here, no matter where your husband is living. Even if your permanent home is not in Britain you can get a divorce here if you have been in residence for at least one year.

IF YOU GET A DIVORCE ABROAD

the decree may not be recognized under English law. The reasons are too complex to explain here. If you have been granted a divorce abroad and you want to remarry in England, take the divorce document to your registry office and the Registrar will advise you whether or not it is valid. If you are in difficulties, get further advice from a solicitor.

## Arrangements for your children after divorce

This is explained in the section on children (p. 321).

## Division of property after divorce

This is explained in the section on property (pp. 375–80).

## Getting maintenance when you divorce

Your husband will probably have to pay money to help maintain any children of the family. He may also have to pay money to maintain you.

### *What is maintenance?*

Maintenance takes the form of regular payments of money, and the amount you get will depend on the financial circumstances of you and your husband. You and your husband have equal responsibility to support each other and your children. So it is just possible that he could claim maintenance from you. This would only happen if you were earning a good wage and he had a good reason for not being able to support himself. The situation is unlikely to occur, and we have assumed throughout this section that you are in a position to claim maintenance from him.

There... that should look after your maintenance problems, m'dear

## When can you claim maintenance?

You can ask for maintenance to be paid as a temporary arrangement while your divorce is going through. Then, when the case has been heard and the decree nisi granted, you can claim maintenance as part of a permanent settlement.

## Maintenance during divorce proceedings

When you file your divorce petition you can include in it a request for maintenance to be paid from the date of filing the petition until the date when the divorce is granted. If your husband does not agree, you can apply for legal aid and get a solicitor to represent you. Your request will be heard by the Court Registrar after you have filed the petition. He will consider any evidence submitted by you and your husband – this is usually submitted in the form of affidavits (sworn statements) drawn up by your respective solicitors. If he accepts that your request is reasonable, he will then make an order for maintenance.

### HOW MUCH WILL YOU GET?

The law simply states that you should be given as much maintenance as the court thinks reasonable. In practice, this tends to be less than you would get after the divorce. However, when the final order is made after the divorce, you may get a lump sum to cover the expenses you have incurred during divorce proceedings; or the final order of maintenance may be backdated.

## Final order of maintenance after divorce

Once your divorce is granted, the court has far wider powers to make financial provision for you and your children. It can order:

1. Periodical payments (i.e. maintenance).
2. Secured periodical payments: this means setting up a trust fund

so that payments can be made out of it which are not dependent on your husband's future income and which can continue after his death.

3. Payment of lump sums.
4. Arrangements about who should live in the family home, or how it should be divided between you. This is explained in detail on pp. 375–80.

Unsecured payments will normally last from the time when you make the application for maintenance until the death of you or your husband. Secured payments will last until your own death. But if you remarry all maintenance payments to you will stop. The only exception is where the court has ordered a lump sum to be paid in instalments: if you remarry before the instalments have finished, the full sum must still be paid.

### PROVISION FOR CHILDREN

The court can also order periodical payments, secured periodical payments, lump sums and property settlements for any 'child of the family'. This means any child born to you and your husband or adopted by you, and any other child who has been treated by both of you as a child of the family, except a foster child.

The court can order payments before or after the divorce. It can even order them if divorce proceedings are dismissed. Payments will normally last until the child leaves school. The court may order payments to continue beyond that if the child goes on to college, training or an apprenticeship.

### HOW MUCH WILL YOU GET?

Arrangements about the division of family property are made at the same time as arrangements about maintenance. If you are awarded generous maintenance payments, you can normally expect to get less in the way of property, and vice versa.

The court is supposed to take certain factors into consideration before it decides how much maintenance to award. These are:

1. The income, earning capacity, property and other financial resources which you and your husband are likely to have in the foreseeable future.
2. The financial needs, obligations and responsibilities which you and your husband have or are likely to have in the foreseeable future. 'Needs' might include your expenses for education. 'Obligations' might be unpaid debts, hire purchase payments, the support of your children by a previous marriage, or the support of your husband's wife and children by a previous marriage. 'Responsibilities' might include the moral obligation of your husband to support a woman he is living with but hasn't yet married.
3. The standard of living of the family before the marriage broke down. It is a general rule that your standard of living should be maintained at the same standard as your husband's.
4. How old you and your husband were when you got married and how long the marriage lasted. If you were divorced by your husband after many years, you might have trouble finding a job, so you could expect to get a higher rate of maintenance than if you had been divorced when you were young, after a short marriage, when you could be expected to fend for yourself, as the following case illustrates:

Sir George Baker, President of the Family Division of the High Court, cut the maintenance awarded by magistrates to a 21-year-old wife deserted after five months of marriage from £3 to 10p. He said: 'In these days of Women's Lib there is no reason why a wife whose marriage has not lasted long and has no child, should have a bread ticket for life.' He added that the wife 'had not lost anything by the cessation of cohabitation'. [28 February 1973]

5. Any physical or mental disability that either of you may have.
6. The amount that you and your husband have each contributed to the welfare of your family. If you have been looking after the home and caring for your family, this would be counted as a

...and remember to maintain your ex wife at the same standard of living as yourself

contribution – on which basis you might also be able to claim a lump-sum payment or a property settlement.

7. The importance to you and your husband of any benefit that would be lost on divorce. For instance, you might lose your right to a widow's pension under your husband's occupational pension scheme. You can be compensated for this loss if your husband gives you a lump sum to provide you with an income after retirement. Get your solicitor's advice about this.

8. The way that you and your husband have behaved. Although 'irretrievable breakdown of marriage' is now the only ground on which anyone can get a divorce, if the judge considers you to be 'guilty' of 'gross conduct' and your husband comparatively blameless, he may award you less maintenance than if you appeared to be 'innocent'.

For all these considerations, the 'one-third' rule, that a wife should receive one third of the parties' joint income, normally applies (pp. 376, 384). In fact, when most marriages break up there is simply not enough money to support two families, and the husband, wife and children all suffer.

### If you remarry

You will no longer be able to claim any maintenance for yourself if you remarry, but your former husband should continue to support his children.

### An important thing to remember:

If a divorce court orders your husband to pay maintenance to you, ask for the order to be *registered with the magistrates' court*. It means that your husband pays his money to the magistrates' court and they post it to you. If he fails to pay, you can then take legal action against him by going to the magistrates' court, as explained on p. 307; or you can sign over payments to the Social Security office (p. 308).

## Getting a matrimonial order from a magistrates' court for maintenance and custody

*The Domestic Proceedings and Magistrates' Court Act 1978, almost all of which came into force on 1 February 1981, has brought the law in the magistrates' courts very much more into line with the law in the divorce courts.*

### What is a matrimonial order?

Applying for a matrimonial order means asking a magistrates' court to make an order saying that your husband must pay maintenance for you and your children; and that you are to have custody of your children.

### What do you have to prove?

To get an order you must prove to the court one of the following facts:

1. Your husband has failed to provide reasonable maintenance for you.
2. He has failed to provide reasonable maintenance for a child of the family.
3. He has behaved towards you in such a way that you cannot reasonably be expected to live with him.
4. Your husband has deserted you. Unlike the divorce procedure, you can apply to the magistrates' court at any time: you don't have to wait until he has deserted you for two years, or until you have been married for three years. A fuller explanation of the legal meaning of 'desertion' is given on p. 283.

### When can you apply?

As a general rule, you should apply for a separation order within six months of the cause of your complaint. You should apply within six months of the most recent incident of your husband's unreasonable behaviour if there were others before that. If your husband has deserted you or is not maintaining you, you can apply at any time.

You can apply while you are still living with your husband: this may help if you want to leave him but can't until you are sure you have some money coming in. But living together after the conduct complained of can still be interpreted by the court as meaning that you can still reasonably be expected to live with your husband, so keep this in mind.

### How to get a matrimonial order

GET A SOLICITOR

You will almost certainly need one. If you don't know how to get hold of one, ask your local Citizens' Advice Bureau or inquire at the magistrates' court. Read the section on 'Going to a solicitor', p. 449.

### APPLY FOR LEGAL AID

If you are not working or if you are earning less than £35 a week you will probably be entitled to free legal aid. Even if you earn considerably more than that you may well be entitled to some legal aid, but you will have to pay a contribution towards it. The amount will depend on your income, your expenses and how many dependants you have. Get your solicitor to help you fill in the legal aid form. Read 'Getting legal aid', p. 452.

### GO TO THE MAGISTRATES' COURT AND APPLY FOR A SUMMONS AGAINST YOUR HUSBAND

Your solicitor will tell you how to do this. You need to go to the magistrates' court and ask the magistrate for a summons explaining briefly the circumstances of your case. Most magistrates hear applications in the morning before the usual court business. Your solicitor may give you a letter addressed to the Clerk of the Court explaining what you want. If you don't have a solicitor the officer at the court will help you with your application. The magistrate will hear the application in private and may ask you a few questions connected with your complaint.

### A DATE WILL BE FIXED FOR THE CASE TO BE HEARD

once your application has been accepted. Your husband will be sent a summons, telling him to appear in court on that day. You must be there too.

### AT THE HEARING

You and your husband will be able to produce evidence and call witnesses to prove your case. Sometimes, particularly in London, the case is not finished at the first hearing, and another date is fixed some weeks ahead.

FINALLY, AN ORDER IS MADE BY THE COURT

The court has power to order any of the following:

1. *Custody of the children.* The court will usually order that either you or your husband has custody of the children. It can at present also order that custody be given to someone who is neither a parent nor a spouse. The magistrates' court can also give actual custody to one party and legal custody (that is, all the rights and duties of custody except physical custody) to the other party.

2. *Access to the children.* The parent who does not have custody is usually allowed to see the children at certain times. The court normally allows this, unless that parent is considered to be a danger to the children. Grandparents too can apply for access.

3. *Maintenance.* Your husband will be ordered to pay a certain amount each week, fortnight or month to help support you and your children. He can also be ordered to pay a lump sum of up to £500 for each of you. If you are in urgent need, the court may make an 'interim order', which normally can last for three months.

## How much maintenance will you get?

In the case of *Gengler vs Gengler* (1976), the High Court said magistrates' courts should work out a wife's maintenance like this: take the husband's gross income, deduct national insurance and travel expenses of work; add it to the wife's income after tax, and divide the total by three. She should get extra maintenance for children. However, in the later case of *Rodewald vs Rodewald* (1977) the Court of Appeal decided that both parties should be assessed on their gross incomes. What is important is to work out the effect of taxation on any order so that the husband or wife does not receive an unjustified tax bonanza. (In reality, husbands often cannot pay the amount ordered and wives are better off on supplementary benefit.)

MAINTENANCE FOR THE CHILDREN ONLY

You can apply just for custody of the children and maintenance for them. To do this, you need only allege that your husband has not been maintaining the children reasonably. Even if you are unsuccessful in this respect, the court can still make an order for their custody and maintenance. The court will consider what is in the best interests of the children and may ask for a report from a probation officer or social worker before deciding (see p. 322). Alternatively, if you and your husband agree about the financial arrangements between you, you can apply for a consent order which will set out your agreement and may have tax advantages. Furthermore, if you and your husband have lived apart for three months, but neither one has deserted the other, and during that time he has been maintaining you, you can get an order that your husband pay you weekly a sum which does not exceed what he has been paying during the preceding three months.

## How long does the maintenance order last?

Maintenance for the children normally lasts until their seventeenth birthday.

If the child goes on from school to college, training or an apprenticeship, or if a child is handicapped, maintenance can be ordered to continue after the child is 18.

If the maintenance order is granted while you are living apart from your husband and you start living with him again, it will not be affected if the order was made directly to the child. However, if the order was made to you for the benefit of the child, it will cease to be effective if you live together with your husband for a continuous period exceeding six months. If a child has been placed in the care of a 'third party', such as a local council, payments still have to be made to support the child, even if the parents are living together.

If you divorce and remarry, you can't get maintenance for yourself, but your ex-husband must continue to support his children.

### How is the maintenance paid?

Your husband pays the maintenance to the court and the court sends it on to you by post. The payments can be made at whatever frequency the magistrates decide, e.g. weekly, fortnightly, monthly. If you want cash rather than a cheque, you can collect the money from court.

### Can you claim maintenance if your husband is abroad?

Yes, you can try; but whether you actually get any money is another question. Many women have a constant struggle (which they often lose) to enforce maintenance orders made against husbands living in Britain. It is at least twice as difficult if your husband lives abroad. Anyway, if you want to try, the procedure varies according to whether he lives in a Commonwealth country or not.

1. *If your husband lives in a Commonwealth country or Eire*, you can make an application for maintenance for yourself and your children at your local magistrates' court, as if he were not abroad (see p. 307). The court does not have to serve your husband with a summons and it hears the case in his absence. When it has considered the evidence, it makes a provisional order for maintenance. This is sent, together with the evidence, to the country where your husband lives. If the courts of that country confirm the order, you are entitled to maintenance. The money should be sent to your local magistrates' court, via the courts in the country where your husband lives. Consult a solicitor; legal aid is available for proceedings in Britain, but not for proceedings abroad (p. 454).
2. *If your husband does not live in a Commonwealth country* you will probably be able to claim maintenance by a different procedure, depending on which country he is in. Check with a solicitor and ask for free legal advice under the 'green form' procedure (p. 454). You will probably have to fill in the appropriate forms at your local magistrates' court office. They

send them, via the Home Secretary, to the country where he is, and your claim is decided according to the laws of that particular land. No legal aid is available, but the clerk at the magistrates' court should help you.

*Note:* If you live in England, Wales, Scotland or Northern Ireland, and your husband lives in another part of the U.K. you can normally claim maintenance through your local magistrates' court, as you would if he were living in the same part of the country as you.

## What happens if the man stops paying maintenance?

This section applies to married and single women who are claiming maintenance from the fathers of their children.

A lot of men stop paying maintenance after a while. If this happens to you there are certain steps you can take to get the money you are owed.

### WHAT TO DO IF THE MAN IS PAYING MAINTENANCE TO THE MAGISTRATES' COURT

(He will be doing this if the magistrates' court ordered the payments in the first place; or if a divorce court ordered the payments and you had them registered with the magistrates' court. The court will forward the payments to you by post, if they arrive.)

Go to the magistrates' court and apply for an 'arrears of maintenance summons'. This means that the man has to appear in court and explain why he hasn't paid. You can't get legal aid at this stage, but all you need do is go along to the court any weekday morning and explain what you want. The court officials will help you. Most magistrates' courts outside London allow you to sign a form asking the Clerk of the Court to apply for it on your behalf. If the man still doesn't pay up, you or the Clerk of the Court can apply for an 'attachment of earnings' order. This means that maintenance is deducted from his wages before he gets his take-home pay. It's a good solution if the man has a steady job. If he hasn't, the payments will probably lapse again when he goes out of work. It will then be very difficult and time-consuming trying to get your money.

What normally happens in a situation like this is that you wait each week to receive your money from the court. If it doesn't turn up, and you have no other money, you have to go to the Social Security office and claim supplementary benefit. (Details about supplementary benefit on p. 189.)

This is a very unsatisfactory situation. Everything happens on a week-to-week basis: one week the maintenance may turn up, the next week it may not. Each week that it doesn't turn up you have to make a special trip to the Social Security office to get enough money to live on. You may not be able to get supplementary benefit immediately – you may have to wait overnight or over a weekend without any money.

But there is one way of avoiding it. The magistrates' clerk (who deals with the administration of maintenance orders) may let you sign over your maintenance payments to the Department of Health and Social Security. This means that the Social Security office becomes responsible for collecting the payments from the man and gives you a supplementary benefit order book. You will be able to cash the orders each week regardless of whether the man has paid up.

It is now official Social Security policy to do this where your maintenance is less than your benefit. But they will probably refuse if your maintenance is higher than your benefit. If you think it would make life easier for you, it is well worth asking them to do it and trying to persuade them to take over the responsibility.

A man can eventually be arrested and prosecuted if he fails to pay maintenance over a long period of time. If convicted, he may be imprisoned for up to three months or fined up to £400. Men who fail to pay maintenance make up many of the 'debtors' who can still be put in prison. It seems absurd that this form of punishment survives long after the idea of imprisoning most debtors has been abandoned as ineffective and unjust. It would not be necessary if all mothers had a right to an adequate, independent income from the state.

WHAT TO DO IF THE MAN IS PAYING MAINTENANCE
DIRECTLY TO YOU

(He will be doing this if the divorce court ordered the payments and you didn't have them registered with the magistrates' court; or if he arranged to pay maintenance without going to court.)

If the divorce court ordered the payments, you will have to go back to the same court to take legal action against the man. This is rather more complicated than going to the magistrates' court and you should get advice from a solicitor.

If the man arranged to pay maintenance by a legal agreement, as explained on p. 310, consult the solicitor who drew up the agreement.

If you simply made an agreement between you, with no legal backing, then all you can do is start divorce or separation proceedings.

## What if you don't want to claim maintenance?

This applies to both married and single women.

If the father of your child has a reasonable income and is reliable, you may get more money from him than if you were getting supplementary benefit. If the payments arrive regularly, you will be spared the ordeal of having to squeeze your day-to-day living expenses out of the Social Security office. However, if the father has a low or unsteady income, or if he is unreliable, he probably won't keep up the maintenance payments, and, because of the uncertainty, it can be even worse than relying totally on supplementary benefit. You may in any case prefer to remain independent of him and not look to him for any part of your income. (Tax on maintenance is explained on p. 120.)

You do *not* have to claim maintenance from the father. Instead, you can claim supplementary benefit and your refusal to pursue the man for maintenance should *not* endanger your right to full benefit, as long as you are not living with him.

The Social Security officials will do all they can to get the father to pay maintenance – because if he does, they will be able to pay you less. When you go to claim supplementary benefit, they will question you about him. If you are not married, they may ask you a lot of personal questions to try to establish his identity. Remember, you do not have to tell them who he is or where he is and you still have a right to claim benefit. If you have no other money, you should be given the full amount for a single person, plus allowances for the children.

If you don't tell the Social Security officials who the man is, they are supposed to try to find out for themselves. Once they know who he is, they may try to persuade you to take legal action against him to make him pay. Don't let them talk you into it if you don't want to: you are quite free to say 'no'. However, the Social Security officials may decide to take legal action themselves. This would mean that they would be responsible for collecting the maintenance and they should still pay the supplementary benefit to you.

## Separation by legal agreement

If you want to arrange a separation order by voluntary, legal agreement, you will need a solicitor. Chapter 12 tells you how to get one (p. 449). Your solicitor will explain the procedure to you and advise you what arrangement would be in your best interests. Make sure he explains your tax position in regard to maintenance payments as this could make a considerable difference to their value (as shown on p. 120).

Your agreement can cover maintenance payments, arrangements about looking after the children and living in the family home, and the division of your belongings.

If your husband doesn't abide by the agreement, inform your solicitor, who will take steps to ensure that he does.

## Judicial separation

This is very rare nowadays and is only useful if you have religious objections to divorce. You may obtain a decree of judicial separation even if you are not domiciled in this country. You apply for it in the same way as you would apply for a divorce. The only differences are:

1. You can apply at any time – you don't have to wait until you have been married three years;
2. At the end of it you are officially separated but the marriage still exists.

## Getting your marriage annulled

This has the same effect as a divorce: it ends the marriage. To get an annulment you must prove that your marriage is not valid. You can do this by establishing one of the following facts:

1. You are too closely related to your husband to be legally married to him. Under the Marriage Act, a woman cannot marry her father, son, uncle, nephew or brother.
2. One of you was under 16 when you married.
3. The marriage ceremony did not comply with the requirements of the Marriage Act of 1949. This may not mean that the marriage is invalid, unless you both knew about it at the time. Even then it may not: for example if you married when you were under 18 without your parents' consent, the marriage would be valid.
4. One of you was already married to someone else.
5. You are both of the same sex.
6. You have not been able to consummate the marriage: this means not having ordinary sexual intercourse.
7. One of you entered into a polygamous marriage abroad while domiciled in England and Wales.
8. One of you refused to consummate the marriage: you will have

to show that whoever refused made a definite decision, not just excuses.

9. One of you was mentally unbalanced when you got married, to the extent of being unfitted to marriage or subject to regular attacks of insanity.

10. The one who is not applying for the annulment was suffering from a contagious form of venereal disease at the time of the marriage and the other did not know.

11. You were pregnant by another man when you got married.

12. One of you did not consent to the marriage. This could be for one of the following reasons:

(a) You were incapable of understanding that a marriage had taken place – for instance: you thought it was a betrothal ceremony; or you were mentally unbalanced and didn't realize you were getting married.

(b) You mistook the identity of the other person.

(c) You were forced to marry against your consent, by threats or violence.

You can't get an annulment for reasons 6–11 if your husband can satisfy the court that you knew there were grounds for claiming one, but led him to believe you wouldn't do so; and that it would be unjust to him if you did. Apply within three years of the marriage if you want an annulment under reasons 8–11.

## Useful things to read

*On Getting Divorced*, edited by Edith Rudinger, £3·95 from the Consumers' Association, 14 Buckingham Street, London WC2 6DS (01 839 1222). A more detailed explanation of the law, the grounds for divorce, the proceedings and financial provision.

*Proceedings for Divorce*, a booklet produced by the Divorce Registry, available from Somerset House, London WC2 and from county courts dealing with divorce.

# 7. Children

## Your rights as a mother

### If you are not married

You are the legal guardian of your children. You automatically have custody of them, which means you have a right to make all the decisions about their upbringing and are responsible for looking after them on a day-to-day basis.

You can only lose your rights over the child if you have it adopted by someone else (more about adoption on p. 354); or if you abandon it, neglect it, or treat it in a way that is unacceptable to the local council, so that it is taken into care (p. 324).

The fact that your child is illegitimate gives it fewer rights of maintenance and inheritance from its father. If born outside the U.K., an illegitimate child has until recently had no entitlement to U.K. citizenship. Now the Home Secretary can give citizenship to the illegitimate child of a British mother and under the new nationality law this may become a right. If you want to make the child legitimate, you can do this by marrying the father; or by adopting the child jointly with your husband (if the man you marry is not the child's father). You will probably not be given permission by the court to adopt the child yourself. The Children's Act 1975 says that the court should not make an adoption order in favour of one parent alone, unless the other parent is dead, cannot be found, or there is some other reason for excluding him or her.

The Law Commission has recommended that the law be changed to give illegitimate children equal status but at the time of writing it is not known whether this will happen.

You can give the child your last name, or the father's, or a combination of the two (or any other last name, if you wish), and enter it on the birth certificate – without the father's consent. The father's own particulars will not be included on the certificate, and the certificate will provide no proof of his paternity, unless he signs the particulars of the birth that you give to the registrar, or signs a statutory declaration confirming that the child is his; or unless you can produce a certified copy of an affiliation order (p. 317). If you wish, you can get a 'short' birth certificate which gives no details of the child's parents.

The father is responsible for supporting the child if he agrees to do so voluntarily; or if you take affiliation proceedings against him (see below).

If you don't agree to allow the father of your child or children to visit them, he can apply to the magistrates' court for 'right of access', which means the right to spend a certain amount of time with the children (say, one day a week and every other weekend). The court will probably rule that he should be allowed to see them unless he has such a bad character that it would be dangerous to let him near them. The father can also apply to court for custody of the children, but the court would be most unlikely to take them away from you unless the father could prove that you are incapable of looking after them (or that you are a lesbian, see p. 243).

## WHAT IF YOU DON'T WANT TO ACKNOWLEDGE THE FATHER?

It can be very difficult for a man to establish that he is the father of your child. He would have to go to court and prove:
– that you accepted payments or gifts from him shortly after the birth of the child; *or*
– that you have acknowledged that he was the father in some other way, in a letter, for example, or by admitting it to people whom he could call as witnesses.

A blood test can only prove that a man is *not* the father of a child: it cannot prove that he *is* the father.

## WHAT IF YOU WANT THE FATHER TO HAVE JOINT RESPONSIBILITY FOR THE CHILD?

Increasingly parents have a stable relationship but do not want to be married. In these cases there seems no reason why they should not share legal responsibility for the children in the same way as a married couple. But at present the law makes this difficult. You cannot have a joint custody order which operates while you are living together, nor are you allowed jointly to adopt the child. The father cannot be appointed guardian while you are alive. If you enter into a formal agreement for joint custody, it seems doubtful that it would be considered legally binding. It is time that the law was changed to permit a joint custody order on the application of the father and mother.

### CLAIMING MAINTENANCE FROM THE FATHER

*If he does not agree to pay* an amount which is acceptable to you, you will have to take affiliation proceedings. This means going to a magistrates' court and proving that he really *is* the father.

You can apply for an affiliation order while you are pregnant, or within three years of the child's birth. You can apply after three years if you can prove that the man paid money towards the maintenance of the child during the year after it was born: contributing to the household budget or giving presents can count. If the man leaves the country and later comes back you can apply up to three years after his return. You cannot apply if you are married to another man and living with him. You can apply if you are separated from your husband.

*If the father agrees to pay* an amount which is acceptable to you, you can both sign an agreement setting out how much he will pay each week. The National Council for One-Parent Families (address, p. 323) has produced a special form which you can use for this purpose. This agreement would be legally binding and you could take court proceedings to enforce it if the father failed to make the agreed payments. It would also be evidence, acceptable in a court of law, that the man had admitted he was the father and had been making payments towards the child's maintenance. If you need to take affiliation proceedings later on, the existence of this agreement will help your claim.

## HOW TO TAKE AFFILIATION PROCEEDINGS

1. Find a solicitor and apply for legal aid. Most women who take affiliation proceedings get legal aid very easily. You can ask one of the officials at the court, or your local Citizens' Advice Bureau, to help you contact a solicitor and fill in the legal aid forms. There is more information about this on p. 452.
2. Your solicitor will help you apply for a summons at the magistrates' court. The application for the summons can be dealt with either by post or by going to court and applying to the magistrate. The hearing is in private. A date is then fixed for the hearing and the father is sent a summons through the post, telling him to appear in court on a certain day.
3. At the hearing you will probably have to give evidence, unless the man admits to the court that he is the father. Your evidence must be backed up, for example by another witness who has heard the man admit that he is the father; or by letters the man has written to you; or by proof that he has already paid money towards the child's maintenance. If the man admits to being the father you don't have to go to court, although it might be useful to be there so that you can give evidence about the amount of money he should pay.

*If the court decides that the man is the father*, it can order him to make weekly payments to you for the maintenance and education of the child; and to pay extra money to offset the expense of the birth. Payments can be backdated to the day of the birth if you made your application within two months of that day. The father has to pay the money to the court, and the court sends the money to you each week through the post. A lump sum of up to £500 can be awarded, and payments of maintenance can last until the child is 16, or 18 if still in full-time education.

Alternatively, the court may order the payments to be transferred – either to the local council, if your child has been taken into care; or to the Supplementary Benefits Commission ('Social Security'), if you are receiving regular payments of supplementary benefit.

If you marry, the father must continue to pay maintenance for the child. But if the child is adopted by anyone else but you alone, he no longer has to pay.

### WHAT HAPPENS IF THE FATHER STOPS PAYING MAINTENANCE?

You may find that the father does not make his maintenance payments regularly. One in ten illegitimate children is covered by an affiliation order, and in half of those cases the fathers pay up irregularly or not at all.

If this happens to you, you can go to the magistrates' court and ask the Clerk of the Court to apply for an 'arrears of maintenance' summons. If that doesn't work you can apply for an 'attachment of earnings' order. If that doesn't work, you can ask your local Social Security office to take over responsibility for collecting the maintenance and give you a supplementary benefit order book so that you can cash the orders each week, whether or not the maintenance arrives. All this is explained under the heading 'What happens if the man stops paying maintenance?' (p. 307).

### IF THE FATHER DIES

You may be able to claim a share in his estate (that is, if he leaves anything behind). Under the Inheritance (Provision for Family and Dependants) Act 1975, 'any person who immediately before the death of the deceased was receiving substantial contributions in money or money's worth can apply for a share in the estate'. It is entirely up to the judge to decide who should get a share and how large or small the share should be; and he has to take the conduct of the applicant into account.

(See also 'If the man you are living with dies', p. 390, and 'Widows' inheritance', p. 182.)

WHAT IF YOU DON'T WANT TO CLAIM MAINTENANCE
FROM THE FATHER?

See p. 309.

### If you are married

Until 1973, the legal guardian of a legitimate child was still the father. This meant that he had a right to take all the major decisions about the way his child was brought up. If the mother disagreed, she could only challenge his decision by going to court and applying for custody of the child.

But in 1973 the Guardianship Act was passed, which gave the mother the same legal rights and authority over her child as the father and established that the rights and authority of both parents 'shall be equal and exercisable by either without the other'. So you, the mother, can now make major decisions affecting your child in the father's absence and without his consent. He can do the same without your consent. If you disagree, either of you can apply to the court to have the matter settled there. The court's decision need not entail the awarding of custody to either parent.

You and your husband are equally responsible for supporting your children and you are both equally liable to be prosecuted if you fail to look after them properly, or treat them cruelly, or damage their physical or mental health.

### IF YOU AND YOUR HUSBAND SEPARATE
### OR DISAGREE OVER THE CHILDREN

Either one of you can apply to a magistrates' court or county court for custody of the children. You will need a solicitor for this, so read pp. 449–59. The court will give equal consideration to both your claims, but will base its decision on what it thinks would be best for the children. In practice, children usually go to the mother, especially if they are young. The parent who is not given custody of the children is normally allowed to spend a certain amount of time with them. The court will also make arrangements for the children to be financially supported, as explained on p. 298.

### IF YOUR HUSBAND ILL-TREATS YOUR CHILDREN

You can apply for a magistrates' matrimonial order or a divorce because of his behaviour. At the same time, you can apply for custody and maintenance for the children. Consult a social worker.

### TAKING YOUR CHILDREN OUT OF THE COUNTRY

You can put your children on your passport or get them separate passports without the father's consent. He can do so without your consent. Both parents have equal rights to take the children out of the country (unless one has been awarded custody), and where there is a disagreement the matter has to be settled in court.

(Details about a married woman's passport rights are on p. 260.)

### MAKING YOUR CHILDREN WARDS OF COURT

If you think your husband may take your children away from you against your will – particularly if you think he may take them out of the country – and there is no other way of stopping him, you can apply to have them made wards of court. Go straight to a solicitor and insist that he takes out a summons immediately. This is a lot more effective than going to the police or to a magistrates' court. Magistrates' courts now have power to order that a child does not leave England and Wales, but it is not yet possible to say how efficiently or quickly such orders will work. If the first solicitor you see cannot make the child a ward, get him to put you in touch with one who can. You can also apply for legal aid – the solicitor will help you. You should only resort to this in an emergency. It means that the court takes over custody of the children and awards the right of 'care and control' to one parent. The children become wards of court as soon as the solicitor takes out the summons. If the court considers there is a real risk that the children will be taken away from the applicant they will issue a 'Home Office letter'. The Home Office then arranges for a watch to be kept on all ports and airports.

## *If you are getting divorced*

### IF YOU AND YOUR HUSBAND AGREE

about who should keep the children after the divorce, there will be no need to fight it out in court. When the divorce petition is first presented to the court, you must fill in a form explaining what arrangements have been made for the children (for instance, what plans you have made for their education, and how they will divide their time between your husband and you). The judge must approve these arrangements before the divorce is made final. An appoint-ment will be made for you to see the judge in private and explain the arrangements to him. If he is dissatisfied with your proposals, he may send you away to sort out alternative arrangements and fix a date for a second meeting. You will have to submit further written evidence to the court and you may have to make alternative arrangements.

### IF YOU DO NOT AGREE WITH YOUR HUSBAND

about who should keep the children, the court will decide who is going to have custody. You must make an application for custody when you file the divorce petition, or when you acknowledge that a petition has been filed by your husband. This is a complicated matter and you should certainly have a solicitor to deal with it for you and present your case to the court. You can apply for legal aid.

Normally, the court rules that children should stay where they are until the divorce is over, unless there are urgent reasons why they should be moved.

### IF YOUR HUSBAND TAKES THE CHILDREN FROM YOU

without a court order and you had been looking after them you can go straight to court and ask for an order that he return them. It is important to tell your solicitor immediately as the application can usually be made the same day, or at least the day after.

### HOW DOES A COURT DECIDE WHO SHOULD HAVE CUSTODY WHEN PARENTS DISAGREE?

1. A social worker attached to the court will probably investigate the situation. She will visit the homes of you and your husband and talk to you both and to the children, if they are old enough. She will then make a report to the court.
2. If the matter isn't settled before the divorce hearing, there will be another hearing afterwards, in private before the judge.
3. The judge must decide what is in the best interests of the children. This should have nothing to do with who caused the breakdown of the marriage. If the children are small, they will normally go to live with the mother, but this is not a hard and fast rule. The judge will nearly always decide that the children should stay together, as it is very rarely in their interests to be split between the parents.
4. You are more likely to get custody of the children if:

(a) You are living with them at the time when the court makes its decision about custody;

(b) You are living in the family home, or you have established a good home for them somewhere else;

(c) You are living in conventional circumstances.

5. You are less likely to get custody if:

(a) You are not living with the children at the time of the custody decision;

(b) You are living in more cramped conditions than your husband;

(c) You are living in a way that might be considered haphazard or unconventional, or sharing with other people in a communal household.

Normally, the judge grants custody and 'care and control' of the children to one parent. 'Custody' means the right to take long-term decisons affecting their lives (such as what schools they should go to and what religion they should follow). 'Care and control' means the day-to-day responsibility of looking after them. The judge may grant joint custody to both parents and care and control to one (although this would usually be at the request of both parents).

Arrangements about care and custody of the children are sometimes dealt with after the divorce and sometimes before, but if there is any disagreement, make sure you are represented by a solicitor (pp. 449–59).

Divorce is explained in detail on p. 280.

### Further information (for single mothers)

National Council for One-Parent Families, 255 Kentish Town Road, London NW5 (01 267 1361).

Gingerbread, 35 Wellington Street, London WC2 (01 240 0953 and 01 836 4203): some practical help and moral support for single parents.

## How your child could be taken into care

This section applies to married and single parents.

Having your child taken into care means that the social services department of your local council takes over all your responsibilities as a parent. If this happens to a child of yours, she or he may be allowed to stay at home, or may have to move to accommodation approved by the council, such as a hostel or a 'community home'. You and the father still have to pay money to support the child. There are three ways this can happen.

1. You can ask the council to take your child into care, perhaps because you are ill or homeless. The council takes over responsibility for the child until you ask for it to be returned to you. It has no power to keep the child against your wishes unless the child has been in care for more than six months, when you have to give them twenty-eight days' notice.

2. The council can decide to take your child into care because you appear to have abandoned it or to be incapable of looking after it properly. The council must write you a letter telling you what it intends to do. If you consent in writing, the council takes over all your duties as a parent and you have no further rights over the child. The same can happen if the child has been in care for three years or more. If you do not reply and the council cannot find out where you are within the space of a year, it concludes that you have abandoned the child.

   If you object, you should write to the social services department of the council and tell them so. They will then have to take the matter to court, and you will have a chance to put your case to the court. You can probably get legal aid for this so you can have a solicitor to represent you. Ask your Citizens' Advice Bureau about legal aid, and read the section on pp. 449–59.

3. A court may decide that your child is in need of 'care and control' and make a care order placing the child in the care of the local council. Care orders are compulsory: they do not require the parent's consent. They are used as a last resort when

all other measures have failed. They are usually made because the child has been neglected or maltreated, or because the child has done something wrong and the court considers that the parents are not looking after and controlling the child properly. The kind of behaviour by a child which may lead a court to make a care order would be:
– conviction for a number of criminal offences;
– persistently playing truant from school, in the case of children under 16;
– mixing with 'bad company';
– taking drugs;
– sleeping around, in the case of girls only.

If a child is under 16 when a care order is made, the order lasts until the eighteenth birthday. If the child is 16 or over, it will last until the nineteenth birthday. It can be ended sooner if the child (through the parent) or the council makes an application for it to be discharged, and that is accepted by the court.

Your child may be allowed to stay at home after a care order is passed. If your child is sent away to a hostel or community home, she or he can be visited by you and may be allowed home at weekends. You and the father will still have to pay maintenance for the child. Consult a solicitor if you want to oppose a care order – you can apply for legal aid (pp. 452–9). See p. 368 for care orders from the child's point of view.

## Nurseries and other child-care facilities

If you have children under school age, you may not be able to look after them all day every day; or you may not want to. Instead you may be able to arrange for other people to look after them. In this section we describe the different child-care facilities that are likely to be available to you.

*If you want to find out about child-care facilities in your area*, contact the social services department of your local council. For information about nursery education, contact your local education authority. Addresses and phone numbers are listed in the telephone directory under the name of the council.

## Day nurseries run by local councils

These are the only state-run nurseries which cater for children of women who have full-time jobs. They are run by the social services departments of local councils, and they are usually open between 8 a.m. and 6 p.m., including school holidays. They take children from six weeks old to school age. They are not free, but the amount you pay depends on your income. It could vary from £12 to more than £25 a week. Standards vary considerably. Since they are not run by local education authorities, very few have any trained teachers on the staff. Instead, they have trained nurses and nursery nurses. Some try to provide good educational facilities, but many are overworked and under-staffed.

### CAN ANY CHILD GO TO ONE OF THESE DAY NURSERIES?

No. Day nurseries have to give priority to children from 'deprived backgrounds' – which means children of single parents who have to go out to work; children whose mothers are ill; and children who live in poor housing conditions. They may also give priority to children of teachers if there is a shortage of teachers in the area. Places are limited, so you will find it almost impossible to get a place for your child unless you fit into one of these categories. It helps if you have a recommendation from a doctor, health visitor or social worker.

*The official attitude towards full-time care for under-fives* is summed up in the Plowden Report:

We do not believe that full-time nursery places should be provided, even for children who might tolerate separation without harm, except for exceptionally good reasons. We have no reason to suppose that working mothers as a group care any less about the well-being of their children than mothers who do not work . . . but some mothers who are not obliged to work may work full time regardless of their children's welfare. It is no business of the educational service to encourage these mothers to do so. It is true, unfortunately, that the refusal of full-time nursery places for their children may prompt some mothers to make unsuitable arrangements for their children's care during working hours. All the same, we consider that mothers who cannot satisfy the authorities that they have exceptionally good reasons for working should have low priority for full-time nurseries for their children.

The number of local authority day nurseries in England declined from 903 in 1949 to 507 in 1974. The most recent figures (1977) show that there 8·9 places for every 1,000 children under 5. After 1979, day nurseries were closed by a number of local authorities as a result of spending cuts imposed by central government.

## Nursery schools and classes

These are run by local education authorities and staffed by qualified teachers, to provide education for children who have reached the age of 2 but who are not yet 5. (In practice, 2-year-olds are rarely admitted.) Most are part time, from 9.30 a.m. until midday, or from midday until 3.30 p.m. A few are from 9.30 a.m. to 3.30 p.m. but even these are of little use to mothers who have full-time jobs and no one to look after their children after school hours and in the holidays. All are free of charge.

Nursery classes are attached to primary schools. Sometimes the only way to find out about classes in your area is to ask each primary school what it provides.

Nursery education is very scarce and there are long waiting lists for most schools and classes. It may be worth finding out about the ones in your area while your child is still a baby: you may be able to put her or his name on the waiting list. If that doesn't work, try talking to the teacher in charge of the nursery school or class. She or he can usually decide whether to accept children, regardless of the number of applicants.

In January 1973 a government circular stated that nursery education should be available to those children whose parents wanted it, from the beginning of the term after their third birthday until the term after their fifth birthday. It stressed that most children would attend for only half the day, but conceded that a minority of children should, for educational and social reasons, attend for a full day.

The building programme to expand nursery education began in 1974 and capital funds were made available by central government. However, some local authorities did not take up their allocation and since then funds have been drastically cut.

At present it seems that the policy laid down in the 1973 circular will never be implemented and in some areas there are no nurseries at all. If you cannot find a nursery school for your child, contact your local councillor and find out if the council is using up all the government funds available, or if it could be doing more to increase the number of nursery places.

In January 1977 there were 52,260 children in 648 nursery schools and 157,601 children in 3,927 nursery classes. But since then many nursery schools and classes have closed, due to local authority spending cuts.

### Private nursery schools

These have to be registered with the social services department of the local council. Their opening hours vary – some are part time and more like play groups; others are full time and cater for working mothers. In 1977 there were 22,513 places in 799 nurseries. Costs and standards vary: some have trained teachers and others don't. In order to be registered they have to meet certain standards of accommodation, safety and record-keeping. They do not have to meet specified educational standards.

### Pre-school play groups

Play groups are usually run by mothers who want to give their children a chance to play creatively with other children. They are not much use for mothers who work full time, as they normally run from 9.30 a.m. until midday; some are open for two or three mornings a week, others every morning. Prices are around 50p per session. There is often a rota of mothers to help the play-group leader.

Many of the groups are affiliated to the Pre-School Playgroups Association, which exists to promote play groups and public interest in them, to maintain high standards, and to advise people who want to set up new groups. In 1980, a questionnaire sent out by the PPA found that 246,365 children were attending playgroups. Its headquarters are at Alford House, Aveline Street, London SE11 (01 582 8871); and at 16 Sandyford Place, Glasgow G3. (If you write to them, send a stamped addressed envelope with all inquiries.)

Play groups have to be registered with the social services department of the local council, and in order to be accepted for registration they must meet standards of safety and accommodation. Local councils often help play groups by providing grants or accommodation. Many Adult Education Centres provide courses for people who want to train as play-group supervisors – although it is possible to start a play group without being trained.

### Child minders

Child minders are people who look after children in their own homes as a means of income. They are still the most common form of child care used by working mothers. Prices vary (from £10 to more than £15 a week) and so do standards. Some child minders are excellent, but others just do it because they need the money when they don't really have the facilities for the children to play. Child minders are legally obliged to register with the local council, so that the council can check that their homes are safe, particularly against fire risk, and that they are not looking after too many children at once. But many child minders avoid registering so that they can take more children than the council would allow. It's advisable to check first that the child minder you are considering leaving your child with has registered with the council. Contact the social services department.

A child minder who fails to register could, after due warning, be taken to court and fined – unless she is a close relative of the children she is looking after; or unless she is looking after children for no more than two hours a day.

Some local authorities have introduced schemes which include training sessions for child minders and loans of toys and other equipment, and, in some areas, child minders and the children in their care have been linked with particular day nurseries or play groups. It would help if more local authorities introduced schemes of this kind. However, for every registered child minder, there are at least ten who are unregistered and these receive no help at all.

### 'One o'clock clubs', occasional crèches, etc.

'One o'clock clubs' are usually run in parks where there is a play hut available. The idea is that mothers bring their children along between 1 and 3 in the afternoon. Mothers have to stay, but play equipment is provided. The clubs are supervised and the service is free. Some councils run 'Mother and Toddler Clubs' and 'Pram Clubs' along the same lines – in parks or community centres. Sometimes maternity and child welfare centres run crèches once or twice a week for a few hours at a low charge or free. Details of all these facilities from the social services department of your local council.

### Workplace nurseries

There are about ninety workplace nurseries in Britain – most of them in the north, where employers depend on married women workers. They are financed by the employer, although mothers are often charged a fee. There are serious snags to this kind of child care, as it means the mother must take the child to work with her, and home again in the evening when they are both tired, with no time to do shopping on her own. When she changes jobs, she loses her child's place in the nursery. Some workplace nurseries forbid mothers to see their children during the day. These nurseries are better than nothing, but it would be a better idea if employers provided the funds for them, but let them be run by the workers, perhaps through a trade-union committee.

## After-school and holiday care for school-aged children

One of the biggest worries for women who go out to work is what to do with their children from the time school ends to the time they get home from work, and during the school holidays. There's always enough talk about 'latch-key' children turning delinquent to make working women feel guilty, but there's seldom any constructive help available for them.

Only a few councils provide play centres: these are open until about 6.30 p.m. in the term time, and they are open all day, from about 9.00 a.m., in the holidays. Some give the children a light tea in the term time and a midday meal in the holidays. The children are supervised and entertained.

There are a few experimental schemes which provide after-school care for children who attend nursery schools and classes in the Inner London area. The education authority provides the accommodation and the local social services department pays for the staff. If there aren't facilities like this in your area, you could try getting together with other women and asking the council to set one up.

## Combined day nurseries and nursery schools

Some nursery centres which provide both day care and nursery education have been established. There are between forty and fifty in the U.K. There are great differences in the organization of these centres, which tend to reflect the differing priorities of each local authority. Increasingly, nursery centres seek to meet all aspects of children's needs, while parents are encouraged to be closely involved.

## Community nurseries

There are only a few community nurseries in the U.K. These, like nursery centres, combine day care with nursery education; but unlike other forms of day care, they serve a particular community and any child living in the catchment area may use them. A further feature of these nurseries is that parents and workers are closely involved in the management of the nursery. Community nurseries need funds from local authorities and have all been set up only after long and sustained campaigns to persuade local authorities to supply grants.

## Campaigning for child-care facilities

Concern about the poor level of facilities, and in particular about the lack of full-time child-care provision, has prompted a number of child-care campaigns, local and national. Many trade unions have a policy which calls upon central government to allocate funds for the expansion of full-time unified provision, with a greater degree of democratic control. The TUC has published a *Charter on Facilities for the Under-Fives*, of which the main requirements are these:

1. A comprehensive and universal service of care and education for children from 0 to 5 must be made available by public authorities. A national programme for pre-school services must be drawn up by the government jointly with the unions.
2. Pre-school services must be available on demand to all those wishing to make use of them, which will require a major expansion of all pre-school services on the basis recommmended in this report.
3. Pre-school services must be made available free of charge to parents.
4. A statutory duty to provide pre-school services must be placed on local authorities.
5. A service for the under-fives must be based on the principle that there can be no distinction between the education and welfare needs of young children.
6. All pre-school facilities must have flexible hours to meet the needs of

working parents; and for school children a service of extended day and school holiday schemes should be made available.

7. The national plan for extended pre-school services should be based on an extension of nursery centres, combining care, education, health and welfare facilities for under-fives. Centres should co-ordinate all under-fives facilities in their areas. Child minders and play groups should be 'attached' to nursery centres, which should provide them with training and back-up services.

8. Existing facilities should be improved to provide a more comprehensive service – i.e. day nurseries should employ teachers as additional staff, nursery schools and classes should provide an 'extended day' and also facilities in school holidays.

9. Child minders should be employed by local authorities; attached to nursery centres and day nurseries; and provided with back-up services. New legislation on child minding should be introduced laying down minimum national standards. Local authorities should have a statutory duty to administer and enforce such legislation. Where workplace nurseries are provided, this should be on a basis which ensures joint union/parent/employer control and full local authority involvement, plus collectively agreed sufficient safeguards to protect the legitimate interests of the workforce.

10. Consultations should take place between the Department of Education and Science, Department of Health and Social Security, the relevant unions and the Council for National Academic Awards and the Local Government Training Board and the Nursery Nurses Education Board on an improved training and career structure for nursery officers. Discussions on integrated training and service conditions for teachers and nursery staffs should also be encouraged.

11. Discussions on ways of achieving far closer integration of the government departments responsible for under-fives services should take place. Local authorities should also integrate their services. A single development plan with joint funding should be provided.

The full Charter can be obtained from the TUC, Great Russell Street, London WC1.

**Further information**

National Child-Care Campaign, c/o Surrey Docks Child Care Project, Docklands Settlement, Redriffe Road, London SE16.

Addresses of local child-care campaigns from your town hall or local library.

## Education

At every stage of the education system, girls are treated less favourably than boys. Sometimes, discrimination is obvious; sometimes it is so subtle that it passes unnoticed. But it undoubtedly has a profound effect on the way girls and boys grow up and the way their futures are shaped – as these figures indicate:

|  | Girls | Boys |
|---|---|---|
| CSE examinations (summer 1978): |  |  |
| physics | 14,668 | 88,625 |
| technical drawing | 2,383 | 80,768 |
| domestic subjects | 97,000 | 10,719 |
| commerce | 31,337 | 10,059 |
| School leavers with two or more 'A' level passes: |  |  |
| science | 6,880 | 20,640 |
| arts and social science | 24,390 | 18,340 |
| mixed | 8,730 | 12,130 |

Seventy per cent of students taking science courses in further education colleges are male. Less than 40 per cent of university students are female.

The Sex Discrimination Act says it is illegal to treat girls less favourably than boys. But it can only affect the most blatant and straightforward forms of discrimination – as you will see if you read on. It cannot change the attitudes, traditions and patterns of behaviour which play such a crucial role in education. For instance, the Act cannot stop teachers having different expectations of girls and boys (boys will be noisy, can help lift heavy things, are 'naturally' more interested in certain topics; girls are quieter, tidier, and 'naturally' prefer certain types of activity). The law does not oblige schools or teacher-training colleges to introduce the study of sex roles into the curriculum. Nor does it oblige teachers to give particular encouragement to girls embarking on science courses. In areas like these, where the law cannot – and perhaps should not – intrude, it is up to students, teachers and parents to press for changes, through their unions and parent–teacher associations. (More about that on p. 350.) Even in areas which are covered by the law, you may achieve more by organizing campaigns at a local or national level than by taking individual complaints to the county court. However, it's important to know what the Act says, so that you can use it as ammunition to strengthen your case, even if you don't go to court. And, in some circumstances, taking a complaint through the court may prove the most effective course of action.

## What does the Sex Discrimination Act say?

*Chapter One describes the general terms of the Sex Discrimination Act. Since it is relevant to this section, we suggest you read it first.*

In providing education, it is illegal to treat a girl less favourably than a boy would be treated in the same circumstances, by:

1. Admitting her to a school or college on different terms; *or*
2. Refusing to admit her, or ignoring her application; *or*
3. Admitting her, but then refusing her access to classes or courses, or any other benefits, facilities or services provided by the school or college; *or*
4. Treating her unfavourably in any other way.

The Act places a general duty on local education authorities to provide equal educational opportunities for both sexes.

Unlawful discrimination can be *direct* or *indirect* as explained on p. 25.

WHO CAN BE HELD RESPONSIBLE FOR BREAKING THE LAW?

1. The Act covers all schools, colleges and other educational establishments maintained by local education authorities (LEAs). The LEA, or the school managers or governors, can be held responsible, depending on the circumstances of the case.
2. Independent schools ('public' and other fee-paying schools) and special schools (such as those for handicapped children) are also covered. The proprietors can be held responsible.
3. Universities are covered by the Act. The governing body of the university is responsible for any illegal discrimination.
4. Certain other establishments, which have been designated by the Secretary of State for Education, are also covered. These include certain independent polytechnics in London and other establishments which receive grants from the Department of Education and Science, or from local authorities. In each case, the governing body of the establishment can be held responsible.

EDUCATIONAL TRUSTS

The Act allows educational trusts to change their terms (if the trustees choose to do so) in order to open up their benefits to both sexes. For example, the Rhodes Trust has in the past provided scholarships for boys only, as a result of Cecil Rhodes's will. The trustees can now, with the consent of the Secretary of State for Education, award scholarships to girls as well.

EXCEPTIONS

1. Single-sex schools and colleges are still lawful. This means they can go on admitting one sex only. If they admit a small number of the opposite sex (for instance, if a girls' school admits boys to the kindergarten), they must give them equal treatment; but for all other purposes they are exempted from the law.
2. Co-educational schools which provide boarding accommodation

for one sex can continue to do so. Boarding accommodation for both sexes can be separate, but must be equal.

3. Single-sex schools and colleges which are turning co-educational can apply for permission to discriminate by admitting more members of one sex for a limited period.
4. Education provided by charities set up to benefit one sex.
5. Further education courses in physical training are exempted.
6. Girls can be excluded from participating with boys as competitors in a sport where they would – on average – be at a disadvantage because of their physical capacity. It is still not clear whether schools can legally prevent girls taking part in sports such as football.

*Two examples of unlawful discrimination:*

1. Jill and Peter both go to the local mixed comprehensive. Peter does woodwork on Friday afternoons, while Jill does sewing. No girls are allowed to do woodwork; no boys are allowed to do sewing. The school governors are breaking the law.
2. Ann goes to a local girls' school; Jack goes to the local boys' school. The girls' school has poorer science classrooms and more science pupils per teacher than the boys' school. The boys' school has woodwork facilities but no cooking classrooms or teacher. The girls' school provides cooking and home economics lessons, but no woodwork. The governors of each school would *not* be breaking the law, because each school is single-sex. But the local education authority would be breaking the law because it is providing unequal educational facilities for the children in its area.

### ADVERTISING

It is illegal to advertise any form of education in a manner which implies that the advertiser intends to discriminate. For example, a college cannot legally advertise a car mechanics course 'for men'. If you find any illegal advertisements, report them to the Equal Opportunities Commission (address, p. 486). If the advertiser persists in breaking the law, the Commission can apply for a court injunction to stop him. If you think the advertisement amounts to unlawful discrimination against you personally, you may have grounds for taking a complaint to the county court.

## SCHOOL BOOKS

The Act makes no mention of school books, although many of these discriminate against women in a number of ways – some more subtle than others – and reinforce stereotyped views of male and female abilities and roles. Here are some examples:

1. The Oxford Children's Reference Library book, *Science*, shows 107 males in its illustrations, and seventeen females. The males are engaged in a variety of active and scientific pursuits, while almost all the females are engaged in passive and typically feminine pursuits such as combing hair, vacuuming, and mixing a pudding. School children who read the book might gain the impression that science is mainly for boys; and it could add to other influences which discourage girls from studying science or aiming for jobs in the fields of science and engineering.
2. A book called *Famous Writers* in the Macdonald Junior Reference Library mentions thirty-four men and not one woman. This could lead children to believe that women have achieved little or nothing in the literary field; and girls may underrate their own abilities if they have no role models of their own sex.
3. The Ladybird reading books – even the new 'modernized' editions – often show the main characters, Jane and Peter, in stereotypical roles. One illustration in *Things We Like* shows a group of boys playing ball while Jane cheers them in the background:

   > Peter has a red ball.
   > He plays with the boys with the red ball.
   > Jane looks on.
   > That was good, Peter, says Jane.

   This is just one of the many passages in the Ladybird reading scheme which show male characters playing active or leading roles while female characters are passive or supportive. Each passage adds to a general picture of the world which is passed on to children at a most impressionable age.
4. *Tudor Britain* in the series *History Topics and Models* (Evans Brothers) has a chapter on 'Tudors at Work'. In three pages of text, there are only these three references to women:

   > Behind the workroom was the family's living-room; here the master, his wife, family and apprentices had their meals.

Work began at about six-thirty every morning when the master and his wife made sure that the boys were up and busy in the shop and workroom.

The merchant's wife had some pottery and pewter for special occasions.

Women are described in terms of their relationship to men and never as individuals in their own right. *Their* work (preparing food, making clothes, child rearing, etc.), though no less important, is not discussed at all.

It could be argued that schools using books which present such a one-sided view of the world as a compulsory part of the syllabus are in breach of the law. To educate girls to have a more limited view of their roles and abilities than boys is to treat them less favourably. In an advisory booklet issued to all schools, *Do you provide equal educational opportunities?*, the Equal Opportunities Commission says that sexism in school text-books can be discriminatory. It advises schools of the 'need to select text-books which represent balanced sex-role attitudes' and urges them to make representations to publishers 'to amend future editions of text-books'.

At the time of preparing the third edition of this *Guide*, no test case had been brought to court to determine whether or not the compulsory use of sexist school books was unlawful. It seemed unlikely that such a case would succeed. Some publishers are beginning to produce reading schemes and other text-books which are non-sexist. However, the current shortage of funds presents a major problem. Cuts in educational spending mean that many schools can barely afford the most essential teaching materials, let alone to replace whole sets of books because they are sexist (although one may question their priorities). The main hope is that pressure from teachers, parents and pupils will eventually force publishers to change their policy, and as old books wear out, so they will gradually be replaced by new ones which avoid sex, race or class bias.

A technical manual for teachers concerned to end sex-stereotyping in schools is available free from the EOC (address, p. 486).

### How to get your rights

You can make a formal complaint under the Act *only if* you yourself or your child has suffered discrimination. Young people under 18 can only make a complaint through their parent or guardian. A teacher can make a complaint on behalf of her own child, but not on behalf of her students. If a teacher is discriminated against in her job, she can make a complaint to an industrial tribunal under the employment section of the Act (p. 41).

At the time of writing, only one complaint under the education section of the Sex Discrimination Act had reached the county court. This was the case of Helen Whitfield against Croydon Borough Council.

Helen attended a middle-school in Croydon, where she found that a course in woodwork, metalwork and design technology was not open to her because she was a girl. She applied to join the course. Initially, she was turned down, but later when one boy dropped out of the course she was offered a place as a special concession. She refused the offer, because she did not want to be the only girl in a class of boys. She complained under the Sex Discrimination Act, arguing that if boys were admitted automatically to a course, while girls were excluded unless they made a special application, this amounted to 'less favourable treatment' under the terms of the Sex Discrimination Act.

The county court judge took the view that Helen had not really wanted to do the course, and ruled that the school's behaviour was not in breach of the Act. There was no appeal.

Strictly speaking, a county court judgment does not set a legal precedent and cannot dictate the outcome of future cases. However, this decision does appear to legitimize a practice which has become widespread in schools. Traditional 'boys'' and 'girls'' subjects are taught (home economics and technical drawing, for example), often at the same point in the timetable. Both sexes may be told they can opt for either one, but the great majority choose the course which seems most appropriate to their sex. Occasionally a few pupils are unconventional enough to insist on doing the atypical course – and they are allowed in, perhaps grudgingly. The school thereby avoids allegations of unlawful sex discrimination, while perpetuating traditional divisions along sex lines (especially in vocational courses).

The Equal Opportunities Commission takes the view that this practice *is* unlawful; and says in its guidance to schools:

Pupils should not be required to make a special application to study a subject which might be regarded as non-traditional, except in single-sex schools where non-traditional courses are not available.

However, this will remain open to question until another case is taken to court – and won. The chances of this happening do not seem very high. Many parents are intimidated at the thought of going through the complicated legal procedure. They may be worried about 'making trouble' at school which they fear could have an adverse effect on their children; or they may be reluctant to bring a complaint of sex discrimination against a school which is otherwise satisfactory. Much of the fault lies with the enforcement procedures laid down in the Act. It would be more helpful to have a single system of tribunals, dealing with all complaints of sex discrimination as well as claims for equal pay.

If you have a complaint of unlawful discrimination in education, follow the steps described below. It may be best to start off by talking or writing to the body responsible for the school, college or LEA: tell them you think they are breaking the law and that you are considering making a formal complaint. This alone may prompt them to change their ways – particularly if you have the support of teachers, parents or students. In any event, try to get support from one or all of these sources – it will probably increase your chances of ending the discrimination.

MAKING A FORMAL COMPLAINT

If you or your child has been discriminated against, you should (in most cases) complain in writing to the Secretary of State for Education. If nothing is done to your satisfaction within two months, you can make a complaint to the county court within the next six months. If your complaint is against a university or independent school, you should take it straight to the county court, without writing to the Secretary of State. (If your complaint is about an advertisement, report it first to the Equal Opportunities Commission.)

*Read the chapter on the county courts* on p. 461. It tells you how to go through all the necessary steps and what to expect at each stage of the proceedings.

GETTING HELP WITH YOUR CASE

For advice about your rights under the Act, write explaining your particular case to the Equal Opportunities Commission or to the Women's Rights Officer of the National Council for Civil Liberties (addresses, p. 499). For help with preparing your case, you can get advice from a solicitor free or partly free under the 'green form' procedure; or, if you want a solicitor to conduct the case for you and represent you in court, you can apply for legal aid. The amount of free help you get depends on your income and savings. More details about legal advice and aid on pp. 452–9.

You can get someone to represent you in court who is not a qualified lawyer (for instance, you might know of someone who has experience in dealing with sex discrimination cases).

It is worth asking the Equal Opportunities Commission to send you the following free material: leaflets entitled *How to take your case to the county court*; and *How to apply for help with your case*; and a special questionnaire form for setting out the details of your complaint.

PREPARING YOUR CASE

Make sure you collect all relevant information to back up your case. You have a right to put questions to the body responsible for the discrimination, before you go to court. You can do this either by setting out your questions in a letter, or by using one of the special questionnaire forms from the Equal Opportunities Commission. In our opinion, these forms are badly thought-out and off-putting for the average complainant, but you may find that they are better than nothing. The body to whom you send the questions is not obliged to answer them, but if it doesn't, this may count against it when the case is heard. If it does give you answers, you can produce these as evidence in court.

In addition to the questions you ask, collect any relevant information and documents that could back up your complaint. If you know of anyone who witnessed the discrimination, ask them if they would be prepared to go to court to give evidence for you. If they are willing, find out if there are any dates on which they can't go to court, as this may affect the date of the hearing. It may be useful if you can get information about other instances of discrimination by the same school, college or local authority. If it has a bad record, the Equal Opportunities Commission may know about it. You can find out by writing to the Commission.

WHAT CAN YOU GET IF YOU WIN?

There are four things you may be able to get:

1. An order from the court declaring your rights and those of the other side.
2. An injunction to stop the other side discriminating unlawfully (e.g. insisting that a school admit girls to woodwork classes). If they disobey the injunction, they can be fined or imprisoned for contempt of court.
3. Money in compensation for damages.
4. Costs (money to compensate you for legal fees, if you paid any).

It is up to you to decide what kind of injunction (if any) you want the court to make and how much you require in damages. You should decide this in advance and present it to the court on your 'Particulars of Claim' form (p. 464). You should claim any money you think you have lost as a result of the discrimination and you can also claim for 'injury to feelings'.

**IF YOU LOSE**

You will not be asked to pay the other side's costs unless you claimed more than £100 in damages (so be very cautious about this and get legal advice on your chances of winning). If you have definite reasons for thinking that the court's decision was wrong, you have certain rights of appeal. Before appealing, consider the question carefully and get legal advice. Otherwise you may get involved in a lot of extra expense if the appeal is unsuccessful. The court office will explain what you have to do in order to appeal.

*If you have reason to believe that the school, college or local education authority will continue to discriminate unlawfully* – and the court does not issue an injunction which can prevent it – you can report the case to the Equal Opportunities Commission. They can make an investigation and then issue a Non-Discrimination Notice, or apply to court for an injunction. The Commission's powers are described on p. 481.

**FURTHER INFORMATION**

*Sex discrimination in schools* by Harriet Harman, from NCCL, 23–5 Tabard Street, London SE1.

## *What the law says about education generally*

If you have children aged between 5 and 16, you must see that they receive 'efficient, full-time education suitable to [their] age, ability and aptitude'. Your local education authority is obliged to provide this education. What this means in practice for over 90 per cent of children in Britain is that their parents send them to the local state school, where they get whatever's going in the way of education.

### CAN YOU CHOOSE YOUR SCHOOL?

The Education Act says that the Minister of Education has a duty to try to provide education in accordance with the parents' wishes. But the duty is limited to what will incur only 'reasonable public expenditure'. At the time of writing, this was becoming less and less.

Wealthy parents have always been able to choose, of course, but most of us have virtually no choice at all. Each local education authority divides its districts into 'catchment areas' and allots one to each school. It is very difficult to send your child to a school outside the catchment area where you live. If you want to try to persuade the LEA that your child should go to a school outside your area, you should write to the Education Officer and give her your reasons (get the address of the LEA from the telephone directory). If she refuses your request, you can appeal to the Secretary of State for Education, but you may have greater success by getting other parents' support and waging a campaign locally. If you are dissatisfied with the secondary school to which your child is allotted it's worth trying to enlist the support of the primary school head teacher for an appeal to the Education Officer.

### WHAT HAPPENS IF YOUR CHILDREN PLAY TRUANT, OR YOU FAIL TO SEND THEM TO SCHOOL REGULARLY?

If a child of yours has been absent persistently for some weeks, the Educational Welfare Officer will normally visit your home and talk to you. If matters don't improve, you will receive an 'attendance' order, which orders you to send your child to a certain school regularly. If you fail to obey, what happens next depends on whether the absence is considered the parents' or the child's fault. If it is considered the parents' responsibility, you – or more likely your husband – will be summoned to court and may be fined. If this happens, you stand a chance of avoiding conviction if you can prove one of the following to the court:

1. The child was unable to go to school because of illness or some other unavoidable reason (this must have been something that affected the child, not the parent).
2. The child was away from school on days set apart for religious observance by the religion that you follow.
3. The school was not within walking distance and the LEA failed to make suitable arrangements for transport.

In cases of truancy (where the child has taken the initiative in 'bunking off') you will receive a summons for the child to appear before a juvenile court. The court will consider reports on the home background from the social services department and the Educational Welfare Officer, and the child's attendance record from the school. The case may be adjourned for six weeks to see if the child will return to school. If not, she or he may be referred to a Child Guidance Clinic. In extreme cases, your child may be taken into care by the local authority (see p. 324).

TRANSPORT

If your child's school is more than walking distance from your home, the LEA is obliged to provide free transport or to pay travelling expenses there and back. 'Walking distance' means two miles for a child under 8 and three miles for a child over 8, measured by the 'nearest available route'. It makes no difference if the route is unsafe for a child or unfit for wheeled transport.

## POWERS OF THE TEACHERS

Once your child is at school, within school hours, the teachers take over your rights and obligations as a parent and they are therefore allowed to exercise reasonable discipline over the child. The LEA has full responsibility for children while they are at school, and if your child comes to any harm you may be able to sue for damages (you will need a solicitor for this; see pp. 449–59). If a child is sent home early, it is the duty of the school to see that she or he arrives safely.

In theory, teachers have no control over what your child does or wears outside school hours except on the way to and from school. (In theory, they have no power to make children do homework.) In practice, however, teachers can often make children conform by reprimanding or punishing them in school.

## CORPORAL PUNISHMENT

If one person hits another in ordinary circumstances, it is criminal assault. As a parent, however, you have a legal right to hit your children as a form of 'reasonable chastisement'. When you send your child to school, the law says you delegate that right to the teachers.

Most LEAs make their own rules about corporal punishment and schools are supposed to keep records of all corporal punishments that are given to children. In practice, the records are rarely complete and few parents know that they exist. It's worth finding out what punishments are allowed in your child's school. Some LEAs don't allow corporal punishment in certain schools – for instance, the Inner London Education Authority does not allow it in primary or secondary schools.

*If you object to corporal punishment being used in your child's school* there are three things you can do:

1. Any teachers who give out punishments that are more severe

than the LEA rules allow should be reported to the head teacher or to the LEA.

2. If the teacher uses more than reasonable discipline – for instance, by beating a child over the head – she or he can be prosecuted by you for criminal assault. Report the matter to the LEA or get advice from a solicitor (p. 449).

3. Make it clear to the teachers that you do not think it is right for your children to be physically punished and that you do not wish to delegate your power to hit them. If you do this, a teacher who then hits your child may be breaking the law. Write to the Society to Oppose Physical Punishment (STOPP), address, p. 353. They will send you a form which says just that: you sign it and send it to the LEA and to the head teacher of the school. This has never been tested in a court of law, so it is not yet known whether a parent can refuse to delegate her powers in this way.

Sometimes, of course, parents want teachers to be stricter than they are. But parents cannot insist on corporal punishment. A boy in Harrow was awarded an out-of-court settlement of £250 for loss of dignity after a caning at Harrow High School. And at the time of writing, a case is before the European Court of Human Rights on the grounds that belting is a breach of human rights.

EXPULSION

A child under 16 cannot be expelled from a state school, but can be suspended for a limited period or transferred to another school. A child over school-leaving age (16) who is suspended for two weeks can be expelled when the two weeks are up. If your child is suspended or expelled you have a right to appeal against the decision to the school governors or managers. The decision should not be upheld unless there is a valid reason, such as serious misconduct, prolonged absence or failure to work.

RELIGION

All state schools and voluntary schools (that is, most schools where you don't pay fees) have to begin each day with 'collective worship' and must provide a certain amount of religious instruction. If you do not approve of this sort of thing, you can arrange for your child to be withdrawn from morning prayers and religious instruction. (Unfortunately, it seems that a child cannot make a personal decision about this.)

Dear God, please save me from Morning Prayers and Religious Instruction

## *Getting financial help from the local education authority*

Some LEAs are more generous than others. Some will pay for a child to be sent to boarding school if the schools in the area are not suitable. If you are eligible for supplementary benefit (see p. 189), or receiving Family Income Supplement (p. 186) or otherwise considered 'in special need' because of low income, you should also be eligible for grants to help buy school uniform or ordinary school wear, school maintenance grants to help support children over 16 who are still at school, and free school meals. You can get information about these benefits from the education officer of your local education authority or Social Security office.

## IF YOUR CHILD IS HANDICAPPED

Local Education Authorities have a duty to provide special education in special schools, hospitals or elsewhere, for children who are blind, partially sighted, deaf, especially delicate, educationally subnormal, severely physically disabled, epileptic or maladjusted. They have power to make special provision, including transport to and from school, for a disabled child from the age of two onwards. But in fact, special schools are very limited in number and the kind of provision offered to your child will depend on what schools are available in your area.

If the LEA is satisfied that there are special reasons why your child cannot attend a suitable school, they can arrange for a home tutor. This applies to children in hospital or convalescing at home and those who are severely physically disabled. It also covers children awaiting a vacancy at a special school. Home tuition is sometimes provided by LEAs for children who have been sent home from school for being too disruptive. But as home tuition is expensive, this is rarely allowed.

## How can a parent make changes in the school?

A lot of parents feel helpless to make any changes in their children's education – often because their own childhood has left them with a strong aversion to school and an exaggerated sense of the head teacher's authority.

As a parent you of course have every right to make your objections known to the teachers and to suggest changes. This can have a considerable effect inside the school, although it may be some time before you or your children are aware of it. If complaining to the teachers makes no difference, you can complain to the school governors or managers (by writing to them at the school); then appeal to the local education authority; then, if all else fails, appeal to the Secretary of State for Education.

But there is a limit to what can be achieved by complaining through the official channels. Two causes of the shortcomings of the present state education system are: (a) the government does not give it enough money; and (b) most schools are isolated from the activities of the neighbourhood. The first is a matter of local and national politics. The second can be tackled at the level of the individual school – by parents becoming more closely involved with the work of the school and helping to shape policy through the parent–teacher associations. So, rather than writing a letter of complaint, you may find it more effective to get together with the teachers and other parents and work with them to make changes within the school. The important thing is to keep in touch with what is going on at the school and to get to know the teachers. Many primary schools now encourage parents to come into school and help the teachers, for instance by listening to children reading. This is obviously an ideal way of learning what goes on. If you can't do this because you are working all day, or because the school doesn't invite you, you should still try to visit the classroom with your child occasionally, to chat to the teacher and look at the work that is being done.

Another way of making your influence felt is by getting on to the school board of governors or managers, or electing someone else who holds the same views as you. All schools have at least two parent representatives on the board of governors or managers who are elected at a meeting of parents. Once elected, however, they do not have to carry out the electors' wishes. The only other way to become a governor or manager is to be nominated by the local section of a political party.

### How can a student make changes?

School students may be able to influence what goes on if they get together and make their collective views known to the teachers, managers or governors. You can join the National Union of School Students (address, p. 353).

## *Educating your child at home*

It is possible to satisfy the local education authority that you are providing your children with 'full-time, efficient education', etc., by teaching them at home. It helps if you have teaching qualifications or can provide them with a 'tutor' who has. Alison Truefitt, in *How To Set Up a Free School*, describes one successful experiment by a mother in Ealing, West London, a graduate with a teaching diploma who, unusually, had taught in every kind of state school, from infants to grammar:

Her daughter, now seven, and the youngest, took a violent and unaccountable dislike to her state primary school. In fact, she developed a severe school phobia, being sick every morning and so on. When after being ill at home for some time the daughter was due back for the last two weeks of term; and when, seeing the sickness coming on again, her mother said suddenly 'you needn't go back to school at all this term', the child recovered almost visibly.

The child is now extremely happy at home, and starting to read and take an interest in things again, which she had dropped while at school. The mother insists that the child is not in fact withdrawn or particularly shy: 'she talks all the time when we have her friends round here', just that she hated the huge size of the school she was at . . .

The LEA have made no inquiries about what the child is doing [in the way of lessons]. The mother says she does 'very little sitting down and teaching her. Certainly nothing regular.' It is interesting that the Ealing LEA are allowing this situation to continue, though they have 'suggested' that mother and child attend a child guidance clinic, which they are doing in the hope that this will prevent the LEA climbing further on their backs. However, it is unlikely the authority would have taken so liberal a view if they had not been dealing with a professional teacher who clearly knew the ropes.

Since this was written the child returned, of her own free will, to a different school in the same area.

For more information, contact Education Otherwise (address, p. 353).

## Free schools

These represent an ideal which is different from the traditional concept of education: children are given a lot more freedom than in ordinary schools to decide what and how they are going to learn. They are encouraged to learn spontaneously and little authority is exercised by teachers. The longest-established of these is the White Lion Street Free School in Islington, London N1.

## Further information

Advisory Centre for Education (ACE), 18 Victoria Park Square, London EC2 9PB (01 980 4596): for information on most aspects of education, students' and parents' rights.

Children's Books Bulletin, 4 Aldebert Terrace, London SW8: literature on sexism and children's books. Send s.a.e.

National Union of School Students, 3 Endsleigh Street, London WC1 (01 387 1277).

STOPP (Society to Oppose Physical Punishment), 10 Lennox Gardens, Croydon, Surrey CR0 4HR.

Education Otherwise, Field House, Mellis Road, Thrandeston, Nr Diss, Norfolk (037 983 678): for information on educating children otherwise than at school.

*Do you provide equal educational opportunities?* Free booklet from the Equal Opportunities Commission, Overseas House, Quay Street, Manchester M3. Scottish version is also available.

*Where to Look Things Up*: directory of useful addresses in the educational field, from ACE (address above).

*Women and Education, Issue 20*: resource list on non-sexist education from Women and Education, 14 St Brendan's Road, Manchester 20.

*How to set up a Free School*, 40p plus postage from the White Lion Street Free School, 57 White Lion Street, London N1.

## Adoption

In 1978, 12,121 children were adopted. Approximately half were adopted by a parent or relative.

### *If you want to adopt a child*

You can adopt a child through one of many registered adoption agencies. These are either local councils or voluntary societies. You may be able to adopt privately for instance, if you already know the child or its family; if you are related to the child; or if you have made contact with the child through a 'third party', such as a doctor, social worker or a friend. However, adoption through a 'third party' may soon be restricted by law. A complete list of adoption agencies is available from British Agencies for Adoption and Fostering (address, p. 364).

YOU HAVE TO BE VERY CAREFULLY VETTED

if you adopt through an agency. They will want to discuss the matter with you at great length and find out all about you before they decide whether you are a fit person to adopt. You are more likely to be accepted if you fulfil all of the following conditions:

1. You are married. If you are living with a man but not married to him, you cannot adopt as a couple. You may be able to adopt if you are single, but this is a lot more difficult.
2. You are under 40. The age limit for a man is usually higher. If you are in your late thirties, you are more likely to be accepted if you already have children. You must be at least 21.
3. You have a good home and an adequate income to support the child.

4. You are in good physical and mental health and have a satisfactory mental history.
5. The agency (if it is a good one) must be satisfied that you can 'genuinely accept another person's child as your own'.

There is a very long waiting list of parents wanting to adopt healthy white Anglo-Saxon babies and it is getting increasingly difficult to adopt new-born racially mixed babies. Meanwhile, there are a great many older children and children who are non-white or physically or mentally disabled, who cannot find adoptive parents. So, you may find it easier to adopt if you are prepared to accept a child who is non-white, disabled or no longer a small baby.

## RELIGION

Adoption agencies have a legal duty to take into account the natural parents' wishes about religious upbringing when placing a child for adoption – but they are not bound to abide by them. Some adoption societies still insist that adoptive parents practise a certain faith, even when the natural parents have not specified that their children should be brought up in any particular religion.

### HOW LONG WILL IT TAKE?

Prepare yourself for a long wait. It could take two years or more before you are given a child.

### HOW MUCH?

The buying and selling of children is not allowed so it would be illegal for you to accept or offer any money in the course of the adoption, except by paying a contribution towards the cost of the placement, if the agency asks for one. Local councils do not normally charge for arranging adoptions.

### WHAT ABOUT THE NATURAL PARENTS?

You cannot adopt without the consent of the natural mother and father, except in certain circumstances which are explained further on in this section. The natural parents are no longer shrouded in secrecy as they used to be: the adoption agency may talk quite openly about them and give you detailed information about the child and its background. It may arrange for you to meet them, if both sides agree. You will know the mother's name and possibly the father's because you will see the child's birth certificate. But you can, if you choose, conceal your identity from the natural parents.

### ONCE YOU HAVE BEEN ACCEPTED AS A POSSIBLE ADOPTIVE PARENT

You must look after the child for three months before the court can make the adoption order. You must make sure that the social services department of your local council is informed in writing that you are looking after the child with a view to adoption (unless either you or your husband is a parent of the child). You will be visited by a social worker from the council and the court will also appoint a 'guardian *ad litem*' (who may be the same social worker sent by the council) to be responsible for the child during those three months. Either the 'guardian *ad litem*' or another qualified person will interview all the people concerned with the adoption and report to the court whether the adoption arrangements are suitable.

*After three months*, if all goes well, you have to go to court for the legal adoption to take place. Adoption proceedings normally take place in the county court or the magistrates' court. They are heard in private before the judge or magistrate. (Some judges are fond of delivering a lecture at this point.) You can choose to be identified by a serial number rather than by name if you don't want the natural parents to know who you are. If the court is not entirely satisfied that you are ready to adopt the child – for instance, if you don't have proper accommodation – it can make an interim order allowing you to keep the child for up to two years, in the hope that you will be able to improve your circumstances during that time. You must make a fresh application to the Registrar of the county court for a permanent adoption order *at least* two months before the interim order comes to an end.

*When the adoption order is granted*, you take over full rights and responsibilities as the child's parent. The natural parents no longer have any rights over the child. In place of the original birth certificate, you will be sent a copy of the entry in the Adoption Register, which gives the date of the adoption order and the name of the court that made it.

CAN THE CHILD FIND OUT ABOUT ITS NATURAL PARENTS?

If you are over 18 and adopted, you may see your birth records by applying to the Registrar-General, and so find out who your natural parents are. If you were adopted before 12 November 1975, when the Children's Act became law, you can see your birth records but you must have counselling first. This may be done at the Register Office or by a local council or adoption agency. If you were adopted after 12 November 1975, you will be offered a counselling service. If you are under 18 and adopted and you intend to marry you can find out, by applying to the Registrar-General, whether your intended husband is too closely related for a lawful marriage, but you will have to wait until after your eighteenth birthday if you want more information.

## Having your child adopted

If you do this, it is important to understand that you will lose all contact with the child and all your rights as its mother. Obviously it is something you must think about very carefully before you make your decision. Try and talk it over with sympathetic people and don't be afraid to change your mind, even if it's right at the last moment.

*You can arrange an adoption* by contacting one of the adoption agencies. The social services department of your local council may be able to arrange the adoption; otherwise it can put you in touch with an agency that will. If you are not completely satisfied with the first agency you approach, it is worth visiting several until you find a good one.

The agency will want to talk the matter over with you very carefully and at length, to make sure that you really want to have the child adopted and that the adoption will be in the best interests of the child. You will be given a form which explains in simple words what a legal adoption is, and points out that the child may be sent abroad. Before your baby can be placed with an adoptive parent you will be asked to sign the form, stating that you understand exactly what it means.

You must give the agency full details of your background and the baby's; the baby is given a medical examination, and you will need a certificate which states that it is healthy and free from any physical or mental defect. It would be illegal for you to give or take any money from a person who might adopt your child.

You can make certain requests about the way you want the baby to be brought up, for instance that you want it to be brought up in a certain religion, or with other children in the family. You may be able to meet the prospective parents if you want to. However, the adoption agency is not legally bound to meet your requests. So if, for instance, you want your child brought up as a Catholic, it may be best to go to a Catholic agency.

ADOPTION PROCEDURE

During the three-month period when your child lives with the people who want to adopt it, before the adoption order is made, you will be visited by the 'guardian *ad litem*' appointed by the court to supervise the adoption. She will have visited the adoptive parents and checked that everything is going smoothly. She will explain the procedure to you again, and if you still want the child to be adopted you will be asked to sign the final agreement form, which is then presented to the court.

You will probably not have to go to court to give your agreement, but if you have to be interviewed by the court for any reason and you don't want to see the adoptive parents, ask to be interviewed separately.

*You must give your agreement in writing* before the adoption order can be made. If you are married, your husband must also give his agreement. If you are single, the father's agreement is not necessary, but if he is paying maintenance, the court should tell him that the baby might be adopted and give him a chance to make his views known.

*If the father wanted to apply for custody of the child*, he would have to do so before the adoption order is made and he would have to satisfy the court that he could take care of the child. If custody were granted to the father, the child would not be adopted by anyone else and he would take over full rights and responsibilities towards the child.

*You can withdraw your agreement* any time you want to, right up to the day of the final court hearing. Don't sign anything unless you are absolutely convinced that you are doing the right thing. You may withhold your agreement indefinitely. However . . .

*The court can make an adoption order without your agreement* if it is satisfied that:

1. You have persistently failed to fulfil your duties as a parent; *or*
2. You have abandoned or neglected the child; *or*
3. You cannot be found; *or*
4. Your refusal to consent is 'unreasonable'; *or*
5. You are incapable of giving your consent, for instance because of mental illness; *or*
6. You have seriously ill-treated the child and it is unlikely that your conduct would improve if you were to look after the child. (The official language is 'The rehabilitation of the child within the household of the parent or guardian is unlikely'.)

The court can make an order for adoption without the agreement of the married father (or unmarried father, if he has legal custody) for the same reasons.

If you agree at first and then decide that you don't want your child to be adopted, your new decision will be accepted unless it can be shown to be totally unreasonable. If the court is considering granting an adoption order without your agreement, it must tell you its reasons and give you a chance to apply for legal aid and get a solicitor to represent you in court. If the adoption order goes through without your agreement, you should get a solicitor and lodge an appeal *immediately* (read pp. 449–59 on how to get a solicitor and apply for legal aid).

*When could your refusal to agreement be called 'unreasonable'?* This would only happen in exceptional circumstances. Here is one case where the Court of Appeal decided (1 May 1975) that a mother was not unreasonable in withholding her agreement:

An Indian woman had her baby placed with foster parents ten days after it was born. When 3 months, the baby was placed with a couple who wished to adopt her. At this stage the mother agreed to an adoption. The couple already had an adopted son aged 3 and the baby settled down happily and was excellently cared for. When the baby was 9 months old the mother changed her mind. She wanted to take her baby back to India to show her parents and then return and care for her in Britain. A month later the adoption application was heard by the court. The judge said that if he had only to consider the child's welfare he would order that the child remain with the adoptive parents. But the main thing he had to consider was whether the mother was unreasonable to withhold her consent. He was satisfied that she sincerely believed the child would be better off with her and decided that she was reasonable to withhold consent and could therefore keep her child. The Court of Appeal upheld the judge's decision.

The Children's Act, passed in 1975, has redefined the law. It says that the courts must give first consideration to the need to safeguard and promote the welfare of the child throughout its childhood; and if the child is old enough, they should take its feelings and wishes into account. But that is not the only thing they must consider: they should not override the decision of the mother – as long as that decision is reasonable – and all other relevant factors should be taken into account. In another recent case, the principle was established that 'a reasonable parent gives great weight to what is best for the child'. So one factor contributing to a court's decision that a mother is 'unreasonable' might be that she refuses to let her child go to a home which could provide a better life in the material sense.

### Adopting your illegitimate child jointly with your husband

Almost half the adoptions that take place are by one or both of the child's natural parents. In most of these cases, the child was born to a single woman who then married and made the adoption jointly with her husband. This makes the child legitimate and gives the man full parental rights and responsibilities towards the child. However, it is now the practice that, where a woman gains custody of her child in divorce proceedings and then remarries, it is almost always impossible for her new husband to adopt the child. Instead they will be advised to ask the divorce court to consider giving them joint custody.

## How the law is to be changed

When the Children's Act 1975 comes fully into force, the law will change in the following ways. When this edition went to press it had still not been decided when these changes would occur.

1. The system whereby the Secretary of State approves adoption societies will be overhauled. Every local authority must provide a comprehensive adoption service – probably in conjunction with approved adoption societies if there are any in its area. Adoption societies and local authorities which run their own adoption services will be known as adoption agencies.
2. A child must have lived with the adopters for at least twelve months before an Adoption Order can be made, except in the following cases, where it must have lived there for at least three months:
(a) The child is related to the adopters; *or*
(b) The child has been placed with the adopters by an adoption agency.
3. *'Freeing' a child for adoption.* A parent who wants to have her child adopted can choose between:
(a) Agreeing to an adoption by specific adopters (which is all she can do until the new law is implemented); *or*
(b) Agreeing to 'free' the child for adoption by giving the adoption agency the right to choose adoptive parents and giving them parental responsibility and rights over the child until the adoption is completed.

When a parent decides to 'free' the child for adoption, the adoption agency must apply to the court for an order declaring the child 'free'. The application cannot be heard until the child is 6 weeks old. Before making the declaration, the court must ensure that all the child's parents or guardians have consented. If the child is illegitimate and the father doesn't have custody, the court must ensure that he has no intention of applying for custody, or that he would be unlikely to get it if he did apply.

The court can declare a child 'free' for adoption without the parents' or guardians' consent only in the following circumstances:

(i)  the child is already in the care of the adoption agency – that is, the agency has taken over parental rights and responsibilities; *and*

(ii) the child has been placed for adoption or the court is satisfied that it will be soon, and one of the conditions applies whereby the parents' consent for a specific adoption can be waived. These conditions are listed above, pp. 359–60.

If an adoption agency applies to a court to declare your child 'free' *without* your consent, you cannot take the child away unless the person looking after it agrees, or the court gives permission. If you did consent to the application being made, you can take the child away at any time before the court hearing.

Once the court has made the order declaring your child 'free' for adoption, you can say you want nothing more to do with the matter. Otherwise the adoption agency must tell you, within one year and fourteen days of the order being made, whether your child has been adopted and whether it is living with the adoptive parents.

If you did not agree to your child being 'freed' for adoption but the court dispensed with your agreement, you can appeal against the order. If you did agree, and you change your mind after the order has been made, there is nothing you can do unless the child has still not been adopted after a year. You can then apply to the court for the 'freeing' order to be revoked. If you do this, the court must decide whether you would safeguard the child and promote its welfare if it were returned to you. If the child is old enough, the court must also take its wishes and feelings into account. If the court decides not to revoke the 'freeing' order, you cannot appeal against the decision unless the court gives special permission. The adoption agency will not have to tell you whether the child has been adopted later on.

4. *Custodianship Order*. This is an alternative to adoption, whereby

relatives and others who are looking after the children on a long-term basis can apply for legal custody of the children. They then become known as the child's custodians and have all the rights and duties of a parent: this means they can decide where the child lives and how its time is spent. They would not have any right to arrange for the child to emigrate or to agree to its adoption. If you want to apply for a Custodian Order, the child must have first lived with you for at least twelve months, or for at least three months if you are a relative or step-parent. You cannot apply without the consent of the person who already has legal custody of the child – and that would normally be one or both of the parents, or the local authority if the child is in care. But if the child has lived with you for at least three years, you don't need the parents' consent; and once you have applied for the Order, the parents cannot remove the child from your care without permission from court.

If a Custodian Order is made the parents may have access to the child and may be ordered to pay maintenance. The Order remains in force until the child is 18 or until it is revoked by the court. The custodian, parent, guardian or local authority can apply for the Order to be revoked.

## Further information

British Agencies for Adoption and Fostering, 11 Southwark Street, London SE1 1RQ (01 407 8800): for general advice on adoption and fostering; also acts as a co-operative exchange, liaising eighty adoption agencies.

*Adopting a child*: a brief guide for prospective adopters; *Stepchildren and adoption*: information for parents and step-parents following divorce. Both from British Agencies for Adoption and Fostering.

*How to Adopt*: a Consumers' Association publication, from 14 Buckingham Street, London WC2 6DS (01 839 1222).

*The Single Woman's Guide to Pregnancy and Parenthood*, by Patricia Ashdown-Sharp, Penguin Books. Now out of print, but very good so try your library.

## Fostering

Fostering is quite different from adoption. It offers a form of care within a family environment for those children who for a variety of reasons cannot remain in their own family, and for whom adoption is neither desirable nor possible. Very often the children maintain links with their family, and the overriding aim of foster care is to reunite children with their own families or to prepare them for some other more permanent form of care. (This can sometimes be long-term foster care, where a child is expected to stay with the foster family for the majority of its remaining childhood years.)

Most foster-care placements are supervised by social services departments of the local council, but increasingly voluntary organizations such as Barnardo's National Children's Homes and the Church of England Children's Homes are approving their own foster parents.

### If you want your child to be fostered

You can make your own arrangements with private foster parents. They would then be required by law to register with the social services department of the local authority and you should ensure that this has been done. The financial arrangements will be agreed between yourself and the private foster parents.

In certain circumstances you may need the assistance of a social worker, who would then advise you regarding foster care through the social services department. These placements are known as 'Section 1' or voluntary agreement placements. Check up on the law in respect of such placements and be sure of your rights. You may be expected to pay a certain amount towards the cost of care – this will be assessed by your social worker after discussion with you.

It is important to establish and maintain links with the foster parents and to indicate from the outset your desire to visit and keep in contact. Failure to do so could jeopardize your right to have your child back at a later date. If your child remains in care for longer than six months, you may have to give notice before your child can be returned to you. You should also check up on the restrictions relating to children who have been in care for three or five years.

Fostering can be a very successful form of care, in which close relations are developed between foster parents and natural parents.

## Becoming a foster mother

You can do this by applying to the local social services department, or to the local branch of a voluntary organization such as those mentioned above. There are certain requirements which vary from agency to agency. However, there is no law preventing single women, widows or cohabitees from applying, nor are there any age restrictions. Each agency will have its own views regarding suitability, and this will also depend, of course, on the children catered for by that agency. Obviously it would not be desirable to place a very young child, who might be in care for a long time, with an older woman. Careful matching of the child with the family has to take place.

It is important to recognize the essentially temporary nature of foster care. Foster parents will be expected to comply with the law regarding the return of children to their natural parents or to the local authority.

Foster parents are paid a regular sum of money to cover any costs they might incur while caring for their foster children. Agencies are introducing more and more schemes for caring for children with special needs – difficult teenagers or handicapped children, for instance – for which an additional fee might be paid to the foster parents.

## ADOPTION BY FOSTER PARENTS

Foster parents who have had a child for five years or more may make a direct application to the courts to adopt the child. Once notice of intention to apply has been lodged the child may not be removed from the foster parents until after the adoption hearing, except in cases of suspected abuse, etc.

## CUSTODIANSHIP

When the Children's Act 1975 comes fully into force it will allow foster parents to apply for custodianship after the child has been with them for twelve months, with the natural parents' consent, and after three years without their consent. If you are granted custodianship and the child has been living with you for at least three years, the parents cannot then take the child away without permission from the court. If you are granted custodianship you then have legal custody of the child, which gives you power to make all ordinary decisions for the child and the usual parental authority. You do not have the right to arrange for the child to emigrate, nor may you agree to the child being adopted. You may consent to the child's marriage.

The parents may have access and may have to pay maintenance. The custodianship lasts until the child is eighteen or until the court revokes it. The custodian, parent or legal guardian or local authority can apply for the order to be revoked. At the time of writing it is not known when this Act will come fully into force.

## *Further information*

National Foster Care Association, Francis House, Francis Street, London SW1 (01 828 6266/7): this association offers publications, information and advice.

## Leaving home when you're under 18

If you're a girl it's a lot more difficult for you to leave home under 18 than it is for a boy. Your freedom of action is restricted by a set of rules which do not apply to boys of your age: they seem to be based on the assumption that if a boy has sex or leads a wild life, that's normal, but if a girl does the same she is set on the path to disgrace and ruin.

### What could happen if you leave home?

It's not actually illegal for you to leave home, but you are still a 'minor', which means that you are meant to do what your parents say. So a great deal depends on your parents' attitude. If they don't object to your leaving and you manage to keep out of trouble, then you will probably be left alone. But if they do object and they ask the police to find you, or if you do something that brings you to the notice of the police or the social services department of your local council, and they decide you are in need of 'care or control', then you may find yourself in court, even though you haven't broken the law. What may happen in court is explained below.

The law says you can be taken to court because you are in need of 'care' for a number of different reasons, for instance:

1. Your parents think you are beyond their control.
2. You are not going to school regularly (only if you're under 16).
3. The police or your parents think you are in 'moral danger'. In practice, this means having sexual intercourse or being likely to have it when you are under 16 (the age of consent); and even if you are 16 or 17 and legally entitled to have sex, you may be thought to be in 'moral danger' because you are sleeping around, going to clubs late at night, living in a mixed flat or commune, involved in prostitution or taking drugs, sleeping rough outside, or doing anything equally unconventional.

If you are taken to court, you can apply for legal aid to pay for a solicitor to represent you. This could be a great help. Get information about it from your Citizens' Advice Bureau or tell the court officials that you want legal aid. (Legal aid is explained on p. 452.)

### IF THE COURT DECIDES THAT YOU ARE IN NEED OF 'CARE OR CONTROL'

one of the following things could happen:

1. Your parents might have to promise the court to take care of you and exercise proper control over you.
2. The court may pass a supervision order, appointing a social worker to keep an eye on you for a certain period.
3. The court may pass a care order, placing you in the care of the local council (this cannot happen if you are 17 or over). It means that the social services department of the council takes over all responsibility for you and decides whether you should live at home, in a hostel or in a 'community home'. If a care order is passed when you are under 16 it will last until you are 18 or until your marriage. If it is passed when you are 16 it will last until you are 19 or until your marriage.

If you are placed in the care of the council, you can apply for the care order to be ended at any time: you can get legal aid for this, and the solicitor will tell you what to do. If the court agrees to end the care order, it will either let you go completely free, or substitute a supervision order. If the court refuses to end the order you can't apply again for another three months.

More about care orders, from the parents' point of view, on p. 324.

### IF YOU HAVE BEEN SLEEPING WITH A MAN, HE MAY BE PROSECUTED

Again this is only likely to happen if your parents object to your leaving home or if you are in trouble with the police for some other reason. The reasons why the man may be taken to court are explained in the section on sex (p. 212).

### How to avoid trouble when you leave home

You will be less likely to end up in court if you can give the appearance of leading a respectable life – sharing suitable accommodation with a girl friend, holding down a regular job, and mixing with people who look respectable in the eyes of the police and the court – and if you can somehow avoid your parents making a complaint to the police. Things will be a lot more difficult if you are under school-leaving age, as you probably won't have any income, and if you leave school to get a job, this may be a reason for taking you to court.

Once you are 18, you can live where you like.

### Where to get help

Many of the bigger towns and cities now have youth advisory centres, which may be able to help you. Your local Citizens' Advice Bureau should know the address.

# 8. Housing

## Married women: your right to the family home

*First of all, make sure that the home is in your name as well as your husband's*

Whether you buy or rent your home, you should see that it is in *both* your names, for reasons that we will go into below. If you are moving into a new home, make sure it is in your joint names from the beginning. If it isn't, try to get it transferred to joint names. Your landlord (if you rent) may object, but it is worth making an issue of it. If you think of marriage as an equal partnership, you

should look upon this as your right, not just as a safeguard against future hazards – even if you are not paying an equal amount towards it.

Should you and your husband ever split up, your right to stay in the home will be far more secure if it is in joint names. But you will, of course, be equally responsible for keeping up mortgage or rent payments if they fall into arrears.

### Where the home is privately owned

*You have a right to stay in the home* whether it is in your name, his name, or joint names, until you actually get a divorce. If your husband tries to throw you out or forces you to leave, you can get a court order saying that he must let you stay. If you want to do this, get a solicitor and apply for legal aid, as explained on pp. 449–59.

*Your husband has an equal right to stay in the home* even if you are the sole owner. You would only be able to get him out if he were violent or molested you or your children and you applied for a court order (see p. 271).

*If the home is in your husband's name* he can sell it without your permission. However, there are certain steps you can take to prevent him from doing this. You can *register your right of occupation*, either with Her Majesty's Land Registry, or at the Land Charges Registry: your Citizens' Advice Bureau will be able to tell you how to do this, or else you can go straight to a solicitor. You can do this at any time during the marriage while you are living in the home or after you have left. It is wise to register your rights as a matter of course without waiting to see if your marriage runs into difficulties; and if your relationship with your husband becomes unstable you should do it immediately. Your husband will not know that you have done it, although it would be possible for him to find out if he made inquiries.

Once you have registered your right of occupation, your husband cannot sell the house without your consent, until you get a divorce and other arrangements are made by the court, as explained on p. 375. In some circumstances, the house can be sold by the mortgage company if mortgage payments are not kept up, even if you have registered your right of occupation. However, this is not possible if you are occupying the home and you have an equitable interest in it.

It was decided in 1979 that, even if you do not register your interest, mortgage companies may have to ask you about your claim to the house. Mrs Brown, a secretary, and Mrs Boland, a nurse, took their cases to the Court of Appeal when Williams and Glyns Bank had obtained possession orders for their homes. Their husbands had borrowed money from the bank and secured their loans on the houses without telling their wives. Both wives had substantially contributed to the purchase and improvement of their homes, which had been registered in the husbands' names alone.

Lord Denning said in his judgment that 'most wives now are joint owners of the matrimonial home with their husbands. They go out to work just as their husbands do. Their earnings build up the home as much as their husbands' earnings.' He therefore decided that a purchaser or lender should make inquiries of the wife as to her claim to the house. If she discloses her rights they come before the rights of the mortgagee or any other person who claims. If she does not disclose them they come second. 'It seems utterly wrong,' he said, 'that a lender should turn a blind eye to the wife's interest or the possibility of it and afterwards seek to turn her and her family out.'

In these cases the bank was unable to recover the monies from the value of the property except by claiming the mortgage instalments from the husband. Only when and if the husband sold the house with the wife's knowledge would the bank be able to get its share. Although Mrs Brown and Mrs Boland had made actual financial contributions, most wives who occupy the home would be said to have a share in its ownership even if they do not contribute (unless the marriage was very recent): this section therefore should also apply to them. It is nevertheless safer to register your interest in the house.

WHO OWNS WHAT DURING THE MARRIAGE?

Before 1882, a married woman had no right to own property: everything she had belonged to her husband. Since then, married women have been allowed to own property and, as the law stands now, husband and wife each have a right to own separate property.

Too often, this means that the husband, still the main breadwinner in most marriages, owns most of the family's property; while the wife, who stays at home to look after children or has a lower earning capacity if she does go out to work, owns little or nothing. However, it is becoming more common practice among young couples to buy their homes in joint names.

If you get divorced, you may be able to claim a share of the family property which is larger than you actually *own*, because it will be based on your needs, your contribution as a wife and mother and various other considerations. But the law does not recognize that you have a right to a share in the property while the marriage is still in existence, unless it is jointly owned. (See p. 383 for how the law should be changed.) However, there is one exception . . .

*Claiming a share of the family home and property during marriage:*

If the family home and property is in your husband's name you may be able to establish a share in it by applying to court for a calculation of your share, under Section 17 of the Married Women's Property Act. The court can also order that the property is sold. You can also use this section of the Act if the home and property are in both your names but your husband does not agree that you are entitled to your share. You will need a solicitor and you should apply for legal aid (read pp. 449–59).

When working out your share, the court first considers whose name the property is in. As a general rule, the home will belong to your husband if it is in his name, to you if it is in your name and to you both equally if it is in joint names. But this rule can be altered by the following considerations:

– How much money did you each put into the purchase of the house and the repaying of the mortgage?

– When you bought the home, did you intend it to be a joint purchase? In deciding this, the court considers whether the down-payment came from a bank or building society where the account was in joint names or in one name only; and whether you looked for the house together and made the decisions jointly, or whether one of you made all the arrangements.

The proceedings will take several months, possibly even a year. It helps if you can produce your own financial records, with details of your earnings, expenditure and income tax.

You can take these proceedings either during marriage or within three years of the divorce. But if you're getting divorced, it's probably better to claim a share of the property as part of the divorce proceedings, under the Matrimonial Causes Act 1973; it's usually quicker and you are likely to get more. A solicitor will advise you on this.

IF YOU GET DIVORCED

You and your husband may come to a private agreement, before the divorce, over the division of your property: if so, you must tell the court what you have arranged. The court will not discuss the matter any further unless it thinks the arrangements are unfair to either one of you. If you and your husband can't agree, the matter will have to be decided by the court after the divorce, at a private hearing before a judge or registrar.

*What share of property are you entitled to when you get divorced?*

When the court decides what your share in the property should be, it takes the following things into consideration:

1. The factors listed on p. 299, which it also considers when it decides how much maintenance should be paid.
2. How much maintenance you are to be paid as a result of the divorce settlement: if you are awarded generous maintenance payments you can normally expect less in the way of property, and vice versa.

3. What share of the property you are automatically entitled to. This is determined by the calculations listed above, pp. 374–5. They include such things as whose name the home is in; how much each of you has paid towards the down-payment and the mortgage; when you bought the home; and whether you intended it to be a joint purchase. You will also be entitled to a share if you have made major improvements to the home which have added to its value – such as building, painting and decorating.

4. Your contribution to the home in *non-financial* terms. It was the Matrimonial Proceedings and Property Act, passed in 1970, which said, for the first time, that judges should take this factor into account. It was an important breakthrough and many people thought that at last a woman who was unable to pay money towards her home could expect a half-share of the property in recognition of the time she had spent working in the home and looking after her husband and children. However, the judges took a different view. Their interpretation of the Act was established in the case of *Wachtel vs Wachtel* in 1973:

Mrs Wachtel was divorced from her husband, a dentist, after eighteen years of marriage, when they had a son aged 14 and a daughter aged 11. The family property consisted of a home worth £20,000 and Mr Wachtel's income of between £4,000 and £5,000 a year. The divorce court judge ordered that Mrs Wachtel be paid half the value of the home (£10,000) and about half her husband's income. Mr Wachtel appealed. The Court of Appeal considered all the facts of the case – Mrs Wachtel had worked until her son was born, then stayed at home to look after her children and helped her husband in his practice; he put down a salary to her as part of his expenses against tax. In the end, the Appeal Court judges decided that 'the fairest way to start' interpreting the new law was to give the wife one third of the joint income and capital – and awarded Mrs Wachtel just that.

Far from being a starting point, this decision has meant that in the majority of cases, the wife can expect no more than one third if the home is in her husband's name. Judges still seem to believe that a woman's contribution to the home as wife and mother is less valuable than the man's contribution as breadwinner; and that men need more to live on than women. The case of *Harnett vs Harnett,* described below, p. 378, is a typical example of a one-third award to the wife. Another case in 1974 (pp. 384–5) upheld the 'one-third' rule. The case of *Jones vs Jones*, p. 380, illustrates the sort of circumstances in which a wife may get a substantially larger share.

This is unlikely to happen unless:

(a) the husband's conduct has been particularly bad; *or*
(b) he has shown determination not to pay maintenance; *or*
(c) the wife has exceptional needs, such as a large number of children; *or*
(d) it has been a long marriage, and giving the wife only one third of the value of the home would not enable her to have a roof over her head.

## *What arrangements can be made to divide the property?*

Once your share has been established, the property must be divided accordingly. If you and your husband cannot agree how to do this, your lawyers will negotiate with each other and try to work out something that suits both of you as far as possible. Then the judge makes the final ruling. Normally one of the following arrangements are made:

1. The property must be sold, so that you can divide the proceeds.
2. The home is transferred from your husband to you, in which

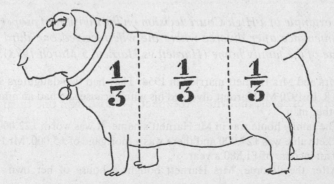

case you own it outright. This is unusual, except where the husband is very rich, or where there is a large mortgage.

3. You are allowed to stay in the home with your children until they grow up: after that you may either sell it and divide the proceeds; buy your husband's share; or return the home to him.

4. Your husband pays you a sum of money for your share of the home, and you go to live elsewhere; or vice versa.

If the home is in joint names and the divorce settlement does not include any arrangement that one of you should have sole rights to live there, then you are both legally entitled to go on living there, unless you can prove to a court that your former husband's presence endangers the physical or mental health of you or your children.

*If you have nowhere to live after the divorce:*

If the divorce settlement leaves you with nowhere to live, you can apply to the court for permission to stay on in the family home. If you have custody of the children it is quite likely that permission will be granted. Even if you have no children living at home, you are likely to be allowed to stay there if your husband already has somewhere else to live and if your share of the proceeds would not be enough for you to buy another home. The reverse is also true. If you have found council or other satisfactory accommodation, you may find your husband is allowed to stay in the home and you have to wait for your share in it.

*An example of a High Court decision on the division of property and maintenance after divorce where the wife received one-third of the value of the family home (Harnett vs Harnett, 5 March 1973):*

Mrs and Mrs Harnett married in 1954. They had two daughters aged 11 and 8. In 1970 Mr Harnett divorced his wife because she had an affair with another man.

The family home was in Mr Harnett's name. It was worth £22,000, as its market value was £27,000 and there was a mortgage of £5,000. Mr Harnett had an income of £1,880 a year.

After the divorce, Mrs Harnett bought a house of her own. It cost

£10,850 and she owed mortgages of £9,650. Mrs Harnett earned £2,124 a year.

Mrs Harnett claimed a share in the value of the family home. She said she had made a substantial contribution to it in money's worth, by her work as a wife and mother during sixteen years of marriage. She also asked the court to make an order that her husband should pay her a lump sum or transfer the house to her for her use.

Mr Harnett was only prepared to pay £4 a week maintenance for each of his daughters. He refused to pay anything to his wife because she had caused the breakdown of the marriage.

The judge decided that a wife's behaviour should only be taken into account in a decision like this if it was obvious that she had set out to destroy the marriage, while her husband was blameless. Mrs Harnett's behaviour had not been that outrageous and the judge decided to ignore it.

The judge ruled that the wife should be entitled to approximately one third of the joint income and capital of husband and wife (although if the husband were rich, the wife might get a smaller proportion); if the wife were awarded high maintenance payments, then she should get less in the way of a lump-sum payment and share of property; and vice versa.

The judge considered Mrs Harnett's claim that she had contributed to the home in money's worth by her work as a wife and mother: he decided that this did not *entitle* her to a share in the home, since housework did not improve the value of the property. He said that Mrs Harnett's contribution as a wife and mother should be taken into account only in deciding how much maintenance she should have.

The judge ordered Mr Harnett to pay £10 a week maintenance to Mrs Harnett for each of the daughters. He also ordered him to give Mrs Harnett £12,500 to pay off the mortgages on her house and provide her with £1,500 cash. He ordered Mrs Harnett to make a legal settlement so that her new house would provide a home for herself and her children until they were 25 or married; and its value would then be equally divided between herself and Mr Harnett.

The judge thought this arrangement was fair, as Mrs Harnett was receiving £1,500 cash plus a half-share in the value of her new house which amounted to £5,500. The total value of her award was £7,000, which was approximately one third of the value of the family home.

*An Appeal Court decision to award the wife the entire value of the family home (Jones vs Jones, 19 December 1974):*

Myrtle and Webster Jones were married in 1958. They had 5 children, now aged between 10 and 16. Mrs Jones got a divorce in November 1972 on the ground of her husband's unreasonable behaviour. In March 1973 she applied to court for an injunction to stop her ex-husband molesting her and her children. The injunction wasn't made because he agreed to leave the home. In June that year he attacked Mrs Jones with a knife and severed the tendons in her right hand. He was sentenced to three years in prison for grievous bodily harm. She was left with 75 per cent disability of her right hand and received £1,800 from the Criminal Injuries Compensation Board. She asked the court to transfer Mr Jones's financial interest in the home to her, since she could not continue her work as a part-time nurse. The house was registered in joint names. She had spent her earnings on housekeeping and had paid mortgage arrears and all mortgage payments since Mr Jones had left. The judge agreed to transfer Mr Jones's share to Mrs Jones, but said that when her youngest child was 18 she should transfer one fifth of its value back to him. The case went to the Appeal Court where it was decided that Mr Jones's conduct had been so grave that it had to be taken into account. Since Mrs Jones was unable to work, she would probably have to sell the house when her youngest child was 18, in order to pay her ex-husband one fifth of its value. It would be unjust to expect her to do this. It was ruled that Mrs Jones should have the entire value of the house.

### Where the home is rented

As a general rule, you have a right to live in the family home, even if the tenancy is in your husband's name, until you actually get divorced, or until the tenancy agreement expires.

IF YOU GET DIVORCED

You can go on living in the home under one of the following circumstances.

1. The tenancy was in your name in the first place.
2. You come to an agreement with your husband to transfer the tenancy to you. If you are in council accommodation, you should ask the council for consent.
3. You are living in private accommodation and the divorce court orders the landlord to transfer the tenancy to your name. If you want this done, get your solicitor to ask the court to order the transfer as part of the divorce settlement. The court does not have to agree to this, but it probably will if you have custody of the children. When deciding whether to agree, the court will take into account the attitude of your landlord and whether the terms of the tenancy forbade your husband to pass it to another tenant. This is known as a 'covenant not to assign'. If there is such a covenant it is doubtful whether the court has power to order a transfer when the landlord objects. It is vital to get the tenancy transferred before your divorce is made absolute. If you leave it until after the divorce, you will have no way of getting the tenancy transferred, unless your husband has left the home and the landlord agrees to do it. Many landlords are reluctant to transfer tenancies: they would rather evict you. However, if you don't get the matter settled during the divorce proceedings and you are living in a fully protected or part-protected tenancy (see pp. 393–5), the best thing to do is pay the rent and say nothing. Once the landlord has accepted rent from you, s/he will find it harder to evict you.

4. If you are living in a council flat or house and the council is willing to transfer the tenancy to you, it must first obtain an order for possession against your husband, under the Housing Act 1980. If he has been a good tenant and paid the rent they may have no grounds to get possession. In this situation you can apply to the divorce court for a transfer of the tenancy and if the court orders it the council will transfer. The court will not normally order it unless it considers the council is being unreasonable.

If the tenancy is in both your names and the divorce court does not order that it should be transferred to one of you, you and your husband both have a right to go on living there. You can only get him out by proving that his continued presence in the home endangers the physical or mental health of you or your children. Here is an example of one divorced woman who succeeded in getting her husband evicted.

W. and H. married in 1950 and had two sons: one was now married and living in his own home; the other, aged 14, was living with his parents in the house they jointly rented from the council.

In July W. obtained an undefended divorce on the grounds of her husband's unreasonable behaviour. She was given custody of her 14-year-old son.

H. continued to live in the house. In November 1972, W. applied through her solicitor to the county court to get a court order to make her husband leave the home. Her application was refused. She appealed to the Court of Appeal. This time she succeeded. But the court said that in cases where a joint tenancy gave husband and wife equal rights to occupy the house, a court order would only be granted where 'it was both imperative and inescapable'. The evidence which decided the court to grant an order in this case consisted of statements from a doctor that the husband's continuing presence in the home was likely to undermine the mental well-being of the wife and the son, and that unless something was done, both the wife and the son would become psychiatric invalids.

### If your husband dies

Details about wills and inheritance are on p. 182.

### How the law concerning family property should be changed

The Law Commission has been looking into ways of making the legal position regarding family property more favourable to the wife. It has produced a report which takes the view that marriage is a form of partnership to which both husband and wife contribute in ways that are different but equally important. It sums up what is considered to be the prevailing view:

We are no longer content with the system whereby a wife's rights in family assets depend on the whim of her husband or on the discretion of the judge. We demand definite property rights, not possible discretionary benefits.

It has put forward two main proposals to improve the situation:

1. *Co-ownership of the matrimonial home.* This means that, unless husband and wife agree to the contrary, they will both be equal owners of the home, simply because they are married. It will not depend on who bought the home or in whose name. The Commission also made certain proposals dealing with ownership of household goods. It suggests that whoever occupies the home should have the right to use all the household goods.
2. *Community of matrimonial property.* This means that husband and wife are free to buy and sell their own things during the marriage, but when the marriage ends, whether by death or divorce, everything they bought during the marriage is shared equally between them. This would be done by calculating the total value of their property and compensating whoever has less, either in money or by transferring particular items. The Commission suggests that certain things might be excluded – such as property owned by the husband or wife before the marriage and property received as a gift or inheritance during marriage.

Unfortunately, there is no sign of these proposals being implemented.

## What are your rights if you have set up home with a man who is not your husband?

### *Where the home is privately owned*

*If the home is in both your names*, you have equal rights to it. If you separate and cannot agree about who should go on living there or how the property should be divided, you can apply to a court to have the matter decided. You will need a solicitor for this and you should apply for legal aid (see pp. 449–59).

*If the home is in your name alone*, you have full rights to it and you can ask the man to leave. If he refuses, you can have him evicted. You must give him 'reasonable notice'.

*If the home is in the man's name*, your rights are very limited indeed. If you separate, you will usually have to go, even if you have children, although you must be given 'reasonable notice'. If you actually agreed to marry the man when the house was bought, and you paid a considerable amount towards it, you may be entitled to a share in it if you take proceedings under Section 17 of the Married Women's Property Act or under Section 30 of the Law of Property Act 1925. (If the property is in your name, the man might establish a share in it by the same means.) The proceedings are explained on pp. 375–8.

Here is an example:

A woman and man had been together for about four years. They had a child but decided to have it adopted. The year after that they raised a mortgage and bought a plot of land together, which they registered in the man's name. They intended to build a house there so that they could live in it when the man got a divorce and was free to marry again. They both saw the architect and they built the house together. The woman did a lot of the manual work – more than most women would normally do.

They both had other work, and each week they put their earnings into a box. Later, the money was transferred to a Trustee Savings Bank in the woman's name so that the man's wife would not find out. For a time they both made mortgage payments. But when the bungalow was finished, they separated. The man lived there for a while and made further mortgage repayments. He then sold it for nearly £2,000.

If the case had been decided twenty or thirty years ago, the woman would have had no claim to the property at all. In fact, the court treated the situation as if the man and woman were an engaged couple, and considered whether they had intended it to be a joint purchase. It decided, in 1974, that, although the woman had only contributed one twelfth of the money towards the home, she should in the circumstances be entitled to one third of the proceeds from the sale.

If you have not made any financial contribution, you may be entitled to a share of the property if you can show that you have done a great deal of work on the home. A Court of Appeal decision in April 1975 (described below) opened the way for cohabitees to make this kind of claim.

Janet met Stuart Eves when she was 19. She had been married to someone else for a year and he was also married. They lived together for four years and had two children. Janet changed her name to Eves by deed poll. They found a house and Stuart told her that it was to be a home for them and the children, but that they could not buy it in joint names as she was too young. He later admitted in court this was untrue. He bought it in his name and made a down payment of £2,400 and borrowed £3,200 on mortgage. The house was dirty and dilapidated. Janet did a great deal of work in the house and garden, much more than many people would do. She stripped wallpaper, painted woodwork and cabinets. She broke up the concrete surface of the front garden and carried the rubble to a skip. With Stuart, she demolished one shed in the back garden and put up another.

She said she considered they were man and wife although at first neither had been free to marry. When they both got their divorces, she suggested marriage but by then Stuart had met another woman, Gloria. He said he was going to marry Gloria and sell the house. Janet went to the magistrates' court and obtained custody of the children and an order that Stuart pay her £5 a week for each child. But she was forced to leave the house when Gloria threatened her with violence and moved in with an Alsatian dog.

Janet claimed a share of the house. The court decided that Stuart had led Janet to believe that the house had been acquired by their joint efforts with the intention that it should be owned for their joint benefit until they were married and throughout their marriage: he should be held to that undertaking. If Janet had not believed she was part-owner she would not have done such hard work on the house (which included wielding a 14 lb sledge hammer). The court decided her share should be one quarter of its value; but as she had remarried her share should be seen primarily as for the benefit of the children; as long as Stuart paid maintenance for them he would not have to sell the house to pay Janet her share.

This is an improvement on the old situation. Before the *Eves vs Eves* decision, you had no rights unless you had paid a lot of money towards the house. But it still leaves you in a far worse position than you would be in if you were actually married – for the following reasons:

1. A wife would normally get at least one third of the family home if there were children and the marriage had lasted any length of time. (But Janet Eves was awarded only one quarter and that was because of the extraordinary hard work she had put in.)
2. A wife would normally be awarded her share of the house for her own benefit and, unless the home was being used for the children or there was a very good reason why her husband could not pay her, she would get the money almost straight away. (But Janet Eves had her share placed in cold storage indefinitely and it was said to be mainly for the benefit of the children.) Another difference is that in a recent case the Court of Appeal said that when the couple are not married the woman's share in the home should be valued when the relationship ends and not, as in cases of married couples, when the court hearing takes place. So the woman loses out on any increase in the value of the property.

If you cannot prove to the court that you have put as much hard work into the house as Janet Eves, and if you cannot make a claim under Section 17 of the Married Women's Property Act because you have made no substantial contribution, you will not be entitled to any share of the property, even if you have children by the man and you have been living in the home with him for a long time. You may, however, be able to show that you have a contractual right to stay in the home. In one case the court decided that there was an agreement between the partners that the woman had a contractual right to remain in the house, with the children, for as long as the children were at school and needed the accommodation. In other circumstances your only right may be to have reasonable notice to leave. See a solicitor about this.

### WHAT STEPS CAN YOU TAKE TO PROTECT YOUR SHARE IN THE HOME?

1.  Make sure the home is bought in joint names.
2.  If the house is going to be bought in the man's name alone, ask for a 'declaration of trust' stating that he is holding it in trust for you both, and defining your share in it.
3.  If you have no declaration of trust, you may later have to prove what you contributed towards the home. Money spent on mortgage repayments, repairs and improvements counts. Money spent on housekeeping or household bills doesn't. Keep a careful record of who pays what.
4.  Have your interest in the property recorded on the title deeds so any purchaser knows you both have an interest and has to pay the purchase monies to both of you rather than just the man. You can only do this if you have a declaration of trust. Ask a solicitor to do it for you by registering a 'caution' if the property is registered or a 'class C(iv)' land charge if it is not.

## Where the home is rented

*If the tenancy is in your name*, you can of course stay, and you can throw the man out at any time; *otherwise*

*If the home is rented from the council:* councils rarely give joint tenancies to unmarried couples. If you've been living in a council house or flat and the tenancy is in the man's name, you can ask the council to try and obtain a possession order against the man. If they have no grounds for doing this, then apply to be rehoused yourself. The council will be obliged to do this, if you have children, as they have a duty to rehouse homeless families.

*A case from the records of the Catholic Housing Aid Society shows what can happen to women in this situation:*

A woman with five children had been living in a council flat with a man who was not her husband. The tenancy was in his name. They had been living together for a long time but over the past few years their relationship had deteriorated. The man had made a number of physical attacks on the woman. She had twice summonsed him for assault. The second time he was given a short prison sentence. She approached the CHAS when he came out of prison and attacked her for a third time.

The council Housing Department firmly refused to transfer the tenancy from the man's name to the woman's: they said they had no proof that the relationship had ended and, besides, the man had always been a reasonable tenant and had paid the rent regularly. (All this time the man was not living in the council flat, but was keeping a second home somewhere else.) The Housing Manager refused to change his mind even after several meetings with the CHAS on the woman's behalf.

At one stage, the man built up a small arrears of rent and the Manager said he would therefore evict him. Wheels were set in motion for this, but they were stopped when the man appeared at the Housing Department and paid the rent he was owing. Eventually, the woman was offered a place to live by a voluntary housing association.

*Another case shows how one woman won the battle to get rehoused by the local authority:*

Mrs A. lived with Mr A. in a council dwelling where the tenancy was in his name. They were unmarried and had two children. It was Mrs A. who had applied for the tenancy and she who had qualified for it, but when the time came to collect the keys, Mr A. went along and so the tenancy was put in his name. Mr A. later became violent and Mrs A. wanted to leave him but had nowhere to go. If she had been married, she could have obtained a divorce and an order giving her custody of her children, in which case the local authority would have transferred the tenancy to her name. But as she was unmarried, she couldn't go through this procedure and at first the local authority said they couldn't help her. Her solicitor then obtained an injunction in the county court, ordering Mr A. not to assault her. This was sent to the Housing Manager, who was asked to accept it as evidence that the relationship had broken down. After some time and persistent pressure from Mrs A. and her solicitor, the local authority agreed to re-house her and then started proceedings to evict Mr A.

*If the home is rented from a private landlord* there is little you can do if the tenancy is in the man's name and the relationship breaks down, unless he agrees to leave. If he does, you may be able to persuade the landlord to transfer the tenancy to your name. However, landlords are reluctant to do this as a rule. They would far rather evict. They are more likely to agree if the tenancy is in both your names. Whatever kind of tenancy you have, the best thing to do is to pay the rent and say nothing. Once the landlord has accepted rent from you he may find it more difficult to evict you, particularly if you are living in fully protected accommodation, and you are prepared to fight for your rights. In certain very limited circumstances you may be able to get a court injunction to stop the man evicting you. If you can prove:

1. That the home was rented on the understanding that you would both live there; *and*
2. That you made a sizeable contribution to the home, either in money terms or in work on the house and care of the man and children; *and, probably,*
3. That you intended to marry,

the court may recognize what is known in legal terminology as a 'constructive trust'. If so, it will grant the injunction. But this wouldn't help much if your relationship had broken down completely and it had become impossible for you to live together. The court would have no power to evict the man and the existence of a 'constructive trust' would not oblige the landlord to treat you as joint tenants. (However, the court might be able to remove the man temporarily under the terms of the Domestic Violence Act, p. 261.)

### *If the man you are living with dies*

If he has not left anything to you in a will, you have no automatic right to inherit anything. But under the Inheritance (Provision for Family and Dependants) Act 1975, you may now be able to claim a share of his estate. The Act set down that any person who immediately before the death of the deceased was receiving substantial contributions in money or money's worth can apply for a share of the estate. This could apply not only to spouses, ex-spouses and children, but to cohabitees and lovers of either sex. But it is entirely up to the judge to decide who should get a share and how large or small the share should be; and he has to take the conduct of the applicant into account (see 'Widows' Inheritance', p. 182).

YOUR RIGHT TO THE MAN'S TENANCY ON HIS DEATH

In October 1975, the Court of Appeal decided that a cohabitee could be counted as a 'member of the family' within the meaning of the Rent Act. This means that you have a right to carry on as tenant after the man's death, provided that the tenancy is already protected by the Rent Act. It makes no difference whether you have children: any woman who has lived with a man for a considerable length of time may be regarded as a 'member of the family'. And a case in 1980 decided that in similar circumstances a man could succeed to a tenancy after his cohabitee's death.

## Finding a place to live – rented accommodation

### *Renting from a private landlord*

You don't have to be a woman to have problems finding a place to live these days. The only thing that helps is money – unless you happen to have a close friendship with an estate agent or a property owner.

But if you are single with young children or if you are pregnant, you will probably find it especially difficult. You can't very easily conceal young children, but if you are pregnant your best bet is to hide the fact from all prospective landlords. Once you get a place, the landlord may try to evict you if he finds out, but there are ways of putting this off for several months (or altogether, in some cases), as you will see if you read the 'Quick guide for tenants' on p. 393.

### Renting from the council

You can find out about this from the housing department of your local council. Councils will normally only house families and old people. A single woman with children counts as a family. A pregnant woman does not, although some councils will house homeless women if they are far advanced in their pregnancy. If you are eligible for council housing and you put your name down on the list, they may eventually provide you with a permanent home. It could mean waiting years and years, but some councils have fewer housing problems than others, and it is always worth putting your name on the list. The address of the housing department is in the telephone directory under the name of the council.

If you are actually homeless and you have children (whether you are married or not) the council has a *duty* to house you. The same is true if you are threatened with homelessness (i.e. if you are likely to become homeless within twenty-eight days), if you are vulnerable through old age or disability, or if you are pregnant – unless you have become homeless intentionally, or you have no local connections. The council will usually fulfil its duty by putting you in low-standard 'half-way' housing but they may eventually find you somewhere more permanent. Don't be too optimistic about it, though!

If you have to go into half-way housing, you may run the risk of having your children taken away from you and placed in the care of the council (more about this on p. 324). You may get a reasonable home more quickly by trying to find private accommodation, or approaching an organization like the Shelter Housing Aid Centre (address below).

### Further information

Shelter Housing Aid Centre, 189a Old Brompton Road, London SW5 (01 373 7276/7841): housing advice and information; helps homeless people find homes, with a special interest in single parents.

## Your rights under the Sex Discrimination Act

*Chapter One describes the general terms of the Sex Discrimination Act. Since it is relevant to this section, we suggest you read it first.*

It is illegal for someone who is selling, letting or managing accommodation to treat a woman less favourably than a man would be treated in the same circumstances. Here are some examples of unlawful discrimination:

1. A landlord refuses to rent you a flat, just because you are a woman.
2. An owner refuses to sell you his house, just because you are a woman.
3. A tenant refuses to sub-let to you, just because you are a woman.
4. The owner or manager of the accommodation offers you less favourable terms, or treats you less favourably than a male tenant or buyer.

Unlawful discrimination can be direct or indirect, as explained on p. 25.

It is also illegal to discriminate against women in granting mortgages (see below, p. 397).

## The Act does not apply in the following situations

1. The owner (or tenant in a case of sub-letting), or a near relative of his, lives on the same premises as the accommodation he is renting or selling; *and*
2. He shares part of that accommodation (other than storage space or access); *and*
3. The premises are small: this means there is room for no more than three households; or, if the premises consist of a single household, there is room for no more than six people.
4. Single-sex housing associations are also exempt.

### How to obtain your rights

If you think someone has discriminated unlawfully against you, you can complain to the county court. The procedure is explained in the chapter on Goods, Facilities and Services, p. 402. See also the section on county courts, p. 461.

## Quick guide for tenants

This guide only applies if you are renting from a private landlord. Once you have found a place to live then the next problem is making sure you can stay there. Some landlords will try anything to squeeze money out of you or force you to leave. It helps to know what your rights are and where to go for help. This depends on what kind of agreement you have with your landlord.

### Fully protected tenants

You are fully protected if your landlord does not live in the same house as you, if you do not pay a substantial part of your rent for special services (such as cleaning the accommodation, rather than just the common parts), and if your tenancy is not for a fixed term. It doesn't matter whether your accommodation is furnished or not.

Most fully protected tenancies of this kind were entered into before the 1980 Housing Act came into force.

## WHAT TO DO IF THE RENT IS TOO HIGH

Apply to the Rent Officer to have a 'fair rent' fixed. But, beware, there is always a chance that the Rent Officer will put the rent up, not down. Before you apply, check the rent register at your local Rent Office (address in the telephone directory): it will show you what is considered a reasonable rent for accommodation like yours. The landlord can always apply to the Rent Officer himself, proposing a higher rent. If he does, you have a chance to argue against his proposal.

If you (or the landlord) apply to the Rent Officer, he will come and inspect the place. A little later he will hold a meeting at his office. You and the landlord can attend and have a right to be represented by a lawyer or friend. The Rent Officer will then fix a rent. If you disagree with the rent he fixes you may appeal to the Rent Assessment Committee: you should be careful about this since, as a general rule, Rent Officers are more generous to tenants than Rent Assessment Committees.

Once a rent has been registered, the landlord cannot put up the rent without going back to the Rent Officer, though he can pass on rates increases to the tenant. The landlord cannot usually go back to the Rent Officer for another two years unless he improves the property. If you have just moved in, it is worth checking the register at the Rent Office, to see whether a rent has already been fixed. If it has and the landlord is charging you more, you can recover any overpayments which you have made in the last two years, either by suing the landlord in the county court (see p. 461) or by withholding your rent in the future until you have recovered the amount.

WHAT TO DO IF THE LANDLORD WANTS YOU OUT

You have an almost unlimited right to stay. Your landlord cannot evict you without a court order. The court may evict you if you don't pay rent for a substantial time; if you damage the property or cause a nuisance; if the landlord wants the accommodation for himself or a member of his family; and in a number of other cases. The court will *not* evict you simply because you and the landlord don't get on, or because the landlord has found someone else who will pay more rent. If you get an eviction notice from your landlord you should see a solicitor straight away (p. 449).

## Protected shorthold tenancies

These are a new kind of tenancy created under the 1980 Housing Act, designed to make it easier for landlords to get rid of tenants. They involve:

1. A fixed term of one to five years.
2. Registration of a fair rent.
3. An almost automatic right for the landlord to reclaim possession when the fixed term expires, or at any time after it has expired.

If you are faced with eviction from a protected shorthold tenancy, there are only two minor safeguards available to you. First, the landlord can't evict you without going to the county court for a possession order. Second, the court has power to delay your eviction for up to three months: you may be able to take advantage of this if your marriage has broken down and you are exercising your right to occupy the premises under the 1967 Matrimonial Homes Act. Consult a solicitor.

## Other fixed-term agreements

If you have a fixed-term agreement which is for longer than five years and/or which began before the 1980 Housing Act came into force, you cannot normally be evicted until the tenancy has expired.

When you move in, check with the Rent Tribunal to see whether a fair rent has been fixed. If not, and you think the rent is too high, you can apply to the Tribunal to have a fair rent fixed. Be cautious: the Tribunal may decide to increase your rent. Once the rent is fixed, the landlord cannot legally increase the rent without making a new application to the Tribunal.

If a rent has already been fixed when you move in and the landlord has been charging you more, you can get your local authority to prosecute the landlord and the court can order the landlord to repay you the extra rent, as well as fining him. Inquire about this at your local authority housing department. Alternatively, you can sue the landlord in the county court to recover the excess rent. But beware, action of this kind may prompt the landlord to evict you as soon as your fixed-term agreement expires. Once faced with eviction, you have no greater safeguards than protected shorthold tenants.

## Other agreements

You have no protection at all if you have taken a tenancy for a holiday; if you are a student in student housing; if you pay a substantial amount of rent for board (meals, etc.); and in a few other limited cases.

Beware of phoney 'holiday lettings'. Some landlords will ask you to sign a holiday letting agreement when you are not on holiday, just to avoid their legal obligations. You will probably have no choice other than to sign the agreement or not get the accommodation. However, try to agree orally with the landlord that you can stay permanently, and try to build up a body of evidence that you can show to a court (e.g. a reference from your previous landlord in the same town and/or from your employer; agreeing with the landlord that you can move in your own furniture; providing a reference from the local bank) to help you establish that the landlord knew you were not really on holiday.

If you feel your rent is too high, there is nothing you can do, except to apply for a rent and rate rebate (see p. 194). The landlord cannot get you out without a court order and he has to serve you with a proper notice to quit.

### *Cautionary note*

The above guide is not a full account of tenants' rights. If you share a flat or are a sub-tenant, your position may be very much more complicated. Beware of phoney 'licence' agreements. Landlords may try to get you to sign a 'licence' agreement which contains provisions about not having exclusive possession, sharing accommodation with the landlord, or something similar even when you in fact have the accommodation to yourself. Like phoney holiday agreements, this can make it even easier for the landlord to get you out when he wants to.

If you are in any doubt about your rights, consult a solicitor. You can get legal advice free or partly free as explained on p. 454.

## Mortgages

### *Your rights under the Sex Discrimination Act*

It is illegal for a building society, local authority or any other organization which grants mortgages, to treat a woman less favourably than a man would be treated in the same circumstances. Unlawful discrimination can be direct or indirect as explained on p. 25. Here are two examples of unlawful discrimination based on actual cases:

1. Jane and Bill Smith approach a building society for a mortgage. Jane earns £5,500 a year as a teacher; Bill earns £5,500 a year as a florist. They have two children, both of school age. They don't intend to have any more. Jane is 29, Bill is 30. The building society says it will take all Bill's earnings into account when deciding how large a mortgage to grant them; but it will not take Jane's earnings into account unless she produces a doctor's certificate to show that she has been sterilized.
2. Rosie and Alan White approach their local council for a mortgage. Rosie who is 26, works as a social worker and earns £6,750 a year. Alan,

who is 25, earns an average of £25 a week: he is busy completing some research and is not in regular employment. They don't plan to have children for several years and Rosie has no intention of giving up her job when they do. They tell this to the council officer but he says he is not prepared to accept Rosie's earnings as the basis for a mortgage because 'she might go off and have a baby'.

*It is still legal* to refuse a mortgage to a woman, or to offer her less favourable terms than a man, for reasons other than the fact that she is female – for instance, because the local council or building society thinks her earnings are too low, her job is insecure, or the house she wants to buy is in poor condition. It is *not* legal to treat a woman less favourably than a man just because the council or mortgage company thinks she will have a baby. It's not easy to tell when a mortgage company is discriminating unlawfully: if it is determined not to grant mortgages to women it can fall back on so many different excuses. Some companies are more enlightened than others. Women who are single, over 30 and earning a good salary in a professional job are, of course, the most likely to get mortgages. But if you don't fit this description, it is still well worth trying if you have a steady income. If you are married, you should insist that the mortgage is based on the same proportion of your salary as your husband's.

*If you think you have been discriminated against,* you can bring a complaint against the council or building society to the county court. The procedure is explained in the chapter on Goods, Facilities and Services, p. 402. See also the section on county courts, p. 461. The general provisions of the Sex Discrimination Act are described in Chapter One.

### What sort of mortgages are available?

There are all sorts of different deals you can make to raise money for a house. Here are the main types of mortgage:

1. *Building society repayment mortgage.* This is the most common type of mortgage. You borrow a sum of money and pay it back

Our policy is only to take
your husband's income
into account, Mrs Thing

over the years, with interest. The maximum time allowed is usually twenty-five years. In the end you spend about twice as much as you originally borrowed. The money you pay for interest is tax-free and you tend to pay this off first, so that the mortgage costs you less in the early years.

Building societies normally lend up to 80 per cent of what they reckon to be the value of the house, but you can get more with a 'mortgage indemnity policy', and this means paying a bit extra. Some of the bigger societies will lend only to people who have been saving with them for at least a few months. Some give less favourable terms if you are buying a house that was built before the war; or if you are buying a flat or 'maisonette'.

The most you could expect to borrow would be three times your yearly income.

2. *Local council repayment mortgage.* This is the same as above, except that you get it from the local council in the area where your new house is.

3. *Option mortgage, from a building society or local council.* This is the best for people who pay little or no tax: the Government subsidizes the loan and you pay less money each month at a lower interest rate. You don't really benefit from an option

mortgage if you are paying enough tax to get full income tax relief. You can switch to an ordinary repayment mortgage later on if your income goes up.

4. *Endowment mortgage.* You buy a life insurance policy from an insurance company and get the loan either from the insurance company or from a building society. There are two varieties: with-profits and without-profits. If you have a with-profits endowment mortgage, you get a sum of money when you finish the payments. It costs more in monthly payments and it's only a good idea if you pay a higher rate of tax. Without-profits endowment mortgages are less expensive than the with-profits variety and generally more expensive than mortgages from building societies or local councils. The main advantage of both varieties is that, if a couple buys a house and the husband dies (and the mortgage is in his name), the mortgage is paid off by the insurance policy, and the house belongs to the wife, without her making any more payments.

If you want to get a mortgage, it's important to shop around until you find the best deal. Don't be discouraged if you are turned down or offered unfavourable terms by a number of companies.

### Useful things to read

*Buying a House or Flat* by L. E. Vickers, published by Penguin, 2nd edn 1981, gives a full description of almost everything a potential house buyer needs to know (although it lacks a feminist perspective!).

*Money Which?* (December 1980) gives a complete breakdown of all the facts and figures on mortgages. Available from local libraries or to members of the Consumers' Association, 14 Buckingham Street, London WC2 6DS.

*Which? Way to Buy, Sell and Move House*, from the Consumers' Association (address as above).

*The Legal Side of Buying a House*, also from the Consumers' Association.

*Saving and Home Buying*, for a detailed breakdown of the costs of home buying and moving, free from the Building Societies Association, 14 Park Street, London W1Y 4AL.

# 9. Goods, Facilities and Services

## Your rights under the Sex Discrimination Act

*Chapter One describes the general terms of the Sex Discrimination Act. Since it is relevant to this section, we suggest you read it first.*

It is illegal, when providing goods, facilities or services to the public, or a section of the public, to treat a woman less favourably than a man would be treated in the same circumstances. This covers – among other things – hotels and boarding houses; pubs and restaurants; banks and insurance companies; credit houses and HP firms; theatres and gymnasiums; transport companies and local authorities. (It also covers accommodation and mortgages, as explained on pp. 392 and 397.)

Discrimination can be *direct* or *indirect*, as shown on p. 25. Here are some examples of unlawful discrimination:

1. You go into the Eagle to buy a drink on a Friday night. The barman tells you that Friday is men's night and refuses to serve you.
2. You go into a restaurant after midnight with a woman friend. The manager asks you to leave. When you ask why, he explains that he has difficulty distinguishing unaccompanied women, who just want a meal, from prostitutes. He does not have the same reservations about single men.
3. You are married and you want to hire a television. The rental firm insists that you get your husband to sign the form.
4. You go into a department store to buy a new bed and ask if you can pay for it by HP. You are told that you can only do so if you provide a male guarantor. (However, this wouldn't be against the law if the store insisted that female *and* male customers provided male guarantors.)

## Advertising

It is illegal to advertise the provision of any goods, facilities or services, in a manner which implies that the advertiser intends to break the law. For example, an advertisement for a men-only bar or for a special insurance policy for 'husbands' would be illegal. If you find an example of this kind of advertising, bring it to the attention of the Equal Opportunities Commission (address, p. 486). It is the duty of the Commission to deal with illegal advertisements. It may be able to apply to a court for an injunction, stopping the advertiser from producing any more of them.

## There are plenty of exceptions to the law

This part of the Act is shot full of holes. There are so many exemptions that it seems that almost anyone who is determined to discriminate against women can carry on doing so. It is still lawful for the following to discriminate against either sex:

1. Private clubs, such as working men's clubs, sports clubs, gaming clubs, night clubs and gentlemen's clubs. New laws against racial discrimination make it illegal for private clubs to discriminate on racial grounds. There is no justification whatever for allowing them to discriminate on grounds of sex. The fact that women cannot join working men's clubs and can enter them only as guests of men, perpetuates myths about the superiority of the male and his prerogative to go out at night with his mates while the wife stays in with the kids. The exclusion of women from gentlemen's clubs, such as the Athenaeum, the Garrick and the Junior Carlton, has approximately the same effect on the upper classes.
2. Political parties: this means women can go on organizing women's sections and women's conferences – in our view a necessary function to encourage political activity among women. Some women are understandably intimidated in the presence of men who are accustomed to dominating political meetings.

3. A religious body can discriminate if it has to do so because of its doctrine, or in order not to offend 'a significant number' of its members. This would allow, for example, special religious services for men only. It is a very vague exemption, which condones sexist practices by religious organizations.

4. Hospitals, prisons, hostels, old people's homes and any other places for people needing special care. Again, a very vague exemption. What constitutes 'special care'? It may be necessary in some cases (hospital patients may prefer segregated wards) but not in others – such as old people's homes, where those needing 'special care' might benefit from mixing with the opposite sex.

5. Facilities for participation in competitive sport, provided that an average woman would be at a disadvantage because of her physical capacity, compared with an average man. This doesn't cover all sports – for instance, it doesn't cover jockeys or darts players.

6. Charities and non-profit-making organizations set up to provide facilities or services for one sex: so the scouts can exclude girls, but a voluntary group set up to help old people cannot discriminate. Single-sex charities and non-profit-making organizations cannot discriminate against the people they employ at their offices, but they may be able to discriminate against the people they employ in their hostels, hospitals or residential centres (see p. 46). This exemption may be necessary in some cases (for instance, to allow meetings of the women's liberation movement to exclude men). But it is far too broad and invites abuse. It could be argued, for instance, that an all-male darts team, based at the local pub, could continue to exclude women without breaking the law, simply by calling itself a non-profit-making body. It might have been better to restrict the exemption to organizations whose functions relate to needs which are exclusive to one sex.

7. Insurance companies and similar bodies which sell life assurance, accident insurance, etc., can go on calculating the risk involved in offering insurance on the basis of 'reasonable actuarial

information'. Actuarial information means general statistics about women and men, such as the number of years they are expected to live, or their likelihood of having motor accidents. So insurance companies could, in theory, offer women life assurance on more favourable terms than men because, statistically speaking, they live (and pay premiums) for longer and have fewer dependants. Likewise, they could offer cheaper motor insurance to women, because they are safer drivers.

8. Facilities and services can be restricted to one sex in order to preserve 'decency and privacy'. This covers lavatories, sauna baths, changing rooms, etc. Considerations of 'decency and privacy' are accepted far too readily – after all, French women and men have been sharing public lavatories for years without any dire consequences. Perhaps it's time we had second thoughts – particularly since the British insistence on separate facilities can have unfavourable repercussions for women in the employment field (see p. 46).

9. There is a general exemption for communal accommodation, where dormitories and bathrooms are shared: it is lawful to exclude one sex for reasons of 'decency or privacy'. Where facilities or services can only be provided effectively for people using communal accommodation (such as treatment at a health farm), it is lawful to exclude one sex from the facilities or services if they are also excluded from the accommodation.

## How to obtain your rights

If you think someone has discriminated against you in one of the ways described in this chapter, you can complain to the county court. At the time of writing, no complaints under this section of the Act had actually reached the courts, so there was no way of telling how it would work out in practice. You may find that it is enough just to tell the organization (or individual) that you think it is breaking the law and that you are considering making a formal complaint to the court. But if that doesn't stop the discrimination, then follow the steps described below:

1. Make your complaint within six months of the date on which the discrimination occurred.

2. *Read the chapter on the county courts* on p. 461. It tells you how to go through all the necessary steps and what to expect at each stage of the proceedings.

3. *Get help with your case.* For advice about your rights under the Act, write explaining your particular case to the Equal Opportunities Commission or to the Women's Rights Officer of the National Council for Civil Liberties (addresses, pp. 448–9).

   For help with preparing your case, you can get advice from a solicitor free or partly free under the 'green form procedure'; or, if you want a solicitor to conduct the case for you and represent you in court, you can apply for legal aid. The amount of free help you can get depends on your income and savings. (More details about legal advice and aid on p. 452.)

   You can get someone to represent you in court who is not a qualified lawyer (for instance, you might know of someone who has experience in dealing with sex discrimination cases).

4. *Prepare your case.* Make sure you collect all relevant information to back up your case. You are allowed to put questions to your opponent before you go to court. You can do this either by setting out your questions in a letter or by using the special questionnaire forms which are available from the Equal Opportunities Commission. In our opinion, these forms are badly thought out and off-putting for the average complainant, but you may find they are better than nothing.

   Your opponent does not have to answer your questions, but if he doesn't, this may count against him when the case is heard. If he does give you answers, you can produce these as evidence in court. In addition to the questions you ask, collect any relevant letters or other documents that will back up your complaint. If you know of anyone who has witnessed the act of discrimination, ask them if they would be prepared to go to court to give evidence for you. If they are willing, find out if there are any dates on which they can't go to court, as this may affect the date of the hearing.

It may be useful if you can get information about other instances of discrimination by the same person or, if it is a company, of general patterns of discrimination by the company in this area. If the Equal Opportunities Commission has already made a complaint to a county court against the organization you are complaining about (unlikely), this could help your case. You can find out by writing to the Commission.

### WHAT CAN YOU GET IF YOU WIN?

There are four things you may be able to get:

1. An order from the court declaring your rights and those of the other person.
2. An injunction to stop the other person discriminating unlawfully (e.g. to stop the restaurant manager refusing to serve women); if the person then disobeys the injunction, he can be fined or imprisoned for contempt of court.
3. Money in compensation for damages.
4. Costs (money to compensate you for legal fees, if you paid any).

It is up to you to decide what kind of injunction (if any) you want the court to make and how much you require in damages. You must decide this in advance and present it to the court on your 'Particulars of Claim' form (see p. 464). Work out how much money you think you have lost as a result of the discrimination; and you can also claim for 'injury to feelings'.

### IF YOU LOSE

You will not be asked to pay the other side's costs unless you claimed more than £100 in damages. So if you are thinking of claiming more than £100, make sure you get legal advice and that you have a strong chance of winning.

If you have definite reasons for thinking that the court's decision was wrong, you have certain rights of appeal. Before appealing, consider the question carefully and get legal advice. Otherwise you may get involved in a lot of extra expense if the appeal is unsuccessful. The court office will explain what you have to do in order to appeal.

*If you have reason to believe that the person or organization will continue to discriminate unlawfully* – and the court does not issue an injunction which can prevent it – you can report the case to the Equal Opportunities Commission. The Commission has power to make an investigation and then issue a Non-Discrimination Notice, or apply to court for an injunction. The Commission's powers are described on p. 481.

## A successful case:

In November 1980, the Court of Appeal ruled that Williams Furniture Ltd had discriminated unlawfully against Mrs June Quinn of Leicester by asking her husband to sign a guarantee before allowing her to buy a suite of furniture by hire purchase.

Mrs Quinn put down a deposit on a three-piece suite. The sales assistant who filled in the hire purchase form asked her if she had a bank account (which she had) and said that her husband would have to complete a guarantee. Mr Quinn did so and Mrs Quinn got the suite. She then put a questionnaire to the store (as provided by the E O C under the terms of the Sex Discrimination Act), which asked them: 'Would you have imposed a guarantor requirement on a married man whose circumstances were, in all material respects, similar to my own?' The answer was 'No'.

In the county court, the judge ruled that the assistant had given Mrs Quinn advice, but did not actually discriminate. However, in the Appeal Court, Lord Denning and Lord Justice O'Connor decided that the judge was wrong: by insisting or requiring, or even suggesting or advising, that Mrs Quinn's husband should sign the guarantee, when a guarantor requirement would not have been imposed on a married man in the same circumstances, Williams Furniture Ltd had discriminated unlawfully. [*The Times*, 18 November 1980]

**The rest of this chapter deals with your rights
as a consumer.**

*Whether we like it or not, it is a fact that in most households the
women have to do most of the shopping. So the rest of this chapter
tells you what your rights are. Most of it applies to men too.*

## Buying by 'HP'

When people talk about buying by HP, they may be referring to
one of several different ways of paying for something by instalments.
The four most common are hire purchase, credit sale, conditional
sale, or personal loan from a finance company. They all differ
slightly in the way they are defined by law and the protection they
offer to the buyer, but they all have certain things in common:

1. You pay for the goods gradually, after you have taken possession
   of them.
2. You normally have to put down a deposit first.
3. You usually end up paying more than you would if you had paid
   it all at once.
4. If you can't keep up payments, you may have to return the
   goods, or you may be taken to court.

If you're asked for a man's signature (as a guarantee) and refused
credit if you don't provide it, remember that the company is
breaking the law unless it also asks male customers to provide a
man's signature.

### When can a company legally refuse you credit?

Companies are free to refuse credit to customers for other reasons
which do not involve sex (or race) discrimination. For instance,
they can do so if they think you are a bad risk because you have
failed to pay debts in the past.

I'm afraid we'll have to have
your husband's signature, too

### *Credit rating: your right to know what is on your file*

Companies that provide credit facilities often consult credit-reference agencies, which keep files on people to show whether or not they are likely to keep up payments. So if, for example, you once failed to pay a debt, this could be on the files of a credit-reference agency. When you next apply to a company for credit the company might refer to the agency and, having found out about your bad debt, refuse to give you credit. In the past, these files were secret: when you applied for credit you had no right to know whether the company was going to contact a credit-reference agency. You couldn't find out what (if anything) was on your file; nor could you change the information, if it were incorrect. Under the Consumer Credit Act 1974 you have a right to know these things. This is what you can do:

1. When you apply to a company for credit, ask them to tell you which credit-reference agency, if any, they are using to check up on you. If you ask within twenty-eight days of applying for credit

and they fail to tell you, the company can be prosecuted and fined up to £200.

2. Contact the credit-reference agency and ask them to show you a copy of their file on you. You will have to pay the agency 25p. (If it turns out that they don't have a file on you, they keep the 25p.)

3. The agency must give you a copy of all the information they keep about you, in 'plain English', even if it is stored on computer tapes. If they fail to do this, they too can be prosecuted and fined up to £200.

4. If you decide the information is wrong and likely to discourage companies from giving you credit, tell the agency that you want them to correct it, or take it off their files altogether. They must tell you within twenty-eight days whether they have done this or not.

5. You can also, if you wish, tell the agency that you want them to add a note of up to 200 words to your file. For instance, you might want them to include an explanation that you failed to keep up certain payments because the goods you were buying were faulty.

6. If the agency doesn't amend its file in the way you want, you can appeal to the Director General of Fair Trading, Field House, Bream's Buildings, London EC4A 1PR.

## The different ways of paying by instalment

1. *Hire Purchase:* if you buy something under a hire purchase agreement, you do not actually *own* it until you have paid the last instalment. This puts the company you have bought it from in a particularly powerful position, but you are quite well protected under the Hire Purchase Act, if the sum involved is less than £5,000.

2. *Conditional Sale:* this is almost exactly the same as a hire purchase agreement and gives you the same protection under the Hire Purchase Act. The company owns the goods until you

have fulfilled certain conditions, which normally include paying most or all of the instalments.

3. *Credit Sale:* this way, the goods become yours as soon as you sign the agreement. You have limited protection under the Hire Purchase Act, if the sum involved is between £30 and £5,000.

4. *Personal Loan from a Finance Company:* this method is becoming more and more common. Two separate deals are involved: you buy from the seller and borrow from the finance company. It may seem to be the same as a hire purchase deal, but it isn't. You are not protected under the Hire Purchase Act.

5. *Trading Checks:* you get a 'trading check' (which is like a money voucher and issued by a finance company), either from the shop where you want to buy, or directly from the finance company. You use the check to buy the goods and then pay for the check by instalments. You can only use it in shops which have an arrangement to use trading checks. You are not protected by the Hire Purchase Act.

*Read any agreement very carefully*, especially the small print. If you don't understand it, don't sign. Get help first from your Citizens' Advice Bureau, or your local Consumer Advice Centre, if there is one in your area.

### Can you cancel an agreement once you have signed it?

You can if it is a hire purchase, conditional sale or credit sale agreement, within the limits of the Hire Purchase Act; *and* if you signed the agreement at home. If so, you should be sent a copy of the agreement within seven days of signing it and within the following three days you can notify the seller that you want to cancel. You should return the goods and refuse delivery of any that haven't yet arrived. If you have paid a deposit, you should get it back in full.

## What if you can't keep up the payments?

UNDER A HIRE PURCHASE OR CONDITIONAL SALE AGREEMENT

If you have paid less than one-third of the total price, the company which owns the goods can come and take them away. If you have paid more than one third and the total sum is less than £2,000, the goods can't be taken away unless *you* formally end the agreement and allow them to be taken away; or the company gets a court order.

If you want to end the agreement and you have paid half the total cost (or can add enough money to make up that amount) you can ask the company to take the goods away; then you will only be liable for any damage you may have done to the goods. If you have not paid half the total cost, the company will take the goods away and you may still have to pay any back instalments you have missed. If the company repossesses the goods without a court order and you have already paid one third of the total cost, you may be able to reclaim all the money you have paid so far. If the company obtains a court order, then the court has power to vary the payments owed to take account of your financial circumstances, but the goods must be returned. So it may be better to wait and let them take you to court – the judge may settle the matter in a way which is more favourable to you. Get a solicitor and apply for legal aid (pp. 449–59).

UNDER ANY OTHER CREDIT AGREEMENT

You own the goods, so nobody can take them away but neither can you return them. You can sell them yourself or come to an arrangement with the company to sell them if you want to raise money to pay off the debt. Otherwise, the company you owe the money to will have to take you to court if it wants to recover the debt.

## General shopping

### Making a down-payment

It is important to find out whether you are making a part-payment or a deposit. If you make a *part-payment*, this is part of the agreed price and you can claim some or all of it back if the sale falls through. If you make a *deposit* this is a separate agreement which is supposed to reassure the seller that you are serious about wanting to buy. Unless you agree in the first place that it is in part-payment and recoverable, you may not be able to claim it back if the sale falls through. Never give a deposit if you can avoid doing so. Anyway, keep it as small as possible. You are not entitled to the return of your deposit unless the goods prove to be faulty or the seller breaks the contract in some other way.

### If goods are wrongly described

The seller is breaking the law. If you buy something that turns out to be different from its description (on the packet or in the brochure, for instance) you can demand your money back. If you don't get it, consult your Citizens' Advice Bureau or Consumer Advice Centre, or go to a solicitor (p. 449).

This applies to price tags too. It is illegal to indicate that goods are cheaper than they actually are. If a shopkeeper says that goods are cut-price, they must have been sold at the higher price for twenty-eight consecutive days during the past six months.

### Safety of goods

Some goods have to meet certain standards of safety laid down by law. These include gas, oil and electric heaters, children's night-dresses, carry cot stands, electric blankets and all household electrical appliances, cooking utensils, ceramic and enamel ware, pencils, chalks and crayons, and toys. Celluloid is not allowed in toys except in the paint that is used on them and in ping-pong balls.

The amount of arsenic, lead and certain other heavy metals is restricted in paint used on toys. If you buy anything which you find is dangerous, complain to the Environmental Health Inspector or the trading standards department of your local authority.

## Faulty goods

If you buy something which is faulty, you can usually claim compensation from the person who sold it to you. The Sale of Goods Act 1979 gives the buyer considerable protection. It says that anything which is sold must be of a 'merchantable' quality, and goes on to define the word as follows: 'An article sold must be as fit for the purpose for which articles of that kind are commonly bought, as is reasonable to expect, having regard to the description applied to it, and the price paid (if this is relevant) and any other factors.' So if you buy something which does not come up to these standards, you can claim compensation.

You will probably not be able to claim compensation if:

1. The seller specifically points out a particular defect to you.
2. You examined the article before buying it.
3. You bought something at an auction (unless the article does not fit the description in the sales catalogue).
4. You bought something, such as a second-hand car, from a private person in answer to a newspaper advertisement. Here you can only claim compensation if it does not fit the description which the seller gives you.

THE SELLER MAY OFFER TO COMPENSATE YOU IN ONE OF THE FOLLOWING WAYS:

1. By repairing the article so that the fault is corrected and its value, appearance and usefulness are not affected.
2. By replacing the article with a similar one which isn't faulty.
3. By replacing it with a different article.
4. By taking it back and refunding the purchase price.

5. By letting you keep it and refunding part of the purchase price, depending on how serious the fault is.
6. By giving you a credit note. If you are given a credit note, read it carefully. It may not be valid beyond a certain date. If there is no date on it, it is valid for six years.

If the seller's offer suits you, you can of course accept. But you may decide to refuse the offer and take the matter to court. If you do this the court will award compensation in cash terms only. The award may amount to the full price you paid for the goods. It may be less if you have had some use out of the goods; and it may be more if extra damage has been caused by the faultiness of the goods. For instance, if you bought a washing machine and it broke down after six months, you may get less cash compensation because you have had some use out of it. If, on the other hand, the machine overflowed and damaged your kitchen floor, you might get extra.

It's unlikely that the seller would offer you extra money – but in some circumstances it may be worth accepting his offer rather than going to court and risking being awarded less than you originally paid. The seller might, for instance, offer to replace a faulty washing machine with a new one after you have had six months' use out of it. Once you have accepted his offer, you can't change your mind and ask for a different form of compensation.

### WHAT TO DO IF YOU WANT TO TAKE THE MATTER TO COURT

If you have a claim for less than £200, you can have it settled by the Registrar of the county court without using a solicitor. It will cost you little beyond the price of issuing a summons: this is usually 10 per cent of your claim; even if you lose the case you will not be asked to pay any legal costs, although if you are calling witnesses you may have to pay their expenses. This procedure, introduced in 1973, is designed to help people with small claims. Get details from your Citizens' Advice Bureau or Consumer Advice Centre.

If your claim is for more than £200, you will probably need a solicitor if you want to take the matter to court. This could be very expensive – because you may have to pay your own legal costs and, if you lose the case, those of your opponent. If you win the case, your opponent may be ordered to pay your costs, but not necessarily. So be cautious. Before you embark on the claim, make sure you get advice from a solicitor under the 'green form' procedure described on p. 454, or from your Citizens' Advice Bureau or Consumer Advice Centre.

### IF YOU RETURN GOODS WHICH ARE NOT FAULTY

simply because you have changed your mind and no longer want them, or because you made a mistake about colour or size, you must accept whatever compensation the seller offers you (if any), or keep the goods. You have no legal right to return them.

### IF YOU BUY SOMETHING WHICH HAS A MANUFACTURER'S GUARANTEE

read the wording carefully. You may have to sign it and send it back before it has any effect or it may apply immediately. Whether or not you accept a manufacturer's guarantee (by signing and returning it), you can still claim compensation for faulty goods as described in the previous section. Accepting a guarantee cannot take away your rights against the seller.

## *If you take something to be repaired and don't collect it*

If you take something to be repaired, serviced or cleaned and you don't collect it, the person you left it with can eventually dispose of it, *if*:

1. He has a sign prominently displayed in his shop: this must meet conditions laid down in the Torts (Interference with Goods) Act 1977.

2. He tells you that the article is ready for collection, and how much it will cost.
3. He tells you that it will be sold if you don't pay within a specified time.
4. He sends you a registered letter saying that the article is to be sold, fourteen days before he plans to sell it.

### *If you are sent goods you haven't ordered and you don't want*

You are not obliged to return the goods or pay for them. The person who sent them has six months to collect them: if he doesn't, they automatically become yours. Alternatively, you can write (any time within five months after they arrive) saying that you didn't order them and giving your name and an address where they can be collected: if he doesn't collect them within thirty days of receiving your letter, they become yours. In either case reasonable access must be allowed for collection. (This is laid down in the Unsolicited Goods and Services Act 1971.)

## Cutting off the gas or electricity

THE GAS BOARD

can cut off your supply if you haven't paid your bill within twenty-eight days, but it must give you written notice seven days beforehand and twenty-four hours' notice if a Gas Board official has to come into your home to remove pipes.

THE ELECTRICITY BOARD

gives you twenty-one days' notice, then after a further seven days, it will send you written notice saying that if you don't pay your bill the supply will be cut off. Unless it has to force entry into your home, it need not give twenty-four hours' notice before an official comes to disconnect the supply.

IF YOU CAN'T AFFORD TO PAY YOUR BILL

go to your local gas or electricity showrooms and ask whether you can arrange to pay by instalments. The sooner you do this, the greater your chances of avoiding disconnection of the supply. If you are dissatisfied with the response you get, you can take up the matter with the Electricity Consultative Council or the Gas Consumer Council. You will find the appropriate address on the back of the bill. If you are threatened with having the supply cut off, go to your local Social Security office and explain what has happened. They may be able to pay the bill for you (see pp. 189–97).

IF THE WORST COMES TO THE WORST

an official will call at your home to cut off the supply. At this point a convincing sob-story can stay execution. Or you can pretend to be out. A social worker from the social services department of the council may intervene on your behalf if there are children in the house. If the official can't get in, he will have to get a warrant from a court to authorize an entry. In order to get a warrant he will have to satisfy the court that you have been given at least twenty-four hours' notice and that all the preliminary proceedings have been carried out as the law requires; and give information under oath explaining why the warrant is necessary. But in the case of an emergency, the Gas or Electricity Board can get an entry warrant simply by convincing the magistrate that life or property is at risk. Once the supply is cut off, you will have to pay to get it reconnected.

IF YOUR HOME IS ENTERED BY FORCE

the Gas or Electricity Board must repair any damage they do, or pay you compensation. If they force entry while you are away, they should leave your home as securely locked as it was when they arrived.

## Further information

Consumer Advice Centres: These offer free advice on consumer problems and help with complaints against retailers, manufacturers and finance companies. To find out if there is one near you, look in the telephone directory, where it may be listed under the name of your local council; or telephone the inquiries department of your local council. By 1981 many had closed down as a result of government cuts.

Consumers' Association, 14 Buckingham Street, London WC2 6DS (01 839 1222) for information on consumer subjects. It has produced a large number of useful booklets which are available to the general public and also publishes *Which?* magazine. Otherwise, consumer advice is available to members only.

# 10. Women and Immigration

The immigration laws are extremely complicated and open to widely different interpretations. They discriminate against men and women alike. We will not attempt here to give a full account of the law, but to provide a few basic guidelines and draw attention to the aspects that have particular significance for women.

The Home Office appears to be unaware that women immigrants exist except as wives and dependants – as a random quotation from the 1980 Statement of Changes in the Immigration Rules will illustrate:

Where the passenger is a citizen of the United Kingdom and Colonies, holding a United Kingdom passport, and presents a special voucher issued to him by a British Government representative overseas . . . he is to be admitted for settlement, as are his dependants if they have obtained entry certificates for that purpose . . .

But despite the impression given by the Home Office, women are supposed to be allowed to enter Britain independently, under the same conditions as men. The Sex Discrimination Act does not affect the immigration laws.

## Conditions for entering Britain

Briefly, the following rules apply. You can enter the country without restrictions if you are a 'patrial'. This category includes citizens of the U.K. and Colonies who were born, adopted, registered or naturalized in Britain, or have a parent or grandparent who was born here. If you are a Commonwealth citizen with one parent who is a citizen of the United Kingdom and born in Britain, you are a patrial. If you are a Commonwealth citizen with one grandparent born here, you can enter and work without a work permit, although you are not a patrial.

All other people are subject to immigration control. There are three main categories and each is treated in a different way:

1. Citizens of the Common Market countries.
2. Commonwealth citizens.
3. Other non-Commonwealth citizens.

Citizens of the Common Market are free to come and work in the U.K., although they may be refused re-entry or an extension of stay if they have been claiming supplementary benefit here. But everyone else is considerably restricted – black people most of all. Normally you cannot enter without an entry certificate, visa or work permit, and these are often very hard to come by.

### *Here are a few general points worth noting*

1. If you are uncertain about your right to enter or settle in Britain, don't automatically believe what the Home Office tells you. They may not have considered all the facts that could be used to construct a case in your favour. The best thing to do is to contact one of the organizations that specialize in helping immigrants. These are the Joint Council for the Welfare of Immigrants, the U.K. Immigrants Advisory Service, and the National Council for Civil Liberties. Or inquire at a neighbourhood law centre, if there is one near you. (Addresses, p. 500.)
2. If you think you may have difficulty getting into the country, always try to arrange for friends to meet you at the port of entry and try to arrive on a weekday, during office hours, so that an advice agency can be contacted.
3. If you are entering as a student, the immigration authorities will not automatically let you in because you have been accepted for a full-time course of study: they will also want proof of your ability to study the course and evidence that you have financial support and accommodation. So be prepared for that and bring with you whatever documentary evidence you have. The Home

Office constantly refuses applications from people who enter Britain as visitors and want to remain as students.

4. If you are allowed to work with a work permit which has been issued for a specific job with a specific employer, initially for a year, you have a right to change your job, provided your new job is the same type as that for which the permit was issued. Before you take your new job, you must get permission from the Department of Employment.

5. If you do not have a right to stay here permanently, don't leave the country without first checking that you will be able to come back. It is best to take with you all the documents you had when you came in before: for instance, if you came in as a 'dependent wife', you might need to show copies of your marriage certificate and your husband's work permit. If your permission to stay is about to expire, and you apply for an extension, it is unwise to travel abroad when your application is still being considered. Indeed, the act of leaving the country will cancel your application and on your return you will have to convince the immigration authorities that you qualify to re-enter.

6. Employers don't always check whether their employees have work permits. If you work without a permit, you are committing an offence, but your employer is not.

## Rules which affect women who are subject to immigration control

### ENTERING BRITAIN WITH YOUR HUSBAND

If your husband gets permission to enter Britain (to work, study or settle there) you can enter with him as his dependant, under the same conditions as him – although he may first have to prove that he is able to support and accommodate you. You will be allowed to work under the same conditions as he is. Your children under 18 can enter as well.

If you have been living with a man 'in permanent association', but are not married to him, you can come to Britain with him if the immigration authorities decide that your 'permanent association' with him is accepted as the equivalent of marriage in the country you come from. They will certainly not let you in on this basis if you come from the 'white Commonwealth' or from any country, such as India, where marriage is the norm.

## IF YOUR HUSBAND COMES TO BRITAIN FIRST AND YOU PLAN TO JOIN HIM

There may be a very long delay before you are given an entry certificate or visa. In October 1975 women in Bangladesh had to wait two years for an interview; those in India nine months; and those in Pakistan for eighteen months. However, if you are a Commonwealth citizen and your husband is a patrial, you can accompany him or come to join him, even without an entry certificate. Instead of an entry clearance certificate you should ask for a 'certificate of patriality', which you can request at any port of entry. If you do this, it's important to bring with you very strong, reliable documentary evidence to show that you are a Commonwealth citizen married to a patrial.

## IF YOU MIGRATE TO BRITAIN CAN YOUR HUSBAND JOIN YOU?

The immigration rules were changed in 1979 to allow foreign husbands to join women who are settled in Britain *only if* the woman was born in the U.K. or has a parent born in the U.K.; and if the immigration authorities are satisfied that the marriage is genuine, not primarily for the purpose of gaining settlement in the U.K., and that the partners have met. The husband must first obtain an entry certificate and they can apply for one at any overseas British post. They can expect to suffer the same delays.

CAN YOU BRING YOUR CHILDREN?

You can bring your children with you, or send for them to join you, under the following circumstances:

1. You can show that you are able to support and accommodate them; *and*
2. You and the father of the child *both* have permission to settle in Britain. (This condition applies even if the child is illegitimate, despite the fact that, in all other aspects of British law, a mother has sole rights over her illegitimate child.) *Or*
3. You can prove to the immigration authorities that you have had *sole responsibility* for the child. If your child has been living with a grandparent, or has maintained some contact with the father, you will find it extremely difficult to prove that you have had sole responsibility, even if you have been supporting the child financially. The authorities are not prepared to waive the rule unless a child is 'desperately unhappy and finds life intolerable in his own country'. Ironically, the result is that a child who is actually disturbed stands a better chance of being admitted than a child who is well adjusted.

These regulations apply to children under 18. Generally, children over 18 must qualify for admission in their own right. However, an unmarried and fully dependent son under 21, or an unmarried daughter under 21 who formed part of the family unit overseas, may be admitted *provided that* the whole family is migrating to the United Kingdom.

ENTERING WITHOUT PROPER PERMISSION TO STAY

There are many cases of non-patrial British passport-holders who have entered Britain without proper permission and who cannot be sent back to their country of origin (such as Kenyan and Ugandan Asians). They are usually given permission to stay for a short period and have to reapply when the period expires. If a man does this his wife may be allowed to join him on the same conditions.

## NON-BRITISH WOMEN WHO MARRY MEN WHO ARE PERMANENTLY SETTLED IN BRITAIN

These women have a right to settle with their husbands in Britain. This is one way to be granted permission to stay here permanently, although the Home Office resolved early in 1977 to clamp down on 'marriages of convenience'. Once you are married you can apply for registration as a U.K. citizen. If you get divorced later you still have a right to stay.

## NON-BRITISH MEN WHO MARRY WOMEN BORN IN BRITAIN, OR WITH A PARENT BORN IN BRITAIN

Such men have a right to remain in Britain with their wives once the marriage has taken place. They will not automatically be entitled to citizenship. No such right exists for non-British men who marry women who were not born in Britain, or who do not have a British-born parent.

### IF YOU ARE ENGAGED TO BE MARRIED

As a woman, you will be allowed to enter Britain to marry your fiancé, if he is settled in Britain and you can satisfy the immigration authorities that you will get married within a reasonable time. He will have to show that he can support and accommodate you. You will normally be admitted for up to three months. Once you get married you can apply to the Home Office for a right to permanent residence (or, if your husband only has a temporary right to stay, for permission to stay as long as he does). If you don't get married within three months, you can apply for permission to stay longer, but you will have to give a good reason why the marriage has been delayed and provide evidence that it will take place soon.

NATIONALITY OF YOUR CHILDREN

If you were born in the U.K. but your husband was not, and you give birth to a child while you are abroad, your child cannot automatically take British nationality. You can apply to register the child as a U.K. citizen if the father has no well-founded objection. If the child is illegitimate and you do not declare the father's name, your child may then be a 'stateless person', if the rules of the country where it was born do not allow it to adopt the nationality of that country and if you fail to have it registered as a U.K. citizen. If your child is born in the U.K., even if your stay is temporary and you are not a U.K. citizen, the child has the status of a patrial.

APPLYING FOR QUOTA VOUCHERS

Citizens of the U.K. and former colonies who have registered themselves overseas can apply for quota vouchers which enable them to enter and settle in Britain. (Only a limited number are issued each year – in 1980 5,000 were available, but not all were used.) Applications must come from the 'head of the household'. Women are not recognized as heads of household unless their husbands are dead or invalid and incapable of supporting the family; or they are single, divorced or separated and self-supporting.

DEPORTATION

If you are married and your husband is deported, you are likely to be deported with him, unless you have permission to stay in your own right (for instance, as the holder of a work permit); or unless you can prove that you have been living apart from your husband and you are not dependent on him.

If you are deported, your husband will probably be allowed to stay, provided he has permission to stay in his own right.

'AU PAIR' GIRLS

The Home Office makes special provision for 'au pair' girls to enter Britain – doubtless to keep middle-class households comfortably equipped with cheap domestic labour. According to the Immigration Rules, ' "au pair" is an arrangement under which European girls aged 17–27 may come to the United Kingdom to learn the English language and to live for a time as a member of a resident English-speaking family'. No mention of 'au pair' boys. The arrangement can include part-time domestic work (although in practice it often amounts to full-time drudgery). You can stay twelve months as an 'au pair' girl, and this can be extended for one more year but no longer. If you come to Britain as an 'au pair', you cannot change to any other form of employment. If you don't qualify as an 'au pair', you can't get a work permit for a domestic job.

THE PLIGHT OF FILIPINO WOMEN

Although it was the general rule in the 1970s that only 'patrials' and citizens of the EEC could come to Britain to work (except for skilled jobs where no other applicants were available), a special quota allowed others to enter as resident domestic workers and nursing auxiliaries. The quota was initially introduced because of a labour shortage: it came to an end in 1980. Most of those who came to fill the quota were Filipino women, recruited by employment agencies in the Philippines. To get permission to enter, they had to say they were single and had no children, and to produce a reference to show they had experience of the kind of work they were to do in Britain. However, the agencies, who obtained work permits on their behalf, often misled them about these requirements, or encouraged them to say they were single and childless when they were not.

These women came to Britain because they were desperate for work (in order to support the children they were not supposed to have). If they stayed four years, the restriction on their stay was lifted, as they no longer had to live on their employers' premises. Unaware that they had broken the rules many of them applied to the Home Office at that stage for permission to bring their children to live with them in Britain. Until 1978, the Home Office usually agreed, but after that, as part of the government's clamp-down on immigration, it changed its tune. Not only did it refuse to allow the women to bring in their children, but it declared that they were 'illegal entrants'. Their failure to admit that they had children made their permission to enter void, said the Home Office; they would therefore be 'removed' from the country. A person who is removed in this manner has no right of appeal to a tribunal or court until after being deported.

A campaign developed to support these women and save them from being deported. Many of them were represented by the trade unions, who became involved in the issue of immigration for the first time. There were challenges in the courts, but the courts upheld the Home Office practice. In an important test case, Mrs Claveria was told she was an illegal entrant because she had not revealed the existence of her three children when she obtained her work permit, which in 1973 allowed her to enter Britain as a resident domestic. She was removed to the Philippines in March 1980. In another case, the court ruled that people were illegal entrants not only if they gave false information, but also if they failed to give any information which the Home Office later decided was relevant. The Filipino women thus became 'illegal entrants' by failing to say they had children or were married, even if they had never been asked if this was so, and they did not know they had to reveal such details.

The Home Office said they could only stay on 'exceptional compassionate grounds'. Yet this did not prevent the 'removal' of many women who had worked hard in Britain, in unpopular jobs and at low wages, scrimping and saving in order to support their children and establish a home for them in this country. It is one of the most shameful episodes in our country's treatment of immigrants.

At the time of preparing the third edition of this Guide, the

Home Office was still deporting Filipino women. Women who are in danger of 'removal' should contact the Migrant Action Group, 68 Charlton Street, London NW1; the JCWI (address below); or the TUC, Great Russell Street, London WC1.

## How to appeal

If you do not agree with any decision taken by the immigration authorities, you may be able to appeal – first to an adjudicator and, in certain cases, to the Immigration Appeals Tribunal. You will need help with your appeal, but legal aid is not available and few solicitors know much about immigration law. It would be best to contact one of the organizations listed below.

## The laws are soon to be changed

It is expected that the laws of nationality and citizenship will be changed before the end of the parliamentary session in 1981. The government published its proposals in a White Paper in July 1980. The main changes which affect women are:

1. Non-patrial women and men who marry U.K. citizens can apply for U.K. citizenship after three years of marriage. No more automatic right for non-patrial women to settle in Britain when they marry a British man.
2. Children born outside the U.K. can inherit U.K. nationality from either parent, if that parent was born in the U.K.

## Further information

Joint Council for the Welfare of Immigrants (JCWI), 44 Theobalds Road, London WC1 (01 405 5527/8): an independent organization, giving advice and legal help to immigrants.

U.K. Immigrants Advisory Service (UKIAS), 7th Floor, Bretten-ham House, Savoy Street, Strand, London WC2E 7EN (01 240

5176): for advice and help with immigration problems and appeals. Set up and grant-aided by the Government, but claims to be independent.

The National Council for Civil Liberties (NCCL), 23–5 Tabard Street, London SE1, may also be able to help in limited circumstances.

# 11. Women and Prison

In 1979 there were, on average, 1,458 women in prison and 40,762 men. That is, one woman for every twenty-eight men. So we have assumed that there are a lot more women with husbands and other male relatives in prison than there are women prisoners, and have dealt with the subjects in that order.

## Prisoners' wives

(This section also applies if you are the 'common-law' wife of a prisoner: you are normally regarded as a 'common-law' wife if you have been living with a man for more than two years as though you were married, without actually going through the ceremony. Much of the information should be useful to anyone who has a close friend or relative in prison.)

### Perhaps the most useful thing to know in the first place is where you can get information, help and advice

1. *Your local probation service* should be able to help you make sense of all the official rules and regulations that surround prisons, such as how to arrange visits. It may be a useful source of advice if you run into financial difficulties and other practical problems. Most probation services are now expanding the work they do with prisoners' families and run a variety of schemes, such as co-operative buying of basic groceries, coffee-mornings and other meetings for unsupported wives (not just prisoners' wives), and transport for taking families to out-of-the-way prisons. You will find the address and phone number of the probation service in the telephone directory.

2. *The welfare officers at the prison* will be able to tell you how the Prison Rules are put into practice in that particular prison (this varies very much from one prison to another); to help you with your visits; and to deal with any problems or queries you may have in connection with the prison. They can also be a source of more general help and information. You can write to a welfare officer at the prison address, or arrange for a meeting when you come to visit your husband.

3. *The social services department* of your local authority may be a useful source of help if you have difficulties connected with your home or your family and other social problems. Its address and phone number are in the telephone directory under the heading of your local authority.

4. *Your local Social Security office* is the place to go if you need money. You won't get much, but it may keep you just above the breadline. If you ask at your local Post Office, they will give you the address. More is said about Social Security on p. 189.

5. *Citizens' Advice Bureaux* are a good source of information and advice on most practical problems. If you have to go to court (for instance if you have trouble with your landlord, or if you want to start divorce proceedings), your Citizens' Advice Bureau will help you get in touch with a solicitor and apply for legal aid. You will find the address of your nearest CAB in the telephone directory.

6. *The Prisoners' Wives and Families Society* gives advice on legal and other problems; has a short-stay hostel for homeless prisoners' families; and provides overnight accommodation for those visiting London prisons. They can sometimes help with furniture and clothing (address, p. 448).

7. *The Prisoners' Wives Service* visits prisoners' families in the London area. It aims to build up supportive friendships with prisoners' wives and tell them their statutory rights (address, p. p. 448).

8. *NACRO (National Association for the Care and Resettlement of Offenders)* is a registered charity which gives help to prisoners and their families both before and after release from prison. It

may sometimes be able to help where government departments cannot, although it often refers people to probation officers (address, p. 448).

## Is your husband on remand or has he been given a prison sentence?

If your husband has not yet been given a prison sentence by the court, then he is in prison 'on remand'. This means that he has certain privileges. You can write to him and visit him more often. The rules applying to prisoners on remand are described on p. 447.

*The rest of this section is written with particular reference to the wives of men who are serving prison sentences. But the prison rules which are mentioned apply also to women who are serving prison sentences.*

*Remember:* generally speaking, prisoners don't have automatic *rights* – they have only *privileges*. The way they are treated and the way the prison rules are interpreted vary greatly from one prison to another.

### Visits

HOW OFTEN ARE VISITS ALLOWED?

In theory, a prisoner is allowed one visit every four weeks. Before you can make a visit you must get a Visiting Order from the prison governor. If you don't know how to get one, your husband should know how to arrange it; otherwise ask your local probation officer or write or phone to the governor at the prison.

Three individuals can be named on each Visiting Order. If a prisoner's wife or common-law wife is named, the order covers any children of the marriage.

In practice, some prisons allow visits every two or three weeks. On rare occasions, prison welfare officers can arrange special visits, but this depends very much on the whim of the prison governor.

Until recently, prisoners' wives were allowed to make extra visits if they were helping their husbands with appeals. But in December 1972 the Home Office introduced new rules which put an end to this, by giving unlimited access to legal advisers helping prisoners with appeals to any court, but excluding anyone who is not a qualified legal adviser.

Mrs Margaret Tuttle, of Muswell Hill, London, is a typical case. Her husband is in Gartree, near Leicester, serving an 18-year sentence for armed robbery, malicious wounding and carrying an offensive weapon. He is appealing against his sentence and Mrs Tuttle is also trying to get together new evidence which would allow him a new trial . . . Until the new Home Office rules were introduced last month, Mrs Tuttle used to visit her husband twice a month. 'One visit we reserved for seeing each other, for talking about my problems with the house and social security, for example, and for Jimmy, my husband, to see our 22-month-old son . . . The second we used to talk about his appeal. It is 100 miles from London to his prison. No lawyer has the time to make that trip many times. I used to see the lawyer and act as a go-between. Prisoners do not like writing to their solicitors because all their letters are read. What people do not seem to realize is that they don't just lock prisoners away – they "lock away" prisoners' families as well.' [From the *Guardian*, 23 January 1973]

## WHAT ARE THE CONDITIONS?

A visit is supposed to last for thirty minutes and usually takes place in 'closed conditions' – which is rather like sitting on opposite sides of a Post Office counter with a glass window between you and your husband and inadequate partitions to separate you from a long row of other visitors.

In practice, conditions vary enormously. In open prisons, visits may take place in cafeteria-like rooms and last up to two and a half hours. In some other prisons, visits last for thirty minutes in cramped conditions with no privacy. In long-stay prisons, governors tend to be fairly liberal about the way visits are conducted.

Most prisons allow you to hold hands, but nothing more. Some do not even allow that. Nothing is supposed to change hands

between you and your husband, although some prisons let visitors give inmates cigarettes and sweets. It is worth finding out about this from the prison welfare officer before you make your first visit. Prisoners are searched before and after visits to make sure that they have not been given anything they should not have.

Visits are rarely in private and the Prison Rules say that they must take place within the sight, but not necessarily in the hearing, of a prison officer. In practice, there are always officers on duty but they tend to be too busy to pay attention to any particular visit. Nevertheless, wives tend to feel that they are very exposed during their visits. It is worth asking the welfare officer which visiting days are likely to be the quietest, as this can make an enormous difference.

## WHAT ARE THE FACILITIES FOR WIVES AND CHILDREN?

Again, this varies a great deal from one prison to another. Some prisons provide toys and voluntary helpers to run play groups for children on visits; and some have special facilities for mothers with babies. Others have very poor facilities. One of the biggest problems is that families often have to wait a long time before they can go in to see the prisoner: this can be a bit harrowing, so take toys if you have children with you. Many prisons are a long way from public transport routes, but welfare officers at the prison can often help with local transport.

## IF YOU CAN'T AFFORD TO MAKE THE VISIT

If you are already receiving supplementary benefit and you are the wife or common-law wife of a prisoner, or the closest relative of a prisoner who is not married, you can get fares for monthly visits paid by the Social Security office. If you have any children by the prisoner, their fares will be paid too. Unfortunately the Social Security will not pay visiting fares for you or your children if you are the fiancée or close friend of a prisoner and you have been living with him for less than two years. If the prison allows fortnightly or three-weekly visits, Social Security will only pay your fares once a month.

The Prisoners' Wives Service, which operates in the London area, is campaigning for each visiting order to be covered by a travel warrant . . . 'We visit over 350 new families each year and of these about 100 are receiving invitations for extra visits. Our families are lucky as there are charities in the London area that will help with the extra fare money. This can be quite substantial. But we are really concerned about all the other wives throughout the country who are not getting help. We feel that to issue a visiting order without the funds to use it is a form of cruelty and means that the rich are in a privileged position and the poor suffer . . . We have approached the Home Office, but they have said that the money is not available to cover these extra visits.' [From *Social Services*, 3 March 1973]

Fares are usually paid in the form of a railway warrant. If you are able to travel by car, you can get a Post Office Giro order for petrol instead of a travel warrant for trains and buses. Not all Social Security offices agree to this willingly – but if you insist they should allow it. You will not be given any other money unless the prison is too far for you to get there and back within a day. It is up to the Social Security officials to decide what is a day's journey: it could mean setting off at 7.00 a.m. and returning at 11.00 p.m. It might be worth insisting on making your visit on a Sunday, as there are fewer trains and you may not be able to get there and back on the same day.

If you have to stay overnight, the Social Security will pay for bed and breakfast but not for anything else. Arrangements have to be made well in advance, and if you write to the prison welfare department, it will usually help you find a hotel or boarding house.

## Letters

IN THEORY, A PRISONER MAY WRITE
ONE LETTER A WEEK

It is posted by second-class mail at public expense. In practice, most prisons allow inmates who are serving sentences of more than a couple of months to pay for two extra letters a week from their earnings. Letters to official sources, such as probation officers and solicitors, are supposed to be issued free in addition to the prisoner's quota of letters to his friends and family. But this rule is not always observed, and some prisons are more lenient about it than others.

Letters written by prisoners have to be a regulation size and written on prison paper. They are posted in plain envelopes which do not give any indication of where they come from. Strictly speaking, air-mail letters should not be identifiable as letters from prison but in fact they sometimes are. In exceptional circumstances, the prison authorities can allow the prisoner to write on plain paper, for instance, if the letter is going to a child under 16.

IN THEORY, PRISONERS ARE ALLOWED TO
RECEIVE ONE LETTER A WEEK

which is restricted in length. Again, in practice they may be allowed to receive more, and restrictions on length are not as rigid as with outgoing letters. Prison officers can be quite cooperative if wives write very long letters at times of family crisis and for other special reasons. All prisons have a private postal address which you can use if you don't want your letters to be identified as going to a prison – you can get this from your local probation officer or from the prison welfare department.

## THERE ARE OFTEN SERIOUS POSTAL DELAYS

If letters aren't getting through in either direction, contact your local probation officer or the welfare officer at the prison: they should be able to tell you whether the delay has simply been caused by the postal service, or by something more serious.

## IF ENGLISH IS NOT YOUR FIRST LANGUAGE

the prison should allow you to write and receive letters in your own language. There is sometimes a bit of a hold-up about this at first, until the prison authorities get used to the idea: after that, things should run smoothly.

## ALL LETTERS TO AND FROM PRISONERS ARE READ BY THE PRISON AUTHORITIES

and if they break any of the rules listed below they will be censored. Like the semi-public visits, the censoring of letters is sometimes a source of great anxiety to wives. It's worth remembering that prison officers have to read so many letters that they are trained to look for specific details and usually fail to take anything else in.

## RESTRICTIONS ON CORRESPONDENCE

1. Letters must not contain information about prison conditions, comment on prison staff, or mention names of other prisoners.
2. A prisoner may not correspond with anyone he did not know at the time of his conviction. This rule covers correspondence about non-legal matters, such as business affairs, and correspondence concerning legal action the prisoner is conducting without the aid of a solicitor. In some circumstances, the rule may be waived – but it's up to the prison authorities to decide when to

grant such a privilege. A prisoner may be allowed to write to the Ombudsman or to the MP for his home constituency, but not to any other MP. The rule does not apply to letters to a solicitor concerning the prisoner's appeal against his conviction or sentence.

3. A prisoner cannot contact a solicitor with a view to starting any legal action (other than an appeal) without the consent of the Home Secretary. If the legal action concerns prison conditions, he will not be allowed to go ahead unless he has first made a complaint through the 'normal channels' within the prison.

## SOME OF THESE RESTRICTIONS CONTRAVENE THE EUROPEAN CONVENTION ON HUMAN RIGHTS

In February 1975, the European Court on Human Rights delivered judgment in the case of a British prisoner, Sidney Elmer Golder. He had appealed to the European Court when the Home Secretary refused to let him consult a solicitor for advice about suing a prison officer for defamation: Golder alleged that the officer wrongly accused him of taking part in a prison disturbance. The Court decided that the Home Secretary had infringed Article 6 of the Convention which states that 'In the determination of his civil rights and obligations . . . everyone is entitled to a fair and public hearing within a reasonable time by an independent and impartial tribunal established by law.' He had also infringed Article 8 of the Convention that 'Everyone has the right to respect for his . . . correspondence.' The court declared that 'impeding someone from even initiating correspondence constitutes the most far-reaching form of interference with the exercise of the right to respect for correspondence'. In response to the decision, the Home Secretary said in August 1975 that 'Henceforth, inmates will be free to seek legal advice about taking civil proceedings and to take such proceedings, provided that where the proposed proceedings concern the administration of establishments the complaint has first been ventilated through the normal existing channels to give management an opportunity to provide a remedy.' This is such a narrow interpretation of the Court's ruling that it leaves prison regulations (as described above) in breach of the spirit of the European Convention – particularly where the censorship of letters is concerned.

### Taking action

If you are dissatisfied with the way your husband is treated while in prison, don't be afraid to make a fuss about it. Here are some of the things you can do:

1. Complain to the prison authorities. Get together with wives and relatives of other inmates in the same prison; it may be easier to approach the prison staff in a group.
2. If the prison authorities don't respond satisfactorily, complain to the Home Office. The phone number of the Prison Department is 01 828 9848.
3. Contact your MP or local councillor; ask them to take up your case with the Home Office.
4. If that has no result, contact your local newspaper or the national press, to publicize the case.
5. Certain organizations take up prisoners' cases. Try approaching PROP or the NCCL (addresses, p. 448).
6. If you think the prison is contravening the European Convention on Human Rights and you have exhausted all other channels, take your complaint to the European Commission on Human Rights. The address is Strasbourg Dedex, France. Get legal advice first (see p. 454).

### Parole

Prisoners may be let out on parole after they have served one third of their sentence or a year, whichever is longer. Each case is reviewed separately by the prison's local review committee and the national Parole Board. It's impossible to find out exactly how a prisoner is assessed or why a decision is taken to grant or refuse parole. The way the system works encourages you to believe that there is nothing you can do to influence the decision. However, it would do no harm – and it *might* help – if you could arrange for letters to be sent confirming that employment and/or housing would be available if parole were granted. Letters should be addressed to the Parole Board, Home Office, Whitehall, London SW1. It may also be worth writing to the local review committee. You can find out the address from the prison welfare officer.

### Money

Unless you have a reasonable income of your own, you are entitled to supplementary benefit in the same way as any single woman. If you have children you will get additional allowances for them. We explain about supplementary benefit on p. 189.

If your husband has home leave you should claim extra money from your Social Security office for the few days he is living with you.

If you have children and you are working you may be entitled to the Family Income Supplement, which is described on p. 186. If – as is likely – you find that supplementary benefit isn't enough to live on, contact your local probation officer or NACRO: they may be able to put you in touch with organizations that can give you additional support. The WRVS (Women's Royal Voluntary Service) can be very helpful.

You can send money to a prisoner. It will be held by the prison authorities as part of his personal property and he will be able to spend it on such things as newspapers, magazines and cards.

### Housing

If you are entitled to supplementary benefit (and you can find out whether you are on p. 190) the Social Security should pay your rent and rates. The local authority may give you a rent rebate: inquire about this at your local housing department (address in the telephone directory under the heading of the local authority).

If you have any trouble with threats of eviction or rent arrears, try to get help immediatcly. Your local probation officer should be able to advise you what to do; otherwise go to your Citizens' Advice Bureau and ask to be put in touch with a solicitor. The Social Security may pay rent arrears, especially if the alternative is to split up the family and place the children in care. In some circumstances, the social services department of the local council will pay rent arrears.

If you have a mortgage, the Social Security will not meet the full payments, but it may arrange to pay a certain amount towards the interest. Either you or your husband should write to the building society as soon as possible to see what can be arranged.

In many ways you are in the same position as a separated wife, so you may find it useful to read the section entitled 'Married women: your right to the family home' on p. 371. For general information on your rights as a tenant, read the section entitled 'Quick guide for tenants' on p. 393.

### Hire purchase and other debts and fines

You are not responsible for your husband's debts. He should write to the company or court to whom he owes money explaining that he is in prison and that he will pay a nominal amount out of his wages. This has the effect of leaving everything in suspended animation until he is released. In the meantime you are freed from the anxiety of having to keep up payments. The same is true of gas and electricity bills and local authority rent arrears: if your husband writes saying that he is responsible and that all he can do is offer a nominal amount – say 10p a month – out of his prison earnings, this is usually accepted. You will only be responsible for bills incurred after his imprisonment and for debts that are in your name.

### Divorce and separation

If you want to start legal proceedings to divorce or separate from your husband, the fact that he is in prison makes no difference – if anything, it makes it easier (although while your husband is in prison he cannot be said to be deserting you, as he has no choice). You will probably be able to get legal aid. We explain how to find a solicitor and apply for legal aid on p. 449; and how to get a divorce or separation on p. 278.

## Women in prison

### What do women go to prison for?

Over half the women who go to prison each year are 'on remand'. That means that they have not actually been sentenced to prison but they are either awaiting trial or have been convicted and are waiting to be sentenced. In 1979, 5,996 women went to prison. Of those, 40 per cent were in prison on remand and the rest were actually sentenced to prison. Fifty-seven per cent were sentenced for various forms of stealing; 7 per cent for charges connected with prostitution; 23 per cent for other, mainly minor offences; and 19 per cent for some sort of violence against other people. Shoplifting sent more women to jail than any other offence – and most shoplifting offences are very small.

So women prisoners are hardly a bunch of dangerous criminals. Less than a handful might need to be locked up for public safety.

The vast majority are in on very short sentences. Allowing for remission (reduction of sentence, which usually amounts to a third) slightly less than 15 per cent of convicted prisoners spend more than a year inside.

There are three closed women's prisons, Holloway in North London, Cookham Wood in Kent and Styal near Manchester. There are also some women in the maximum security wing at Durham prison. There are three open women's prisons: Askham Grange near York, Moor Court near Stoke on Trent and Drake Hall in Staffordshire. Holloway is being rebuilt under an ambitious multi-million-pound plan, due for completion in 1983. One result of there being so few women's prisons is that many of the inmates are a long way from home.

## Rules for women prisoners

Almost all prison rules are the same for women as they are for men, including the rules about visits and letters which are described in the section on Prisoners' Wives (pp. 432–44). Remember that prisoners have *privileges*, not *rights*, and that the way they are treated varies considerably from one prison to another and from one prison officer to another. Two rules apply to women prisoners only:

1. *Women are allowed to wear their own clothes and make-up* and they do not have to have their hair cut. Personal appearance is a matter left to the individual prisoner.
2. *If a woman has a baby* (either before or after she is sent to prison) she is allowed to keep it with her until it is about a year old. This is supposed to be the rule, but prison governors can refuse to let mothers have their babies with them if there isn't enough room. At Askham Grange there is a mother-and-baby unit where mothers can (if there is room) keep their children up to the age of 3 years. But children older than the age limit set by the prison must be taken into the care of the local council if they cannot be looked after by relatives. The official reasoning on

this issue is rather strange: that a child should not be allowed to stay in prison beyond an age where it is aware of its environment. Yet the alternative is to send it away from the mother, probably to another institution.

It costs £140 a week to keep a woman in prison (1979 figures). It costs even more if she has children. In 1976, the price of imprisoning one woman who had four children, whose husband had deserted her, and who was jailed for six months for theft, was £4,141·43. It would obviously be a lot more today.

Research (1976) by Carole Gibb on women with children received in a year into Holloway alone showed that 35 per cent had dependent children (many in Holloway, especially on remand, are young) and that only half of the children normally lived with their mother. This still meant that over 1,000 were separated by their mother going into prison. Over a quarter had to be taken into care, almost another quarter had to move to friends or relatives and nearly half stayed in the same family situation, usually with fathers, grandparents or siblings. A considerable number of these separations proved unnecessary, as the mother was remanded and then not sentenced to prison. The distress, both to mother and children, over such separation is apparent even to the Home Office:

'It is well known that this sort of dispersal has a traumatic effect on the children and may be a cause of their future delinquency or other forms of instability . . . To send a woman to prison is to take her away from her family; the children in particular suffer from this deprivation which can lead to the break up of the home, even where there is a stable marriage' (*Treatment of Women and Girls in Custody*, HMSO 1970). [From a report by RAP (Radical Alternatives to Prison), *Alternatives to Holloway*]

## 'Mad not bad'

There is a tendency for female offenders to be regarded as psychologically disturbed rather than criminal. If a woman prisoner does not conform by obeying rules and regulations, she may be treated as a psychiatric 'case' and possibly even transferred to a psychiatric prison. Tranquillizer drugs are administered in large quantities. A Yorkshire newspaper reported the experiences of one ex-prisoner, 24-year-old Ruth Hall, who had already spent ten years of her life in penal institutions. She first started taking drugs in Holloway:

'I went to the doctor and said I was depressed ... [He] gave me a sleeping draught. When I first started taking it I used to get a buzz off it. Various people on the wing were on Valium and they said they got a buzz from that, so I went to the doctor and asked for some. They don't mind giving you tranquillizers, because it keeps you quiet.

'So I started getting drugs from the doctor and the amounts increased because I used to say the last dose didn't work ... I was drugged up half the time. I did six months, came out, went home and was in a pretty bad state.'

She became addicted to heroin, attempted suicide and was arrested twice more for shoplifting. The first time she went for two years to Styal. The second time she was sent to Holloway on remand. 'I was sent to hospital for medical reports. One doctor saw me for half an hour, another for ten minutes.

'They said I was a psychopath because I was not sorry about anything. I was certified insane and sent to Rampton [a psychiatric prison] ... I questioned and questioned why I was there. All I could get was they didn't know, but I was there because of the law. I remained on admission ward. They couldn't classify me because they said there was no reason for me to be there.'

It took Ruth Hall a year to convince the authorities that she was sane; she was then released. [*Yorkshire Post*, 8 January 1976]

## Prisoners on remand

(This applies to men as well as women, but we thought it worth mentioning since so many women prisoners are on remand.)

If you are on remand you have certain 'privileges', including:

1. You don't have to do prison work if you don't want to (although it may be better than doing nothing).
2. You can send and receive as many letters as you like.
3. You can have as many visits as you like, although you will probably be restricted to one a day.

4. You are allowed to receive some sorts of food from outside the prison.
5. You can buy writing materials, newspapers and books, unless they are considered 'objectionable' by the prison authorities.
6. You can ask for a visit from a doctor or dentist who is not attached to the prison.
7. You can see your legal adviser within normal working hours as often as you need to, in the sight but not in the hearing of a prison officer.

(Read also 'Getting legal aid', pp. 452–9.)

### Further information

Prisoners' Wives and Families Society, 254 Caledonian Road, London N1 (01 278 3981): offers practical help for prisoners' families.

Prisoners' Wives Service, 373a Brixton Road, London SW9 (01 737 0223): visits prisoners' families in the London area.

Preservation of the Rights of Prisoners (PROP), 97 Caledonian Road, London N1 (01 278 3328/542 3744): prisoners' union, campaigning for prisoners' rights.

National Association for the Care and Resettlement of Offenders (NACRO), 169 Clapham Road, London SW9 (01 582 6500): information and help for prisoners, ex-prisoners and prisoners' wives and families.

National Council for Civil Liberties (NCCL), 23–5 Tabard Street, London SE1.

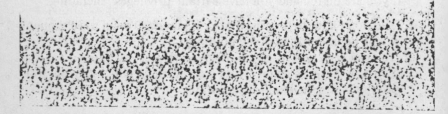

# 12. Approaching the Law

## Going to a solicitor

Throughout this book we have often suggested that you go to a solicitor for help. Most people have never met a solicitor and wouldn't know where to start looking for one. The thought may be a little alarming. But once you know what to do, it really isn't all that difficult.

### What sort of people are they?

The vast majority are men. All practising solicitors are enrolled by the Law Society and at the last count there were 37,832 men and 3,700 women. So under 10 per cent of practising solicitors are women. All solicitors are middle class: most of them were born that way and the rest were educated into it. This is positively encouraged by the legal education system which is extremely conservative. Solicitors tend to wear suits and have their offices in the smarter parts of town. They are not allowed to advertise their services but there are ways of finding out which to go to, as you will see if you read on. Most firms of solicitors expect you to phone or write to make an appointment before you see them, but neighbourhood law centres, described below, p. 452, are more informal. Barristers make up the other half of the legal profession: they are the ones who speak to the judge and jury in the higher courts and advise solicitors on specialist matters; 9 per cent of them are women.)

If all this sounds off-putting, don't worry. It doesn't mean that they won't be helpful to you. Most of them have a reasonable knowledge of the law and some are very sympathetic and obliging.

Two warnings: almost any legal proceedings take a long time; and solicitors are *very* expensive, so you should apply for legal aid to pay your costs (see pp. 452–9).

Go to your nearest Citizens' Advice Bureau and ask for the names of local solicitors who would be prepared to act for you under the legal aid scheme. A national referral list of solicitors operating the legal aid scheme has been prepared for each area and states what kind of work each law firm does – such as divorce, criminal cases or wills, and whether the firm is willing to do emergency work, such as applying for emergency injunctions. Not all firms do legal aid work as they are not paid as much under the scheme as they could charge a private client. If your CAB is a good one, it should be able to tell you which solicitors are best suited to help with your particular case and make an appointment for you. The national referral list is also available at libraries, law centres, town halls and social services departments. If you have a social worker she should be able to help you as well.

You can also go to a magistrates' court or a county court and ask someone in the court office to give you the names and addresses of solicitors who work nearby.

If the case is urgent and you can't contact a solicitor, fill in the appropriate legal aid form (available from the court or from your Citizens' Advice Bureau) and leave a blank space where it asks for the name of your solicitor. Then you will be provided with one.

If you find yourself in court without a solicitor (for instance, if you are arrested and taken to court before you have time to contact one) ask to have the case adjourned: your request will almost certainly be granted. You will then have time to contact a solicitor and apply for legal aid.

### How to change your solicitor

If you don't like the solicitor you've got and you want to get another one to act for you, you are perfectly entitled to do so. Don't be frightened of taking the step – it's quite common. On the other hand, don't be too optimistic: you may find that the second solicitor is no better than the first, because the law itself is a slow, expensive and unsatisfactory business.

*If you're on legal aid*, tell the Clerk of the Court (if you're involved in a criminal case) or the Law Society (if you're involved in a civil case), and ask them to transfer your legal aid to the solicitor of your choice, giving your reasons for wanting to change. Once that is done, the first solicitor will transfer all your papers to the second one. It would be courteous to tell the first solicitor what you intend to do and ask him to transfer the papers, but he will do so even if you don't tell him.

*If you're not on legal aid* you will have to tell the first solicitor to transfer your papers to the second solicitor. He probably won't do this until you pay his bill, and he is entitled to keep all the papers until he gets his money.

The second solicitor will probably not start acting for you until your case has been handed over to him by the first solicitor.

### What to do if you think your solicitor has charged you too much

If you're on legal aid, you probably won't come up against this problem. But if you're not and you think your solicitor's bill is too high, take action right away.

IF YOUR CASE DID NOT GO TO COURT

the first thing to do is to tell the solicitor that you think it's too high. If he doesn't convince you that he has charged the right amount, or agree to reduce the bill, you can ask him to get a certificate from the Law Society stating that in their opinion the sum charged is 'fair and reasonable'. If the Law Society says that a lower sum would be 'fair and reasonable', you will only have to pay that.

Your solicitor cannot take you to court for not paying his bill until he has written to you telling you of the right to ask the Law Society for a certificate. He also has to tell you that you can ask for his bill to be 'taxed'. This means having it checked by the county court or High Court. It may be decided that the bill should be reduced. You should ask for the bill to be taxed within a month of receiving it, but, if you ask after a month and within twelve months, the court may still allow you to have it taxed. The snag is that unless it is decided that you should pay less than five sixths (or in some cases four fifths) of the bill, you will have to pay the costs of having it taxed, which may mean that you have to pay more than the original sum.

You cannot ask for a certificate from the Law Society after you have paid the bill, or after the bill has been taxed.

IF YOUR CASE HAS GONE TO COURT

all you can do is ask the court to tax your bill as described above.

### Neighbourhood law centres

These are places where lawyers make a positive effort to be accessible to the community and offer free legal advice and aid in most cases. If there is one in your area, it would be well worth approaching them to see if they can help you. (For addresses, see p. 500.)

## Getting legal aid

Legal aid is money paid by the state to help cover the cost of having a solicitor to help you with a legal matter. If you want to get help from a solicitor and you are not so rich that you don't have to worry about the bill, you should apply for it. The amount of legal

A person to see you about Legal Aid, sir

aid you get depends on what your income is. If your income is below supplementary benefit level (see p. 190) and your capital below £1,200, legal aid will be free; but even if you have quite a high income you can qualify for free legal aid or legal aid towards which you make some contribution. The amount will depend on your expenses and obligations.

*Married women:* If you are married, your husband's income is counted as part of yours when you are assessed for legal aid, *unless* you are involved in legal action against him. This can be unfair. For instance, a married woman might be injured at work and want to claim compensation from her employer; her husband may think she shouldn't bother; with his income added to hers she is not eligible for legal aid; without his financial support she cannot pursue her claim.

There are three different legal aid schemes.

## 1. Legal advice and assistance

This is a scheme known as the 'green form' procedure. You can get advice and other help (such as writing letters or drawing up documents) from a solicitor, on any legal problem. It is either free or partly free if you fall within the financial limit. You can use it for preparing your case for a tribunal hearing, and even for getting a solicitor to accompany you to the tribunal and advise you on how to put forward your case. But it doesn't cover the cost of a solicitor actually representing you at a court or tribunal, except in domestic proceedings in a magistrates' court when your solicitor can ask for permission for it to cover presentation at court. There is no limit to the amount of advice and assistance you can get under this scheme, but if it amounts to more than £40 worth, the solicitor must get authorization from the Law Society. This limit is extended to £55 for divorce cases.

EXAMPLES OF WHEN IT IS USEFUL

Your landlord threatens you with eviction or puts up the rent, and you want to find out what to do about it.

Your husband has walked out on you and left you without any money. You are uncertain whether to start divorce proceedings or to sue him for maintenance.

You have had your supplementary benefit book taken away because you are suspected of living with a man: you want help to prepare an appeal to the supplementary benefits appeal tribunal.

HOW DO YOU GET IT?

Ask your solicitor for the application form. It is a simple form which the solicitor will fill in for you. You will qualify if your 'disposable' income is less than £85 a week and your 'disposable' capital is less than £600. However, you may still have to pay a contribution. For instance, if your disposable income is £62 a week, you may have to contribute up to £25; but if your weekly disposable income is £45, the most you will have to contribute is £5.

WHAT DOES 'DISPOSABLE' INCOME AND CAPITAL MEAN?

*Your disposable income* is your total weekly income including Child Benefit, *not counting* tax, National Insurance contributions, allowances for dependants and certain other expenses.

*Your disposable capital* is the money you have saved or invested *not counting* the value of your furniture, part or all of the value of your house, debts and certain other sums.

It is very complicated to work all this out and you should try to get help with it from your solicitor or the Citizens' Advice Bureau.

## 2. Civil legal aid

Civil legal aid is money to cover all or part of the cost of having a solicitor act for you if you are involved in a civil case. It is administered by the Law Society.

*What is a civil case?* A civil case is a non-criminal case where one private individual or group of individuals sues another. Most of the areas of law dealt with in this book would involve civil cases, for instance divorce, separation, affiliation proceedings, adoption and consumer disputes.

*You will get legal aid if* you can convince the Law Society's Legal Aid Committee that you have good reason for proceeding with your case; and you satisfy the financial conditions. Legal aid will be totally free if:

(a) you are on supplementary benefit or Family Income Supplement; *or*
(b) your annual disposable income is £1,700 or less and you have no more than £1,200 disposable capital.

You will get legal aid to cover *part* of your costs if:

(a) your annual disposable income is between £1,700 and £4,075; *and*

(b) your disposable capital is between £1,200 and £2,500.

You will certainly not get legal aid if your disposable income is over £4,075 and you will probably not get it if your disposable capital is over £2,500.

HOW TO APPLY

1. It is advisable to get legal advice first, to find out whether you have a strong enough case to make it worth going ahead. You can get this under the 'legal advice and assistance scheme' described on p. 454.
2. You can get the form which has to be filled in to start court proceedings and apply for legal aid, from your solicitor, Citizens' Advice Bureau or the nearest Law Society's legal aid area office (addresses are in the telephone directory).
3. The form is long and complicated to fill in. If you already have a solicitor s/he will probably help you, otherwise you can get help from your Citizens' Advice Bureau. Send the form off as soon as possible to the Secretary at the Law Society's legal aid area office.
4. The financial section of the form is sent on to the Supplementary Benefits Commission: they assess your financial situation and tell the Law Society what is the maximum amount you can afford to pay. They will probably want to interview you.
5. The Legal Aid Committee will then decide whether or not to grant you legal aid.

*If you are granted legal aid*, you will be told how much the case is likely to cost and what your contribution is likely to be. You will also be told what is the maximum you will be expected to pay if the case turns out to be more expensive. If you accept this decision you must tell the Law Society within twenty-eight days, and you will then be given a legal aid certificate. It usually takes two or three months from the time you apply to the time you are granted the certificate. Your solicitor can then go ahead with your case. You will normally be expected to pay your contributions (if any) in monthly instalments.

*You can apply for an emergency certificate* if your case is urgent, by filling in a special form (available from your solicitor, Citizens' Advice Bureau or the Law Society's legal aid area office). It is best to find a solicitor to act for you before you apply: you can organize this through the 'legal advice and assistance scheme' described on p. 454. If your case is very urgent, legal aid can be granted on the same day as you apply.

*You can appeal* to the Law Society's legal aid area committee if you are refused legal aid. You should do this within four days of hearing the decision. You cannot appeal against the financial arrangements, only against the decision that your case is not strong enough to merit legal aid. Tell them about any new evidence or information that you think might be relevant. If your financial circumstances change, it is worth making a fresh application for legal aid.

*Is it worth going ahead if you can't get legal aid?* If you win your case, your legal costs will normally be paid by your opponent unless he or she is legally aided. So if you have a strong case it may be worth going ahead and borrowing the money if necessary. Your solicitor will advise you on this.

### 3. Criminal legal aid

Criminal legal aid is money to cover the cost of having a solicitor represent you if you are involved in a criminal case.

*What is a criminal case?* A criminal case is one where a person is prosecuted by the police for breaking the law, for instance for dangerous driving, shoplifting or soliciting.

If you are prosecuted by the police, be sure to get a solicitor, unless the case is very trivial indeed. If you intend to plead 'Not Guilty', don't assume that your innocence will protect you. It is quite possible that false evidence may be given against you –

deliberately or accidentally. Beware of pleading 'Guilty' until you have spoken to a solicitor. S/he may advise you against it, or present 'mitigating' factors to the court so that you have a chance of getting a reduced sentence. So if you are taken to court and you don't have a solicitor, tell the magistrate that you want a solicitor and legal aid, and ask for the case to be adjourned. If you don't know of a solicitor, you will be provided with one.

If you end up being tried without a solicitor, and the magistrate is considering sending you to prison, he *must* ask you if you want legal aid. It's rather absurd that he is not obliged to offer you this until you have been convicted, but, whatever happens, don't refuse his offer.

### IF YOU ARE NOT LEGALLY REPRESENTED IN COURT, YOU ARE MORE LIKELY TO GO TO PRISON

This fact was clearly shown in a book called *Silent in Court* by Susan Dell – a study of women prisoners in Holloway and how they had been represented in court before they were sentenced. Only 17 per cent of women who were sent to Holloway from magistrates' courts had been legally represented. (Eighty per cent of Holloway's inmates come from magistrates' courts.) The book was written before the new ruling which obliges magistrates to offer legal aid before sending anyone to prison, but it shows the importance of being properly represented in court. Susan Dell says:

An inexperienced defendant is at a disadvantage in court even if well-educated and articulate, but for those who have little education, who are scared, nervous and unable to express themselves in the kind of language they believe is expected in courts, the handicap can be crippling, particularly if they wish to deny the offence or plead mitigating circumstances.

The mere presence of someone to speak on behalf of the person in court, even if it is just to state the basic facts of the case and ask for bail, can have a significant effect on the number sent to prison on remand or under sentence. The study shows that an alarming number of women who were convicted but not represented in court later claimed that they were not guilty. Most of them had pleaded guilty in court, either on the advice of the police or because they didn't see any point in putting up a fight ('it's their word against mine') and wanted to 'get it over', or simply because they didn't understand what was going on.

YOU WILL BE GRANTED LEGAL AID IF THE COURT DECIDES:

(a) that it is in the interests of justice that you should have it; *and*
(b) that you cannot afford to pay the cost of your defence yourself.

You will get legal aid entirely free if:

(a) you are receiving supplementary benefit; *or*
(b) your net income over the last year was not more than £815 after deducting tax, National Insurance, rent, rates and allowances for dependants; and your capital is not more than £75. The value of the matrimonial home or your interest in your main dwelling is disregarded.

But people who have more money than that often get legal aid free. Practice varies from one court order to another. Generally speaking, free legal aid is a lot easier to get than it would seem from the official requirements listed above. Free legal aid is granted almost automatically for trials in the higher courts (the Crown Courts or Central Criminal Court).

If you are not granted legal aid entirely free, you will have to pay a contribution towards your legal costs.

HOW TO APPLY

Apply as soon as possible. The application form is more straightforward than the one for civil legal aid. It is available from court offices and Citizens' Advice Bureaux. It is best to fill it in on the spot, so that you can get help if you need it. If you are in prison, you are supposed to be given the form automatically, but you'll probably have to ask for it.

If you don't have time to apply for legal aid before you are taken to court, tell the magistrate as soon as possible. He will either consider your application immediately, or adjourn the case.

The clerk of the court will probably consider your application first. If he is against granting you legal aid, he must refer it to the magistrate. If the magistrate refuses legal aid, you cannot appeal against his decision, but you may be able to make a fresh application later.

*If you are granted legal aid*, but you have to pay part of the costs, you may be asked to make a down-payment before the case is heard. But this doesn't often happen and the down-payment is likely to be about £25, though it may vary according to your means. When the case has been concluded, the magistrate or judge may order you to pay a contribution towards the cost. If you are acquitted your costs should be paid for you.

In the higher courts, a legal aid order will cover the cost of a solicitor and barrister, but in the lower courts it will usually only cover a solicitor. But if it is a complex case, your solicitor can apply for the legal aid order to cover the barrister as well.

### Further information

*Civil Liberty: The NCCL Guide* includes chapters on arrest, bail and questioning; court procedure; and legal aid. A Penguin Handbook, obtainable from bookshops or from the National Council for Civil Liberties, 23–5 Tabard Street, London SE1.

*Legal Aid Guide*, free from your local Citizens' Advice Bureau or from the Law Society, Chancery Lane, London WC2.

## The different kinds of civil courts

At many points in this book we have mentioned the civil courts. The diagram on p. 462 summarizes the different kinds of cases dealt with in different civil courts, and the way in which an

individual case may move from one court to another if the parties concerned are not satisfied with the first decision. If a case is 'defended' it means that the case you are bringing against somebody is challenged by them.

## Taking a complaint to the county court or sheriff court

The account that follows is reproduced, with slight adaptations from *Rights for Women* by Patricia Hewitt, with kind permission from the National Council for Civil Liberties. It is designed to help you make a complaint under the Sex Discrimination Act: all complaints of unlawful discrimination which do *not* concern employment or training go to the county court, or the sheriff court in Scotland. But it applies equally to other complaints that are made to the county courts, such as claims against manufacturers or retailers (p. 416). It describes what is *supposed* to happen. Don't be surprised if your own experience is somewhat different. You may find the procedure is slower, more complicated and more intimidating than the impression given here. Like it or not, the courts operate on the assumption that everyone who brings a case should have a lawyer. People who try to do without are unlikely to be welcomed or made to feel at ease. A lot will depend on the personalities and opinions of the people you encounter at the court. Helpful court officials and a registrar or judge who does not

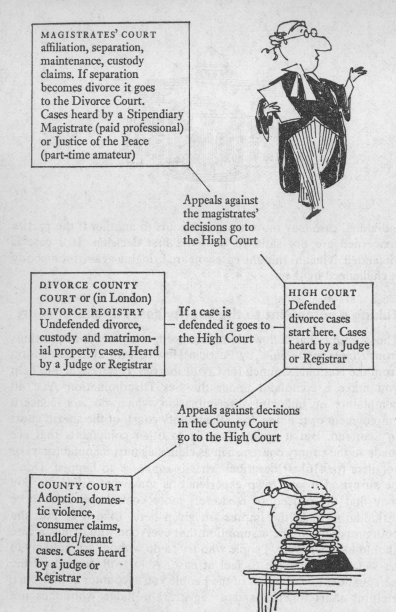

**MAGISTRATES' COURT** affiliation, separation, maintenance, custody claims. If separation becomes divorce it goes to the Divorce Court. Cases heard by a Stipendiary Magistrate (paid professional) or Justice of the Peace (part-time amateur)

Appeals against the magistrates' decisions go to the High Court

**DIVORCE COUNTY COURT** or (in London) **DIVORCE REGISTRY** Undefended divorce, custody and matrimonial property cases. Heard by a Judge or Registrar

If a case is defended it goes to the High Court

**HIGH COURT** Defended divorce cases start here. Cases heard by a Judge or Registrar

Appeals against decisions in the County Court go to the High Court

**COUNTY COURT** Adoption, domestic violence, consumer claims, landlord/tenant cases. Cases heard by a judge or Registrar

disapprove of women bringing cases without professional help, could obviously make things a lot easier for you.

## PLAINTIFF AND DEFENDANT

If you make a complaint to the county court, you are the *plaintiff*; the person against whom you are complaining is the *defendant*. There can be more than one plaintiff and more than one defendant involved in a case. Before you make your complaint, you have to decide who the defendant will be in your case. You also have to get full details of his name and address, since the court has to ensure that the summons (that is, your complaint) reaches him. It is not the court's job to check the accuracy of the name and address.

## LIMITED COMPANIES

You may be complaining against a limited company (e.g. a television rental firm which has refused to let you rent a TV without your husband's signature). A limited company usually has the word 'Limited' or 'Ltd' after its name. This word should be on its writing paper or invoice, or you can find it in the telephone directory. In the case of a limited company, the summons has to be delivered or sent to the 'registered office', which may not be the address at which you have been dealing with the company. Always check the address by contacting the Companies Register, Companies House, 55–71 City Road, London EC1Y 1BB (01 253 9393).

## FIRMS

If the firm's name does not include 'Ltd', it is probably a one-person business or a partnership. In this case you can use the address at which the firm carries on business or where one of the partners lives. You may have been dealing with a particular partner but, if one partner has entered into a contract for his firm, then all the partners are liable. The best thing to do is to sue the firm without naming the partners individually; if you sue one of the partners and win, but he is unable to pay you, you won't then be able to sue the others, whereas if you sue the firm you can be more certain of getting compensation if you win. If the name of the firm does not include the full names of the partners, you should be able to get the full details from the Registry of Business Names at Pembroke House, 40–56 City Road, London EC1Y 2DN.

#### 'PARTICULARS OF CLAIM'

When you start an action you must give the court written details of what you are claiming. This is called the 'particulars of claim' and should set out quite briefly the facts of the situation which support your claim. You don't have to set out the whole story, but simply enough to tell the defendant why you are making the claim and how much you want him to pay you. The particulars should be headed with the name of the court, with a space for the 'plaint number' (i.e. the number by which your case is identified) which will be allocated when you issue the summons. Below this the names of the plaintiff and the defendant are set out. There is a specimen particulars of claim on page 475.

You then have to set out a brief statement of the facts of your claim and the sum of money or other remedy for which you are suing. It is usual to write in the third person (referring to yourself as 'the plaintiff' . . . 'she') and to set out your claim in numbered paragraphs. If you have trouble wording your claim, the court office will be able to help.

The particulars of your claim don't have to be typewritten, provided that your writing is clear. You will need one copy for the court, and one copy for each defendant. You should make sure that you also keep a copy for your own use.

#### CHOOSING THE RIGHT COURT

England and Wales are divided into districts in each of which there is a county court. You can start court proceedings in the district where the defendant lives, or where the action which led to your complaint took place. If you do not know which is the right court to go to, you should inquire at the nearest county court office. County courts are usually listed in the telephone directory under 'courts'.

## THE 'REQUEST'

To start your action, you must fill in a form called a 'request'. The court needs this in order to prepare a summons, which is the document that the defendant receives from the court telling him about your claim and what he has to do. A request form can be got from any county court office and the court staff will help you complete it. A court bailiff usually serves the summons on the defendant by post. You can serve the summons yourself, but it is better to let the court do it for you. That way, you are sure that the summons will be properly served.

## COURT FEES

When you hand in your completed request form to the court you will also have to pay the court fee in cash. Court fees are based on the amount of damages you are claiming. The minimum fee is £4. The maximum fee is now £29. If you are asking for an injunction this will cost you £15, plus £2 if you wish the court bailiff to serve the injunction.

## THE PRE-TRIAL REVIEW

The pre-trial review usually takes place in private and is informal. It is really a discussion between the registrar of the court, who acts instead of the judge, and the plaintiff and defendant, to decide how the action should be dealt with.

The date for the pre-trial review is normally some six weeks after the issue of the summons. Therefore seven days prior to the hearing of the pre-trial review if no defence has been received you should write to the court and to all other parties stating that on the hearing of the pre-trial review you will apply for an order that the defendants, having failed to serve their defence, be debarred from defending. The registrar then has the power, on the hearing of the pre-trial review, to make a judgment for the amount claimed.

Unless you attend the pre-trial review, your case may be dropped. If this happens you can ask the court to restore the case and hear it another day. The registrar decides whether or not to restore the case. If he does, he may ask you to pay any expense that the defendant has been put to as a result of your failure to turn up in court. If he refuses to restore your case you will have to start all over again in order to make your complaint.

If the defendant does not attend the pre-trial review, you may be able to have the case decided there and then. You will probably have to give evidence, in which case the registrar will ask you to stand up and take the oath or affirm. You can then sit down and tell the registrar the facts of the case. You should remember to bring with you any letters, bills, receipts or other pieces of information which will help you to prove your case. If the registrar is satisfied that you have proved your case, he will give a decision and record the judgment.

If you and the defendant attend the pre-trial review, the registrar will look at the papers that you have both submitted. If he thinks that your 'Particulars of Claim' don't give enough information, he may ask you to explain the matter more fully; he may then deal with the defendant's defence in the same way, or, if the defendant has not submitted one, he will find out whether he has a defence and if so, what it is. However this rarely happens in practice. If you want more information from the defendant at this stage, you should say so.

You may find that you have left something out of your 'Particulars of Claim', or that as a result of further inquiries you want to alter them. You can do this before the pre-trial review simply by amending your 'Particulars of Claim' and sending copies to the defendant and the court (and keeping a copy for yourself). If you want to alter them at the pre-trial review you must ask the registrar for permission.

### DIRECTIONS FOR TRIAL

At the pre-trial review the registrar gives directions which may be needed to prepare the action for trial and save unnecessary costs and expense. If the defendant wants to dispute your claim and has not filed a defence, and the registrar is not prepared to debar the defendant from defending, the registrar will normally order that a defence be filed within a certain time (usually fourteen days) and that he should not be allowed to defend the action if he fails to obey the order.

This is supposed to stop a defendant who has failed to file a defence from turning up at the trial and asking to be heard; and it may save you the expense of bringing witnesses to court, who would not be needed if the action were undefended. But the defendant can ask to have more time to file his defence, if he can't do it within the time given; if you object, he can apply to the registrar who decides whether or not he should be given extra time.

### FURTHER DETAILS OF YOUR CLAIM AND THE DEFENCE

You are entitled to know the facts on which your opponent is relying to defend the case. And he is entitled to know the facts on which you base your complaint. Without this information, neither of you would know what witnesses or documents to bring to court. It is possible that the registrar, without being asked, may tell you or the defendant to supply extra details, but you should also consider whether you need to know anything more about the defence. Either side can ask the other for more details.

## PRODUCTION OF DOCUMENTS

Although neither you nor the defendant can be required to say in advance what evidence you will call in support of your case, you can be ordered to produce all the documents which you have that are relevant to the case. With some exceptions, each of you must, if ordered by the registrar or court, disclose to the other side all the documents that you are going to produce in court. This is called an order for 'discovery'.

If necessary, the registrar will order you both to exchange lists of all your documents within a stated time and allow each of you to inspect the documents disclosed. Nowadays, many solicitors find it simpler to send each other photocopies of their client's documents, rather than go to the trouble of exchanging lists, especially where there are only a few documents involved. You are, of course, allowed to charge the defendant a reasonable price for supplying copies.

If an order for mutual discovery is made, its meaning in simple terms is that each party must prepare a list of any documents such as letters, invoices, receipts, agreements or anything else in writing having a bearing on the case, but excluding what are known as 'privileged documents' such as witnesses' statements or letters passing between you and your own lawyers.

## FURTHER HELP

Although the registrar cannot help you in preparing your case, he can (if asked) indicate in general terms the sort of evidence you will need to prove your claim. He might suggest that you should try and find a witness who could support a particular aspect of your case, or that you should produce certain documents at the hearing. If you are in doubt, do not hesitate to consult the registrar.

DATE OF THE HEARING

The registrar will fix a date for the trial. You should tell the registrar if there are any dates when, because of a holiday or work commitment, you or your witnesses cannot appear at court.

If, at a later date, you have to ask for the date to be changed, then you may have to pay any extra expense which the defendant incurs as a result. If it is necessary to change the date, write to the defendant as soon as possible and see if he will agree. If he does, you can write to the court enclosing his letter of agreement and ask for a new date. If he refuses, you will have to make an application to the court, in writing, for a new date.

PREPARING YOUR CASE

When your case is heard, the court has to consider the evidence which is presented to it. It then has to decide on the balance of probabilities whether or not you have proved your case. 'Balance of probabilities' means that, in order for you to win, the judge has to decide that it is more probable than not that your complaint is justified in the eyes of the law. Sometimes the evidence is so finely balanced that it is almost impossible to say who is in the right. In such a case, the court is entitled to say that you have lost your case, because it is up to you to prove your claim. It is therefore vitally important that you give the court all the evidence you can to support your complaint.

WITNESSES

It may well be that you and the defendant are the most important witnesses (perhaps the only ones). Each of you gives your version of what happened: your stories may conflict in many respects. If possible, you should bring along any other people who saw or heard what happened or who can support your story. If you are relying on witnesses, it is essential that they come to court so that they can give their evidence on oath and can be questioned by the defendant and the court.

For various reasons, witnesses are sometimes reluctant to come to court. When you ask people to act as a witness, find out whether they are prepared to come to court without being served with a witness summons. Ask them whether there are any dates when they cannot attend court – this could affect the date of the hearing. If any witnesses are not prepared to come to court voluntarily, they can be compelled to do so. Tell the court office you want to serve a witness summons. The court staff will help you fill in the necessary form. You will have to produce the plaint note, and pay a small fee for the summons. You will also have to pay the court the money for the witness's expenses (travel to and from the court and loss of time at work); the court office will tell you how much this is.

You must be prepared to pay your witness's expenses. But if you win, the defendant will usually have to pay all or part of these expenses. The court decides what is a reasonable sum to cover travelling and other expenses involved, and the time lost attending court.

DOCUMENTS

Although spoken evidence from witnesses is most important, documents can sometimes make all the difference between success and failure. Letters written by you or the defendant, contracts and agreements, bills, invoices and receipts, bank statements and so on, could all be vital to your case. Remember to bring them with you when your case is heard, with copies for the judge.

THE HEARING

Make sure you know where the county court is. They normally open at 10 a.m. for a 10.30 start. Try and arrive at 10 a.m. so that you can find out which court room you will be in, and have time to discuss the case with your lawyer if you have one. Give your name to the usher so that he knows where you are when the case is called. The usher normally wears a black gown.

There may be other cases before yours, and you must expect to spend the day at court. It is a good idea to sit in court rather than wait outside, so that you can see how other cases are dealt with, and hear the sort of questions that are put to witnesses.

There is no reason why you should not bring along a friend or relative to help you conduct the case yourself. The court can allow another person to address the court on your behalf (this person is called a 'McKenzie' after a case of that name which established the right to have a non-lawyer present your case). Help of this kind can be very useful especially if you are feeling nervous. But you will still have to give evidence yourself.

## THE COURT

The judge will sit at the front, facing the court: he wears a wig and purple gown. The clerk of the court sits in front of him. If there are any barristers or solicitors appearing in court, then they sit at the front facing the judge. Barristers wear a wig and a black gown; solicitors wear a gown, but no wig if they are conducting the case.

## GIVING EVIDENCE

When you come to give evidence in your case, you should come forward to the witness box where you will be asked to take the oath or affirm. Tell the judge about your claim from the beginning. If you have a lawyer representing you s/he will help you by asking questions. Try not to get excited and do not exaggerate. A person who stays calm and reasonable makes a better impression than one who is angry or incoherent. Remember to pause between sentences because the judge will be making a note – in longhand – of what you say. It is a good idea to watch his pencil; when he stops writing, you can go on speaking.

When telling your story, it may be difficult to avoid repeating what someone else told you when the defendant wasn't present.

This is known as 'hearsay' evidence, and generally speaking, it is not allowed. If you simply want to repeat what someone said to you in order to explain what happened next, the way to get round the problem is to say 'As a result of what Mr X told me, I did so and so'. This is very difficult to remember, and when the time comes you will probably launch into details of what Mr X. actually said. So don't be surprised if the judge stops you. The reason why what Mr X. told you is not allowed, is that the truth of what he said cannot be tested unless Mr X. is in court to be questioned. On the other hand, you are entitled to say what the defendant or his witness said because they can be asked about it when they give evidence.

CROSS-EXAMINATION

When you have finished telling your story, the judge will ask the defendant or his lawyer if he wishes to ask any questions. In the same way, when the defendant or any of his witnesses gives evidence, you or your lawyer will be asked if you wish to question him.

There is nothing quite so dramatic as a devastating cross-examination, when the evidence given by a witness is utterly discredited. But cross-examination is a difficult art. Unless there are particular questions you want to ask, it may be wiser to remain silent.

Most judges dealing with cases where both you and the defendant are in court prefer to hear what each party has to say and then, if any explanations are necessary or there are points which need clarification, to question each of you in turn. At the same time, he will give each of you an opportunity to qualify or explain anything you have already said.

You should try and take a full note of the evidence given by the other party's witnesses and mark the passages in that evidence which are of particular importance and which you will want to refer to when you cross-examine the witness.

However, if it is necessary for you to challenge evidence given by witnesses called on behalf of the defendants it is good tactics to get the witness to agree with you on matters that are common ground.

There is no need to get aggressive when cross-examining a witness. It is best to keep calm and collected even when you totally disagree with that witness's answer. From time to time it will be necessary to pin-point the differences between that witness's evidence and the evidence that was given in your favour. You should be as clear as possible with your questions so as to get the most useful answers from the witness during cross-examination.

## SPEECHES AND JUDGMENT

At the end of the evidence your lawyer and the defendant's lawyer may address the judge. If you don't have a lawyer, the judge should ask you, or your 'McKenzie', whether you have anything you want to say. If you want to, you can use this opportunity to sum up your complaint and stress the points which seem most important to you.

The judge will usually give his judgment straight away. If it is a difficult case or if he wishes to consider any point of law, he may reserve his judgment. You will then be sent notice of a further date to attend court when judgment will be given.

## COSTS AND EXPENSES

If you win your case, you should ask the court to pay your expenses in addition to any damages you have been awarded.

Your expenses may include the following items:

1. Lawyers fees (if any);
2. Court fees;
3. Witness expenses. In addition to the expenses for your witnesses, you can claim for your own expenses as a witness (travelling costs and loss of time at work);
4. Out of pocket expenses. You may claim the expenses involved in making searches in public registers, such as the Companies Register. You may also claim fares, telephone calls or any other expenditure that the court considers were reasonably necessary for the preparation of your case. If you have had to spend a

night away from home to attend the hearing, or take a meal in a restaurant during the trial, you can also claim these costs.

## PAYING THE OTHER SIDE'S COSTS

If you lose, you may have to pay your opponent's costs. The legal fees which he can claim from you depend on the amount of damages which you were asking for. If you were asking for less than £100, he won't normally be able to ask you to pay his legal fees. But if you were claiming more than that, you could have to pay a large amount of money. For instance, if you were claiming over £500, the case could have cost your opponent over £100 in legal fees – and if you lose, you could be ordered to pay that.

When deciding how much to claim in the first place, you should, if possible, get legal advice on how likely you are to win, and you should take into account the possibility of having to pay your opponent's legal costs if you claim more than £100 and lose.

## YOUR RIGHT TO APPEAL

If you have definite reason for thinking that the court's decision is wrong, you have certain rights of appeal. Before appealing, you should consider the question carefully and take legal advice. Otherwise, you may get involved in a lot of extra expense if the appeal is unsuccessful. The court office will explain what you have to do in order to appeal from the court's decision, and will tell you the time within which this must be done.

---

**Explanatory Notes to Model Particulars of Claim:**

1. In other words, the manager or person who served you at the showroom.

2. In order to check which section of which Act you are claiming under, you should ask your local Citizens' Advice Bureau, or a solicitor, or the Equal Opportunities Commission (in cases of sex discrimination only).

3. The court office, or a lawyer, will be able to advise you on how much you should claim. Damages are awarded on 'scales', which are also used as the basis for working out legal costs. If you claim a certain amount, and are awarded a figure on a lower scale, then you will not be able to get your legal costs paid by your opponent. You cannot be given more than you claim.

MODEL PARTICULARS OF CLAIM

---

IN THE ........ COUNTY COURT Plaint Number:

BETWEEN          JANE SMITH          Plaintiff

and

CHAUVINIST TV RENTAL CO LTD Defendants

### PARTICULARS OF CLAIM

1. On ............ (date) the plaintiff visited the showrooms of the defendants at ........... (address) and requested the hire of a television set.
2. The plaintiff completed the form of agreement to hire and explained that she was employed as a secretary on a salary of £184 a month.
3. The defendants, through their servant or agent,[1] then asked the plaintiff to produce a male guarantor.
4. The plaintiff explained that she had been employed in her present job for over a year and had previously held similar jobs. She offered to produce evidence from her employer.
5. The defendants, through their servant or agent, refused to enter into a hiring agreement without a male guarantor.
6. The defendants are in breach of Section 29 of the Sex Discrimination Act 1975.[2]
7. By reason of the matters aforesaid, the plaintiff has suffered loss and damage.

### AND THE PLAINTIFF CLAIMS

1. An injunction requiring the defendants to stop discriminating unlawfully against the plaintiff on grounds of sex.
2. Damages limited to £ ........[3]
3. Costs.

date                             (your signature)

## A brief guide to magistrates' courts

### What cases do they hear?

1. *Criminal cases.* All criminal cases have to start in a magistrates' court (these include charges of prostitution, p. 244, and shoplifting, p. 444). If the charge is more serious there is a further hearing in a crown court.
2. *Civil cases.* These include family cases; granting of separation and maintenance orders (p. 301); custody (p. 322); adoption applications (p. 354) and affiliation proceedings (p. 317); magistrates' courts also hear civil assault cases, where a private person takes out a summons against another person for assault.

### Juvenile courts

These are often attached to magistrates' courts. They have magistrates who specialize in juvenile cases and the procedure is different. Besides hearing criminal charges against children and young people under seventeen, they also hear applications for care orders (pp. 324, 368).

### Who are the magistrates?

They are either professional lawyers, chosen from barristers with some years' experience; or they are non-legal nominees of local political parties, known as lay magistrates or 'Justices of the Peace'. If the magistrate is a professional he will usually judge cases on his own. Justices of the Peace normally sit in threes and never alone. The clerk of the court is a lawyer who advises magistrates on the law. In some cases, the clerk seems to be more in charge than the magistrate.

### You can apply for legal aid

for proceedings in magistrates' courts (p. 452). Below we give a brief description of the procedure in civil and criminal cases, to give you an idea of what happens, in case you have to conduct your own case without a solicitor's help. In any event it's best to get legal advice (p. 454).

### Procedure in criminal cases

If you have to appear in a magistrates' court on a criminal charge brought by the police, you will first have been charged in a police station. Unless the charge is very serious, you should be let out on bail (release from custody) and told when to appear in court. It is important to turn up in court at the correct time, otherwise the magistrate will probably issue a warrant for your arrest and once arrested you may not be allowed bail. If you are ill or really cannot turn up for a good reason, make sure that the police or the court are notified.

When you get to court you may be locked in a cell until it is time for your case to be heard: this is known as 'surrendering to your bail'. Some courts allow you to wait outside the courtroom. If, when you appear in court, you admit the charge and plead 'Guilty', your case will normally be dealt with there and then. If you deny it and plead 'Not Guilty', your case will be adjourned to another day. The police may try to persuade you to plead 'Guilty' even when you do not think you are. They may tell you that you will only receive a small fine if you plead 'Guilty', whereas you will be dealt with more severely if you deny the charges. Unless you are absolutely sure you are guilty and it is a minor offence such as a traffic offence or being drunk and disorderly, it is always best to get a solicitor's advice before pleading 'Guilty'. If you tell the court you want your case to be adjourned so that you can seek legal advice, your request should be granted.

IF YOU PLEAD 'GUILTY'

The police officer concerned will normally give the court an account of your case and there will be no need for witnesses to give evidence under oath. You can ask the police officer questions if you want to, and you have a right to address the court (in order to explain to the court why you acted in the way you did) before the verdict of 'Guilty' is entered in your name and the court decides what sentence to give you.

IF YOU PLEAD 'NOT GUILTY'

The case against you has to be proved beyond all reasonable doubt. The police and any witnesses they call have to give their evidence under oath. You have a right to ask them questions about their evidence (cross-examine); then you in turn give your evidence under oath and call any witnesses you have to support your case. You may make a closing speech to the court, pointing out why you are not guilty.

If you have not been charged by the police – for instance, if a store is prosecuting you for shoplifting – then the store detective may conduct the case without the police being involved.

Written statements from witnesses are not normally accepted as evidence unless you have sent their statements to the prosecution before the hearing and there has been no request for the witnesses to appear in court. If you want to do this, the statement has to be on a special form: check with the court officials or a solicitor. If a witness will not come to court willingly, you can apply to court for a summons ordering her or him to appear. You have to give the summons to the witness, together with sufficient money to pay travelling expenses to court.

You will almost certainly be offered bail when your case is adjourned, unless the court has reason to believe that you may commit another offence; that you will abscond; or that it is necessary to detain you for your own safety. If bail if refused the magistrate must tell you why. You have a right to re-apply for bail each time you appear in court and you can also appeal to a High Court judge, but no legal aid is available for this.

## THE RIGHT TO TRIAL BY JURY

If you are charged with a more serious offence, such as theft, you will be asked by the court whether you wish to be tried by judge and jury in the crown court or dealt with by the magistrates' court. If you are charged with a very serious offence such as causing grievous bodily harm or manslaughter, you are automatically tried by judge and jury, though there will be a preliminary hearing in the magistrates' court. There is a higher acquittal rate in jury trials because juries are less inclined than magistrates to believe police evidence. You have to wait longer for a trial by jury. If you do not have legal aid, they are very expensive, but if you are charged with a serious offence you will normally receive legal aid. If you are convicted, you may receive a more severe sentence if you have chosen trial by jury than you would have done if your case had been heard in the magistrates' court.

## APPEAL

If you are convicted you can appeal *either* to the crown court, where a judge will re-hear your case and all the evidence; *or* to the Court of Appeal, on a point of law only.

## Procedure in civil cases

First of all you have to apply for a summons (this is explained on p. 465). You do this at a private hearing in front of a magistrate, usually between 9.30 and 10.30 a.m., before the courts hear their ordinary cases. A summons is then served on the other person (e.g. your husband) by the court and a date is fixed for the hearing. The only people who can be present at the hearing are you, the other party to the case, your respective lawyers, court officials and social workers. You will have to give evidence and call your witnesses, if you have any. Written statements are not normally allowed, as in criminal proceedings (p. 477). Try to make sure that all your witnesses are in court and can give their evidence there and then. If the case concerns children, it will be adjourned so that a social worker can prepare a welfare report. In civil proceedings you have to prove your case 'on the balance of probabilities', which means that the standard of proof is not as high as in criminal cases.

# 13. The Equal Opportunities Commission

The EOC was set up in 1975 to monitor the workings of the Sex Discrimination and Equal Pay Acts, to fight discrimination and to promote equal opportunities. It is based in Manchester, with small offices in Glasgow and Cardiff and a London press office. At the time of preparing the third edition of this Guide, the EOC had an annual budget of £2 million and 171 employees. Its fourteen commissioners meet monthly to decide policy. It is in danger of having its funds cut by the government.

## What does the EOC do?

We list below the powers given to the EOC under the Sex Discrimination Act. However, this list alone would not explain what the Commission actually does, because it does not make full use of all of its powers. Its performance has certainly improved since the early years of its life, but it still falls far short of the ideal of a vigorous campaigning body which many women envisaged in 1975. The following passage from the *New Statesman* (1 December 1978) helps to explain some of its difficulties:

The EOC was set up according to the same unwritten rules by which most Commissions and 'quangos' are established. These rules are designed first and foremost to satisfy the interest groups which carry most weight with the government, and only secondly to enable the organization to exercise its statutory duties and powers. Thus, the Labour Party's Women's Officer became chairman and a Tory Shadow Minister's wife became deputy chairman – which may have kept the two parties happy but may not have been the best recipe for a strong, united leadership . . . There was a battle over whether the TUC and CBI should have two or three places on the Commission. In the end they won three each, making an 'industrial block' which could outweigh other alliances or interest groups. The Education establishment had to be satisfied next, then Scotland, Wales and finally the Home Office itself. The notion that the Commission might be filled by individuals most noted for their enthusiasm and ability to work for equality was not entertained. It was intended to be (and still is, with some notable exceptions) a disunited group of the 'Great and the Good', with prior and sometimes conflicting allegiances, approaching their statutory task with a passionate caution.

The description remained appropriate in 1981, although Lady Elspeth Howe, 'the Tory Shadow Minister's wife', had been replaced by Jane Findley (another Conservative).

## The formal powers of the EOC

1. *It can make formal investigations.* The Commission can make formal investigations into areas where discrimination is suspected. The scope of these inquiries can be broad – such as employment patterns in one region of Britain; or narrow – such as the practices of one particular company or individual. The Commission can investigate any form of behaviour which is unlawful under the terms of the Sex Discrimination or Equal Pay Acts, including 'discriminatory practices' explained on p. 26 It can also conduct investigations into areas not covered by the law, but where discrimination is suspected. In making formal investigations, it can compel people to supply information, orally or in writing. If anyone refuses the Commission can apply for a court order which requires them to obey. If they disobey the court order, they can be fined up to £400.
2. *It can recommend a course of action.* Following or during a formal investigation, the Commission can recommend that a person or organization behaves in a different way, in order to promote equal opportunity.
3. *It can recommend changes in the law.* The Commission can recommend changes in the law as a result of its investigations.

4. *It can issue Non-Discrimination Notices.* If the Commission decides, after a formal investigation, that someone has been breaking the Sex Discrimination or Equal Pay Act, it can issue a Non-Discrimination Notice. (The one exception is in the field of education, where the EOC has no power to issue a Non-Discrimination Notice.)

The notice tells the person named in it to stop breaking the law. If this means he has to change certain practices or arrangements, then he must let the people concerned know what changes he has made and he must let the Commission know too. The Notice may also ask for specific information to help the Commission check that it is being obeyed. So if, for example, a Notice were served on an employer who had broken the Sex Discrimination Act by refusing to promote women to higher grades, the Notice would require that he informed his employees that promotion would be available for women in the future. It might also require that he told the Commission when women were promoted.

A person who receives a Non-Discrimination Notice can appeal against it within six weeks. He would have to show that the Notice was unreasonable, either because it was based on false information, or for some other reason. If the Notice concerned employment, or training, he would appeal to the industrial tribunal; if it concerned anything else, he would appeal to the county court. If there is no appeal, the Notice becomes final after six weeks. If there is an appeal, the Notice becomes final when it has been dismissed or abandoned. If at any time within the next five years, the Commission thinks that the Notice is not being obeyed, it can conduct a formal investigation and apply for an injunction to enforce the Notice, as explained below.

5. *It can apply for injunctions.* The Commission can apply for an injunction to stop a person breaking the Sex Discrimination or Equal Pay Act. An injunction is an order from a county court, which orders someone to stop acting in a particular way. If that person disobeys the injunction, he is 'in contempt of court' and the Commission can apply to court to have him sent to prison.

The Commission can apply for an injunction in the following circumstances:

(a) It has issued a Non-Discrimination Notice and it has reason to believe that the Notice is not being obeyed.

(b) An individual has successfully brought a complaint under the Sex Discrimination or Equal Pay Act and the Commission thinks that the employer or organization concerned will not stop breaking the law.

(c) The Commission thinks that someone has broken either of the laws and is likely to go on doing so. In this case it can apply for an injunction without any need for a Non-Discrimination Notice or a complaint from a member of the public. But it must first bring a complaint itself, under the relevant Act, to an industrial tribunal or court. If the complaint is successful, the Commission can apply to court for an injunction straight away, and the case need not be heard again. The tribunal finding is sufficient evidence for the county court to grant an injunction.

(d) The Commission can apply for an injunction against anyone who has broken the law by:

(i) publishing an advertisement which shows that the advertiser intends to discriminate unlawfully (see p. 30); *or*

(ii) by instructing an employee or agent to discriminate unlawfully; *or*

(iii) by putting pressure on anyone else to discriminate unlawfully.
     In these circumstances, it is normally up to the Commission to take action to stop a breach of the law. It can apply for an injunction without issuing a Non-Discrimination Notice (if it hasn't already done so) and without taking a complaint to a court or tribunal.

6. *It can help individual cases.* The Commission can help individuals bring complaints of sex discrimination or unequal pay to industrial tribunals or county courts. It will normally do this only where there is an important principle involved – and where there is uncertainty about how the law should be interpreted and a test case is needed to settle the matter.

7. *It can fund education and research projects* aimed at promoting equal opportunity.

8. *It can advise the government* on areas of law not touched by the Sex Discrimination Act. It thus has scope to campaign for equality in areas such as tax, social security, pensions, immigration, parental leave and child care.

## How has the EOC used its powers?

There is not room here to give a full critique of the EOC's failures and achievements. A brief summary will have to suffice. In the first five years of its life, the EOC started six formal investigations, issued one Non-Discrimination Notice and no injunctions. It gave some form of backing to 273 cases that went before industrial tribunals and county courts, fifty-eight that went to the Employment Appeals Tribunal, nineteen to the Court of Appeal, five to the House of Lords and five to the European Court of Justice. It funded more than eighty research or education projects, and set up a large library, open to the public, at its Manchester headquarters. It produced detailed proposals on taxation, maternity rights, child care, social security, retirement age and protective legislation. And it has published guidelines for employees and employers, as well as for schools and advertisers, on how to keep within the law and promote equal opportunities.

## How can the EOC help you?

You can't just telephone or write to the Commission with a complaint of discrimination and expect it to ensure that justice is done – it doesn't work like that. It handles a lot of inquiries from the public and if you write asking for advice about your rights under the Sex Discrimination or Equal Pay Act, it should be able to give you the right answers. If you want to bring a complaint under one of the Acts, there are three ways the EOC can help:

1. *By sending you free literature* to help you pursue your case. It publishes useful guides explaining how to take your case to an industrial tribunal and county court; a questionnaire form to

help you set out the details of your complaint; and a form you can fill in to apply for assistance from the EOC.

2. *By assisting you with the initial stages of your case.*

3. *By giving full financial backing to your case,* which may be continued through all the stages of appeal. (You will probably not get full financial backing unless your case is considered to be an important test of the law.)

4. *By approaching the person or people whom you are accusing of breaking the law* and helping to obtain a settlement – either by encouraging them to change their ways, or by persuading them to pay you some compensation. A great many cases have been settled 'out of court' after approach from the EOC.

5. *By starting a formal investigation* into the alleged discrimination. (Sometimes the EOC can persuade an employer, school or other organization to cease discriminating by threatening to start a formal investigation.)

It is always worth asking the EOC for help and advice. You may be fobbed off; on the other hand, you may be pleasantly surprised.


### Further information

Addresses of the EOC: Main office, Overseas House, Quay Street, Manchester M3 3NH (061 833 9244); Cardiff: Caerwys House, Windsor Place, Cardiff CF1 1LB (0222 43552); Glasgow: 249 West George Street, Glasgow G2 4QE (041 226 4591).

Free publications (not an inclusive list):

*What is the EOC and how can it help me?*
*Equal opportunities: an employee's guide*
*How to prepare your own case for an industrial tribunal*
*Credit for women*
*Housing, Goods, Facilities and Services*
*Fresh Start: a guide to training opportunities for women*
*Do you provide equal educational opportunities?*

# 14. Tribunals

You might have to appeal to a tribunal if you have a dispute with your landlord, or if you disagree with a decision that has been made about your right to National Insurance or supplementary benefits, if you have a complaint of sex discrimination, or for a number of other reasons. Here are some notes to give you an idea of what to expect.

Tribunals are not like law courts. They are supposed to be informal. They are designed so that ordinary people can appeal to them without having to get advice from a lawyer, and without having to spend any money. They can settle cases a lot more quickly than law courts – a complex case might take as much as two days, but most cases are settled much more quickly than that.

It all sounds great. But the truth is that in almost any tribunal hearing, you, the person who is appealing, will have to argue your case against people who are experts in the field. You will have to understand a lot of complicated rules and regulations if you are going to get the better of them. So you may be at a considerable disadvantage if you just turn up on your own and rely on their good will and understanding. Legal aid is not available for tribunal hearings (although it should be) but under the 'green form' procedure, described on p. 454, you can get considerable help from a solicitor without actually having legal representation at the hearing. Otherwise, take a friend or a representative from your trade union, the Child Poverty Action Group, or anyone you can find who has experience of the way tribunals work.

## Industrial tribunals

Industrial tribunals deal with:

1. Complaints of discrimination on grounds of sex or marriage in employment and training, under the Sex Discrimination Act 1975 (p. 41). Other sex discrimination cases go to the county court (p. 461).
2. Applications for equal pay under the Equal Pay Act 1975 (p. 69).
3. Complaints of unfair dismissal under the Employment Protection Act 1978 (p. 100).
4. Complaints relating to maternity pay and the right to return to work after childbirth, under the Employment Protection Act 1978 (p. 91).
5. Complaints relating to redundancy, under the Employment Protection Act 1978.

APPLYING TO THE TRIBUNAL

To make your complaint, get the application form from your local employment office or Job Centre (address in the telephone directory under Department of Employment) or from the office of Industrial Tribunals. Fill it in and send it to the Secretary of the Tribunals, Central Office of Industrial Tribunals, 93 Ebury Bridge Road, London SW1. (In Scotland, the address is St Andrew's House, 141 West Mile Street, Glasgow G1 2RU.) On the form, you have to name the employer against whom you are complaining: it is important to get this right. If, for instance, you have been discriminated against by the manager of a firm, name the *firm* not the manager; if you win you are more likely to get compensation from a company than from an individual. The same is true if you have a complaint against an employment agency or trade union: name the organization, not the person you happened to deal with.

Even if you do not name the relevant Act on the form, the

tribunal will sort that out for you. Just describe what happened and why you are lodging a complaint.

## GETTING HELP WITH YOUR CASE

If you belong to a trade union, ask your shop steward or union official to help you with your case. She or he should be present during the conciliation stage and present your case to the tribunal. You can also get legal advice, either through your union, or by going to a solicitor and asking for advice under the 'green form' procedure. You may get help by writing to the Equal Opportunities Commission (address, p. 486).

## THE 'CONCILIATION' STAGE

In most cases, the tribunal sends copies of your complaint to the Advisory, Conciliation and Arbitration Service (ACAS); it also sends copies to the employer. An officer from ACAS will probably contact you and try to arrange a conciliation. You may be asked to a meeting with the conciliation officer and the employer. A great many cases are settled this way. However, you don't have to agree to a settlement at this stage. Don't be talked into it unless you are absolutely sure you have achieved the results you wanted. If there is no conciliation, your complaint is heard by the industrial tribunal. You will be told the date of the hearing, with at least fourteen days' warning. If you or any important witnesses can't make the date fixed for the hearing, you can apply to have it changed: write to the clerk of the tribunal as soon as possible. If you ask for an adjournment on the day of the hearing, it may be granted, but you might have to pay whatever costs the employer incurred on that day, which could be high if he is legally represented.

## PREPARING YOUR CASE

Collect all relevant documents, letters and, if you have any witnesses to back up your story, make sure they can attend the tribunal hearing. You can, if you wish, prepare a written statement of your case, setting out all the evidence and the decision you want the tribunal to make. A lawyer may help you with this if you ask for advice under the 'green form' procedure (p. 454). It's essential to prepare your case carefully and turn up at the tribunal in person.

## AT THE HEARING

The procedure is fairly formal. The tribunal consists of three people, a chairperson, who is a lawyer, and two lay (non-legal) members – one representing management, the other a trade unionist representing workers. Only 23 per cent of the lay members are women, but it is government policy to aim at having at least one woman on every tribunal hearing sex discrimination and equal pay cases. Which side puts its case first depends on whether you or the employer must prove the case. If you have to prove the case, as you would in an equal pay case, you state your case first, and vice versa.

You will be asked to swear an oath or affirm. You then go into the witness stand to give your evidence. You are asked to state your case first (this is done by your union representative, if you have one): state the facts of the case and tell the tribunal what decision you want it to make – for instance, that the employer has discriminated unlawfully, that he should stop doing so, and that you should be paid a certain sum in compensation. Draw the tribunal's attention to all the relevant documents and call your witnesses to give evidence.

The tribunal and the employer (or his representative) will probably question you. You can question the employer when he has presented his side of the case.

The tribunal must give its decision, with full reasons, in writing. A copy is sent to you.

AFTER THE HEARING

You can claim travelling expenses and compensation for loss of earnings: see the clerk of the tribunal about this. If you have any other expenses, such as legal fees, you will have to pay them yourself, whether you win or lose. The only exception is where the tribunal thinks that one side (you or the employer) has acted 'frivolously or vexatiously', in which case the tribunal will order that side to pay the other's costs. But this rarely happens.

IF YOU LOSE

There are two things you can do:

1. You can ask to have the case *reviewed* for any of five reasons:
(a) The tribunal staff made a mistake in handling your complaint;
(b) Either you or the employer did not receive notice of the hearing;
(c) The tribunal made its decision in your absence, or the employer's absence;
(d) New evidence has become available, which could not have been known or foreseen at the time when the tribunal heard the case; or
(e) The 'interests of justice' require a review.

   Apply for a review within fourteen days of the date the decision is registered (the date is on the copy of the decision which you receive). If your application is accepted, the tribunal will rehear the case. This means further arguments can be presented and the tribunal can change its decision; *or*
2. You can *appeal* against the tribunal's decision if you think it involved a mistaken interpretation of the law. (You cannot ask for a *review* for this reason.) Appeal within forty-two days to the Employment Appeals Tribunal. You will almost certainly need a lawyer's help if you appeal. Legal aid is available (p. 452) but if you are not eligible, try to get help through your union or the Equal Opportunities Commission; or if you can afford it,

pay a lawyer's fees yourself, but first get legal advice on your chances of winning.

## National Insurance tribunals

You can appeal to this tribunal if you are claiming a National Insurance benefit (such as unemployment benefit or maternity allowance) and you disagree with the decision made by the National Insurance officer – because he is not giving you enough, or giving you nothing at all. You must appeal within twenty-eight days from the date that the decision is sent to you. (If you appeal late, you have to show 'good cause' for the delay.)

Get an application form from your local National Insurance office. That is normally in the same place as the Social Security office. You return the completed form. Or you can simply write to them saying you wish to appeal against their decision, giving the date when it was made and your reason for appealing (i.e. that they are not giving you enough benefit). You will then be told the date of the hearing.

The tribunal consists of three members: a chairperson, who is usually a lawyer, and two others, one representing employers and the self-employed, and one nominated by trade unions. None of the members of the tribunal is employed by the DHSS. You will sit at the same table as the tribunal members and you will not have to take an oath or stand up when you are giving evidence.

The tribunal knows the basic facts of the case before the hearing starts. You are allowed to call witnesses and produce documentary evidence such as letters, doctor's certificates, pay-slips, time sheets, etc. The tribunal will ask you questions and the National Insurance officer will probably do so as well. You may question witnesses and study documents produced by the Insurance officer.

The tribunal may tell you its decision at the hearing. A written statement, which will include the tribunal's reasons for the decision, will be sent to you. You can appeal against the tribunal's decision to the Social Security Commissioner, but appealing is a complicated business, so you should first get expert advice from a solicitor or your trade union. If the tribunal's decision is not unanimous, you have three months in which to appeal. If it is unanimous, you must get leave to appeal either from the chairperson of the tribunal or from the Social Security Commissioner. When you have got leave to appeal, you have three months to make the appeal itself.

## Supplementary Benefit appeal tribunals

If you think you are not getting enough supplementary benefit and you are entitled to more, make an appeal to this tribunal. You should appeal within twenty-one days of the decision you disagreed with. Get an application form from your local Social Security office or simply write a letter to them saying 'I wish to appeal against the decision made on [date], as my benefit is not enough.' You will be told the date of the hearing.

The tribunal consists of a chairperson and two other members from panels representing workers and employers. The chairperson is rarely a lawyer. The hearing will be in private unless you give permission for research workers to attend. It is just as informal as the National Insurance tribunal.

You are allowed to produce documents and witnesses to back up your case, and to question the Supplementary Benefits officers and any witnesses they produce. You may be asked questions by the members of the tribunal and by the Supplementary Benefits officers.

You will hear the tribunal's decision at the end of the hearing, or later by post. They are obliged to give their reasons for the decision, in writing. You may be able to appeal to the Social Security Commissioner if the tribunal has made a mistake on a point of law, but you should get expert advice on this.

You can claim travelling expenses and compensation for loss of earnings. See the clerk of the tribunal about this.

## Rent tribunal

You can appeal to this tribunal if you are living in certain types of rented accommodation and you think your rent is too high. (See p. 393 for details of relevant tenancies.) Application forms are available from your local Citizens' Advice Bureau or from the tribunal office. You will be told the date of the hearing.

Members of the tribunal are selected from panels appointed by the Department of the Environment and the Lord Chancellor. The chairperson is a lawyer. The hearing will be less formal than a law court, but more formal than some other tribunals. The chairperson and members sit at one table and you and your landlord sit at separate tables with your representatives. Nobody has to speak under oath.

The members of the tribunal visit your home on the morning of the hearing. Make sure you are there so you can draw their attention to relevant details that might affect the rent. At the hearing, you are allowed to call witnesses and produce documents such as letters, plans and rent books. The tribunal will question you. You or your representative may question the landlord and his witnesses; he may question you.

The tribunal gives its decision either at the end of the hearing or later, by post. You should always ask for its reasons, in case you have grounds for an appeal. You may appeal to the High Court if you think the tribunal has made a mistake on a point of law. But get expert advice first.

## Rent Officer and Rent Assessment Committee

If you live in 'fully protected' rented accommodation (see p. 393), you can't appeal to the rent tribunal if you think your rent is too high. Instead you can apply to the Rent Officer and, if you don't agree with his decision, to the Rent Assessment Committee. (Your landlord can also apply if he wants to put the rent up).

First of all, apply to the Rent Officer. Application forms are available from your Citizens' Advice Bureau or from the Rent

Office (address in the telephone directory). You must say that you think the present rent is too high and suggest a new rent.

When the Rent Officer gets your application, he will notify the landlord. He will visit your home and do a brief survey. Point out any defects to him at this stage. He will then call you and the landlord to a meeting at his office. The discussion will be fairly informal. You are each allowed to have someone to represent you, and to produce documentary evidence. After the meeting, the Rent Officer will decide on a 'fair rent', notify you and the landlord, and register the rent.

If you don't agree with Rent Officer's decision, you must send a written objection to him within twenty-eight days. The case will then be referred to the Rent Assessment Committee. If you get to this stage you will really need expert advice from a surveyor or valuer. Ask your Citizens' Advice Bureau how to get in touch with one.

Members of the Rent Assessment Committee are chosen from panels nominated by the Minister for the Environment and the Lord Chancellor: the chairperson is a lawyer. The hearing is fairly formal – comparable to a rent tribunal.

The committee may first ask you and your landlord for further information. It will then give you both a date before which you must submit your case in writing or ask for an oral hearing. If either of you asks for an oral hearing, there will be one. Each of you will have a chance to argue against the other's case. The committee usually inspects the premises before the hearing. You will be allowed to call expert witnesses, such as a surveyor, and if the landlord calls witnesses, you can question them.

The committee then either confirms the Rent Officer's decision or decides on a new 'fair rent' which is then registered. You should always ask the committee to give reasons for its decision, in case you have grounds for an appeal. You can appeal to the High Court, but only on a point of law, and you would need a solicitor's help for this.

### Other tribunals

We don't have enough space to discuss all the tribunals here. The others are:

Immigration Appeal Tribunal – for appeals against decisions of Immigration Officers and the Home Office concerning the entry of immigrants, etc.

Medical Appeal Tribunal – to determine compensation if you are injured at work.

Mental Health Review Tribunal – for appeals for discharge from mental institutions.

Tribunals of the National Health Service – for complaints against doctors, dentists, etc.

Local Valuation Courts – for disputes over rates.
Ask your local Citizens' Advice Bureau.

# Appendix 1

# Organizations for help and advice

Many of the addresses listed below apply not just to England and to Wales but to all parts of the U.K. Special addresses for Scotland and Northern Ireland are listed separately at the end.

*Abortion Law Reform Association* (ALRA), 88a Islington High Street, London N1 (01 359 5200): campaigns for a woman's right to choose.

*Advisory, Conciliation and Arbitration Service,* head office at Cleland House, Page Street, London SW1 (01 211 3000): for inquiries about the employment provisions of the Sex Discrimination Act and the Equal Pay Act. Regional addresses on p. 63.

*Advisory Centre for Education* (ACE), 18 Victoria Park Square, London EC2 9PB (01 980 4596): for information on most aspects of education, students' and parents' rights.

*Age Concern,* 60 Pitcairn Road, Mitcham, Surrey CR4 3LL (01 640 5431): information and campaigning centre for old people's welfare rights.

*British Agencies for Adoption and Fostering,* 11 Southwark Street, London SE1 1RQ (01 407 8800): for general advice on adoption and fostering; also acts as a co-operative exchange, liaising 80 adoption agencies.

*British Pregnancy Advisory Service,* headquarters at Austy Manor, Wootton Wawen, Solihull, West Midlands, B95 6DA (05642 3225). See p. 232 for main regional telephone numbers. Charitable organization for counselling, pregnancy testing, abortion, sterilization, vasectomy, artificial insemination.

*Brook Advisory Centres,* London headquarters at 153a East Street, London SE17 (01 708 1234). Other Brook Centres at 233 Tottenham Court Road, London W1 (01 580 2991), and in Coventry, Bristol, Birmingham, Cambridge, Liverpool and Edinburgh – addresses in local telephone directories. A charitable organization, funded by the N HS, for contraceptive advice, counselling, pregnancy testing and abortion referrals.

*Building Societies Association*, 14 Park Street, London W1 (01 629 0515): for information about mortgages.

*Catholic Aid Housing Society*, see Shelter Housing Aid Centre.

*Child Poverty Action Group* (CPAG), 1 Macklin Street, London WC2 (01 242 3225/9149): information on welfare benefits.

*Children's Books Bulletin*, 4 Aldebert Terrace, London SW8 1BH: research and information on sexism and children's books.

*Citizens' Advice Bureaux*, headquarters at National Citizens' Advice Bureaux Council, 110 Drury Lane, London WC2 (01 836 9231): many bureaux throughout the country, which give advice on a wide range of subjects including legal aid, welfare benefits, landlord and tenant law, family law, consumer and other legal problems.

*Citizens' Rights Office*, 1 Macklin Street, London WC2 (01 405 4517): helps poorer families with legal problems such as appeals to tribunals and provides practical advice on welfare rights, etc.

*Consumers' Association*, 14 Buckingham Street, London WC2 6DS (01 839 1222): for information on consumer subjects; publications are available to the general public, but it caters mainly for members.

*CO-ORD*, The Co-ordinating Committee in Defence of the 1967 Abortion Act, 27–35 Mortimer Street, London W1 (01 580 9360).

*English Collective of Prostitutes*, P.O. Box 287, London NW6.

*Equal Opportunities Commission*, Overseas House, Quay Street, Manchester M3 3HN (061 833 9244): see p. 486 for regional addresses.

*Family Planning Association*, headquarters at 27–35 Mortimer Street, London W1 (01 636 7866): provides information on all aspects of contraception, sexuality and related problems.

*Gingerbread*, 35 Wellington Street, London WC2 (01 240 0953): practical help and moral support for single parents. Many local groups.

*Industrial Tribunals, Central Office of*, 93 Ebury Bridge Road, London SW1.

*Joint Council for the Welfare of Immigrants* (JCWI), 44 Theobalds Road, London WC1 (01 405 5527/8): advice and legal help for immigrants.

*Law Centres*, see Neighbourhood Law Centres.

*Law Society*, Chancery Lane, London WC2 (01 242 1222).

*Marie Stopes House, The 'Well Woman Centre'*, 108 Whitfield Street, London W1 (01 388 0662): charitable organization for contraception, pregnancy testing, counselling, abortion, sterilization, vasectomy, help with minor gynaecological problems, psycho-sexual therapy.

*National Abortion Campaign* (NAC), 374 Gray's Inn Road, London WC1X 8BB (01 278 0153): campaigning for a woman's right to choose.

*National Association for the Care and Resettlement of Offenders* (NACRO), 169 Clapham Road, London SW9 (01 582 6500): information and help for prisoners, ex-prisoners and prisoners' wives.

*National Council for Civil Liberties* (NCCL) 23–5 Tabard Street, London SE1: campaigning organization for protection of civil rights; separate Rights for Women section, with special expertise in sex discrimination and equal pay legislation.

*National Council for One-Parent Families*, 255 Kentish Town Road, London NW5 (01 267 1361): help for one-parent families.

*National Foster Care Association*, Francis House, Francis Street, London SW1 (01 828 6266): advice and moral support for foster parents.

*National Organization for the Widowed and their Children*, Cruse House, 126 Sheen Road, Richmond, Surrey TW9 1UR (01 940 4818/9047): provides counselling in bereavement, advice on practical problems and opportunities for social contact.

*National Union of School Students* (NUSS), 3 Endsleigh Street, London WC1 (01 387 1277).

*National Women's Aid Federation*, 374 Gray's Inn Road, London WC1 (01 837 9316): help for battered women, co-ordinates local women's aid centres.

*Neighbourhood Law Centres* – for general information you can contact Law Centres Federation, 164 North Gower Street, London NW1 (01 387 8570).

Other Law Centres:

Adamsdown Community and Advice Centre, 103/4 Clifton Street, Adamsdown, Cardiff (0222 498117).

Belfast Law Centre, 14 University Street, Belfast (0232 46984).

Benwell Community Law Project, 85 Adelaide Terrace, Newcastle on Tyne NE4 8BB (0632 731210).

Bradford Law Centre, St Patrick's Centre, Sedgefield Terrace, Bradford BD1 2RU (0274 306617).

Brent Community Law Centre, 190 Willesden High Road, London NW10 (01 451 1122).

Bristol Resource Centre, 62 Bedminster Parade, Bristol BS3 4HL (0272 667933).

Brixton Community Law Centre, 506–8 Brixton Road, London SW9 (01 733 4245).

Camden Community Law Centre, 146 Kentish Town Road, London NW1 (01 485 6672).

Clapham Law Project, c/o Clapham Community Project, St Anne's Hall, Venn Street, London SW4 (01 622 8789).

Coventry Legal and Income Rights Centre, 62 Lower Ford Street, Coventry (0203 23051).

Hackney Law Centre, 236–8 Mare Street, London E8 (01 986 8446).

Hammersmith and Fulham Law Centre, 106–8 King Street, London W6 (01 741 1450/1476).

Handsworth Law Centre, 220 Soho Road, Birmingham 21 (021 554 0868).

Harehills and Chapeltown Law Centre, 128 Roundhay Road, Leeds LS8 5AJ (0532 491100).

Hounslow Law Centre, 13 Balfern Grove, Chiswick, London W4.

Newham Rights Centre, 309 Barking Road, London E6 (01 471 8226).

North Islington Law Centre, 161 Hornsey Road, London N7 (01 607 2461).

North Kensington Law Centre, 74 Goldborne Road, London W10 (01 969 7473).

North Lambeth Law Project, 381 Kennington Lane, London SE11 (01 582 4425).

North Lewisham Law Centre, 28 Deptford High Street, London SE8 (01 692 5355).

North Manchester Law Centre, Community Service Centre, Paget Street, Manchester 10 (061 205 5040).

North Wales Employment Resource and Advice Centre, 1st and 2nd Floors, Bradford House, St Dinbych, Llanwrst, Gwynedd (0492 641280).

Paddington Advice and Law Centre, 441 Harrow Road, London W10 (01 960 4481).

Plumstead Law Centre, 105 Plumstead High Street, London SE18 (01 855 3513).

Saltley Action Centre, 2 Alum Rock Road, Birmingham 8 (021 328 2307).

Sandwell Law Centre, 19a Birmingham Street, Oldbury, Warley, West Midlands, B69 4 EB (021 552 6121).

Small Heath Law Centre, 477 Coventry Road, Birmingham 10 (021 773 8121).

South Islington Law Centre, 166 Upper Street, London N1 (01 359 5401).

South Manchester Law Centre, 595 Stockport Road, Manchester 12 (061 225 5111).

South Wales Anti-Poverty Action Centre, Bethseda Chapel, Bethseda Street, Merthyr Tydfil (0685 6252).

Southwark Law Project, 29 Lordship Lane, London SE22 (01 693 0610).

Tottenham Law Centre, 15 West Green Road, London N15 (01 802 0911).

Tower Hamlets Law Centre, 341 Commercial Road, London E1 (01 791 0741).

Wandsworth Legal Resource Project, 248 Lavender Hill, London SW11 (01 228 9462).

West Hampstead Community Law Centre, 220–22 Belsize Road, London NW6 (01 328 4501/4523).

*Occupational Pensions Board*, Executive Office, Apex Tower, High Street, New Malden (01 942 8949).

*Pre-School Playgroups Association*, Alford House, Aveline Street, London SE11 (01 582 8871): advice on how to set up play groups.

*Pregnancy Advisory Service* (PAS), 40 Margaret Street, London W1 (01 409 1281), charitable organization for pregnancy testing, counselling, abortion.

*Preservation of the Rights of Prisoners* (PROP), 97 Caledonian Road,

London N1 (01 278 3328/542 3744): prisoners' union, campaigning for prisoners' rights.

*Prisoners' Wives and Families Society*, 254 Caledonian Road, London N1 (01 278 3981): help and advice for prisoners' families.

*Prisoners' Wives Service*, 373a Brixton Road, London SW9 7DE (01 737 0223): counselling and welfare rights for prisoners' wives in the London area.

*Rape Crisis Centre*, c/o P.O. Box 42, London N6 5BU (24-hour service on 01 340 6145, or during office hours 340 6913): advice and counselling service. For those outside London, see p. 242.

*Release*, 1 Elgin Avenue, London W9 (01 289 1123): advice on drugs, immigration, abortion and general criminal/legal problems.

*Shelter Housing Aid Centre* (SHAC), 189a Old Brompton Road, London SW5 (01 373 7276/7841): advice on housing (now incorporates Catholic Housing Aid Society).

*Society to Oppose Physical Punishment* (STOPP), 10 Lennox Gardens, Croydon, Surrey CR0 4HR (01 686 3622): campaigns against corporal punishment in schools.

*Trades Union Congress* (TUC), 23–8 Great Russell Street, London WC1 (01 636 4030); information on trade unions.

*U.K. Immigrants Advisory Service* (UKIAS), 7th floor, Brettenham House, Savoy Street, London WC2 (01 240 5176): advice and help with immigration problems and appeals.

*White Lion School*, 57 White Lion Street, London N1 (01 837 6379): free school. Open to visitors 7.00–9.00 p.m. Tuesdays.

*Women's Forum* (National Council for Voluntary Organizations), 26 Bedford Square, London WC1 (01 636 4066): publishes a comprehensive list of women's organizations, price £1·20, including postage and packing.

*The Women's Place*, 48 William IV Street, London WC1 (01 836 6081): for information (to women only) on the women's liberation movement and addresses of local groups. Open after 12 a.m.

*Woman's Right to Choose*, 88a Islington High Street, London N1 (01 359 5209).

# Appendix 2

# Notes on Scotland and Northern Ireland

The laws in Scotland and Northern Ireland differ considerably from those in England and Wales. These notes are an attempt to highlight the differences where they are most marked. They should be read with reference to the relevant sections of the main text.

## Scotland

There is now a separate guide to women's rights in Scotland, which is considerably more detailed and comprehensive than the following brief notes can be. Called *Scottish Woman's Place: A Practical Guide and Critical Comment On Women's Rights in Scotland* by Eveline Hunter, it is published by EUSPB, 1 Buccleuch Place, Edinburgh (£1·95).

### General notes

Certain terms and expressions which recur throughout the book are different in Scotland:

1. There are no magistrates' courts in Scotland. The Scottish equivalent are the sheriff courts for civil cases and district courts for criminal cases.
2. The legal advice procedure known as the *'green form' procedure* in England and Wales is in fact the *'pink form' procedure* in Scotland.
3. 'Barristers' are called *'advocates'*.
4. A court 'injunction' is known as an *'interdict'*.
5. 'Maintenance' is known as *'aliment'*.

(The terms in numbers 4 and 5 are not exact equivalents and some areas of the law in which they occur differ between Scotland and England.)

### Money (p. 115)

All the subjects dealt with under this heading apply to Scotland except the following:

WIDOWS' INHERITANCE (p. 182)

You can claim 'legal rights' if your husband leaves you little or nothing in his will. You are entitled to one third of his moveable estate (that is, not including houses or land), while the children, including illegitimate and adopted children, share another third between them. If there are no children your share is increased to one half. Likewise, the children's share would be increased to one half if there were no widow. If you think you have a claim, consult a solicitor immediately.

If your husband dies without leaving a will and there are no children, you are entitled to:

1. The house in which you live and its furnishings;
2. Cash up to £16,000; *and*
3. One half of the remaining moveable estate (i.e. not counting houses or land).

If there are children, your cash entitlement is reduced to £8,000 plus the house and furnishings and one third of the remaining moveable estate, while the children inherit the rest of the estate.

If you are divorced, you can get nothing from your ex-husband's estate.

The executors named in your husband's will (or you as his widow if there is no will) should apply to the sheriff court for 'Confirmation': this enables them to distribute the estate. It is advisable to get a solicitor to help, particularly if your husband hasn't left a will.

A man has the same rights if his wife dies before him.

### Sex (p. 210)

SEX UNDER 18 (p. 210)

In Scotland you will not be taken to court if you are under 17 and having sexual intercourse or 'in danger' of having it, because the whole procedure for dealing with juvenile offenders and children in need of supervision is different. If you are under 16 and you are considered to be exposed to moral danger, you may be brought before a Children's Panel and put under a supervision order. The procedure is explained more fully below on pp. 514–16. There is no assumption in Scots law that a boy under 14 is incapable of sexual intercourse. He has to be under 8 before he is assumed incapable.

CONTRACEPTION (p. 214)

If you are under 16 it is not illegal (as it is in England) for a doctor to give you a medical examination or treatment without your parents' consent. Health Boards have responsibility for family planning.

Generally you cannot get contraception via the domiciliary service unless you are disabled and you have been referred to the health visitor from a hospital you have attended, but domiciliary services in some areas will visit women in their own homes in particular circumstances.

Doctors in Scotland don't normally ask for your husband's consent before fitting an IUD. Your husband's consent is usually sought before sterilization, but there is no legal requirement for this.

ABORTION (p. 223)

The 28-week time limit for legal abortions does not apply in Scotland, although in practice few doctors will terminate a pregnancy after this stage.

RAPE (p. 233)

The law on rape is different in Scotland, although there are a number of similarities. The definition of rape is stricter: there must be actual penetration by a man's penis into the vagina. Ejaculation is not necessary, although the existence of sperm would be useful evidence. Sexual assaults falling short of penetration would not be rape in its legal sense but would be indecent assault, which is a lesser offence.

Intercourse must be forced on you against your will. Physical violence is not necessary, although there is less chance of conviction without such evidence. Saying 'no' is not sufficient in itself. Your attacker could defend himself by persuading the jury that *he thought* you consented to sex and *he had reasonable grounds* for thinking so. The English decision given in the case of *D.P.P. vs Morgan* (p. 236) does not apply in Scotland.

Boys under 14 are not considered incapable of sexual intercourse.

Current legal opinion is that a man can be guilty of raping his wife whether they live together or not, but there have been no recent cases to confirm this.

Rape victims in Scotland can still be questioned on their sexual past in court in order to discredit them as witnesses of good character. The names of rape victims can be published, although the press in Scotland have agreed not to use their names. Police questioning is similar to that in England.

There are two rape crisis centres, in Glasgow (041 331 2811) and in Edinburgh (031 556 9437).

PROSTITUTION (p. 244)

The English procedure for cautioning and arresting prostitutes does not apply. A man who solicits a woman to have sexual intercourse with him is usually charged under the local authority bye-laws.

## Marriage (p. 247)

In Scotland it is possible to be legally married without going through an official ceremony of any kind, if:

1. You have lived with the same man for a long time; *and*
2. You are both free to marry; *and*
3. You consider yourselves married; *and*
4. Your acquaintances consider you married.

This is known as 'cohabitation with habit and repute'. It does not mean that the growing numbers of younger couples who make no secret of the fact that they are just living together will find themselves 'married' in this way. But it may affect older women who have always considered themselves married and use the man's name. It could help them claim a widow's pension and a widow's share of the property when the man dies. Claims can be made directly to the Social Security office for pensions, but it may be necessary to get a 'declarator' from the Court of Session confirming your married status before making a claim, as of right, for a wife's or widow's benefits.

## GETTING MARRIED IN SCOTLAND (p. 254)

Marriage banns have now been abolished, but a notice of your intention to marry will be displayed at the registry office. Provided that the registrar is satisfied you are legally entitled to marry each other he will give you a marriage schedule after fourteen days (or sooner in exceptional circumstances and if agreed by the Registrar General). Once you have a schedule you can be married in a registry office or in any recognized religious ceremony.

## GETTING MARRIED UNDER 18 (p. 252)

You can get married anywhere in Scotland without your parents' consent provided you are over 16 and you or your partner have lived in Scotland for at least fifteen days.

A useful booklet entitled *Marriage in Scotland* is available from General Register House, Edinburgh EH1 3YT.

Here's a wee giftee for our Silver Habit & Repute Anniversary, hen

CHANGING YOUR NAME (p. 255)

You cannot change your name in Scotland by deed poll or by making a statement before a Commissioner of Oaths. But you can change your name just by calling yourself by another name and you can, if you wish, record your change of name with the Registrar of Births, Marriages and Deaths. This might be useful if you want proof that you have changed your name, for instance, for a bank or insurance company.

THE FAMILY HOME AND OTHER POSSESSIONS (p. 256)

It is very important to have the family home in both your names (whether it is owned or rented) since you have virtually no protection if the home is in your husband's name and your marriage breaks down.

The respective rights of you and your husband to possessions and money are similar to those in England, with one exception: if your husband has been the only one to earn money from employment, any furniture bought for the home may be considered his – even if you paid for it out of housekeeping money. If he gets into debt, it could be sold to pay his creditors.

DOMESTIC VIOLENCE (p. 261)

There are three kinds of legal action used against violent husbands in Scotland, none of which is very effective.

1. An interdict is a sheriff court order prohibiting your husband from molesting you or entering your house. You cannot normally get this order *unless you are living apart*. An interim interdict can be granted within a week of your solicitor raising the action, but for a full interdict you would have to show that your husband has been violent towards you and is likely to be so again. To establish this you would need witnesses, but the standard of evidence required is less than that for criminal proceedings.

   Breach of interdict is not a criminal offence so your husband would not be prosecuted if he later pestered you unless there is evidence of physical assault. You would have to instruct your solicitor to raise an action for breach of interdict which could result in him being fined.

2. Lawburrows is an old Scottish remedy which is not often used. You

must ask the sheriff court to order your husband to promise a sum of money as security against his future good behaviour. He does not have to pay the money unless he later assaults you. This can be used whether you are living together or not, but if you are still cohabiting you are obviously penalized if he later has to hand over the money.

3. It is a criminal offence for your husband to assault or threaten you. You cannot bring a private prosecution yourself; this must be done by the procurator fiscal after a police report. Although there must be witnesses they need not have actually seen the assault itself. Neighbours hearing you scream or seeing your injuries immediately afterwards could be sufficient corroboration. The police themselves can be witnesses. Nevertheless it remains very difficult in most cases to provide sufficient corroboration of assault.

There is no equivalent to the exclusion orders granted by the English courts although the Scottish Law Commission has drafted a bill which would extend this protection to Scottish women. There are a number of refuges for battered women throughout Scotland run by women's aid groups (addresses, p. 522).

### Divorce and separation (p. 278)

You can apply for a divorce any time after you have been married – there is no need to wait for three years.

The Divorce (Scotland) Act 1976 which came into force on 1 January 1977 enables you to get a divorce in Scotland on similar grounds to those in England, with five important differences:

1. Divorce after five years' separation without the consent of the other spouse can be refused only where grave *financial* hardship is involved.
2. If you have applied for a divorce because your husband has deserted you, the fact that you have sexual intercourse with another man does not prevent you pursuing the divorce on grounds of desertion.
3. If you are divorcing your husband because of his adultery you do not have to prove that you find it intolerable to live with him. However, if you live with him for more than three months after you discovered the adultery, this will be taken as evidence that you condoned it, and you will not be able to apply for a divorce on this ground. To show that his behaviour implied that he was committing adultery, you will need

evidence from two witnesses. A statement made by your husband to an inquiry agent, confessing adultery, would *not* be accepted as evidence.

4. If you are divorcing your husband for unreasonable behaviour, you will need witnesses to back up your evidence. Unreasonable behaviour can be either active or passive: active behaviour could involve physical violence, persistent nagging or taunting, while passive behaviour could occur if your husband was reduced to a 'vegetable' state as a result of an accident or illness.

5. Decisions about custody of the children and financial settlements take place at the divorce hearing and the decree, once granted, takes effect immediately. However, a period of twenty-one days is allowed for a possible appeal, so it would be unwise to remarry until this period has ended.

Although the grounds for getting a divorce are similar in Scotland and England, the procedure is very different. There is no equivalent to the inexpensive English divorce by petition. All actions are heard in the Court of Session in Edinburgh and you must use both a solicitor and an advocate. Even completely undefended divorce actions cost at least £250. Legal aid is available for both defended and undefended actions.

Where the divorce is uncontested and there is no dispute over custody or financial arrangements you need not appear personally in court. Your solicitor will take sworn statements from you and your witnesses and these affidavits will be presented to court.

### ARRANGEMENTS FOR YOUR CHILDREN AFTER DIVORCE (p. 293)

This is explained above.

### DIVISION OF PROPERTY AFTER DIVORCE (p. 295)

This is explained above, p. 508.

### GETTING MAINTENANCE WHEN YOU DIVORCE (p. 296)

In Scotland, maintenance is known as 'aliment'. As in England, you can apply for aliment as soon as you have raised your divorce action to cover the period before the divorce hearing. Permanent financial arrangements are made at the actual hearing, so it is very important to make your application beforehand. Either your or your husband can apply for the following:

1. *A capital sum.* The amount is reached by working out who owns what in the home and then dividing up the rest between the spouses, using rough and ready rules rather than any exact formula. The capital sum awarded cannot be adjusted later when the husband's or wife's circumstances change.
2. *Periodical allowance.* In theory this is supposed to ensure that you are able to enjoy the same standard of living after the divorce. In fact this is difficult to achieve, as your husband's income is unlikely to be able to support two households in the same style as before. Normally you can expect roughly between a quarter and a fifth of your husband's gross income. The court will only award what he can reasonably afford, even if you find this inadequate. The amount awarded is affected by considerations such as who was responsible for the marriage breaking down, what you each earn, and your respective needs.
3. *Aliment.* Whichever parent has custody of the children may apply for an award of aliment for them. This is given for adopted and illegitimate children of either partner as well as children of the marriage.

*After the divorce* if circumstances change either you or your former husband can ask the court to change the periodical allowance, the aliment for the children, and the custody and access arrangements. You cannot register the awards of periodic allowance or aliment with the sheriff court (as you can with the magistrates' court in England) so if the payments are in arrears you will have to ask a solicitor to help you.

The periodic allowance ends if you remarry. If your husband dies you may still be able to receive the periodic allowance from his estate. Aliment for the children continues even if you remarry and only ends when they reach 16 or when they are capable of earning their own living.

GETTING MAINTENANCE AND CUSTODY WITHOUT DIVORCE (p. 301)

A man is obliged to maintain his wife and children; in Scotland a woman is not obliged to maintain her husband and children unless he is unable to earn his own living and she has adequate means of her own. You can go to the sheriff court and claim aliment for yourself and your children if:

1. Your husband has deserted you; *or*

2. You are living apart by mutual consent; *or*
3. You are living apart from him without his consent, for what the court considers to be a good reason (e.g. he has assaulted you).

Questions of custody and access to the children are usually settled at the same time.

### SEPARATION BY AGREEMENT (p. 310)

Voluntary separation agreements may not be legally enforceable in Scotland and are rarely used.

Useful reading:
*Marriage, Divorce and Family*, an introduction to Scots family law, by David Nichols, from the Scottish Association of Citizens' Advice Bureaux, address p. 521.

### NULLITY (p. 311)

Refusal to consummate the marriage is not a ground for nullity in Scotland. The partner must have been incapable of sexual intercourse at the time of marriage. Your husband cannot get an annulment if you were pregnant by another man at the time of the marriage, and neither of you can get an annulment because the other has venereal disease in a communicable form.

## Children (p. 314)

### IF YOU ARE NOT MARRIED (p. 314)

You and the father have equal legal responsibility to support the child.

### CLAIMING MAINTENANCE FROM THE FATHER (p. 316)

If the father of your child refuses to accept responsibility and you want him to support the child financially, you must go to the sheriff court for an order of 'affiliation and aliment'. You can do this during the last three months of your pregnancy or at any time after the birth of your child – though it is better to go to court within five years of the birth. If you are married to another man you can still apply but you will have to convince the court that your husband cannot be the father. If a number of men could be the father and you don't know which is, you won't be able to get aliment from any of them.

What to do:

1. Go to a solicitor and apply for legal aid (see p. 519).
2. If you apply during the last three months of your pregnancy you will have to sign a declaration that the man against whom you are bringing the action is the father. You will also have to get a doctor's statement confirming that you are pregnant and giving the expected date of birth. The advantage of applying before the birth is that you can get money promptly after the birth. You might also want to apply then if the father looks as if he is about to 'disappear'.
3. At the hearing you will probably have to give evidence even if the man does not defend the action. The court will have to be satisfied that the man is the father and if the action is defended your evidence will have to be backed up by other evidence, such as a witness who has heard the man admit that he is the father.

*If the court decides that the man is the father*, it can make an order declaring this and order him to make regular payments to you for the maintenance of the child. You can also get extra expenses to offset the expense of the birth. If your child is not yet born the court won't make any order until after the birth unless the action is undefended or the man admits that he is the father: in this case, the court may order an immediate payment to cover the expenses of the birth. The father has to pay the money to you. He may arrange to do so in cash or by postal orders. The court does not collect the money for you.

If you marry, the father must continue to pay maintenance for the child. If the child is adopted by you or anyone else, he no longer has to pay (unless he adopts the child jointly with you). He does not usually have to pay after the child is 16. If the child dies before 16, the father is liable to share the funeral expenses with you.

MAKING YOUR CHILDREN WARDS OF COURT (p. 320)

You can't do this in Scotland. Instead, you can ask the court to 'interdict' your husband from taking the children away. It will be easier to get an interdict if you have already been awarded custody. See a solicitor and ask her to start proceedings immediately.

IF YOU ARE GETTING DIVORCED (p. 321)

1. If you and your husband agree about who should keep the children after the divorce, there will be no need to fight it out in court. The arrangements you have agreed upon may be set out in a document, signed on your behalf by your respective lawyers. If there is no written agreement, you will need someone else to back up your evidence to the court about the arrangements you have made. If the judge isn't satisfied, he can postpone granting the divorce and put off the hearing to another date, to give time for other arrangements to be made.
2. If you do not agree with your husband, an advocate from the court may investigate the situation, instead of a social worker.
3. Arrangements for custody are normally made at the divorce hearing, not afterwards.
4. It is not the practice in Scotland to distinguish between 'custody' and 'care and control'. One parent gets both; the other parent is normally allowed access to the child, as in England.

HOW YOUR CHILD COULD BE TAKEN INTO CARE (p. 324)

The first two ways that this can happen are the same as in England, except that a local council cannot keep your child against your wishes; and it is the Social Work Department (rather than Social Services) that takes children into care.

The third way is entirely different in Scotland. Young people under the age of 16 who get into trouble with the law, or young people whose parents or guardians are not considered to be looking after them properly, are dealt with by a system of *reporters* and *children's panels*, set up under the Social Work (Scotland) Act 1968 and put into practice in 1971. Reporters are appointed by the local authorities. Usually they are lawyers or have experience in social work. Members of children's panels are appointed by the Secretary of State for Scotland on the recommendation of the children's panel advisory committees; members are drawn from a cross-section of the community to represent different age and occupational groups.

If a child under 16 commits an offence or seems to be in trouble for some other reason, she is normally referred to the reporter by the police or the Social Work Department or the school head or school council. Children up to the age of 18 may also be dealt with in this way if they are under a supervision requirement imposed by a children's hearing (see below). The reporter investigates the case and may decide:

1. To take no further action; *or*
2. To refer the case to the Social Work Department to arrange for the advice, guidance and assistance of the child and family on a voluntary basis; *or*
3. To refer the case to a children's hearing.

In some parts of Scotland she may instead arrange with the police to give the child's parents a warning that if a similar incident happens again the child may have to attend a hearing.

Most cases which come before the reporter are referred to a children's hearing on one or more of the nine conditions that can form the 'grounds of referral'. Your child (if not yet 16) may be considered to be in need of 'compulsory measures of care', for one or more of the following reasons:

1. The child is beyond your control.
2. Through lack of parental control the child is falling into bad company, is exposed to moral danger or suffering unnecessarily, or having her health or development seriously harmed.
3. The child is truanting from school; *or*
4. Has committed an offence; *or*
5. Has been the victim of a sexual offence.

If the reporter refers your child to a hearing, you will receive a copy of the 'grounds for referral' a week beforehand. You are under a duty to attend the hearing with your child. The children's panel at the hearing has three members, at least one of whom must be a man and one a woman. You, your child, the reporter and a social worker attend the hearing – the Social Work Department provide the social background report which forms the basis of the discussion at the hearing. You and your child may each bring a relative or friend to help in the discussion.

The chairperson reads out the grounds for referral and if you or your child disputes them, the case may go to the sheriff court to establish the facts. You may claim legal aid for this procedure. If the court finds the facts are true, the case is referred back to the hearing. The hearing may decide to make no order or to impose either of two types of supervision requirement. Under the first type, your child is supervised by a social worker while living at home or with a relative or a foster parent. Under the second type, the child is sent to be supervised in a residential home or school. The hearing also has power to issue a warrant for the detention of a child in a place of safety as a temporary measure.

If you or your child wish to appeal against any decision, either of you can ask for written reasons for the decision from the reporter and appeal to the sheriff court within twenty-one days of the hearing.

The supervision requirement has to be reviewed whenever the local authority recommends; or (after at least three months' supervision) at the request of the child or parent; and, in any event, after a year. It automatically lapses on the child's eighteenth birthday.

In certain circumstances a local council may 'assume parental rights' over a child who is already in its care as a result of any of the three procedures mentioned above. If you do not give written consent to this the council must write to you explaining what it is doing. If you object you should tell the council in writing and consult a solicitor. Your objections may, if necessary, be considered by the sheriff. If the local authority assumes parental rights you lose almost all your rights over the child, although you are still liable to pay aliment. The council may let you take over 'care and control' of the child for a trial period and it may give you back your parental rights if this seems to be best for the child. If, at any time, you want the situation changed, see a solicitor and make formal objections to the sheriff who has powers to alter the position.

### LEAVING HOME WHEN YOU'RE UNDER 18 (p. 368)

If you are under 16, you may have to go before a children's hearing, in situations where, in England, you would be taken to court (see above). If you are aged between 16 and 18, children's hearings have no jurisdiction over you unless they have already made a supervision order for you.

### EDUCATION (p. 334)

Parents in Scotland should complain to the Secretary of State for Scotland about any unlawful discrimination in schools.

### CORPORAL PUNISHMENT (p. 347)

There is a code of practice on the use of corporal punishment in Scottish schools which some regions have adopted as official policy. Only a leather belt may be used, and only on the palms of the hands.

## Housing (p. 371)

MARRIED WOMEN: YOUR RIGHT TO THE FAMILY HOME (p. 371)

The law on matrimonial property is extremely complicated in Scotland. Here are two general points which show that it is even more important for Scottish women to ensure that the family home is in joint names.

1. Where the home is privately owned and it is in your husband's name, you have no rights to it at all: he can evict you if he wishes, although this may enable you to divorce him for desertion. You have no right to occupy the matrimonial home after divorce, even if you have children; and the court cannot transfer the home to you, although it can award part of its value to you in a lump sum on divorce.
2. Where your home is rented and the tenancy is in your husband's name, he can evict you and the court has no power to transfer the tenancy to you if you separate or divorce. A local authority is less likely to transfer a tenancy to you if it is in your husband's name than if it is in joint names.

In rare cases where the home is in the wife's name the situation is reversed and the husband has no rights to it. The Scottish Law Commission has drafted a bill which would give women roughly the same rights to their home as women in England.

WHAT ARE YOUR RIGHTS IF YOU SET UP HOME WITH A MAN WHO IS NOT YOUR HUSBAND? (p. 384)

If you are considered married 'by cohabitation and repute', as explained above (p. 506), you have the same rights as a married woman. If not, you are in the same position as an unmarried woman in England.

RENTING FROM THE COUNCIL (p. 390)

District councils now have a legal duty to help you if you are homeless. Their duties are similar to those described for England and Wales. Some councils in Scotland refuse to house separated women until they pay off rent arrears owed by their husbands on other council tenancies. Resist this. You are not legally responsible for your husband's debts. Other councils may refuse to house you until you are actually divorced, if your husband already has a council home. If you are in this situation, get in touch with

Shelter, your local advice centre, or Citizens' Advice Bureau. It is now unlawful for local authorities to make repayment of your husband's rent arrears a condition of transferring the tenancy to you. If this happens to you it would be wise to seek advice from Shelter or a solicitor.

QUICK GUIDE FOR TENANTS (p. 393)

Fixed short tenancies for periods of between one and five years have now been introduced in Scotland. The tenancy can be 'short' only if you have been told beforehand in writing that it is fixed and only if a fair rent is registered on the premises. After the fixed period is ended the landlord can get a court order removing you from the property. The law on short tenancies is now roughly similar in Scotland and England.

## Goods, facilities and services (p. 402)

THE PROCEDURE FOR SMALL CLAIMS (p. 416)

This does not apply in Scotland, but there is now a comparatively quick and simple procedure called 'summary cause' for bringing claims involving less than £500 to the sheriff court, either on your own or with a solicitor's help. Ask your Citizens' Advice Bureau about this.

IF YOU CAN'T AFFORD TO PAY YOUR FUEL BILL (p. 419)

In Scotland, the fuel boards, social work departments and Social Security Office have a liaison scheme whereby they can hold up disconnection while your case is examined. Contact your local Social Services department. Mothers with children are supposed to get special consideration.

## Women and prison (p. 432)

There is no probation service in Scotland. The social work departments of local authorities are the nearest equivalent. Instead of prison welfare officers, there are social workers attached to prisons. Wives are not excluded from extra visits in connection with prisoners' appeals. Legal advisers have virtually unlimited access and there can be visits from any other people provided these are in connection with the appeal. There is now only one women's prison in Scotland – Cornton Vale.

The Scottish Association for the Care and Resettlement of Offenders (SACRO) is at 110 West Bow, Edinburgh EH1 2HH (031 225 5232).

## Approaching the law (p. 449)

### LAWYERS (p. 449)

Scottish solicitors belong to the Law Society of Scotland, 26 Drumsheugh Gardens, Edinburgh. If you think your solicitor has charged you too much, there is no rule in Scotland which says you must challenge the bill within a month or else pay up in full. Nor does the Scottish Law Society provide any certificate to confirm that the sum charged is fair and reasonable. It does, however, offer to scrutinize informally accounts relating to conveyancing and general business. It will not look at accounts relating to litigation (such as a divorce). If you want to query a litigation account, contact your local Citizens' Advice Bureau. They have been supplied with information on this matter and should be able to help. If you have any other complaints about the way your solicitor has handled your case, write to the Law Society of Scotland, or contact your local CAB.

Barristers are known as *advocates* in Scotland. Any complaint against an advocate should be addressed to the Dean of the Faculty of Advocates, Advocates Library, Parliament House, Edinburgh EH1 1RF.

### LEGAL ADVICE AND ASSISTANCE (p. 454)

The *'green form'* procedure is known as the *'pink form'* procedure in Scotland. Otherwise, this is the same as in England.

### CIVIL LEGAL AID (p. 455)

This is administered in Scotland by the Law Society of Scotland through its Legal Aid Central Committee. Legal aid is granted by local Legal Aid Committees or, in the case of proceedings in the Court of Session (such as a divorce) by the Supreme Court Committee in Edinburgh. The conditions of eligibility for legal aid are broadly similar to those in England. If you want to appeal against a decision of a Legal Aid Committee or the Supreme Court Committee, you can appeal to the Central Committee within fifteen days of hearing the decision. You cannot appeal to the Central Committee against an assessment of your means by the Supplementary Benefits

Commission, but you can ask the Supreme Court Committee to re-assess your means or to supply a breakdown of their assessment.

CRIMINAL LEGAL AID (p. 457)

If you are arrested and brought before a district or sheriff court without being released on bail you have a right to free legal advice and representation from the duty solicitor at court. If you have been released on police bail, you should ask to consult the duty solicitor, although you do not have the same automatic right. In 'summary' cases, where the maximum penalty is six months' imprisonment, your right to free representation continues until you make your plea of 'Not Guilty' or 'Guilty' and, in the latter case, until the solicitor has made a plea in mitigation (i.e. for a light penalty). After this, you are granted legal aid if you satisfy the financial conditions and it is considered to be 'in the interests of justice' that you should have legal aid. In more serious cases which carry a penalty of more than six months' imprisonment, your free representation lasts until you are granted bail or committed for trial by jury. After this, you are granted legal aid if you satisfy the financial conditions.

Once you are granted legal aid you will not be asked to make any financial contribution. In no criminal cases will you be asked to contribute to the cost of the prosecution – whether or not you are granted legal aid.

TRIBUNALS (p. 488)

These operate as in England, with only very minor differences. There are no Mental Health Review Tribunals in Scotland; instead the sheriff performs a similar function and a Mental Welfare Commission exists to protect the interests of mental patients and to inquire into allegations of ill-treatment or improper detention.

CIVIL COURTS (p. 461)

The two main civil courts in Scotland are the sheriff court and the Court of Session, which is divided into an 'Outer House' and an 'Inner House'. There are fifty sheriff courts in Scotland. These deal with matters such as separation, affiliation, aliment, custody, adoption, consumer claims, landlord and tenant, debts. Appeals from the sheriff court go to the sheriff principal (there are six altogether); and from there to the Inner House of the Court of Session; while in some cases they go straight to the Inner House. The Outer House of the Court of Session deals with divorce and allied matters such as matrimonial property and custody of children. Appeals from the Outer House go to the Inner House of the Court of Session.

## Further information

*Advisory, Conciliation and Arbitration Service*, Franborough House, 123–57 Bothwell Street, Glasgow G2 7JR (041 204 2677).
*British Pregnancy Advisory Service*, 245 North Street, Glasgow (041 204 1832).
*Brook Advisory Centre*, Lower Gilmore Place, Edinburgh (031 229 5320).
*Child Poverty Action Group*, 234 West Regent Street, Glasgow (postal address).
*Citizens' Rights Office*, 132 Laurieston Place, Edinburgh (031 228 6688).
*Cruse* (for widows), 212 Bath Street, Glasgow (041 332 1299) or 35 Drummond Street, Edinburgh (031 556 6163).
*Equal Opportunities Commission*, 249 West George Street, Glasgow (041 226 4591).
*Family Planning Association*, 2 Claremont Terrace, Glasgow (041 332 9144).
*Gingerbread*, 38 Berkeley Street, Glasgow (041 248 6840) or 37 Buccleuch Place, Edinburgh (031 667 0720).
*Gay Centres*, 534 Sauchiehall Street, Glasgow (041 332 1725) or 60 Broughton Street, Edinburgh (031 556 3673).
*National Childbirth Trust*, Glasgow (041 334 5922) or Edinburgh (031 225 4043).
*Pre-School Playgroups Association*, 192 St Vincent Street, Glasgow (041 221 9388).
*Rape Crisis Centres*, Glasgow (041 331 2811) or Edinburgh (031 556 9437).
*Rent Registration Offices*, 141 West Nile Street, Glasgow (041 332 6981), 6–7 Coates Place, Edinburgh (031 225 1200), 47 Holburn Street, Aberdeen (0224 25288) or 26 East Dock Street, Dundee (0382 24082).
*Scottish Association of Citizens' Advice Bureaux*, 12 Queen Street, Edinburgh (031 225 5323), does not handle personal queries but will give you the address of your local CAB.
*Scottish Association for the Care and Resettlement of Offenders*, 38 Cleveland Street, Glasgow (041 226 3547).
*Scottish Convention of Women*, chairwoman Maida Hart, 40 East Barnton Avenue, Edinburgh.
*Scottish Council for Civil Liberties*, 146 Holland Street, Glasgow (041 332 5960).
*Scottish Council for Single Homeless*, 93 Hope Street, Glasgow (041 248 3813).
*Scottish Council for Single Parents*, 44 Albany Street, Edinburgh (031 556 3899).
*Shelter Housing Aid Centres*, 53 St Vincent Crescent, Glasgow (041 221 8995), 88a George Street, Edinburgh (031 225 6058) or 48 Marischal Street, Aberdeen (0224 53586).

*Women's Aid*, 11 Colme Street, Edinburgh (031 225 8011), will give you the address
of local groups.
*Women's Centre*, 57 Miller Street, Glasgow (041 221 1177) or 160 Fountainbridge,
Edinburgh (031 229 0053).

## Northern Ireland

Legislation and services in Northern Ireland are often very different from
provisions in England and Wales. And at the time of writing (January
1981) many important changes are in the pipeline. For these reasons you
should, wherever possible, consult the organizations listed on p. 528 to
ensure that you act on accurate and up-to-date information.

### Sex Discrimination

Legislation is similar but Northern Ireland has its own Equal Opportunities
Commission at Lindsay House, Callendar Street, Belfast (0232 42752). The
Fair Employment Agency (same address) deals with complaints of dis-
crimination on religious grounds.

### Work (p. 32)

Northern Ireland's Equal Pay Act is much the same as the English Act and
has the same weaknesses. Complaints are dealt with by industrial tribunals
and their decisions can be taken to the Court of Appeal on a point of law.
Forms for making complaints are available from local offices of the
Department of Manpower Services (address, p. 528).

Protective legislation and provisions relating to maternity rights, unfair
dismissal, etc. are identical to provisions in England and Wales.

### Money (p. 115)

WIDOWS' INHERITANCE (p. 182)

If your husband dies without making a will, your inheritance rights are
limited. He may also die after making a will which provides inadequately
for you and/or your children. In either case you can apply to the court for
an order to give you more under the new Inheritance (Provision for Family
and Dependants) Order. Separated and divorced women can also apply.

SUPPLEMENTARY BENEFIT (p. 189)

Tax and social security are virtually identical to the U.K., but to get supplementary benefit you must have lived in the United Kingdom for five years prior to making a claim. The other major difference is the Payment for Debt Act 1971, under which deductions can be made at source from social security payments (and from the wages of public employees) if you are in arrears with rent, gas or electricity. For help on these or other points contact the Belfast Community Law Centre (address, p. 528).

## Sex (p. 210)

SEX UNDER 18 (p. 210)

The age of consent in Northern Ireland is 17. It doesn't make sense, of course, as people can get married at 16.

CONTRACEPTION (p. 214)

Family planning advice can be a problem as many doctors are still unsympathetic to single women. The addresses of family planning clinics are listed in the phone book under 'Health and Personal Social Services' (and see p. 528).

ABORTION (p. 223)

Abortion is only available in exceptional circumstances and you are advised to contact the British Pregnancy Advisory Service direct (address, p. 232), or the Ulster Pregnancy Advisory Service (address, p. 529). If there is a Women's Aid group near you they will give advice and support, but the main problem for the thousands of women who go to England each year for abortions is money – fares and the fee bring the cost to around £150 minimum and it is often difficult to get help on this.

RAPE (p. 233)

The law on rape was updated in 1978. The Sexual Offences (Northern Ireland) Order provides that a man cannot argue that he believed the woman consented no matter how unreasonable this belief is, and, except in certain circumstances, the Order prohibits publicity of the names of rape victims.

## Marriage (p. 247), Divorce and Separation (p. 278)

Parental consent is required for anyone wishing to marry under the age of 18.

At present Northern Ireland has no special legislation to protect battered women, but changes are expected in the near future. For advice or accommodation women should phone Women's Aid groups (addresses, p. 529).

When women come to Northern Ireland there is often confusion about whether or not they can petition for *separation* or *divorce*. The position is that, regardless of where the husband is living, after one year's residence they can apply for separation or divorce under Northern Ireland legislation. If you return to Northern Ireland after living elsewhere you may not need to wait a year if you can claim domicile – that is, that Northern Ireland is your home to which you always intended to return.

Since April 1979, as a result of the 1978 Matrimonial Causes Order, the law on divorce has greatly improved. Petitions are still heard in the High Court, Belfast (though this will be changed soon) and you may have difficulty getting a solicitor if you live outside Belfast. Again, however, Women's Aid should be able to help on this. Divorce is now granted on the sole ground that the marriage has broken down irretrievably. To prove this evidence must be presented that the respondent (your husband if you are divorcing him) has committed adultery, or has behaved in such a way that the petitioner (you) cannot reasonably be expected to live with him, or has deserted the petitioner for two years, or that the couple have lived apart for two years, or five years if one partner objects to the divorce being granted. In Northern Ireland the High Court now has wide-ranging powers to give women a better deal over any property of the marriage, and husbands trying to avoid a fair share-out by, for example, selling the house, can be stopped by the courts.

Women's rights to the house whilst married are non-existent in Northern Ireland (there is not yet an equivalent to the 1967 Matrimonial Homes

Act), but the minute a woman files a petition for divorce she does acquire substantial rights. As a result, women here may need to seek advice and act quickly to prevent the home from being sold over their heads. Two other differences are that there is no postal divorce, and in divorce proceedings where there are children involved the court has to bring in a social worker to report on the suitability of whatever arrangements are proposed for their care. Apart from these points, divorce is now much the same as in England.

Under the 1979 Domestic Proceedings Order for Northern Ireland, separation orders are granted on the grounds of adultery, unreasonable behaviour, desertion and failure to maintain, and married women subject to violence or the threat of violence will be able to ask the court to exclude husbands from the home and area. The 1979 Order does not cover common-law wives who will be left without protection unless the government agrees to close this loophole. For information on this whole area and how far things have got contact your nearest Women's Aid group (address, p. 529).

Women with religious objections to divorce should petition the High Court for judicial separation – the grounds are exactly the same as for divorce and the same orders for property and financial support can be made by the court. Maintenance is much the same as in England and if there are difficulties an attachment of earnings order can be made.

For further information on family law contact Belfast Women's Law and Research Group (M. Clarke, 0232 660449).

### Children (p. 314)

YOUR RIGHTS AS A MOTHER (p. 314)

We hope changes will be made soon but at present in Northern Ireland parents do not have equal rights with regard to children – effectively they belong to the husband, unless as a result of separation or divorce the court gives custody to the woman.

HOW YOUR CHILD COULD BE TAKEN INTO CARE (p. 324)

Again changes are expected, but at present under the Children and Young Persons Act 1968, the Health and Social Services Boards have a duty to take into care children who have been lost or abandoned, or whose parents are unable to care for them for some reason. If you place your child in care voluntarily, she or he cannot be kept in care against your wishes without a court order.

A court will grant an order if it decides that your child is in need of care, protection or control. To reach this decision it must be satisfied that 'the child is not receiving such care and protection and guidance as a good parent may reasonably be expected to give'. In addition, the court must be satisfied that one of a number of conditions has been met: these include such things as the child 'falling into bad association'; being 'exposed to moral danger'; or being likely to experience unnecessary suffering. The conditions listed under the Act do not include the child committing an offence. If the court decides that 'care and protection' are required, it can send the child to a training school; commit her or him to the care of the Area Board; make a Supervision Order; or order you, the parent, to exercise proper care in future.

### NURSERIES AND OTHER CHILD-CARE FACILITIES (p. 325)

There are no state nurseries providing all-day care in Northern Ireland and the number of places in play groups and nursery education is, proportionately, much lower than that in England and Wales. In 1978 a substantial expansion of facilities was proposed by government but there is no likelihood of this happening now. For information on what is available in your area contact your local social services department, listed under 'Health and Personal Social Services' in the phone book.

### ADOPTION (p. 354)

Northern Ireland law will probably come into line with the law in England and Wales soon, but until then the 1967 Act still applies. An adoption order cannot be made without the consent of the parent or guardian, but the court can act without consent if it decides that the parent or guardian:

1. Has abandoned, ill-treated or neglected the child; *or*
2. Cannot be found; *or*
3. Is incapable of giving consent; *or*
4. Has failed persistently to carry out the obligations of a parent or guardian; *or*
5. 'Is withholding his consent unreasonably' – what is unreasonable depends on the court; *or*

6. Is one 'whose consent ought in the opinion of the court to be dispensed with'.

In all decisions, the court's paramount consideration must be the welfare of the child.

## Housing (p. 371)

The Matrimonial Homes Act does not apply in Northern Ireland, which means that a married woman cannot register an interest in her home when it is in her husband's name.

If you live in an owner-occupied house and it is not in joint names you can only establish rights to it by starting divorce proceedings. If you are a Northern Ireland Housing Executive tenant the Executive does grant joint tenancies, though if you are not working this might be a problem as you will be liable for half of any arrears. On separation or divorce the tenancy should go to the person with custody of the children. If you have to move into a Women's Aid refuge you can be rehoused (in some areas quite quickly) from the refuge, provided that a social worker's report supports your housing application.

If you are a tenant in the private sector under the Rent Order of 1978 the court may be able to transfer the tenancy to you if you become separated or divorced, if your accommodation is a statutory or protected tenancy.

Rent rebates, rate rebates and rent allowances are available in Northern Ireland. The Rent Order of 1978 also gave greater security of tenure to private tenants in statutory or protected tenancies: it establishes rent assessment committees to fix rents; it imposes duties on landlords in connection with repairs; and it prevents eviction without a court order. The 1978 Order is so complicated, however, that you should contact your nearest advice centre on all these points, or phone the Belfast Community Law Centre (p. 528).

## Goods, facilities and services (p. 402)

For advice and assistance phone the information officer, Northern Ireland Consumer Council, Belfast (0232 746151), or write to Mary Clarke, Consumer Desk, BBC, Ormeau Avenue, Belfast.

## Approaching the law (p. 449)

GETTING LEGAL AID (p. 452)

The legal aid scheme provides three kinds of help:

1. Up to £25 worth of legal advice and assistance in the form of drafting documents or writing letters.
2. Legal aid for civil proceedings – divorce, separation, etc.
3. Legal aid for criminal proceedings.

In all cases, whether you get help free or have to pay a proportion of the cost depends on your dispensable income. For further information (names and addresses of solicitors, whether or not you will have to pay, etc.) contact your nearest Citizens' Advice Bureau or the legal aid department of the Incorporated Law Society of Northern Ireland (address below).

### Further information

*Belfast Community Law Centre*, 14 University Street, Belfast (0232 46984).

*Belfast Housing Aid Society*, 16 Howard Street, Belfast BT1 7PA (0232 45640/22013).

*Belfast Women's Centre*, 18 Donegal Street, Belfast (0232 43363).

*Catholic Down and Connor Marriage Advisory Service*, 11 College Square North, Belfast (0232 41606): advice on marital problems and approved methods of birth control.

*Citizens' Advice Bureaux*, Northern Ireland headquarters, 28 Bedford Street, Belfast BT2 7FE (0232 43986).

*Department of Manpower Services*, Industrial Relations Division, Netherleigh, Massey Avenue, Belfast 4 (0232 63244).

*Down and Connor Family Welfare Society*, 43 Falls Road, Belfast 12 (0232 43601).

*Equal Opportunities Commission*, Lindsay House, Callendar Street, Belfast (0232 42752).

*Family Planning Association of Northern Ireland*, 47 Botanic Avenue, Belfast 7 (0232 25488).

*Incorporated Law Society of Northern Ireland*, Legal Aid Department, Law Courts Buildings, Chichester Street, Belfast (0232 35111).

*Northern Ireland Civil Rights Association*, 2 Marquis Street, Belfast (0232 23351): for general advice on civil liberties.

*Northern Ireland Child Poverty Action Group*, c/o Eileen Evason, Social Administration Department, New University of Ulster, Coleraine, Co. Londonderry.

*Northern Ireland Consumer Council*, Belfast (0232 647151).
*Northern Ireland Housing Executive*, 1 College Square, Belfast (0232 40588).
*Ulster Pregnancy Advisory Association*, 388a Lisburn Road, Belfast (0232 667345).
*Women's Aid refuges for battered women*: telephone Belfast (0232) 662385, Portrush (0265) 823195, Londonderry (0504) 65967, Strabane (0504) 882261.

# Appendix 3

# A draft contract for marriage or living together

If you live with a man, whether you are married or not, you may find that there are many ways in which your rights are not protected. One way of tackling this problem is to come to a clear agreement about the terms of your relationship at the outset, preferably before you move in together or marry, and draw up a legal contract setting out in black and white exactly what your rights and responsibilities will be. Love and understanding may not solve all your problems and you may find it very useful to devote some hard, clear thinking to the subject and to commit your understanding to paper.

Below, we give an example of a contract drawn up by one (imaginary) couple. Gloria and Sam are getting married but you could make a similar contract if you just wanted to live together. However, there is a danger that the courts would not enforce a 'cohabitation contract' because they might consider it immoral in threatening the institution of marriage!

It's up to you to decide which terms to include. For instance, you might want to have a joint family name instead of keeping separate names. You might want to include an agreement that you will devote a certain amount of time to discussing your relationship, so that channels of communication are kept open. You might want to include a clause providing that you should review the agreement from time to time to see if you wish to amend it. There will probably be areas of your relationship that you do not want to deal with in legal contract – such as religion and sexual fidelity.

A contract of this kind has not yet been tested in the courts of Britain, so it is impossible to know exactly how far it would be legally enforceable. Some of the terms would be more acceptable in a court of law than others. For example, the law cannot and will not enforce an agreement to share housework, to look after children, or to oblige one partner to encourage the other in the pursuit of training or a career. However, if you are married and your husband has consistently flouted these terms of the agreement you might (if things got that bad) be able to use this as part of the evidence of his unreasonable behaviour in divorce proceedings.

Terms dealing with property rights would have more legal force. As a clear expression of the intent of both parties to set out specific property rights, they would normally be enforceable in a court of law. Courts dealing with divorce and separation would have to overrule the agreement if they considered the terms were not fair and equitable, but the terms stated in the sample contract would probably be upheld by the courts.

In any event, a contract is a useful way of reminding you both of the agreement you made at the start of your relationship. In the event of a disagreement, it could have considerable force in helping you and the man to work out your own solutions without having to go to court. And, if the relationship does break down, it could make it easier to sort out money matters and other practical arrangements, which can otherwise cause great difficulty.

In order for the contract to have as much legal force as possible, it's best to have it drawn up by a solicitor. Some solicitors may be surprised at your request, or may even refuse to deal with it – so you may have to look for one who is sympathetic. If you show the solicitor the sample contract given here it will help to explain the sort of thing you want.

THIS AGREEMENT IS made on the 1st day of January BETWEEN GLORIA SMITH of Manchester, England (hereinafter called 'the Woman') and SAM BLOGGS of London, England (hereinafter called 'the Man'). WHEREAS:—

1. The Woman and Man intend to marry.
2. The Woman and Man wish to enter into an Agreement which they intend to be legally binding upon them, as to their own respective rights within marriage, obligations towards each other, obligations towards any children of the marriage and interest in any property owned jointly and separately by them.
3. The Woman and Man wish to establish the principle that they both have equal rights in all matters concerning their life together and their respective development as individuals and that all such matters should be settled between them in mutual agreement.
4. The said principle shall be the guiding principle even when it conflicts with financial considerations.

NOW in consideration of the above agreement and of the intended marriage IT IS HEREBY AGREED:—

1. The Woman and Man agree that each shall be entitled to retain for all purposes after the marriage their own respective names before the marriage. They agree

that when they have children they will adopt a joint family name, there being no prior assumption that this should be the name of the Man.

2. The Woman and Man shall each be entitled to work and to engage in vocational and social activities as each chooses. Should either of them who has not previously been working outside the home decide to take up an occupation, or should either of them decide to continue her or his education, they agree to support each other in attaining their objectives.

3. The Woman and Man agree to plan their lives in such a way that the Woman may combine her work and any vocational and social activities with motherhood and that the upbringing of any children of the marriage shall not disrupt or restrict the work and vocational and social activities of one party more than of the other.

4. The Woman and Man agree that the responsibility for the upbringing of any children of the marriage and for the domestic work of the home shall be shared equally between them.

5. The Woman and Man agree that they shall decide jointly where the family home shall be with equal consideration as to the needs of each. The fact that one of them may earn more than the other as a result of employment in a certain place shall not allow that one to decide where they shall live.

6. The Woman and Man agree that they shall have equal interests in any premises occupied by them as the family home so that if the legal title to such premises is vested in one party such title shall be held in trust for both parties in equal shares.

7. The Woman and Man agree that all property owned separately by them before the marriage shall remain their separate property unless such property shall be occupied as the family home, in which case the above clause applies. Any property owned jointly by them before the marriage shall remain their joint property and on sale the proceeds shall belong to them in equal shares.

8. The Woman and Man agree that all property acquired after the marriage for their joint use shall be jointly owned. All property acquired after the marriage for the sole use of either party shall remain separate property of that party.

9. (a) The Woman and Man agree that while they both maintain separate bank accounts the monies in each bank account shall belong to the party whose name it is in.
(b) Should they decide at any time to open a joint bank account the monies in that account shall belong to both in equal shares.
(c) If at any time one of them is not in full-time paid employment because of childbirth or responsibilities of caring for the children of the marriage, they both shall transfer all monies into a joint bank account but failing this half the monies earned during such a period by the one who is employed shall belong to the other.

10. The Woman and Man shall, as far as it is reasonable to do so, share equally in the management and control of any jointly held income and property.

11. The Woman and Man agree that they shall be equally liable to meet the common expenses of the family home including all necessary outgoings such as rent and mortgage payments, rates, electricity and the expenses of maintaining the children, in proportion to their respective incomes.

IN WITNESS whereof the parties have hereunto set their hands and seals the day and year first above written.
SIGNED SEALED AND DELIVERED
by the said GLORIA SMITH in the presence of

          Witness  .....................
          Address  .....................
          Occupation  ................

SIGNED SEALED AND DELIVERED
by the said SAM BLOGGS in the presence of

          Witness  .....................
          Address  .....................
          Occupation  ................

# Index

*Certain organizations which appear with great frequency in the text have not been included in the index except for their main entries. Examples: Citizens' Advice Bureaux; Industrial Tribunals; Social Security offices.*

## Vindication of the Rights of Woman
Mary Wollstonecraft
*Edited by Miriam Kramnick*

Walpole described her as 'a hyena in petticoats'. Her *Vindication* was received with a mixture of outrage and enthusiasm. In an age of ferment, Mary Wollstonecraft took the prevailing egalitarian principles and dared to apply them to women.

Subsequent feminists tended to lose sight of her radical objectives, but it is a tribute to her forceful insight that they are finally returning to the arguments so passionately expressed in this remarkable book.

## Three Guineas
Virginia Woolf

A witty, elegant and lucid polemic which magnificently argues the case for sexual equality and for women's liberation. Far from being – as might be expected – a rarefied treatise on Bloomsbury's notions of 'literature', *Three Guineas* is an extremely pertinent and well-aimed opening shot in the battle which still rages today.

## From Hand to Mouth
Marianne Herzog

This book describes the lives of quiet desperation led by thousands of women exploited in factories.

*From Hand to Mouth* is an account of the experiences of Marianne Herzog and others on the production line in some West German factories which are household names – Philips, Siemens, Telefunken. Backbreaking piecework, boredom, fear of unemployment and coping with ill health, shopping, home and family are all part of the hand-to-mouth existence of these factory workers.

## Housewife
Ann Oakley

'In an interesting, carefully researched and well-written study, Ann Oakley traces the historical development of the housewife role, examines the present-day situation of women as housewives, not only in terms of how society sees them, but more importantly, how they see themselves, an analysis dramatically illustrated by four case histories' – *Hibernia*

## Scream Quietly or the Neighbours Will Hear
Erin Pizzey

Erin Pizzey's struggle to open, and keep open, her refuge for battered wives in Chiswick has become a national issue, opening up to public scrutiny a problem that has been, hitherto, conveniently swept under the carpet.

## Dutiful Daughters
Women talk about their lives
*Edited by Jean McCrindle and Sheila Rowbotham*

'As remarkable and immediate as Oscar Lewis's *Children of Sanchez* . . . an extraordinary compilation of the voices and memoirs of women over the past half century' – Emma Tennant in the *Guardian*

## The Wise Wound
Menstruation & Everywoman
*Penelope Shuttle and Peter Redgrove*

'An important, brave and exciting exploration into territory that belongs to all of us, and nobody could read it without a sense of discovery' – Margaret Drabble in the *Listener*

## The Ambivalence of Abortion
Linda Bird Francke

In interviews with men and women of all ages and social groups, Linda Bird Francke describes the human experience of abortion, and in doing so casts new light on one of the most controversial and complicated issues of our time.